BITTEN *by the* ROWING BUG

Challenges of an Untamed River

BITTEN

— *by the* —

ROWING BUG

Challenges of an Untamed River

Karl Drlica

LUMINARE PRESS

WWW.LUMINAREPRESS.COM

Luminare Press
442 Charnelton St.
Eugene, OR 97401
www.luminarepress.com

LCCN: 2023920429
ISBN: 979-8-88679-340-6

This work is dedicated to Ilene Wagner
for many decades of partnership.

TABLE *of* CONTENTS

Prologue

Bitten by the Rowing Bug began when my parents decided to sell their Oregon home and move into smaller quarters. My dad had been the rowing coach at Oregon State University for thirty years. He and the previous coach of twenty years had saved every scrap of paper that crossed their desks: photos, student reports, correspondence, histories, news clippings, and notes on tense conversations. My dad thought they were valuable: a college archive should want them. When he failed to interest an archive, his collection went into a dozen boxes that were stored nearby in my sister's garage. There they sat for ten years.

In the meantime, my wife, Ilene, and I decided to move from New York City to California. On a steamy August day, furniture and several hundred boxes of treasures—baby clothes, Legos, and children's books for yet non-existent grand-children—came down the elevator from an eleventh-story apartment. Our elder son Alex and two of my work colleagues sweated with us as we moved the boxes across the busy sidewalk to the curb on Second Avenue. The rented truck was close: I had grabbed a parking spot by following the street sweeper as it forced parked cars to leave the curb. After thirty-five years of New York City and hours of packing, we headed back to California.

Our first stop was at our little vacation home in the Poconos. There we attached a trailer to the truck and another trailer to our old Honda. All vehicles were filled to the brim, with overflow tied to the roof of the Honda. As we pulled out, I cut a corner too close, put a truck wheel in a ditch, and almost rolled the rental. The load shifted, but we were in a hurry. Let it ride.

Eastern Pennsylvania has hills that, after a hundred miles, challenged the Honda and its load. According to the driver, "But dad, I didn't exceed 3,000 rpm," as our little caravan came to a halt. A tow truck took us into the woods, and scenes from the movie *Deliverance* came to mind as we pulled up to a barn-turned-garage. The tow driver and a few of his buddies gathered around, poking at the Honda's engine, confirming death.

Alex jumped into the rental truck and took off for a conference in Chicago: we would find the truck and its trailer in the hotel parking lot. Keys would be at the front desk.

We considered replacing the Honda with a rental, but the local outlet was closed for the weekend. And the motel was full. We were stuck. The tow driver felt sorry for us, or more likely he saw a way to make a fast buck: he offered to sell us his dad's car. He'd add a hitch to it so we could pull our trailer. We gave him the Honda; a credit card and a local notary got us back on the road.

Seven days later we pulled up at Ilene's family home in Oakland. Tenants, who had vacated a few days before, left the house ready for us. But the modest two-bedroom home was not large enough. Our 300-plus boxes filled the basement and garage, floor to ceiling. Narrow paths among the stacks gave access to doors, much like an overstocked thrift store I had patronized in New York City.

After a year, the garage and basement were still packed, but not as densely. That was when my sister Karen decided that a decade was long enough for her to store our dad's rowing archive. A dozen more boxes were added to the Oakland pile.

By 2018 I had winnowed the pile to fifty boxes that almost fit on shelves. They'd all fit if I tossed my dad's archive. It was only paper. It held no deep secret that required shredding. Indeed, it could go directly into the recycle bin.

I moved the archive boxes to the center of the basement. Out of curiosity, I opened the top box and glanced at old news clippings. Memories surfaced. My dad (Karl Drlica) and his mentor

(Ed Stevens) had been a pair of fanatics who had been bitten by the rowing bug. With volunteer student labor, they had built a rowing campus by repurposing everything from scrap lumber to naval vessels. In the process, the elite, expensive sport of rowing became available to "any who wanted it", including young women. I felt compelled to write a summary before I threw the collection away.

Most of the events occurred in Corvallis, a small college town in Western Oregon. These were times of national insecurity, as school children like me learned to dive into muddy roadside ditches in case the Soviets dropped atomic bombs on us. The two coaches had an unpaid task: to teach self-sufficiency and help preserve American-style democracy (for decades the coaches, who worried about Communism, encouraged their students to run the intercollegiate rowing program via elected officers).

Rowing was a lure to capture college students for training in problem solving. Many of the early problems centered on manual skills: fighting floods, reconstructing buildings, and fabricating racing shells. Later, the effort focused on political struggles, as the crew sought to expand a river-based program deemed too dangerous and expensive by University administrators.

When I mentioned the archive to Astrid Hancock, the trail-blazing women's coach of the 1960s, her memories also surfaced. We decided to add our own memories to the summary. We then solicited recollections from former rowers and scoured the internet for background. Once this organizing was complete, I offered the collection and my summary to Oregon State University.

I thought I was finished writing when the University Archives accepted the collection. I'd made space in our basement for other "treasures". But within a month I found myself converting the archival summary into a more readable form. What emerged was a description of the struggles of a rowing coach against both an unrelenting western river and University administrators. The administrators were initially concerned with cost and safety; later they resisted equal treatment for male and female rowers. The coaches failed to stop the floods, but they found ways to influence the University and to also win races. Then came rower rebellion and the conclusion of the archive.

For readers unfamiliar with the river, I have included a map locating relevant events. I also added a glossary for readers unfamiliar with rowing terms used sixty years ago.

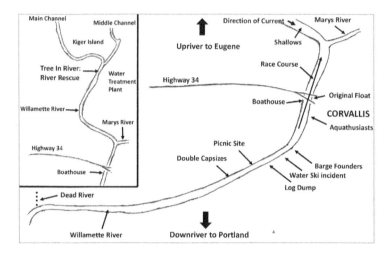

Sketch showing Willamette River near Corvallis, Oregon. Locations of features and events mentioned in the text are noted. Map is drawn with river flowing down (north) to Portland. Inset shows upstream portion of river where a rescue occurred.

──── *Chapter 1* ────

FLOOD DUTY

"Incoming!" shouted Carl as he pointed upstream from midway along the log-raft dock. I wiped the rain off my glasses and stared through the dark, searching for the threat. I was about fifty feet from the upstream end of the dock: I'd be the first to deal with whatever it was. Lights from the town, a hundred yards across the river, reflected off low clouds, giving just enough light to see the bridge pier that forced flood water and its cargo of debris directly at us. Off to my right, in midstream, were standing waves and whirlpools created by the flow rejoining after splitting to pass the pier. The river vibrated the dock under my feet, but I had no fear: I knew how to swim and was ignorant of hypothermia.

Carl had spotted the limbs of a large tree bearing down on us. Light flickering from small waves surrounded a black object headed for the dock. Within a few seconds I saw its limbs and then its trunk. It was coming butt first; no roots stuck out. The tree must have been cut down and left close to the river where flood waters picked it up. Now the current drove it at our dock like a battering ram.

I had only a few seconds to reach the upper end of the dock, thrust the pointed end of my logger's pike pole at the tree, and drive its butt out into the main flow. The rain-soaked deck, which was only a few inches above the swirling river, was barely visible; it was so slick I had to shuffle to reach the point of impending impact. Like a pole vaulter, I gripped my twelve-foot pike with both hands; a rush of adrenalin lightened the pole to almost nothing.

At the end of the dock I braced for my thrust at the log. I could almost hear my dad instructing, "Don't try to stop a big drifter head on. Can't be done. Push it out and down river. Like a judo move." I waited a few seconds, until the tree was about ten feet away. It was only two feet in diameter, not very big compared to some of the monster logs that came down the river. If I could move it out a few inches, its butt might miss the corner of the dock. Then I'd force the rest of the tree out, but I'd need help. I yelled at Carl and my dad for help.

I aimed my thrust a few inches upstream from the butt. Solid contact. The pole recoiled, driven by the momentum of the log, forcing me back. But my feet held firm. I got my weight onto the pole and pushed. The log moved, just enough to clear the corner of the dock. I pulled my spiked pike free and set for another thrust, just as Carl and my dad came along side. The three of us drove pike poles at the trunk, forcing it about a foot off the dock. We walked the drifting tree downstream, pushing it farther out, trying to get it far enough that upstream branches would miss the dock.

Within a few seconds I was midway along the dock and ready for another thrust, this time with all my weight. My aim was a little high, rolling the tree about ninety degrees and submerging the trunk. I pulled out my pike, and the tree rolled back up, revealing a long split. Even in the dim light the white core of the tree was clearly visible.

"No good for anything but firewood," exclaimed my dad, a master of salvage. "Let it go; get it out of here!" He had considered roping the tree as it passed, saving it for some future project.

We had the tree several feet off the dock when it rolled again, bringing a large branch scraping along the deck.

"Get the top," yelled Carl. "We've got this end."

I pulled my pole free, dodged the limb, and headed back up the dock. When I got close to the end, I thrust at the tree again, got a solid hit, and pushed. The tree moved away. I got a new grip and pushed it even farther, this time reaching the end of my pole. I could do no more.

I glanced down the dock. I could see the branches moving out into the main current. Carl was now about twenty feet downstream, giving his final push. His profile was distinctive, as nobody else on the rowing team wore an Army hat. My dad was farther down the dock, a silhouette marked by the red glow of a cigarette. He had already reached the end of his pole.

I turned and looked upstream for another drifter and saw nothing. We could rest.

Later that night a few small stumps came along, but no big trees. By morning, the depth marker painted on piling showed a drop in the water level. The emergency was over: when a flood receded, most of the debris got hung up in the brush along the river banks. We could go home.

For hours we'd been in a world of our own, cut off from land by flood water rushing between the dock and land, submerging the riverbank, the ramps to the dock, and the access road. Tall trees were the only vegetation visible in the early morning light, as dark brown flood water covered hundreds of acres of farmland.[O-40]

The flood had put the dock about fifty feet farther out into the main flow; flooded fields separated us from our cars by about two hundred yards. Our only access to the dock was by a small rowboat that barely held the three of us. The previous evening Carl had rowed us out to the dock as I knelt in the bow and my dad sat in the stern. We had encountered little current while in the fields, but as we approached the dock, the river took over. Carl rowed hard to get across the fast water, heading slightly upstream to keep from being swept past a dock that was barely visible in the dark. Now we were heading back in daylight, but again Carl would have to row hard, this time to reach the slow water in the fields.

Flooded field outside the main river channel. In the background is the approach to one of the two bridges spanning the river at the time the photo was taken. Building is the locker room used by women rowers.[K-6]

We climbed into the rowboat, pushed off, and Carl angled upstream. The current seemed to push us to the slow water. The light rain had not let up, and our soaked coats were heavy. Mine did little to keep out the cold as I huddled in the bow of the little boat, enduring the seemingly endless, fifteen-minute ride to the foot of the bridge. When we reached dry land, we jumped out, dragged the boat ashore, and tied it to a tree in case the water came back up before we returned.

Until the late 1960s, Oregon's Willamette River was untamed by flood-control dams. Cold, seemingly endless rain made floods common. The worst came when a warm Chinook wind melted the snowpack in the Cascade Range. Originally called "snow eaters", these winds produced floods that would shut down the state for several days, as highways were covered and bridges were washed out. The college's rowing facilities were vulnerable, as flood water sent debris smashing into the docks. Buildup of debris against the docks and floating sheds multiplied the river's power.

In the early 1960s I was still a teenager, eager to test myself against the river. Carl Bower was a few years older; he had more respect for the river. My dad was the leader of the team. As head rowing coach at Oregon State University, he assumed that fighting floods was part of his job. He manned all-night vigils in freezing rain to protect docks that he treated as his own. Indeed, he and his volunteers had built them. Carl was his assistant. I was tagging along for adventure and to help my dad.

Coach Karl Drlica (left) and Assistant Coach Carl Bower (right) using pike poles to push logs away from the training barge house.[G-20a] Drlica is wearing a tie, which indicates a sense of urgency or he would have changed out of his suit before working on the dock. Carl is wearing his Army hat.

My dad was always looking for ways to blunt the effects of the river. One of his ideas was to reduce the threat from flood debris by deflecting it with a log boom. The boom was a simple idea: tie several large logs end-to-end with one end cabled to a tree on the bank and the other to the upstream end of a barge he'd obtained from the Navy. The goal was for the boom to divert debris out into the main current. It was imperfect, as some drifting logs rolled under the boom and got wedged under a barge or dock. When the river was high, debris could even get around the boom, as the water reached far up the bank.

Protective log boom. View of crew facilities under normal water conditions, circa 1962. Shown are two large barges for storing racing shells and the log boom extending upstream. At high water, the barges rose almost to the top of the piling. Photo is taken looking downstream.[O-118a]

I remember pushing drifting trees away from the dock before the barges were in place. The danger had been a bit greater then, because the dock was held by cables to trees on the bank rather than by piling. When the water level rose above the attachment points on the trees, the upstream edge of the dock was pulled under the surface. The river current vibrated the submerged section, slick from several days' accumulation of river slime. I could easily slip on the slime and slide into the icy river. But I couldn't leave the debris to my dad—from my perspective, he was old, maybe a little over forty. And I knew he couldn't see the drifting trees as well as I could. Indeed, we rarely played catch with a baseball, because he could barely see the ball.

Many times I imagined the cables to the dock snapping and sending the dock and me down river. Carl and my dad were unconcerned about the cables giving out, because they'd tied and inspected the cables themselves. Instead, they focused on pushing debris away from the dock unless it looked useful as building material. Sometimes even entire buildings would pass by. But often Carl and my dad were disappointed, as most promising items were beyond the reach of their long, hooked pike poles.[K-23]

Barge used for storage and repair of racing shells during a flood. Note the angled prow on the upstream (left) end. [G-25] *A motorboat trapped under the overhang capsized, sending five people under the barge. The dock described in the text is upstream (left) from the barge. A second dock plus sheds for storing coaching launches and training barge are downstream (right) from the barge. Vegetation in the foreground delineates the top of the riverbank, which is approximately five feet below the water surface.*

Missing from the effort were life jackets. Decades later, Carl mentioned that life jackets posed a danger: he and my dad thought the bulky "Mae West" jackets were dangerous. If they got sucked under the downstream barge, the jacket might catch on something under water. Moreover, in those days we were less safety conscious. Nobody wore bicycle helmets, and seat belts in cars were still optional.

By the early 1960s, my nearly blind father had already spent more than a decade protecting the crew docks from flood damage. Since I grew up watching this, I assumed that was what crew coaches did. I didn't know that most coaches never confront such challenges. Nor did I realize that his energy and drive extended beyond physically protecting the rowing program. He was also fighting to make both men's and women's rowing permanent parts of the University. It wasn't until many decades later that I recognized the uniqueness of the Oregon State rowing program.

Chapter 2

BITTEN

The river was slower in the summer, as were most activities in Corvallis. On a warm August day in 1960, I thought I deserved to lie in a hammock and do nothing—I had worked hard to finish high school. I was content listening to Elvis on a suitcase-sized portable radio, shaded by a willow tree behind the family home. The house was a two-story box covered with gray asbestos shingles; its backyard and my tree were surrounded by an impenetrable hedge of cedars that I had to trim every year. The lawn was so thick that I needed help from my younger brother and two sisters to mow it. They seemed to enjoy pulling a rope tied to the push mower. Beyond the hedge was our one-acre "farm". My mom thought that if the kids had enough rabbits, chickens, and sheep to tend, they'd stay out of trouble. The neighbors rarely complained, although donkey braying can be jarring.

Just as I was settling in, rocking back and forth, my dad walked up. He was a medium-sized guy with wavy blond hair, very Scandinavian looking. He was looking for someone to give him a ride to the boathouse, three miles to the east on the other side of Corvallis. I might be that someone. Even with glasses he couldn't see well enough to get a driver's license, so driving him wasn't unusual. I could be back in my hammock in twenty minutes, but I didn't like the idea of putting on shoes.

Coach Drlica, circa 1960.[O-141]

He sensed my teenage sloth; I'm sure he thought that doing nothing was a waste of time. He seemed to be in constant motion. That day he didn't have any emergencies, so he decided to bribe me for a ride.

"What about trying a single?" he asked, referring to a one-person racing shell. Since I'd worked at the boathouse to earn college money, I knew what he was talking about. He'd recently added several old, wooden, single sculls to his boat collection, and one had been rebuilt to plug leaks. I'd never been in a racing shell; I doubt that I'd even seen a crew race or expressed any interest in rowing. But I saw this as an offer, as he rarely had recreational time for his kids.

"It might be fun," he said. "But you'll need to put on a swimsuit."

His tone implied that I wouldn't be able to keep the boat upright. That challenge got me out of the hammock: I'd show him who has balance.

That was the extent of our conversation. My dad tended to be instructive, not chatty. He'd say things like, "Here's how you do it." He never asked, "What'd you do in school today?" School was my mom's job.

We jumped into the family station wagon, a 1958 blue and white Plymouth. We buckled the seat belts my dad had constructed from army surplus parachutes, and by habit I checked the toy turtle on the dashboard. I made sure it was in the small depression where it lived. For a year I had been challenged with driving smoothly enough to keep the turtle in its pen.

We were headed from the southwest side of town to the boathouse on the eastern edge. As I backed out of our driveway and turned right (north), I barely noticed the walnut orchard across the street. Our part of town was a mosaic of college and private properties.

After a quarter mile I stopped at the main road from Corvallis to the Coast. Across was a large, empty field, perhaps ten to fifteen acres. It was fenced like a pasture, but it never seemed to contain animals. Unused land was common in and around Corvallis. In the nineteenth century, the Federal Government had given land to colleges in exchange for teaching science, engineering, and practical agriculture; military training was mandatory.

If I drove straight, I would pass sheep barns, pig farm, dairy barns, and an abattoir. I chose to turn right, but it didn't matter, since all roads seemed to lead to the boathouse. Either way I had to work through downtown Corvallis and cross the old Van Buren Street Bridge. I skirted the apparent pasture, passed the mom-and-pop Oak Creek Market, a few homes, and the College football stadium with its enormous gravel parking lot.

Along the route was a mountain of sawdust that seemed to cover half an acre twenty feet high. The College heated its buildings by burning this waste product supplied by the many lumber mills in the area. I'd seen workers driving tractors over the sawdust pile and had heard rumors that a tractor fell into a burning hole created by spontaneous combustion. We also burned sawdust to heat our home, and I had been instructed to keep matches out of the storage room.

Neither of us said much as I drove past the southern edge of the College, east toward the riverbank. When I got close to the river, I turned left to pass through the fifteen or twenty blocks of stores and car dealerships that constituted the town. Near the north end we reached the approach to the historic steel bridge spanning the river. This old, narrow bridge wasn't built for modern cars; several on-coming cars forced me to slowly squeeze by.

Corvallis rowing landmarks, mid-twentieth century. Left: aerial view of Willamette River Bridge, looking northwest (downriver) during a crew race, ca. 1936.[O-102] Right: Oregon State boathouse, circa 1960. The approach to the bridge is nearby on the right. The river is out of view, 200 yards to the left.[A-39]

Immediately across the bridge, off to the left at the edge of a large gravel lot, was the unassuming, single-story boathouse. After traffic cleared, I pulled into the empty lot. The boathouse had two sections. On the left was a boat repair shop; on the right was the shell bay where racing shells and oars were stored. I parked in front of the repair shop; we got out and walked the few steps to the barn-like sliding doors of the shell bay. My dad opened the padlock on the doors, and I pulled them open.

Inside was a long, narrow room, perhaps twenty feet wide and seventy feet long. The room was dark, as little light entered from the window or the open door. My dad flipped on overhead lights, revealing a dozen eight-oared racing shells resting on racks attached to the walls. In the center of the room was a narrow, one-person racing shell upside down on a pair of sawhorse-like slings. The single, as we called the boat, was about fifteen inches at its widest spot and stretched almost thirty feet before tapering to points at its ends. The wooden hull had been newly varnished, and the fine wood grain made the boat a piece of art. Two metal outriggers, one on each side, extended about two feet from the boat. Each outrigger sported a shiny brass oarlock at its outboard end. This was the boat that would test my balance.

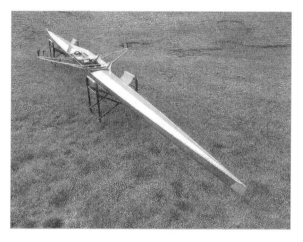

Example of a one-person, wooden racing shell.[O-187b]

My dad walked to the back of the room where oars were standing upright in racks. I followed and picked out a pair of short ones, nine-footers. I knew that I'd need two, one for each hand. Roughly three feet from the handle of each oar was a six-inch leather strip wrapped around the oar shaft. That was where the oar rested in the oarlock.

As I held the two oars, my dad commented, "Port and starboard are different; nails in the leathers go up."

I saw the line of nails where the ends of the leather strip met. By accident I had picked what I needed, one port and one starboard oar. When I looked down the oar shafts, I noticed that the curved blades would each grab water only if the nails in the leathers were up. That way the nails wouldn't rub on the oarlock during the stroke.

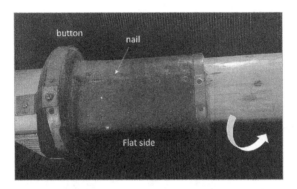

Portion of port-side racing shell oar. Shown is a top view in which the blade is to the right; when in the water, it would be perpendicular to the water surface. White arrow indicates direction of rotation when the oar blade is removed from the water.[O-120]

"Grab the end of the boat," my dad said. "We'll carry it to the river. But don't bump into anything. The skin is only cardboard thick and easily punctured. I gripped both oars with my right hand as we walked to the boat. My dad lifted the end farthest from the door; I grabbed the sharp end of the stern with my left hand, easily raising the thirty-pound racing boat off its slings. I slowly led the way out of the boathouse, carefully avoiding out-riggers poking from racing shells resting along the walls.

With one hand holding the boat, my dad used his other to pull the doors closed and lock them. We'd be 200 yards away at the river and couldn't keep an eye on the expensive racing shells.

The gravel path to the river was bordered by knee-high weeds that had dried under the summer sun. The path took us past the raised bridge approach on our left and a farmhouse on our right. As we approached the river, we passed giant logs set on a slight rise to our right. They were arranged to support a boathouse that was never built. Beyond the logs was a row of trees, a mixture of tall cottonwoods and brushy willows. The willows gave the river its characteristic smell.

Our trail ended at a steep wooden ramp reaching out to the long, narrow dock. Since it floated on logs, my dad called the dock a float. I was familiar with the float, because I helped my dad protect it from drifting logs during winter floods. Now the river was gentle, curling around the edge of the float in pleasant eddies that invited a swim.

We walked slowly down the ramp, protecting the fragile boat while paying close attention to the edge of the ramp, as there were no guard rails. When we got to the float, I set the two oars against a sawhorse located on the bank side. Then we continued to the float's edge where the brown water flowed a few inches below the deck. We turned the boat over and gently set it on flowing water, bow upstream to the left. One outrigger extended over the deck of the float while the other stuck far out over the water.

My dad knelt next to the shell and held the closest outrigger with one hand to keep the boat from being taken by the current.

"Smear some Crisco on the leathers," he instructed.

I found an open can of the cooking fat nailed to the sawhorse, dipped two fingers into the white goop, and applied it liberally to the leathers of the two oars. The excess I wiped on my shorts.

I carried the oars to the boat and set them both on the float. I leaned down and grabbed the nearest oarlock, the one overlapping the float, and flipped up the free end of the keeper bar. That opened the oarlock, and I set the shaft of the port oar into its oarlock.

"Flip the bar down into the slot," my dad instructed. "Then tighten the nut on the end. Make sure the keeper is locked tight. If your oar pops out, you'll go swimming. Then do the same with the other oar. I've got the boat."

Closed oarlock.[O-124d]. When the lock nut on the left is loosened, the keeper bar swings up to the right, opening the oarlock.

Once the oar was locked in, I pulled the shaft so the oar was perpendicular to the boat, resting its blade on the float.

To reach the outboard oarlock, I'd have to stretch out over the water. I crawled close to the boat and looked for a spot in the boat to place a hand for support. The sliding seat ran on a pair of rails supported by a wooden structure that looked like a miniature railroad trestle. A wooden plate, about the size of a foot, was attached to the framework between the rails near their stern end. From a kneeling position I gently placed my right hand on the plate as I prepared to stretch my left arm out to the oarlock. The boat bobbed like a cork under my touch. I was afraid to put much weight on the boat, so I kept most of it on my knees, safely on the float. I reached far out over the water, stretching one leg to provide a counterweight—I could barely reach the oarlock with my left hand. I fumbled with the keeper bar, but I got it loose and flipped it up. My dad pushed the starboard oar blade out to the oarlock, and I set the shaft in the oarlock, pulled the keeper bar down, and tightened the nut. I scooted back to the safety of the float. Then I pulled the oar handle toward me, bringing the outboard oar perpendicular to the boat, resting out of the water on the sides of the boat. Both oars were locked in and ready to go once I pushed the outer oar to where its leather fit in the oarlock.

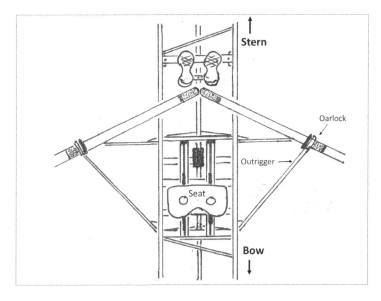

Diagram of a racing shell cockpit rigged for sculling. The seat moves on wheels along metal tracks.[O-117]

I tested the water with my hand; it was cool but not cold. That was what I expected, since I'd been in the river many times that summer. The water was turbid due to silt, which we called clean dirt. In the early 1960s, we didn't worry about water pollution: we couldn't see the agricultural chemicals in the water.

I slipped off my shoes, set them back from the edge of the float, and stood next to the boat, facing the stern. I crouched and grabbed the starboard oar in my left hand, pushing the oar out until its leather fit snugly in the oarlock. The oarlock was tilted slightly, giving the starboard blade an angle that made it skim the surface of the flowing river. I noticed that the oar handles overlapped by about six inches: one hand would have to pass over the other on each stroke, a striking contrast to the common rowboat in which ends of the oars are often separated by a foot-long gap.

"Grab both oar handles in your left hand," my dad instructed. "Then put your left foot on the plate in the boat just to the stern of the seat," he said, pointing to where I had previously placed my hand for support when I stretched to reach the outboard oarlock. I gently stepped, keeping my right foot and weight on the float.

"Now reach down and grab the boat with your right hand," he continued. As I bent over, my weight shifted to the boat. It bobbed in the water but didn't tip, as my dad held it tightly.

"Now squat on your left leg, place your right foot in the stretcher boot, and lower yourself onto the seat. I'm holding the boat; you won't tip over."

I quickly got my right foot into the footrest and plopped onto the seat. Then I put my left foot into the left shoe of the footrest. With a little squirming I settled into the center of the seat, legs flat, an oar in each hand.

"Left over right, thumbs on the ends," were my dad's next instructions. The left oarlock was slightly higher than the right to give the left oar handle room to pass over the right one.

I was ready to take on the river, even though the right (port) blade still rested on the float. I was more curious than nervous. At worst I would go for a swim. And how hard could this be? During a family vacation, I had found it easy to row a wide-bodied rental boat on a calm lake.

My dad shifted his grip from the outrigger to the blade of my port oar. I held on tightly, and he pushed me firmly out into the current, slightly upstream. My left oar continued to skim the moving water, and soon my right did the same. I was on my own, sitting on what felt like a telephone pole that could easily roll—only the oar blades resting flat on the water kept me upright.

"Don't let the blades sink," my dad commanded. "If they go too far under, you'll swim."

I drifted downstream at half walking speed, with the float about ten feet from my port blade, blades still flat on the water to keep me from tipping over. I raised my left hand a few inches—instantly the boat listed to port; right hand up, down went the shell on the left side. The boat was tightly linked to my hands, to my slightest movement. A wrong move, even a sneeze, could tip the boat over. All bravado was gone.

As the boat and I drifted toward the end of the float, I knew I'd have to take a stroke to stay even. My dad didn't have a motorboat ready for rescue.

"Roll (turn) your blades perpendicular to the water," my dad shouted from the float. "Then raise your hands and put the blades in. Pull gently, evenly. Get the blades out of the water by dropping your hands into your lap. Then turn the oars by dropping your wrists. That will put the blades flat on the water."

I rolled the blades perpendicular to the surface, set them in the water, and gently pulled. The shell leaped ahead; the blades came out of the water as my hands dropped down. At the same time, my wrists went into my lap, the oars rotated, and the blades seemed to naturally skim the surface. I felt so powerful, in control of boat and river. That must have been when the rowing bug bit me.

The shell waited for the next instruction from my hands. With newfound confidence I again rolled the blades to where I thought they were perpendicular, slipped them into the water, and pulled, harder than the first time. I wanted a bigger jump from the boat. Suddenly I found myself spitting out river water. The shell had tipped to port, dumping me into the river so quickly I barely had time to catch my breath.

The boat rolled back up, shipping no water. I could almost hear it laughing at me. I quickly grabbed the port outrigger and started side-stroking toward the float, working hard to reach it before we drifted past the end. The bow of the shell got close enough for my dad to grab and pull me in. I let go of the boat, gripped the wooden decking of the float, and pulled myself out.

In a very matter-of-fact way he said, "Your port blade wasn't completely rolled up (perpendicular) when you pulled; you knifed in and went too deep when you pulled." He knew that would happen.

I got back in the boat, and he again pushed me off the float. Again, I began with tiny strokes. I got in several before the boat dumped me. It was me versus the boat, but I knew I could bring it under control—if I were very careful.

On my third try I kept up with the current using baby strokes. The shell surged forward every time I pulled even slightly. I had never felt a boat that was so responsive.

Somehow, I ended up in the middle of the river, a hundred feet from safety. I don't know how I got there. I was concentrating on putting the oars in the water squarely, keeping the boat on an even keel by pulling gently. A bystander on the far bank must have thought I knew what I was doing, as he yelled for me to get my oars off the water between strokes. I didn't dare—I let them skim the surface as I reached for each stroke. I gradually worked my way back across the current; after about ten minutes I angled toward the float.

Racing shell in the middle of the river.[O-133a]

"Head upstream," my dad called out, wanting me to come to the dock at a shallow angle rather than head on. I took several tiny strokes with my right hand, pulling the bow around to head upstream while still angling toward the float. When my bow reached the float, my dad again grabbed it, keeping me from bashing the boat into the wooden dock. He didn't ask how I felt. He knew. I had learned to glide on water under my own power. I felt like a water strider.

Chapter 3

AT THE BOATHOUSE

A lthough I didn't get into a racing shell until I was 17, the boathouse had already been a part of life for a decade. When my younger siblings and I were little, my mom couldn't leave us alone when she drove to the boathouse to pick up Dad for dinner. We all piled into our maroon, 1950 Studebaker and rode, in the dark and rain, to the boathouse.

After crossing the narrow bridge and making the left turn into the boathouse parking lot, my mom would pull up to the boathouse door and wait in the car for my dad. Soon she was fuming: my dad was never ready to go. Initially I was assigned the task of running through the rain to tell him we were waiting. He was always talking with someone, often with his mentor Ed Stevens, the coach before my dad. Stevens had retired in 1950, but he was usually at the boathouse, repairing wooden racing shells and offering advice.

Within a few years, my little brother, Steve, grew big enough to jump out of the car and sprint through the rain to the shop section of the boathouse, the side where boats were built and repaired. Then my sister Karen wanted the honors. I was happy to stay dry and count the raindrops as they pounded the roof of the car.

Karen Drlica, 1950s[O-143]

Karen would yell at Dad that we were here. Then she'd find a broom and sweep the sawdust off the floor. The workshop was about eighty feet long and twenty wide, with windows along the outer wall. A narrow boat stand ran for sixty feet through the center of the room; power saws and a planer, mostly along the inner wall, produced piles of sawdust. When Karen's sweeping was done, she'd find a chair to push against the long workbench. She'd climb onto the chair and then the bench to hang tools on the wall where their shapes were stenciled. Next, she'd run to Dad's office at the back of the building, often finding him talking with someone as he sat on the metal desk he'd built years before. I'm sure she pestered him for the dime he promised her for sweeping and putting tools away.

Sometimes Karen and Steve would put training-barge seats on the floor of the large room where the racing shells were stored. There they would sit on the seats and race. Karen recalled, "We could get the speed up going backwards toward the door, between the rows of shells, pushing with our feet. Dad asked only that we not use the racing shell seats. They were more delicate than the training-barge seats, which ran on heavy roller-skate wheels. Dad was concerned that we might put flat spots on the wheels when we skidded. Once in a while we'd fall off or hit a greasy outrigger from a shell on the bottom rack."

Some boathouse events were etched into vivid memories. Karen recalled, "When I was six or seven, I was sent in by Mom to get Dad. I was told by someone to check in the shower room. I climbed up the three steps to the raised room and burst in. ... I was met with BIG guys being embarrassed by a little girl in their midst. They ran to hide and yelled at Dad; I spun around and went out the door as fast as I could. But I had a message to deliver, so I waited on the steps. Soon Dad came to the door, I relayed the message, and no more was said."

My dad sometimes took us to the boathouse on weekends as a treat or maybe to babysit. In the summer, we ran up and down the ramps and floats. He had no concern for dangers of the river, nor did we. Indeed, years later he allowed dozens of boats to row in the rainy darkness even during high water.

He may have naively thought he could get some work done if he gave us projects, mostly woodworking. He started Karen on a model sailboat that she remembered painting, along with her clothes, blue. I liked running the saws and especially the planer, which was an incredible machine. And we'd spend hours working (playing) with the lathe, making fancy clubs and other wooden implements for mock battles.

In 1958 the family bought a Plymouth station wagon and kept the old Studebaker, which my dad would occasionally drive to the boathouse, always on back streets because his eyesight was so poor he couldn't get a license. From time to time one of the kids would go with him. Like many parents, he enjoyed introducing his children to new things, but sometimes he overdid it.

Karen recalled, "One of the highlights for me was going to the boathouse with him and sitting on his lap steering the car in the parking lot on the way home. I ran the car up the bank (bridge approach) on the way out of the boathouse (parking lot) while looking at something we were talking about and almost rolled the car. We didn't have seat belts, and that scared Dad so much that I wasn't allowed to 'drive' the car until I reached age fifteen. I can't recall being aware of the danger; I wasn't very upset about not driving. I did learn to take risks from dad though, and to be bold and outspoken."[O-183]

I eventually grew old enough to take on the driving chore, picking Dad up for dinner and taking him back to work after we ate. That was the role model: get a job you can never finish, but one you enjoy so much that every free moment is spent trying to finish.

After a few more years, my dad took to bicycle to relieve the stress of having a driver waiting for him, pushing him to hurry. Corvallis is largely flat, and we all rode bicycles. But the winter wind and rain made riding a challenge and even dangerous. Indeed, Suzanne Wilkins, a member of the women's crew, died when hit by a car on her way home from rowing practice.[O-157] My dad suffered a long-lasting shoulder injury when hit by a drunk driver in the middle of a clear, dry day.

Coach Drlica, undated photo showing the bicycle
he was riding when hit by a car.[O-142]

Parked cars seemed to get in my way when the wind forced me to keep my head down. We often rode at night; my dad had a light on his bike, but in those days bicycle lights were dim. I didn't feel that they did any good. I went without a light until forced to get one by recurring nightmares in which police were chasing me for no light.

As I grew older, I performed odd jobs at the boathouse. I think my dad wanted me to learn practical skills. My tasks included making replacement parts for wooden racing shells and placing empty oil drums under the docks to counter the water-soaked logs. He made sure I knew how to roll logs with a peavy, a stout wooden pole with a hinged metal hook near the end for gripping logs. I also hauled scrap lumber the two miles from the college campus to the boathouse. We needed it to build floating sheds for coaching launches. When he had me transport used towels and gym clothing from the boathouse to campus, he unknowingly introduced me to microbiology, "Wash your hands. You don't know where those towels have been." That was the most useful lesson.

I never saw an administrator from the University visit the boathouse. My dad seemed to have his own little universe in which salvaging and self-sufficiency were central to the culture. To understand the development of this culture, I step back forty years to introduce Ed Stevens, the Oregon State coach who preceded my dad and became his mentor.

---- Chapter 4 ----

ED STEVENS, LOCAL ROWING HERO

E d Stevens' obituary[O-23,A-47] made *The New York Times*, but it was brief—a quarter-column piece that mentioned him as a Harvard crew coach in the pre-television days when Ivy League rowing was a big-time spectator sport. It also pointed out that he was the first paid rowing coach at Oregon Agricultural College, an obscure western school that later became Oregon State College and in 1961, Oregon State University. Not mentioned was Stevens' personification of American self-sufficiency. The Great Depression made resources so scarce that Stevens became a master of salvage as he built a rowing program on a river plagued by floods. In 1935 he wrote,

> "As getters of something for nothing,
> we hold all records. We became the village
> nuisance, and folks locked the door
> whenever we came in sight."[A-44]

Along the way, he taught many hundreds of young Oregonians manual skills that included repurposing a railroad depot and building racing shells.

The obituary also failed to mention the unprecedented philosophical shift Stevens made after leaving Harvard: from win-at-all-costs rowing to crew for the average person. In the highly competitive atmosphere of Harvard rowing, he stated, "Anyone who loafs will be pulled out of the boat". In Corvallis, he shifted to "We never cut the squad: rowing is for any and all who want it". To him it made no difference whether the rower had two left hands and weighed 120 pounds or 220 pounds. Part of "wanting it" included boathouse construction and dock repair. Indeed, some students preferred to work on the facilities and build boats rather than pull an oar. There was room for everyone at the Oregon State boathouse.[A-3]

My dad first met Stevens in 1936, when Stevens was 51 years old. "Stevens was a big man, standing well over six feet and weighing more than 200 pounds." Early pictures show him to be a typical heavy-weight varsity oarsman, tall and muscular.

Ed Stevens 1909.[A-1]

Stevens grew up near Cortland, New York, [A-11,O-23] a town of 10,000 people located about thirty miles south of Syracuse. In the horse-and-buggy days of the late 19th century, Cortland was largely a farming community with a bit of light industry (manufacture of wire window screens). Stevens probably came from the farming sector, since references to agriculture appear at many points in his career. As a farm kid he must have milked the cows, cleaned out the barn, and harvested hay. In winter, he was likely responsible for splitting firewood and stoking the fire in the stove.

Stevens often wrote about the virtues of Oregon weather. I imagine he was comparing Oregon winters to the brutal winters of Upstate New York. I understand his willingness to trade piles of snow for mud puddles, since I lived in Upstate New York for several years. I pulled more vehicles out of snowbanks than I care to remember.

After completing high school, Stevens probably worked on the farm for several years, since he was 20 years old when he left for college in 1905. He didn't go far, twenty miles east to Ithaca and Cornell University. He was a farm boy, initially looking to the agricultural school for tips on growing crops and raising farm animals. But soon after arriving he began to study law.

In the early 20th century, crew races were major events. Spectators often exceeded 50,000; trains with bleachers mounted on flatcars paralleled racecourses. The thousands of fans at the finish line made such a roar that adrenalin surged in every crew. This milieu made it easy for oarsmen and coaches to recruit new rowers to their teams, especially at Cornell where the crew was winning almost all its races. Moreover, a varsity letter winner would be a "big man on campus". Stevens joined the crew.

Stevens was a collector of material written about himself. Thus, we know from local newspaper accounts when he returned home to visit his parents and the position he rowed in the Cornell boat. He even annotated some clippings with notes in the margins.

Cornell's coach, Pop Courtney, was a legendary, hard-driving man who had been a professional single sculler of some note.[A-43,O-73] As a coach, he dominated American rowing: his eight-oared crews won eleven collegiate championships from 1901 to 1916. Surprisingly, he chose his crews partly on moral character. He would readily substitute to maintain cohesiveness within his crew. He also believed strongly that poor diet and tobacco use interfered with the ability of young men to work hard. And he was tough—he kicked a whole crew off the team for eating strawberry shortcake shortly before a race (he won the race with substitutes).

Pop Courtney, photo taken between
1910 and 1915.[O-105]

Stevens rowed in the Cornell varsity boat for three years (1907-1909). In 1907 and 1909 the crew won the IRA (collegiate) championship; in 1908 it placed third. He knew how to win races. As reported years later, in 1908-1909 Stevens "held down [the] number 5 and number 7 [seats] in the Cornell eight [depending on the year]."[A-1,A-22,A-31] These positions, plus number 6, are sometimes called the engine room, because the largest, strongest of the team row there.

In the early twentieth century, varsity crews competed in grueling four-mile races. Stevens later complained to my dad that four miles was unreasonably far (currently most races are sprints of 2,000 meters, about 1.25 miles). Stevens was not alone in his complaint, as opinion pieces in newspapers condemned the long races.[A-47] To make his point, Stevens saved a clipping from the *Providence Tribune* describing the last part of a four-mile race:

"I read that the stroke pulled three times without touching the water and that after the oar slipped from his hands, he [still] went through the motions before he collapsed …"

Stevens was a conscientious student, and after rowing practice he had his friends place ice-cold towels on his head to keep him awake. Even then, he was often too tired to study.[A-43] To him, being fit enough for four-mile races was not worth the local prestige. Stevens began to think that the teamwork aspect of rowing, the part he loved, could be experienced without such extreme commitment.[A-43] There must be a better way, one that would allow more young men to participate in his favorite sport and also do well in school.

I never rowed a four-mile race, but many decades after retiring from competition I gained an appreciation for Stevens' complaint. While sculling in Berkeley's Aquatic Park, a narrow lagoon a mile long and about 100 yards wide, I had completed the first two miles of my workout when I noticed a much faster sculler leaving the dock and coming up behind me. He was on a routine row, taking no notice of me. I decided that I wouldn't let him pass. We had to make a 180° turn every mile; by hurrying on the turns, I was able to stay ahead. After three miles, my arms and legs were numb, but they kept my boat moving. The main problem was my lungs. They ached like never before, worse than sprinting in freezing weather. After another half mile I realized that something was wrong: my lungs shouldn't hurt this much. I was still ahead, but I lost track of my course. Suddenly I was dead in the water. I had run into the bank. Fortunately! I had to rest my lungs. As my "opponent" passed, he asked whether I was OK. I mumbled yes. I was still upright, able to row to the dock and crawl out of the boat.

At the dock, another sculler saw me kneeling in a daze. He walked down to the dock, and I blurted, "Lungs hurt." He picked up my boat, carried it to the boathouse, and I stumbled after, vomiting several times. I don't remember getting into my car, but somehow

I got up to speed on the I-80 freeway and managed to cross three lanes of traffic without getting hit. At home I crawled into bed without removing my clothes and stayed there for two days.

Stevens graduated from Cornell in 1909 with a persisting interest in agriculture and a law degree he'd never use. He remained at Cornell for a year or so to take advanced agriculture classes, and Pop Courtney kept him on as an assistant coach.[A-47,O-46] Courtney must have recognized Stevens' understanding of the sport, since assistant coaches were responsible for teaching the next generation of oarsmen how to win races. In the process, Stevens adopted Courtney's training philosophy as his own.

By 1910 railroad travel had opened the West Coast to newcomers. Oregon was seen as a land of opportunity for many, including my own grandparents. One pair had come directly from Europe, the other overland from the Midwest. The Willamette Valley offered fertile farmland at a time when most Americans were farmers, and the forests were ripe for logging. Stevens joined the migration, first to Idaho and, in 1912, further west to Portland.[O-23]

Portland sits at the confluence of the Willamette and Columbia Rivers, about 100 miles inland from the Pacific Ocean. Both rivers are navigable, which allowed Portland to become a port city, exporting lumber and agricultural products. The towns of the Willamette Valley, scattered along 100 miles of river, were connected by steamboats. Roads, where they existed, were little more than dirt tracks in the summer and lines of mud the rest of the year.

When Stevens arrived, most of the streets of Portland were unpaved, and automobiles were a novelty (a 1910 photo of Portland shows streets full of horse-drawn wagons). But soon Portland's thriving population of 200,000 began to convert the streets from mud to pavement. At about the same time (1911-1923), the world's longest paved highway (US-99) was built, passing through the towns of the Willamette Valley as the road stretched from Mexico to Canada. That ended most river travel.

Front Street, Portland, Oregon 1910.[O-98]

For many years, the Portland elite sent their sons east to Ivy League colleges. When the young men returned home for summer vacation, they missed rowing. In the late 1870s, thirty of them banded together, purchased racing shells, and rented a storage shed. They began rowing on the Willamette River, which was wide enough for racing shells to dart in and out among the ocean-going ships that populated the port. When Stevens arrived, he immediately made his way to the boathouse. He soon began to ply the river with experienced oarsmen. He felt at home in Portland.

Rowing paid no salary, so Stevens had to find a job. College graduates were uncommon in the West, especially those with a law degree. But Stevens must have been uncomfortable about the actual practice of law, because he never pursued it profession-ally (next to rowing, Stevens preferred farming). To support his rowing passion, Stevens took a job with the telephone company and farmed on the side. The telephone system was still new, especially in sparsely populated Eastern Oregon. Until 1917, Stevens was the telephone traffic chief for the eastern part of the state. He seemed to be adapting to Oregon life, and in 1915 he married Grace Pierce in Oregon City, a small town located on the Willamette River a few miles south of Portland. [O-23]

The move westward had not decreased Stevens' desire to win. Soon after he joined the Portland Rowing Club, it began beating its arch-rival, the Vancouver (B.C.) Rowing Club. However, farming, Stevens' day job, and a new wife forced rowing into a secondary role. Fred Newell, one of Steven's rowing partners, wrote,[A-53] "I first got acquainted with Steve (Stevens) in 1914. ... He would row for a year or two and then drop out of sight."

Newell was a wiry young man who was well established in Portland athletic circles, having run the anchor leg of a 1907 relay from Salem to Portland (his team was trounced in the 50-mile race by a Native American team from the government school in Salem).[O-3] Decades later, Newell recalled Stevens' passion for rowing.[A-53]

"I was Captain of our [rowing] club in 1919 and 1920 and wanted to build up a senior four-oared crew. I needed a good stroke man. ... While trying to figure out who I could pick up, I happened to hear Steve (Stevens) was working on a farm out in the country. I finally got him located and drove out and talked to him. Boy! Did he jump at the chance. He quit his job and came into town all excited to row. Got himself a job working in a local flour mill. He was very limited in cash; also, he and his first wife had broken up, and he was on his own (they remarried each other in 1925). We gave him an attic room in our clubhouse ... to sleep in. As I recall, he made our clubhouse a sort of headquarters, picking up small jobs here and there. He rowed for us ... and needless to say, he was a good, powerful oarsman."

Stevens likely worked for a ship-building firm in Portland, at least in 1918 and 1919. The firm published a booklet touting the feats of its employees, including the fact that in 1918 Stevens was a frame bender. The frames that Stevens bent were equivalent to the ribs of a canoe. In ship construction, long strips of steel were bent so one end attached perpendicular to the keel, while the other end connected to the deck. Metal plates of the hull were then welded to the frames, which in traditional ships were placed two to three feet apart. Stevens was not afraid of hard, physical work.

Lithograph of frame bending.[A-26]

In response to a challenge from eastern shipbuilding companies, the Portland firm wrote a short piece about frame bending.[A-32]

"It is the same story told by the same old crew. ... Here's their showing, remembering that it is made by a gang of six men only, composed of a leader and five helpers. In eight hours they bend, bevel, and set to mold 51 nine-inch side frames averaging 28 feet in length. ... [They] hold the world's record for bending ship's channel frames for 1918."

Frame bending team (left to right: Cole, Stevens, Fitzwater, Kennedy, Stutsman, and Coon; kneeling: Peets). In the foreground are two frames that have been bent.[A-25]

Stevens was a competitor, even on the farm. His ship-building employer pointed out that Stevens used frame-bending money to purchase a small dairy herd in which his bull was thought to be "… one of the best ever produced, not only in this state, but anywhere."[A-24]

Soon Stevens convinced his parents to move to Oregon to help with the farm, making it easier for him to concentrate on rowing. He became a local hero, as much as an oarsman can. Particularly noteworthy was a race at the 1919 Peace Regatta held at the Wigwam Inn. This luxury resort, located at the upper end of a long fjord north of Vancouver B.C., was beginning to attract visitors who appreciated the "rich man's sport." Prior to the race, Stevens' employer wrote, "… if they win—we will show you this Apollo in his true 'form.'"[O-11]

Ed Stevens in 1919[A-22]

Stevens stroked a four-oared shell without coxswain to an overwhelming victory over two Canadian crews (four boat lengths of open water).[A-21, A-22, O-11]

The following rhyme, concerning bets made against Stevens, became popular (Mickey Coon was a fellow frame bender):

> Stevens is the boy who rows,
> Every day his fame grows and grows.
> All this Western country knows
> Portland has the team that goes.
> Mickey Coon bet some of his clothes
> That Stevens wouldn't show his nose,
> But Stevens tore through all of his foes
> And left them all to nurse their woes.[A-22]

Caricature from the rowing archive that depicts Stevens' rowing intensity.[C-53]

I noticed in the race report that the Portland crew rowed a remarkably straight course, even without a coxswain to steer. The toe of the right stretcher boot in the bow position was built to slide from side to side. Thin cables and tiny pulleys connected that toe to a small rudder at the stern. Thus, the bow oarsman steered the boat by moving his foot, watching the wake and alignment of shoreline points behind the boat to determine course corrections.

Four decades later, when the boat was a brittle antique, I rowed bow, constantly looking over my shoulder for river debris that could sink us. When recalling that experience, I wondered why I rowed bow. In the traditional arrangement of rowers, port and starboard alternate, with the one nearest to the stern designated as the stroke. The stroke, who was often the most skilled of the team, set the pace. In the 1960s, the stroke generally rowed port, which would put the bow oarsman on starboard. I never rowed starboard: that would have been like a righthanded person throwing a ball with the left hand.

Newell wanted Stevens to row stroke. Since Stevens rowed starboard, the boat must have been rigged opposite to the usual way of the 1960s, as seen in an old photo.[A-22] That explained how I rowed bow from the port side.

Four without cox, Stevens rowing stroke on starboard.[A-22] Rowing number 3 was Louis H. Mills, a varsity oarsman from Harvard (class of 1914), a native of Portland, and later an important ally in obtaining a boathouse. Mills actively promoted Stevens for a coaching job at Harvard.[A-53]

Stevens' leadership skills and knowledge of rowing impressed his Portland colleagues, leading to his election as Captain of the Rowing Club. When the head coaching job at Harvard opened, the Portland group convinced Stevens to apply.[A-17] By the spring of 1923, Harvard crews had suffered through two losing seasons, and the school looked west for new coaching blood (the University of Washington was highly competitive in eastern regattas, so looking west made sense). Fred Newell recalled that Stevens received endorsements from George Pocock and Rusty Callow, both Seattle rowing notables.[A-53] Stevens was offered the position, and that fall he moved east, leaving his parents in charge of the farm. He must have corresponded with his first wife, since two years later he returned for a visit, they remarried, and she moved east with him.[A-53]

Stevens took along two assistants, Fred Newell and Sam Shaw. Shaw had been captain of the previous year's championship Washington crew and came highly recommended by his Seattle mentors. Harvard supplied three more coaches to help Stevens handle a very large rowing program (more than 400 students).

Stevens received a warm reception at Harvard, but why not? He was an Ivy Leaguer with a law degree; he had Ivy League coaching experience under the legendary Pop Courtney, and he knew how to win races. To assure that Stevens was one of their own, Harvard awarded him an honorary degree. That allowed the school to claim that all of their head coaches were alumni.[A-10] Stevens was pleased, especially to have full control over the rowing program.[A-18]

Press photo of Stevens as the new Harvard coach, 1923.[O-115a]

The turnout for crew was excellent in the fall of 1923 (160 men for varsity). Stevens set out to teach a new type of stroke in which the power came from the legs, not from laying back at the end of the pull.[A-30,O-73,O-129] The new style allowed strong leg muscles to be fully utilized. Moreover, at the end of the stroke, hands and oar handle were pushed quickly out of the lap, allowing the rower to get in more strokes per minute. The Portland Rowing Club and the University of Washington had adopted the new style with considerable success: Stevens and his coaching staff were experts.

Stevens was a "hands-on" coach. According to the local press, he took "An oar himself in the 'A' crew for several weeks" and "Never before in Harvard rowing have the crews had such a splendid start."[A-30]

I can imagine the thoughts running through the minds of young oarsmen, each of whom thought he was the pinnacle of manhood—the power the old man applied to an oar put them to shame. The message was clear: leg drive.

The Harvard student newspaper captured the overall mood: "It can now be said that Harvard has a true system of rowing. Every crew that leaves the boathouse uses the same stroke. The whole staff of coaches is working in unison for the races in the spring. … They [even] act like aspirants for seats in the boat, taking part in every activity designed to improve the crews … there is every indication of a new era in University crew."[A16,A30]

When winter came, the Charles River iced over, but there would be no break for Stevens' crew. An indoor rowing tank was available for those who were "interested", meaning anyone who really wanted to make the team. The tank was equipped with outriggers, oars, and sliding seats to simulate rowing. A motor had recently been installed in the tank to push the water at two to four miles per hour, and mirrors were mounted on the walls around the tank to allow oarsmen to correct their own form.[A-12,A-19]

Newspaper photo of Stevens testing the ice.[A-20]

By making aspects of training voluntary, Stevens was giving self-motivated men a chance to stand out. Developing self-sufficiency within a crew is important, because crew races lack time-outs, substitutions, and real-time coaching. Stevens looked for men who could "figure it out". He was patient and observant, knowing that building a winning crew of self-motivated oarsmen would take several years.

Stevens coached the Harvard crews for almost three years, turning the win-loss record around. In the beginning he stressed conditioning, especially running. One news photo shows Newell leading a hundred or so oarsmen on a three-mile jog (running was not part of rowing programs at the time).[A-15,A-53] Running in snow storms was definitely new—a news article pointed out that four of 109 oarsmen were afraid to run in a storm. The report continued, "[The group] left the boathouse at 5:15 o'clock [p.m.], crossed Anderson Bridge and followed up to the Cambridge bank of the Charles [River]. They stumbled through the slush almost to the Brighton Bridge. In crossing the ice, several men fell down, but the pack continued, cursing on its way back along

Soldiers Field Road to the Newell Boathouse, where they were clocked in 37 minutes from the starting time."[A-15] Stevens noted in the margin of the news clipping that he had extended that particular run to five miles from the usual three or four.[A-15,O-26]

According to the *Boston Globe*, "The running is all done at a slow jog to get the legs into trim and chiefly to give the men a chance to breathe the air deeply. Coach Stevens believes this latter especially necessary, as his material is chiefly city boys whose lives have very little outdoor time in them: … this work in the open makes them peppier and better in every way." [A-8]

Newspaper photo of Coach Newell leading the Harvard crew on its afternoon run (Newell is wearing a Portland Rowing Club (PRC) sweatshirt).[A-8]

Although running was at a jog, Stevens was demanding in the boats, announcing, "If a man loafs, he will be pulled out."[A-29] Newell summarized their perspective when he later noted, "I've seen the time when I took 20-mile rows. That puts on rowing muscle."

The new rowing style also focused on controlling the movement of the sliding seat, arguing that ramming the seat into the stern stops would check the run of the boat. In another innovative move, Stevens had aspirants for the eight-oared varsity boat row four-oared shells, claiming that fours would challenge the oarsmen to develop their skills faster (it's easier to feel your own contribution in a four than in an eight-oared shell).

Stevens remarked, "Rowing in an eight-oared shell after having worked in a four is like transferring from a peanut [shell] to a tub." [A-7] In those days, switching between fours and eights was unheard of.[A-7,A-9]

Stevens acknowledged that teaching a new stroke was difficult, saying that it's easier to teach a new technique to a novice, since an experienced oarsman first must unlearn the old technique.[A-18] Rowing muscles are trained for a rapid, repetitive movement that must be executed almost automatically. Changing from one automatic movement to another takes many miles of work.

In the 1920s, Harvard had a rule requiring all students to participate in athletics, and Stevens was an acknowledged winner. The combination may explain why 465 men turned out for crew at various levels.[A-7,A-18] To deal with so many students, Stevens had five assistant coaches.[A-18] Newell handled the lightweight crew (under 150 pounds in the 1920s;[A-14] weight is unrestricted for heavyweight crews). Shaw coached the freshmen[A-29] and helped Stevens with the varsity. The freshman team was also mentored by Burton Haines, who was beginning a 33-year run as a Harvard crew coach. Ed Brown, who had coached at Harvard for fourteen years, directed the class crews (sub-varsity level teams based on the year in school). Class crews raced other Ivy League schools and were a source of future varsity oarsmen.[A-19] Harvard also had a large sculling program (one oar in each hand). Ed Wachter, the basketball coach and eventual Basketball Hall of Fame member, was retained from the previous year to coach sculling. All were teaching the new style of stroke.

Shortly after arriving, Newell wrote home that each coach had a launch and attendant for his own use and that Harvard had two boathouses filled with "about forty-two eights, six fours, five doubles, and an awful slew of singles."[O-61] Newell's report was complemented by a news article stating that 30 eight-oared shells and 125 singles could be on the river at the same time.[A-7] Stevens was in charge of a serious sport at Harvard.

Stevens was strongly principled and had strict training rules. For example, *The Boston Globe* (March 5, 1924) reported: "The squads all went into strict training this week, and no exception will be made except to allow the men to attend special dances, such as the junior prom, but these will be limited to one affair now before the outdoor season. After that, all such events will be taboo."[A-8]

In addition to winning races, Stevens wanted his oarsmen to do well in school, which was a problem because training for four-mile varsity races was grueling. "I would rather have an ordinary oarsman whose scholastic standing is high than a star rower who does not stand so well in his studies."[A-18] I imagine that he applied pressure for studies, perhaps at the expense of socializing.

According to my dad, Stevens had an aversion to alcohol consumption by his oarsmen, which is consistent with the tough stance reported in the newspapers. Moreover, Stevens likely accepted Pop Courtney's philosophy, which at the time was quite radical, as athletes commonly drank beer rather than water during training.[O-73]

I doubt that Stevens had much empathy for oarsmen who failed to behave according to standards he thought necessary to win crew races. Unlike Stevens, many of his oarsmen were from the elite, upper crust of society; they had little experience with the demands of hard, cooperative, physical work. Stevens had replacements for nonconformists.

After two years, Harvard was winning races. Then, mid-season in the third year, several varsity oarsmen were caught drinking before a big race. I imagine that Stevens consulted briefly with Newell and Shaw, and they probably agreed that such action severely eroded crew unity. Stevens kicked the offenders off the team.[J-1,J-21] That's what Pop Courtney would have done.

A firestorm followed among alumni and members of the crew—this crew was their big chance to beat Yale in *The Race*. The entire season depended on winning *The Race*, the oldest collegiate athletic competition in the United States. In preparation for *The Race*, Yale and Harvard crews sequester themselves for a month at training camps near the race site. Every waking moment is focused on winning *The Race* (described in *The Shell Game*).[O-71] Harvard had not won since 1920—the crew and alumni were tired of being embarrassed year after year.

Normally universities support winning coaches in disputes with students. But according to my dad, the father of one of the expelled oarsmen was a strong financial supporter of Harvard athletics. Consequently, the Harvard administration was reluctant to strongly back Stevens. Wasn't the punishment a bit harsh?

Something was wrong when future leaders of America, a country that espoused rule of law, wouldn't obey rules and function as a team. Letting oarsmen decide how the team should be run would send the wrong message to these young men. In addition, having a wealthy parent bail out a miscreant child did not sit well with Stevens and Newell. Stevens had also been wondering whether rowing should be mainly for the elite of America, the polo-playing class sheltered from rules. Moreover, philosophical discussions with Harvard professors were beginning to undermine the traditional values ascribed to competitive athletics.

Neither Stevens nor Newell was wedded to an East-Coast career, even though they were winning big races. Stevens had gone west before; he could do it again. He knew that he and his recently remarried wife would do just fine in Oregon. The two coaches quit, pretty much on the spot.

According to the local press, "The subsequent resignation of Stevens, not in a huff, but as a dignified action when it became patent that nothing constructive could be done while the oarsmen nursed their grouch, will not make it easier for the next coach. Perhaps it will not make it easier for coaches of other Harvard sports. ... [T]he recent insubordination has been generally disapproved by former oarsmen and graduates in general. ... One former Harvard rowing captain declared to this writer only a few days ago that he believed it one of the most unfair actions taken by any squad of college athletes. ... The boys, at least the ones with whom the unrest started, declared they didn't think the crews were making the progress they should make under Stevens."[A-47]

Claiming insufficient progress was an attempt by Eastern society to save face. Newspaper reporters were not fooled, implying that insufficient progress was not a valid reason for a revolt. Harvard was beginning to win races after the dismal record prior to Stevens' leadership (according to Newell, his lightweight crews beat arch-rival Yale in four out of five races).[A-68] Ironically, the same complaint about insufficient progress was leveled at my dad when Oregon State crews started to win races.

Ed Brown took over coaching duties when Stevens and Newell left mid-season. By then the crew was well versed in Stevens' new stroke; moreover, men in the freshman crews were ready to move up and continue the program in subsequent years. Brown continued with Stevens' ideas, and the crew won many of its races in 1926. Although they lost *The Race* to Yale, the following year the Stevens-trained crew won convincingly, by more than a boat length. That was the only time in a ten-year span that Harvard won *The Race*.

There is no doubt that Stevens was a world-class coach, in addition to being a Portland rowing hero and a man of uncompromising standards. News clippings suggested that Stevens might quickly get another coaching job, most likely in Minnesota or at Cornell.[A-47] Newell was also highly respected in rowing circles. In the middle of the Harvard junket, he had taken a year off to coach a beginning Portland-based Reed College crew. That team beat a University of Washington crew. But Stevens and Newell were finished with the East.

While at Harvard, Newell had taken advanced courses in accounting and banking [O-61] that made him readily employable in Portland. Stevens had taken graduate courses in law,[O-61] but he couldn't see himself arguing for clients. Instead, he went back to the farm his parents had been tending. But the bite of the rowing bug left a lasting mark on Stevens and Newell—neither could keep his hands out of rowing, whether invited or not.

——— *Chapter 5* ———

EARLY DAYS AT THE COW COLLEGE

I n the 1920s and 1930s, the Universities of Washington and California had powerhouse crews, as they do today. They routinely won national championships and Olympic gold medals. The Portland, Victoria, and Vancouver Rowing Clubs were also strong, but the West Coast had few other rowing programs. In 1926, a new rowing club formed around a small band of students at Oregon State.

The College is centered on a slight rise in Corvallis, a largely flat county seat situated midway along the north-flowing Willamette River. At the time, about 7,500 people inhabited this typical valley town in which maples and sycamores lined residential streets.[O-60] Corvallis traffic tended to move at or below the speed limit; horns rarely honked, even when jaywalkers stopped traffic. The town was sleepy.

As a college town, Corvallis supported three movie theaters, but few restaurants of note: dining out was beyond the budgets of most. Underage drinkers used their vehicles as liquor venues, and the roadside ditches were the resting places for empty beer bottles. Students of drinking age would rendezvous at the Peacock, a dimly lit, quiet downtown tavern. Only college football games brought the town to life.

Downtown Corvallis, 1939.[O-99]

About twenty miles to the west are the heavily forested hills of the Coast Range, and thirty miles farther west is the Pacific Ocean. Loaded log trucks poured down the roads that wind through the hills to the coast, leaving behind large swaths of bare mountain sides—clear-cutting was said to give young Douglas firs the sunlight they need to quickly repopulate the forest. Some log trucks would unload at sawmills near Corvallis, while others would proceed to the river where they dumped their logs. Those logs were grouped into large rafts that then moved downriver to other mills. Wood scrap and sawdust were incinerated in large beehive burners with little concern for air pollution.

The land east of Corvallis had been flattened by river floods, leaving rich farmland that stretched thirty or forty miles to the Cascade Range. Summers were dry enough for farmers to harvest hay without worrying about rain fostering mold that could spoil the crop. To assure that pests were suppressed, the stubble was burned in a late-summer ritual that filled the valley with smoke.

The volcanos of the Oregon Cascades had been dead for centuries, although Mt. Hood, near Portland, still fumed enough to make me sick at the 10,000-foot mark. The range stopped most rain clouds that then fed dense forests and in turn log trucks and sawmills.

The college in Corvallis emphasized forestry and agriculture. It was also the engineering center for Oregon; humanities were hardly studied, as they were assigned to the arch-rival University of Oregon. The University is located in the small city of Eugene, about 40 road-miles upstream from Corvallis. Eugene residents commonly referred to Oregon State as the Cow College and to Corvallis as a cow town, devoid of intellectual activity. The College did indeed attract students seeking practical knowledge rather than pie-in-the-sky theory.

The river at Corvallis is remarkably straight for about a mile, far enough for crew races if headed upstream. On the western (Corvallis) side, the bank is high, perhaps 30 or 40 feet. On the eastern, farmland side the bank is low and easily crested by high water. When viewed from above or on maps, Corvallis is seen on the outside of a wide, sweeping bend in the river. The inside of the bend, the eastern side, is in the river's flood plain. Few people were foolish enough to build in the flood plain unless they could find, or build, a hill to escape the floods. A notable exception was the Oregon Electric Railway. The railway had a low-lying depot directly across the river from Corvallis.

Midway along the straight stretch of river is a turntable bridge that connects Corvallis with the farmland to the east. Two large piers support the bridge, which for many years accommodated two narrow lanes of traffic. Pedestrians were restricted to a dilapidated wooden walkway on the upriver side. I used the walkway, but always with some trepidation. It seemed dangerously close to falling apart and dropping my bicycle and me far down to the river.

In the mid-1920s, a tall young man named Robert Young[B-1] moved from Canada to Corvallis to study engineering. Young had learned to row in Vancouver, B.C.; when he saw the river at Corvallis, he immediately visualized racing shells skimming over the river surface. His enthusiasm spread to his engineering friends, and they asked Ky Ebright, the new coach at Cal Berkeley,

to part with two old eight-oared racing shells. Ebright agreed to
help start the new crew in Corvallis.

*Willamette River at Corvallis. Current flows from top to bottom,
with the town on the west (right) bank. The Marys River joins
the Willamette at the bend in the upper right corner of the
photo. Upstream and downstream the river makes a sharp
turn to the left.*[K-1]

*Summertime view of the eastern, turntable pier of the Van Buren
Street Bridge. During high water, drifting trees would catch on
the pier and collect debris. When the pile got large enough, it
would break free and threaten the crew facilities immediately
downstream.*[K-2]

Ebright's decision to give away two boats probably involved some self-interest. He'd been a coxswain and assistant coach for Washington, the dominant force in the small West Coast rowing community. When Stanford got discouraged and stopped rowing in 1921,[O-76] Washington had only Cal to race. In 1924, Ebright took the Cal coaching job largely to provide competition for Washington. He feared that if Cal also quit rowing, there would be no West Coast competition for Washington; it too would fall.[O-74] Starting crew at Oregon State would help rowing at the University of Washington by providing local competition.

Ky Ebright, 1930.[O-104]

When Ebright began at Cal, he had seven eight-oared racing shells,[O-74] some of which had been handed down from Stanford. Giving two to Oregon State seems quite generous, but his remaining fleet was sufficient—in 1928 and 1932 his crews won the premier eight-oared event of the Olympic Games. His 1932 crew whipped a water-logged Washington team by 18 boat-lengths.

In the spring of 1926, Ed Stevens and Fred Newell returned to Portland, Stevens to his farm and Newell to an executive position with the YMCA. Both resumed rowing, mainly for pleasure, since they were then 40 years old. When College administrators in Corvallis learned that their students were planning to start a rowing program, they invited members of the Portland Rowing Club to assess the Corvallis prospects.

Fred Newell, undated photo.[A-52] *He stopped rowing at age 76 when he "got too stiff."*[A-49]

Newell recalled, "I first went there before Steve (Stevens) got into the picture. Some of the professors [from the small school] 'sidled up' to me and would quietly ask, 'Isn't the current too fast?' I had misgivings on it myself but would not admit it. I realized to maneuver a 60-foot shell in fast water was a real trick. I didn't want those 'birds' to kill the possibility of getting the sport of rowing under way."[A-53]

The eddies and cross-currents are obvious from the river bank. Even for someone who has rowed across them a thousand times, they're a bit ominous. Crossing an eddy line makes the boat feel like it's slipping out from under you, somewhat like a bicycle running over a short strip of ice.

Eddy downstream from bridge pier at low water.[O-103]

Newell kept quiet about the eddies, and the two racing shells began their trip north. Ebright sent the boats by rail, because the roads between Berkeley and Corvallis were primitive. The two shells needed to cross mountains that had threatened pioneers only a few decades earlier. To accommodate the long racing shells, a special, extra-long car was added to a train carrying the Cal football team to a game in Seattle.

Top view of eight-oared shell. Bow and stern portions were covered by varnished silk that was easily punctured. Oarlocks were placed about two feet away from the shell on outriggers bolted to the sides of the boat. Coxswain in the stern steered the boat using a pair of thin ropes connected to a small rudder. Rowers are numbered from the bow, with number eight being the stroke.[C-69]

Ebright wrote detailed instructions.[A-60] "Remember that these shells are very fragile and must be handled with the utmost care. As we had to get them ready on the spur of the moment, we had to break off some of the bolts, as they were rusty (outriggers, which were bolted to the sides of the shells, had been removed for transport). Just get some new bolts and they will be better anyway. The boats are in condition to row, as we have been using them. We have not used the *Bruin* just lately, so it has dried out and will leak badly at the first few times it is used but will then swell and close up."

In addition to the two boats, Ebright included two rudders, sixteen oars, and sixteen outriggers marked for placement in the appropriate spots. "The shells can be removed from the small door at the end of the car. Keep the horses (similar to sawhorses with canvas slings to hold a shell) for your own use. Again, remember that these shells are no thicker than a cigar box, and the lightest blow will crack them (they were about 3/32 of an inch or 2 mm thick). So, use great care in handling them. When resting, they should be supported in three places, as they are in the car. They can be carried overhead or at arm's length by the gunnel boards but do not, under any condition, put any pressure on the ends farther out than the cockpit extends. Be very careful."

Ebright's next words should have raised second thoughts about a grass-roots program, "... [these] boats are not the best in the world, but new ones are very expensive ... we have a man who spends all his time keeping our boats in shape, and no boat can be rowed day after day without attention."

Who in Corvallis was going the fix the parts that were certain to break? What about cracks in the hulls from encounters with river debris?

Enthusiasm trumped common sense, and the two shells were dropped off at the train depot in Albany (12 miles from Corvallis), lashed to 50-foot telephone poles, and driven by truck to the College.

Not everyone in Corvallis welcomed the arrival of racing shells. A new sport meant that College money would be reduced for other sports. Moreover, the best athletes might go for crew (in those days, athletes were recruited from the resident student population, which was about 3,000 males at Oregon State). Base-ball was in decline at the College, and in a desperate bid to keep their sport alive, baseball advocates met the racing shells with bats and axes.[J-1] Their intent was clear: break the shells and stop the sport before it could get traction.

Rowing enthusiasts had been alerted. I can imagine the scene when the truck pulled into Corvallis with the shells. The future rowers and their friends would have formed a protective shield around the boats. It's likely that a few punches were thrown along with considerable shouting, and the baseball supporters soon backed off. The boats were untied, lifted off the truck, and carried to a campus dormitory. There they were slipped through a narrow doorway and stored in a long hallway.

Fear of rowing also extended to football, because it competed for the same athletes. Fred Newell later wrote, "I haven't forgotten how the football coach 'bucked' the sport when it was first getting started up your way. If it hadn't been for the then Director of Athletics being interested in rowing getting off to a start … it surely would have gone up the flue (chimney). He enquired for me at the Multnomah Athletic Club (in Portland), and for a few times I met with him there and we would discuss the sport and its prospects."[A-51]

Prospects for the student-driven activity were uncertain, since in a couple of years Robert Young would graduate and move away. On the positive side, the opposition from the football coach, Paul Schissler,[A-68,A-81] could be handled: football was a fall sport, and crew races were mainly in the spring. Athletes could do both. At Harvard, some of Stevens' varsity oarsmen were also on the football team and missed fall rowing practice; Ky Ebright mentioned that one of his Olympic oarsmen played football in the Rose Bowl.[O-74] The College decided to provide minimal support and wait.

The active opposition to rowing soon quieted, and the fifty-year struggle to fully establish competitive rowing at Oregon State began. With two shells for inspiration, the Corvallis students invited members of the Portland Rowing Club to test the boats.

The students had rented a storage shed high on the Corvallis-side riverbank, and in late November 1926 they gathered to see whether the river was too swift for rowing. I imagine that the boats were carried out of the shed and set on slings for inspection. A few minor repairs were made, outriggers were bolted to the sides of the shells, and wing bolts holding the stretcher boots to the boat were tightened. Seats were examined to make sure their wheels rolled freely. Soon the boats were ready to test.

The riverbank on the Corvallis side is steep, but immediately downstream from the turntable bridge was an abandoned ferry slip, a cut in the bank that allowed easy access to the river. After a boat passed inspection, it would have been rolled over to put the hull side up; then it was lifted to rest the gunnels on oarsmen's shoulders so the boat could be carried down the gradual incline to the water. The oarsmen waded into the water and raised the shell high above their heads; then each oarsman grabbed the internal structure with one hand. The other hand held the gunnel as the shell was rolled and lowered to the water, bow upstream.

Many questions would have arisen. How fast would the boats fill with water? Would the current be too swift for the oarsmen to get back? What about eddies below the bridge piers? Could floating debris be avoided?

A standard riverbank launching was probably used. Several men, standing in cold water above their knees, held the boat a few feet from the bank to avoid resting any part on land. Oars were locked into the oarlocks and rested, out of the water, on the gunnels. One by one the oarsmen waded out to the boat, faced the stern, and leaned back over the boat as they reached backwards to grab a gunnel with each hand. Then each man would raise himself up and onto a seat, careful not to put a foot in the bottom of the boat. As each man settled into the boat, he pushed his oar out to rest the blade on the water or, for the starboard oars, on the bank. Finally, the cox was carried to the shell and placed on his seat. Members of the crowd on shore would have grabbed the starboard oar blades and pushed the boat out into the river, cheering and making room for the second shell.

The current was not a serious impediment, although, as Ebright had warned, periodic bailing was needed.

J.C. Othus was one of the spectators. Othus, who was on the faculty of the Mechanics and Materials Department at the College, had rowed in the Cornell varsity boat a decade earlier, and like Stevens, his coach was Pop Courtney (Othus lettered in 1917). Othus knew rowing. He mentioned to Young that he had rowed at Cornell, and Young talked him into being a volunteer coach.[A-60]

Photo of Robert Young (left) and Coach J.C. Othus (right) taken from a brochure.[B-9] Othus had rowed at Cornell. He later (1948) was the rowing coach at the University of Portland.[B-8]

Another spectator was Bud Kearns, Head of the Physical Education Department. He saw opportunity: a highly qualified coach for free, enthusiastic students who were willing to literally fight for their sport, and two free racing shells. If physical education interest proved strong, intercollegiate racing would follow. He gave rowing official sanction, but funding would be only for PE classes. All support for an intercollegiate program had to come from the students, as it did for the next forty years.

Since two delicate racing shells were too precious for training beginners, a local carpenter was commissioned to build a box-like training barge, complete with outriggers, oarlocks, and sliding seats. The barge was long enough for eight rowing stations on each side of a wooden walkway. Othus and Young would walk along the aisle and teach, one-on-one.

First training barge.[O-78]

When the training barge was launched (February 4, 1927), the student newspaper reported that the "men worked together" for the first time. Regular classes in rowing started two days later. Some of the beginners must have been anxious about getting back to shore, since a barge full of novices would make little headway against the winter current.

Two hundred college men were drawn to the river during the first year, and support from the rowing community was strong. Washington coach Rusty Callow commented, apparently ignoring the seasonal floods, "OAC (Oregon Agricultural College) has probably the best possibilities for a real crew among any of the schools on the Pacific Coast, because of the fine material and splendid place for practice … Washington will back OAC in any program to be put over and will always be willing to cooperate with the College."[A-60] Washington did help, but it was another four decades before a Washington coach acknowledged that Oregon State had a real crew[N-7] (as a point of reference, by the early 1960s we were racing Washington's first varsity boat but losing by thirty seconds—that's ten boat lengths (600 feet) or almost out of sight on a hazy day).

Wading into the river to launch wouldn't work on a daily basis, so in early 1927 the crew decided to build a float. They needed to gather logs, tie them together, and then construct a deck. They learned that a farmer on Kiger Island had a few trees to sell (Kiger Island is a 2,000-acre plot formed by a split in the river a few miles upstream from Corvallis; see map in Front Matter).

Handling logs was so routine for young men in Oregon that details of the logging expedition were not recorded. I imagine that they bought several Douglas firs, the major timber in the area. These trees can be 250 feet tall with straight trunks eight feet in diameter at the base. In dense stands, branches are found only at the top, making it easy to clean a log for a raft. I don't know whether the oarsmen bought such tall trees, since most of the old-growth firs had been harvested by 1927. Nevertheless, felling even a smaller Douglas fir can be dangerous if the butt kicks out when the final cut is made. Moreover, there is always uncertainty about where the tree will actually fall.

The crew probably floated the logs to Corvallis. Since Kiger Island is flat, the oarsmen couldn't roll or pull the logs downhill to reach the river. They likely relied on the farmer and his tractor or team of horses to drag the logs to the river.

According to the school newspaper, the first official use of a shell occurred a year later (March 28, 1928). That first workout was "rather rough, as the men were not accustomed to the balance of the small boat." Rather rough meant that the boat tipped from side to side, making it almost impossible to either reach the water on the side that was up or get the oar out of the water on the side that was down.

The newspaper also reported the completion of a second float and removal of debris from the "clubhouse" following a "high water".[A-60] The challenge of the river was being felt, but as a routine part of life—the article didn't bother to point out that the "high water", which I would call a flood, had taken away the first float and forced evacuation of the "clubhouse".

Although high water was a common occurrence, a flood of the late 1920s was exceptional. The east side of the river at Corvallis, which was largely farmland, was completely covered by the river. The few buildings in the area, in particular the Oregon Electric Train Depot, reported water up to the windows. The water level soon dropped, and rowing resumed. Only catastrophe could keep the men off the water.

Oregon Electric Depot illustrating its vulnerability to floods (1923). The night before this photo was taken, the water was two feet higher than in the photo. The Depot became the boathouse in 1932.[O-144]

Othus and Young had a productive 1928 season,[B-3] but without a launch, Othus had to coach from the float, yelling through a three-foot-long director's megaphone as the crew passed by. By having only two or four men row against the current, Othus could have the crew almost stationary in front of the dock.

Othus would have focused on several parts of the stroke. One is how the rowers put the oar blade in the water. This movement, which is called the catch, is followed by a strong pull until the oar handle comes near the chest. Then the hands are dropped to raise the blade out of the water, and immediately after, one hand turns the oar handle so the blade is feathered, *i.e.*, rolled parallel to the water surface. The oar handle is quickly pushed away from the chest, followed by the upper body leaning toward the stern of the boat. The sliding seat moves toward the stern as the knees rise. The goal is to move the rower out of the bow quickly once the stroke is finished. The sliding seat slows as the rower enters a crouching position, preparing for another catch. One hand rolls the oar blade perpendicular to the water, and then the blade goes in. A pause before the catch gives the rower a bit of rest, which is important in long races.

Newell, living 85 miles away in Portland, was happy to help Othus and Young. Here was a new crew that could use his advice. He talked with oarsmen by telephone after 9 p.m., when rates were reduced, but even so, telephone communication was expensive. Consequently, in April 1929 he began writing letters to Young.[A-57] I include a few excerpts to emphasize the seemingly minor movements thought to make a boat go fast.

Newell began with the recovery, the portion of the stroke in which the rower slides toward the stern with the oar blade out of the water and feathered. "Keep the back straight and the shoulders squared naturally for the firm, quick grip of the water.

"If men rush or anticipate the catch or do not appear on time, insist upon their going more slowly and carefully the last three or four inches [on the sliding seat] while reaching for the water. Get this—sneak up on the slide the last bit, and at the same time reach for the water with a quick grip and not a hard chop, which puts a hole in the water with a lot of bubbles and nothing to pull against."

I found his simple hint about leg drive useful when my mind started to drift in a race: "Your legs are not doing their share of work unless you feel an awful pressure against the stretcher (footrest) with the bottom of your feet at the start of your stroke."

In the 1920s, the sport of rowing had few rules—the fastest boat with eight oarsmen and a cox wins. That left room for creativity, which Newell revealed in his suggestions about the stroke position, the rower in the stern. "The stroke oarsman is like the leader of an orchestra; he sets the pace and must save his steam so he can raise the stroke [rate] when necessary (rowing faster, at a higher rate, is similar to a sprint in a foot race). The stroke oar [blade] should be ¼ inch less in width than the others so the work will be easier on him than on the rest. Don't let the crew know that your oar blade is less. It might not have a favorable effect."

Decades later, my dad, as coach, assigned an oar to Brian Finn, the stroke of one of our boats. Brian loved that oar, and he often wondered why he seemed to have a special talent for raising the stroke rate near the end of a race.[O-135] My dad was always alert for ways to make boats move faster.

Except for shaving the stroke's blade, the style espoused by Newell was popular for many decades. Fifty years later, with shorter races, part of my dad's problem with his crews centered on shortening the stroke so the rate could be raised by half a dozen strokes per minute.

On May 4 Newell sent newspaper photos of Yale crews to illustrate some of his points. Then he jumped to coordination "Here is one thing that helps to pull a crew together. Have the cox call out 'Finish together! Swing together, all together!' The word together to ring out at the finish of the stroke. If they are careful to finish together and get the blades out clean together, the boat should slide along on an even keel, what you want. ... If the cox squints his eyes, he can see more clearly if the blades are together or not. No doubt you have found out I am 'nuts' on rowing by this time, so please pardon all my correspondence, which is unsolicited."

In my experience, keeping a narrow, round-bottomed boat "on an even keel" is difficult with eight large bodies sliding back and forth, often with heavy heads tilting to one side or the other. When the boat was down on my side, the oar handle would be in my lap at the finish of the stroke. I couldn't push it down farther to get my blade out of the water. When the boat was down on the other side, my oar handle was level with my eyes, too high for me to catch the water. When another boat pulled next to us, our cox would scream at us to pull harder, and we would get even more ragged.

Young must have been happy to get advice from a former Harvard coach, as he saved the many letters from Newell. On May 12 Newell wrote, "I read in today's *Oregonian* that you won the [class crew] finals by 10 lengths. That looks good."

That victory qualified Young's crew to race against the University of Washington later in May. Newell sensed that Young could beat Washington, so he kept sending advice, along with an acknowledgement: "Sometimes I wonder if I have got an awful 'crust' to bother you with my ramblings, but believe me, I want to get rowing firmly established at Oregon State College."

His crust extended to convincing a friend at Harvard to mail 20 pairs of rowing trunks to the Corvallis team. "How this all happens is that through the year over 800 men row back there. They have 55 eight-oared shells, and many, when they quit rowing, throw all of their stuff on the floor."

The race against Washington was remembered several years later by Stevens,[O-15] who served as the race starter.[B-3] As was customary, the starter rode in the official's motorboat that followed the race, giving Stevens a good view. The race involved a technical detail called "catching a crab" that I need to describe before relating Stevens' recollection.

In a normal stroke, your hands are near your chest as you finish pulling on the oar. To get the oar blade out of the water, you drop your hands into your lap to lift the blade. If the blade does not come out of the water cleanly, the water can catch it and drive the handle at your face. Since your legs are flat, you can lay back and allow the oar handle to whip past your head—if you are quick. The blade ends up pinned against the side of the boat, overlapping the oar of the person rowing two positions toward the stern. You have caught a crab.

Although your oar handle is far out over the outrigger, you can lean out, grab the handle, and pull it back. The moving boat makes that difficult. If the cox calls a halt, you can get your oar back into position and resume rowing. You're still in the boat, but the crab probably cost you the race. And if the rower behind you, toward the bow, was not alert, you could have been stabbed in the back with his/her oar handle when you tried to avoid your own.

A reverse crab is worse. With a normal stroke, the oar stays feathered throughout the recovery and preferably off the water. As you prepare for the catch, you are crouched up over your knees, a precarious position. If the water catches a feathered blade during the recovery, the oar handle will slam into your chest, pick you up, and throw you out of the boat. Your momentum will send you under the surface, so outriggers and oars will generally miss your head as the shell quickly passes by. Your oar blade ends up pinned to the side of the shell, acting as a brake. You are left far behind the boat.

Stevens began, "Back in '28 or maybe it was '29, it's immaterial. A smart, smooth-rowing Washington freshman crew and their charming young freshman coach, Mr. Tom Bolles (later famous coach at Harvard), came down to Corvallis to put the jolly old sport of rowing across and incidentally give the baby a dutiful spanking. They made a grand sight and could hit a stroke of 34 to 36 [per minute] and then some.

Tom Bolles, Washington freshman coach.[O-175]

"The College boys were also a sight to be seen. As 'Old Man' Courtney used to say, they looked like a flock of ducks, and they could not row over 29 [strokes per minute] to save their lives, but we lined them up and the battle raged. The frosh flashed their 34 and then they whooped it to 36, but the doggoned Beavers (Oregon State) kept edging ahead. The young coach was most disturbed. He couldn't figure what made that pesky Oregon State boat keep right-side up, much less make progress. We know he was in a quandary over it, because he asked us about it not less than a dozen times during the race (coaches were often in the officials' launch with the starter and referee). Well, they were our guests, so we only licked them by about 6 feet. You know how it is. The darn frosh put on a last-minute drive and nearly hogged the picture.

Senior class crew, 1929. Robert Young is at the far left.[B-1]

"We didn't exactly swallow our heart during those last few seconds, we just nearly choked to death on the blamed thing. We had no more than got that jumping heart back where it belongs than it bobbed back up again. We looked at the Oregon State boat, and it only had 7 men in it. What the heck. Had we rowed that race with only 7 men and if so, where did we lose him? Holy Socks, it was the stroke oar that was missing. We must have been excited by this time. Bob Young, Oregon State Rowing Club President and stroke oar, poked his head up out of the water about 20 feet behind the boat and swam ashore. He had caught a reverse crab at the end of the race, and it heaved him clean out of the boat."

It's fair to ask how Oregon State could win if they had such poor form. According to newspaper accounts, Oregon State took an early lead in the 2.5-mile race, which started at the log dump and finished at the bridge. After 1.5 miles, Oregon State led by open water. My guess is that they surprised themselves by getting ahead and simply wouldn't give up. Huge crowds lining the river banks certainly pumped energy into the crew.[B-3]

Newell was so excited he couldn't wait a week to send his next letter, firing it off the next day, "… My hat is off to you and your gang…"

Newell was already thinking ahead to the next race, probably with Sacramento Junior College.[B-3] His advice was typical of the 1920s, "Take care of yourself and don't go stale this coming week (going stale is an emotional state in which the athlete no longer cares about winning). Take it easy most of the time and an occasional sprint to keep the wind good. If you could get a light rubdown every night before turning in, it would do you good. Be careful what you eat and do it slowly."

Newell kept up the advice with a phone call on May 27. His new instruction was to keep "… eyes in the boat—Saturday they were not."

I always had trouble keeping my eyes in the boat. My arms and legs ached; breath was short. Knowing that I was ahead made me pull harder. But looking out tended to upset the balance of the boat; moreover, the loss of concentration meant a less efficient stroke.

Page from 1929 Campus Weekend brochure.[B-9] *The crew was composed entirely of engineering students.*[B-3]

Two days later, Newell invited Young and the crew to a celebration in Portland, "Tell Coach Othus to put on his best bib and tucker and strut his stuff." Then Newell went on like a mother hen about the upcoming race in Seattle. "If it looks like rough water, raise the riggers ¼ inch and everybody feather high, and for God's sake don't catch a crab. Just before the start of a race, every man should tighten thumb screws on his stretchers" (footrests were bolted through holes in the frame of the boat using thumb screws so their position could be adjusted for different leg lengths).

Washington won the rematch in Seattle, and Newell followed with a supportive letter. Stevens was also keeping tabs on the new program, but other than being a starter at the Corvallis and Seattle races,[B-6] he was not actively involved. Newell mentioned to Young that Stevens had moved to Salem where he was working in an auto-repair shop. That was only 35 miles from Corvallis, and Young might want to go visit. Perhaps "Steve" would have some tips.[A-53]

Oregon State victories of 1928 and 1929 were big news in the Seattle newspapers.[B-6] The Washington crews were good, but Cal was giving them stiff competition. And now a beginning crew from Corvallis beat their freshman team. The Washington coaches were quick to point out that it was their third freshman boat that lost in Corvallis. Many years later, my dad's response to similar Washington excuses was, "It's up to you who represents your school."

By 1929, crew was firmly established in Corvallis, headlining the Campus Weekend brochure.[B-1] But Coach Othus took sabbatical leave, and Young graduated. That left a coaching vacuum. Newell was too far away to do more than write letters. The Great Depression was beginning, and nobody had cash. Many were out of work. The business slow-down put extra time in Stevens' hands. He began driving to Corvallis several times a week to fix racing shells; soon he was in charge of a program that was pulling itself up by its bootstraps. Among his problems was a boat shed that was about to collapse.

---- Chapter 6 ----

THE RAILROAD DEPOT

B y the fall of 1929, the Oregon State Rowing Club had enough momentum to recruit new oarsmen and schedule races. But Coach Othus left the campus, and few students knew how to repair the fragile racing shells. Moreover, the Great Depression made money too tight for the College to hire a coach or repairman. Stevens had moved from Portland to Salem where he had founded a plant nursery business that was slow to start. To pay bills, he began working in a Salem auto repair shop where he was the chief tire salesman. None of his jobs was going well. When he learned that the racing shells in Corvallis were breaking down, he began driving there to keep the boats afloat. With his typical use of the 'imperial we', he wrote one of his few understatements, "Our frequent visits to the campus helped stimulate interest; advice, tempered by years of experience, was of material assistance."

At about the same time, Clair Langton became the new head of the Physical Education Department at the College. He was in his early thirties, looking to build a program. Rowing offered an opportunity to do something new, to put his department on the map. Some East Coast schools had what amounted to intramural rowing programs, but few taught rowing as a physical education class. Langton now had hundreds of interested students, two racing shells, oars, and a training barge. However, he had nobody to manage a PE rowing program.

Clair V. Langton, ca. 1930s.[A-33]

I imagine that soon after Langton arrived, Stevens walked into his office full of ideas. Stevens was never shy about making new contacts. Langton must have recognized the educational treasure: he had a winning Harvard coach working for free. Moreover, the integrity Stevens had shown at Harvard must have appealed to Langton. Stevens convinced Langton that the real heart of rowing, the teamwork aspect, could be experienced by PE crews.

In 1931 Langton "hired" Stevens without salary to teach rowing to the masses. In his spare time, Stevens repaired racing shells, advised the Rowing Club, and tried to earn a living selling tires. The Department had no money for salary, but it did pay what amounted to gas and oil for transportation (3.7 cents per mile). For more than two years Stevens drove from Salem to Corvallis two afternoons per week to coach the crews and repair boats.

Stevens later wrote, "Of course we could not afford it, but heck! You can't throw a bunch of boys like that down. ... [We were] fully convinced that there are better ways of handling athletic activities than those in general use and saw at once an opportunity to develop rowing on a more liberal basis, concentrating on the recreational angle and placing competitive rowing in a secondary position. Notwithstanding the doleful predictions of failure, we decided to make whatever personal sacrifice was necessary ... to bring it to a successful conclusion. Most important, it could be done without a large cash outlay."[11]

Stevens had made a philosophical shift from winning-at-all-costs to rowing-for-everyone. This was a significant switch, because in those days American rowing was, like polo, strictly a rich *man's* sport. Stevens' shift also fit the environment, as the small college in Corvallis lacked rich young men.

For 35 years Langton's PE support gave crew an institutional base that allowed volunteerism to build an intercollegiate program. Stevens wrote of Langton, "No one else on our campus has ever been more appreciative of the sport of rowing than he. It is he who always stood four square when the course was the roughest."[A-44]

I suspect that Langton gave crew a disproportionate share of the PE budget, although there was never enough money for equipment and fighting floods. Langton also assured the success of rowing by giving male students only two options for satisfying their freshman PE requirement: general gym or rowing. Crew quickly became very popular; by 1935, 300-400 students participated in rowing at any given time (10% of the male student body).[J-14]

That year, 1935, Arthur Orr was elected Rowing Club President. Orr had been a varsity coxswain at the University of Wisconsin and later trained under a Canadian Olympic coach.[C-19] In Corvallis, Orr was assistant comptroller at the College; whether he was also a student is unknown. Orr convinced Stevens to write a history of a program that was only nine years old.[A-44, A-48] The resulting document, which spanned twenty typed pages, provides a sense of the times. It also details how Stevens solved the boathouse problem. Stevens' history begins with a rather loose treatment of the facts.

*Newspaper photo of Arthur Orr (left) and
Ed Stevens (right), 1935.*[0-46]

"The boys, under the direction of Young, formed the OSC
Rowing Club, duly elected Young president, taxed themselves
$2 per term dues, rented an old shed on the riverbank for $12
per month, and training began. Of course, no one knew how
to row … nor did they have any float from which to launch the
shells, but these facts presented no serious obstacle to that gang.

"[They] waded into the creek up to their waists, climbed into
the shells, and sailed away. Of course, the boats leaked plenty,
and the men became quite proficient in estimating how far they
could row down the river and still return without going ashore
to dump out the boat, or even sinking on occasion. Neither did
it matter that the old shed boathouse leaked like a sieve and that
it had no floor, only a mud bank slanting so much that on wet
days it was no small feat to get a shell either in or out. The doors
could not be closed because mud slides had buried the lower
ends a couple of feet deep in mud. There was no place to dress
or leave clothing if one did change. If an oarsman got wet, he
went home wet and liked it.

"One day the boys got an SOS: the water was four feet deep in the crew shed, and all hands to the rescue. Parading around in ice water up to one's middle in only one's BVD's (underwear) is no fun, but the old tubs were likely to float away, as there was nothing to do but fish them out and lug them on to the campus and store them in the basement of old Kidder Hall. Try packing a pair of sixty-foot shells over a mile [on city streets] and then poke them through a hole (doorway) so small that they had to be turned edgeways [for the outriggers to pass through], and with shrubbery so placed that the shells have to be shoved cornerwise through the door. [Tell me if] you are still enthusiastic about rowing—eh, well, these kids were; they liked it."

The river had challenged them, even taking away the float they had just built. But they kept going. Soon after Stevens took over, the University of Washington gave him an old eight-oared, wide-bodied training boat. Stevens recalled, "This was indeed fortunate, because wear and tear, plus the ravages of time—lots of time—was taking toll on the old crates. While we had three boats, only two were available. The third acted as a source of spare parts to keep the others in service. We spoke of the influence of time. These boats are Ward boats built at Foxboro, New Jersey, and since the last Ward boat to be built, so far as we know, was in 1908 and neither of this pair was the last one, your guess as to their age is as good as ours."

While old shells can be rowed, they are hardly suitable for racing, because they tend to twist. Moreover, they had ribs, and the hull between the ribs became wavy, decreasing speed. These particular boats were old when Stanford gave them to Cal. By the time they reached Corvallis, they were antiques, regardless of what Ky Ebright, the Cal coach, said. Stevens made them ready for racing, and in 1936 and 1937 they were used in races with the Sacramento Junior College, the University of British Columbia, and the University of California.

"We finally covered the hulls with cotton cloth, painted them with 'airplane wing dope' and varnish … to make them float.

Broken riggers and rowlocks added to our troubles. We had few tools with which to make repairs. Among the prized possessions of the author is a hand drill whose origin was in a ten-cent store. For several months, the drill in it, in active use, was a nail flattened and filed to a point.

"We heard that there was a Depression, but that meant nothing to us. We'd never known anything else in rowing at OSC. Another Depression more or less wasn't even considered. Frequently it was necessary to choose between lunch and gas to get home and, well, we usually went home. We had to chase what tire business there was or someone else got it. Sometimes it was no good when we did get it, as the customer was 'broke' too."

The boats were not Stevens' only problem. Wooden buildings suffer from Oregon weather, as the dampness encourages the natural rotting by fungi. Floods wash away foundations, and uncontrolled blackberry vines engulf buildings.

"The old shed was about to fall down and smash the boats even if high water didn't float them away. Something had to be done. We had dreamed about a real boathouse, and Professor Othus had even drawn plans for one we had all agreed upon."

To get a boathouse, Stevens had to find money. At the top of his contact list was William Jasper Kerr, President of the College.

"Dr. Kerr had been bitten by the rowing bug and had climbed around on the riverbank to look at a site that was available. We had thoughtfully invited him down to see a class race for which we had borrowed a launch in which to follow the crews. Both crews started out bravely enough with eight oarsmen and a cox in each boat, but an outrigger fell off one of the boats soon after the start and, as it is impossible to row an eight with seven men, we took two boys out of each boat and rowed the race with six men."

As an aside, Stevens mentioned in the last chapter that Robert Young was pitched out of the boat in a 1929 race against Washington, leaving only seven oarsmen; Young's reverse crab occurred close enough to the finish for the crew to complete the race.

Stevens continued, "It was a dog fight all the way, and Dr. Kerr became quite excited. He grabbed his hat and threw it down in the bottom of the boat, from where we rescued it, but not until after he had put his feet on it. Probably while he had his hat off was when the [rowing] bug hit him; anyhow, forever after that he was a real friend of the sport."

Stevens' buddies from the Portland Rowing Club were also on his list. "We went to Portland, called on a prominent businessman and friend of young folks and their activities and presented the facts to him."

Although not named, the businessman was probably E.C. Sammons. Ed Sammons was a Portland success story. According to Fred Newell, Sammons had "come up the hard way". Sammons finished high school at night so he could work during the day as a copy boy at a local newspaper. He soon moved up to sportswriter, which brought him to a regatta on the river. Rowing intrigued him, and he promptly joined the Portland Rowing Club. He learned to row, probably under the guidance of Newell, and raced in a variety of regattas. A local newspaper called Sammons an excellent oarsman; by 1915 or 1916 he became one of the Directors of the Rowing Club. Newell wrote, decades later, that Sammons had the rowing bug in his system.

Edward Sammons, 1919.[O-149]

In 1917, when the country joined World War I, Sammons signed up to fight. Within a year or so, at age 27, he had advanced to Lieutenant Colonel. He was equally talented in business: he rose from assistant cashier to President of the First National Bank.[A-53,O-77] In 1947 Sammons was a key figure in establishing the OSU Foundation, which created a way for private donors to promote activities at Oregon State.

As Stevens recalled, "He immediately offered to get a group together at a dinner and raise a fund to build a boathouse. We were to furnish a list of those to be present at the dinner. For obvious reasons we avoided anyone who might be considered interested or associated with any other sport than rowing or water sports. At the appointed time, we appeared with our list only to be told that, on second thought, we would have to get the approval of the then Director of Athletics (at Oregon State College). This gentleman was interested in other lines of athletic activity, so we didn't have our dinner after all."

While Stevens was rustling around for money, Kerr had included an item in his budget: enough to build the crew house, provide the land for it, and buy some additional equipment. However, the governor of the state cut $500,000 from the higher education budget; Kerr ended up with no money for rowing.

"So, figuratively speaking, our boathouse was a flop. So also was the tire business, and we had more time to think about rowing problems. … In fact, we had more time than anything else. The group rowing had dropped to about thirty-five boys, and the old shed was about to drop also. Fate apparently didn't like the idea of being prodded, but we didn't have anything else to do, because it was during the winter term, and we rowed only spring and fall terms then. We decided we would give the old lady (Fate) a real jab. We would build temporary quarters on the site previously chosen. We obtained permission from the owner of the property and tackled Corvallis businessmen for $380 … to buy materials."

That wouldn't be enough, as Stevens commented, "Score another round for Fate." But this was the turning point for Oregon State rowing—the seed money showed his Portland friends that he was serious.

"While Dame Fate was chuckling to herself over knocking our ears down, we thumbed (hitch-hiked) our way to Portland, called on old Portland Rowing Club men and personal friends of ours, and told them our troubles. They said they had troubles, too, and would we close the door as we went out and leave them to cry peacefully over theirs. We said we'd close the door and stay and cry with them, and we did. And believe it or not, that crying was good. We all felt better."

Two of Stevens' friends decided to finance a luncheon for rowing men. Each put fifty dollars (about eight hundred modern dollars) on the table and invited the others to do likewise. Stevens was astounded, as he wrote, "Page Mr. Ripley, please (*Ripley's Believe It or Not*). Even grads of the (arch-rival) University at Eugene 'chipped in' to help build a sport at the College, something unheard of before.

"We had a hunch we ought to … [get back to Corvallis]—not that we had anything to do, but just one of those unaccountable impulses we occasionally get. Just as we were about to go home [to Salem] in the late afternoon, George Young of the Corvallis Lumber Company came into the office. He said the Oregon Electric Railway had abandoned its line into Corvallis, and the old passenger and freight depot could be bought for lumber to build our boathouse. We learned to heed our hunches a long time ago. We went to look at the depot. It is directly across the river from the old [ferry] landing and right at the end of the bridge. … It looked like a boathouse to us without any moving."

The next morning Stevens was again in Portland, this time to call on the S.P. & S. Railroad Company. A company engineer was sympathetic, but he said they already had an offer of $450 for the station. At the time, Stevens had only $500. "Fifty dollars wasn't much with which to remodel this building, ... so we decided to bring in the reserves for advice."

Front view of the Oregon Electric Depot circa 1933. At the time of this photo, the building was being raised, because floodwaters occasionally reached above the windows. As part of the boathouse renovation, a boat repair shop was constructed along the left side of the station.[G-1]

Stevens and two of his Portland friends "went into a huddle." One, Mr. Cook, "is outspoken, and when we mentioned $450 to buy the shack, he said, 'Buy it? Hell, they ought to give it to you.' We thought that was a good idea, and since Mr. Cook suggested it, he was appointed a committee of one to put it over. We went along to act as seconds."

The fate of the railroad depot passed to Charles Hart, Northwest Vice-President of S.P. & S. It turned out that Hart and Cook had worked together and were very close friends. Hart was also an attorney for the Iron Fireman Manufacturing Company of which Ed Sammons was vice-president. As mentioned earlier, Sammons and Stevens were close friends. Sammons was also chairman of the finance committee of the Oregon State Board of Higher Education. This old boys' club went into a huddle. When they came out, Hart recommended that the S.P. & S. give the Department of Physical Education a lease to the station for $1 per year. Stevens would have full power to make any alteration he deemed necessary.

"Well, we now had a boathouse, the only protected boat landing on the river front, a right-of-way to it, and $500 with which to remodel it; and then, please page Mr. Ripley again, the [College] Registrar called up and wanted to know if we could use student labor to work on the boathouse. Uncle Sam had some sort of student assistance program called the F.E.R.A., and he would very cheerfully pay the boys to work for us. Believe it or not, the Registrar sent us twenty-three students with 25 to 50 work-hours per month for each one. We still did not believe it."

I'm certain Stevens realized that he had created a problem for the College: it now possessed a boathouse that would require money to maintain. But Stevens could mask much of that by his energy and enthusiasm. Moreover, administrators like growth, because that gives them a legacy. Stevens had worked himself into a job, and Langton started a legacy that eventually led to his name being attached to a building on the main campus of Oregon State University.

Stevens continued, "That rowing baby, born back in 1927, had grown up overnight, and somebody had to ride fence on it. Dr. Langton recommended the writer be placed on half-time instructorship. This was good news but spelled more trouble. The Depression had finished up all our personal reserve, and the old salary check did not start for six weeks, and we now had to come to Corvallis every day, 50 miles round trip. So, we fixed up a cot and camped in the boathouse three or four nights a week."

"We were at one and the same time in the house (train depot)-wrecking business, chief of boathouse design, purchasing agent, superintendent and working foreman on the job, as well as coach of rowing. The five hundred dollars wouldn't cover all we needed, as we hornswoggled anything we wanted out of anyone who had it. The Plumbing Department of the College had some used showerheads, porcelain laundry trays, and other fixtures we needed. They expected to be paid for them. They held out for two weeks and gave them to us to get rid of us. As getters of something for nothing, we hold all records. We became the village nuisance, and folks locked the door whenever we came in sight."

Raising the Oregon Electric Depot to withstand future floods. Left: side view; right: rear view. The rear contained a passenger waiting room that was converted into shower and locker facilities. A room for drying wet sweat clothes was constructed on the right.[A-6]

Stevens and his student helpers put in their own water system, drove the well, and even made the well point (a laterally perforated tube driven into the ground to collect water). They built their own sewage system, put in a hot water heater made from an oil barrel (as a firebox) and fifty feet of coiled pipe; they bought a used automatic pump and a steel storage tank for the hot water. From the timbers in the freight platform Stevens built two additional floats. To allow the crews to land after dark, he placed floodlights on the riverbank. Since the train depot suffered from floods, Stevens also raised the whole building thirty inches and set it on a new foundation.

Stevens was quite proud of his students, as seen in the detail he used to describe their activities. Student enthusiasm must have been gratifying, and his project gave a sense of belonging to young men who were away from home for the first time.

Landscaping the boathouse with a caterpillar tractor, as viewed from the back. [O-47] *Beach farmhouse is on the extreme right. The river is beyond the farmhouse.*

Newspaper photo of Stevens and his crew working on the new boathouse. [A-28]

"Hardly one of that gang of students knew which end of a nail to drive in a board, but what they did to the old depot is unbelievable. We now have a shower room and toilets, locker room and storage for 12 shells and oars. Carloads of gravel surrounded the old station, and as we had a very ambitious landscaping program laid out by a student, this [gravel] had to be moved. We had no topsoil, so we dug holes, put in the gravel, and used the soil underneath on top. Students with wheelbarrows moved over 200 [cubic] yards of gravel (roughly 20 dump-truck loads). Later we obtained forty or fifty truckloads of dirt to help fill the low spots. Agriculture students brought down a College caterpillar tractor (motorized earth-moving vehicle), and we borrowed a grader to dig up some of the more densely packed roadway (railroad bed), which had to give way to lawn and shrubbery."

The surrounding grounds were important to Stevens. "There is no money with which to buy shrubs, and we need several hundred; we could find them, as the coach is running a nursery down on his farm in Salem, and there are hundreds of young shrubs in the process of propagation, including fifty young lilacs, fifty or sixty young willows (the pussy kind), as many more spires, weeping willows and locusts, with numerous other odds and ends of shrubs. We need an irrigation system which will cost $150 to $200; as soon as we can promote that, we will begin planting."

The renovation project was well under way by 1934 when the Board of Education sent an inspector to assess the progress. He assured the Board that it had made the right decision in taking on the rail station. Portions of his report read: "... I went all over the property with Albert Cook and Oliver Batcheller, officers of the organization (student members of the Rowing Club). ... The crew house is ideal for the purpose. It is being remodeled largely by the boys themselves. With the gift of the Portland Rowing Club, showers and lockers are being put in along with heating equipment. The railroad has given the boys quantities of ties for fuel."[A-67]

The Board must have been pleased that it had created a hands-on opportunity for the "kids" to learn practical skills.

Rowing continued throughout the renovation process. Heat was required for the building, and hot water was needed for showers. "Every stick in the building was used," wrote Stevens. "If no place was found in the construction, it went into the wood pile. Students with a tractor and saw cut up fifteen cords of wrecking wood (a power saw can be driven by a tractor motor using a belt and pulley system). We have never bought a stick of firewood. Incidentally, we keep up the supply by salvaging logs out of the river. The varsity did not row today, as this is written, so they took turns with a cross-cut saw at the wood pile. ... We frequently spend class periods on inclement days rubbing (sanding) boats to be varnished or at any work necessary."

In 1935 Stevens mentioned, "We recently rebuilt our float and constructed a new approach to it, using materials out of the old approach to the highway bridge across the river. The contractor [who was reconstructing the bridge] needed room to store the lumber. We had the room, and we traded space for about 30,000 feet of bridge timbers. We now have 165 feet of new float available even during periods of high water. Ten cords of [fire] wood were sawed from the odds and ends not otherwise useful. We needed a new battery for the launch, so we sold a few odd planks to a farmer. Other planks went up to the campus to make pits for the horseshoe pitching activity. All this work was done by the instructor and students."

By the mid-1930s Stevens had solved the problem of a boathouse. Along the way, hundreds of students gained manual skills useful in a do-it-yourself era. Stevens also emphasized personal connections, both by example and by encouraging members of the Rowing Club to build a support base. The aphorism passed down to me was, "It's not what you know that's important, but who you know."

Once a project was in place, Stevens led by example and, according to my dad, he empowered young men through his uncanny ability to make them think they initiated the tasks. The tangible products and intense sense of community continued throughout the 1930s as hundreds of students made their way to the boathouse.

Stevens didn't have enough boats for so many students, and the shells he did have required daily maintenance. He couldn't find money to buy new ones, so he made his own. In doing so, he pioneered a new use for plywood: wooden torpedo boats used in World War II. His written history describes the milieu my dad entered as a student.

---- *Chapter 7* ----

ED STEVENS BOAT BUILDER

B y the mid-1930s the country was deep into the Great
Depression. The Willamette Valley produced enough
food, but nobody seemed to have cash. My grandfather
on my mother's side loaded fruit and vegetables into his pickup
truck and drove over the mountains to sell food in Central
Oregon. My mom and her three siblings were sent to live with
other families so the kids could finish high school, and physically
dangerous work was taken on to make ends meet. As a teenager,
one uncle led a team of men that fought forest fires; on at least
one occasion he crawled under gravel to survive a fire that passed
overhead. Another uncle jumped off a runaway log truck that lost
its brakes coming out of the woods. The college students drawn
to the boathouse had similar experiences.

Ed Stevens was lucky: he had a paying job. But keeping his
rowing program going required unpaid, overtime work. For
example, the thin cedar hulls of his racing shells were vulnerable to river debris. Submerged logs and parts of trees regularly
punched holes and split the wood. The other wooden parts of
Stevens' racing shells were also thin and brittle with age. Stretcher
boots, the footrests that hold rowers' feet, were weak points,
as driving pressure from leg muscles broke the arch supports.
Moreover, the bolts attaching the stretchers to the strips of wood
that ran the length of the boats worked lose and wore at the boat
with every stroke.

The sliding seats were also problem areas, as beginning rowers exerted uneven, twisting forces that wreaked havoc with the seats. Moreover, the parts of the seat would wear out—few aspects of rowing are more annoying than seats that don't move smoothly. The wheels were originally brass. They were especially difficult to replace, so new materials were substituted. One was Bakelite, a major component of automobile brakes. One-inch discs were cut out of Bakelite sheets, filling the boathouse with the smell of overheated brake pads.

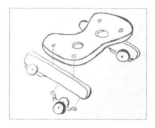

Racing shell seat. Each pair of wheels was connected by a short axel that rolled on a steel strip attached to a vertical piece of wood, called a rail, screwed to the underside of the seat. Thin pieces of copper were bent to form traps that held the axels. The traps were attached by screws to the rails. O-116

Still other problems came from outriggers broken by oarsmen who thought that their extraordinary strength was responsible rather than rust and metal fatigue. Likewise, breaking an oar was thought to reflect strength, but usually the hollow oars were weak, as water under the leathers rotted the wood.

Every evening Stevens repaired equipment, making boats and oars ready for practice the following day. I suspect that he spent 75% of his time fixing equipment. In 1935 he wrote, "A continuous battle is waged to keep the old boats ready for the daily splashing contest. Repairs run all the way from small planking checks (holes and cracks) and replacement of minor parts to holes the size of a boy's foot that he thrust through the thin covering of the shell (novices occasionally thought that you get into a shell by stepping in the bottom). Last fall a rook (freshman) crew wrapped the shell barge (8-oared, wide-bodied training boat) around a pier of the bridge, and we spent our spare time for six weeks thereafter putting it back in service. A half dozen oars with broken blades merit the attention of the coach and his glue pot. Leathers on oars that absorb wear from the rowlocks are continuously wearing out and need replacement, and all equipment has to be kept well varnished to protect it from water."

Crashing a shell into a bridge pier seemed to be taken in stride by Stevens. For him, the noteworthy feature was the six weeks it took to get the boat back into service. Missing was a sense of danger. The broken boat filled with water; by the time the shell cleared the pier, the oarsmen were sitting in the ice-cold river. Fortunately, a logging tugboat was in the area and quickly rescued the boat and its occupants. As coxswain of the boat, my dad was responsible for the collision.

Stevens' narrative continued, "Of course, the really big problem in a rowing set-up is equipment. Shells cost plenty. We knew of one that had seen better days at Washington, but the athletic manager wanted $100 for his intramural fund, so we told our good friend E.C. Sammons about it."

Sammons replied to Stevens, "While you have the opportunity, you better grab that shell. I will guarantee to get you $100 for that purpose. Chisel around and see if you can get it for $50 or $75; but if you have to go to the extent of $100, that's all right."[A-4]

I don't know how well Stevens chiseled, but he got the boat. He wrote, "This helped, but you can't keep two hundred boys going on a few used shells indefinitely. New boats cost $1,000 to $1,250 each (about the price of a new automobile). We needed six new ones, and we had as much chance of getting six or seven thousand dollars as we have of flying to the moon."

Stevens did not get six or seven thousand dollars, but he did create new opportunities. For example, in 1934 he purchased two old four-oared shell barges from the Portland Rowing Club and rebuilt them. The money ($100), which Stevens borrowed, came from the Class of 1934.

Stevens wrote, "We are planning to use [the boats] for inter-fraternity competition ... and expect to repay the loan from the five-dollar entrance fee charged each 'frat' or club that joins the Rowing Club. Since there are twenty-eight fraternities, in addition to several other groups, we expect to soon have the $100 back."

Stevens' stop-gap measures with old boats didn't solve his problems. If anything, they made the problems worse: more boats meant more rowing and more repair. Among his collection of old newspaper clippings was one that mentioned a Cornell coach who built his own racing shells during the winter when the lake at Ithaca was frozen.[A-27] Maybe that was the solution: build shells tough enough to handle the beating delivered by novices and the river.

Stevens was not a boat builder, nor was he paid to be one. He readily fixed broken parts, patched cracks, and renovated buildings. He had even bent frames for ships. But putting together a sixty-foot racing shell from raw materials was a different matter. In principle, he could take apart a shell, copy the pieces, and put together a new boat. But he couldn't spare a shell long enough for that. Working from a blueprint would produce a boat that would float, but would it be strong enough for beginners? Would it sit high enough in the water to withstand small waves? He probably thought, "I'll correct any problem with the next boat."

"We again went into a huddle, this time with an old friend who is an engineering graduate of the University of Washington, now in the employ of the U.S. Navy. This man has a hobby. It is shells—the eight-oared kind. He built one as his thesis when he graduated from the University of Washington. It was a funny looking craft, but it worked. Washington rowing men laughed at it; that is, most of them did. One or two boys who rowed in it didn't. We had seen the boat and knew the design and builder, and we thought well enough of him to recommend his employment by the Harvard Athletic Association during one year of leave from his Navy job. During that year he built two more shells and worked out numerous problems in rowing research. He left Harvard when we did, coming back to his old job [with the Navy]. As a result of our conference, he drew plans for an eight-oared, modified practice shell [that would hold up to rough treatment]."

The Navy man was John Campbell. In theory, the shell he designed would be faster than commercial Pocock boats[1-2] (George Pocock built racing shells in a Seattle workshop that was situated close to sources of spruce and cedar, excellent wood for building racing shells).

Ed Stevens, 1935, attaching the skin of the racing shell to the underlying framework using tiny nails pounded in every inch or so. In the background is the finger-eating band saw that got the better of the author in 1959.[A-5]

"We persuaded the Department of Physical Education to buy material, and we set up an improvised shell-building shop on the shell storage floor. Of course, we had never built a shell. We couldn't even read a blueprint. All of our daylight hours were spoken for by our numerous jobs incidental to a rowing program of this kind. So, all we had left in which to build a shell were the hours after dark. We built an eight, and it is in daily use now (late 1930s). We built two more last summer during vacation with the aid of a student from the Industrial Arts Department. We are not paid to work during the summer vacation, or after dark either, for that matter.

"Every detail (part) of these boats is built here at Oregon State College. Rowing men who are students in industrial arts built the pattern and made the rowlocks and other metal fittings. We made the riggers at the boathouse. Everything about these boats is radically different from the old orthodox shells, and a very sound reason lies behind each change in design. Of course, we are 'balmy', but the Sacramento Junior College crew tried out our funny boat the other day and very promptly requested that they be allowed to use it in the race instead of the [commercial] shell."

Campbell's boat had a rounded bottom, was 10% shorter than a Pocock shell, and had 15% less wetted surface area. To save weight, Campbell removed the heavy wooden, internal shoulders that supported the outriggers bolted to the sides of the boat. Instead, the outriggers passed over the gunnels and attached directly to the long stringer (keelson) in the bottom of the boat. This idea of making outriggers from a single piece of metal predated modern outriggers by many decades.

"As this is being written (approximately 1935), we are laying out the keel for another boat, and we plan to spend our vacation this summer building a new 20-position rook (freshman) training barge. Its estimated speed will be approximately three-fourths the speed of a shell or about twice as fast as our old one. This means greatly improved efficiency in training beginning oarsmen. Our Navy friend drew the plans for it. Our vacation is similar to that of the postman who went for a walk during his day off."

Stevens' history had neglected to point out that he now had a modern, up-to-date shop in which to build racing shells. He had asked the College president for $550 to build a 20 x 108-foot addition onto the boathouse as a shop, office, and drying room for gym clothing. With help from the College, Stevens secured support from Depression-Era Federal public works programs. Once again, he became designer, purchasing agent, superintendent, and supervising foreman in addition to coach of rowing and boat repairman.

Addition of shop wing to the Oregon Electric Depot.[A-6] This wing, which ran the full length of the building, housed a workshop for repairing and building boats. At the back was a small office.

The new section of the boathouse had a workbench 65 feet long along the exterior wall; almost continuous windows provided light. In the center of the room was a boat stand, a long, narrow wooden structure on which shells could be mounted, either for construction or repair.

Stevens noted, "We have small woodworking hand and power machinery, and the total investment is only a little more than $100 for this equipment. Seats for the shells with rollers on which they slide, as well as footrests, built out of several plies of material and bent to the shape of the foot, are part of the products of our boat shop. We are entirely self-contained."

"Interest in this new phase of rowing is so keen we will soon have to build several four-oared boats in addition to the pair we already have. Since this history was written (1935), we have started construction of two new fours for the intramural program. Shells built prior to this time (late 1930s) were planked with cedar and fastened to the frame with copper clout nails (roofing nails). While such material is satisfactory for racing shells, it is far from durable and shatters badly when subjected to hard usage by inexperienced oarsmen. We investigated the use of plastics (fiberglass) and find much to recommend them but had to give up the idea for the present due to scarcity because of the [upcoming] war."

Completed boathouse.[A-39] *The left side housed the boat building/repair shop; the right side housed racing shells.*

Considerable experimentation would have been required for Stevens to develop plastic racing shells, as industrialists working on the problem with boats in general spent five years finding the right resin to mix with the glass fibers. By 1942 they had found a suitable formula, which they demonstrated by producing a fiberglass sailboat.

Stevens was forced to make wooden racing shells strong enough to resist river debris puncturing the hulls and rough handling from beginners damaging everything else. Oregon is a center for wood products research, and Stevens was never shy about sharing his problems with experts. Moreover, he was willing to experiment. After all, he was making boats on his own time. If he failed, no boss would fault him for wasting company time.

"Douglas fir plywood seemed to have some possibilities, but previous experience with it had proven unsatisfactory due to separation [of the wood layers]. Introduction of new waterproof glue (invented in 1934), seemed to solve this problem, so we decided [in about 1937] to give it a trial, notwithstanding the fact that our type and shape of shell requires bending the plank in three planes. Both shells are [now] planked, and this plywood presented less difficulty than did cedar planking. Students were used in the construction of these boats, and two of them will cast the rowlocks this weekend. Others are busy building seats, tracks, stretcher boots, outriggers, etc."

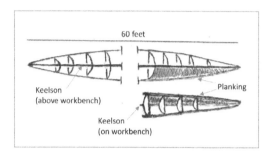

Early stage in racing shell construction.[O-125]

Stevens' narrative was familiar to me, since both my dad and I used the same method. We built wooden racing shells upside down, with three long strips of wood extending the length of the boat. Two strips (side pieces) were placed flat on a long table, attached at the ends and bowed in the center to the shape the boat would assume a few inches above the water line. The third strip, the keelson, also extended the full length but formed an arch above the table. Internal wood bracing held the three pieces in place, and curved bulkheads were placed every few feet to define the shape of the hull when the wooden planking was attached. Pieces of planking were steamed into place, glued to the keelson and one of the side pieces. While the glue was setting up, the planking was nailed with small brass nails every inch or so along the longitudinal strips of wood. Then the new boat was turned right-side up, and internal bracing in the cockpit was completed.

The idea of bending plywood was groundbreaking in the wood products business. Plywood is made by gluing together thin sheets of wood peeled from logs. The rigid product is commonly used for flat surfaces, such as walls and sub-floors beneath tile or linoleum. The strength of plywood also makes it ideal for earthquake-proofing homes by tacking it to exposed studs that would otherwise collapse like dominos in a modest shake. For Stevens, the advantage of a plywood hull was its toughness: it would not split from a collision with river debris. But he didn't know in advance that he could put sharp, complex bends in it.

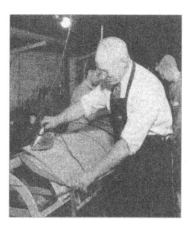

Coach Stevens using a steam iron to shape the hull. The boats were built upside down; Stevens and his crew are attaching the hull (planking) to the frame. My dad is in the right background.[A-69]

Application of plywood planking to frame of four-oared shell. My dad is on the left; Coach Stevens is at the far right.[O-45]

In the late 1930s Stevens used a grant from the Douglas Fir Plywood Association to build four-oared racing shells using 1/8th inch plywood hulls. That would be the ultimate demonstration of a new use for their product.[A-69] From photos we see that he bent the plywood by simply applying a steam iron to wet towels placed on long strips of plywood as they were forced into place on the boat frame.

The plywood association made a color "talking" movie about the process and screened it to thousands of industrialists and industrial arts students. National "science" magazines then picked up the story.[O-107] The publicity paved the way for plywood being used in World War II patrol torpedo (PT) boats (hulls were composed of two one-inch plies arranged diagonally with a glue-impregnated cloth between). Half-a-dozen companies competed for Naval contracts, racing their 70- to 80-foot PT boats off New York's Long Island in a trial called the Plywood Derby (1941). The boats were exceptionally fast, effective war machines; moreover, they continued to float for hours after catastrophic torpedo damage.

PT boat as an advertisement for waterproof wood glue.[O-145]

Two shells built in the 1938-39 season lasted well into the 1960s. These boats were the pride and joy of Langton and his Physical Education Department. During the 1930s Langton frequently brought visiting dignitaries to the boathouse to see his boats and emphasize how this rich-man's sport could be inexpensive (he neglected to mention the substantial volunteer labor).

"We build everything about these boats. ... I doubt if these boats will be materially lighter than other similar boats which use other material for planks, but they are a great deal stronger, will stand very rough treatment, and I believe the fir will take a better finish. No special equipment is needed to apply the plywood planks, and it can be done by anyone with mechanical ability."

Plywood racing shells built by Ed Stevens,
The Timberman, *1941.*[A-69]

These boats were stronger for two reasons. First, the planking was plywood—a crack would not spread. Second, the bow and stern decks were covered with plywood, not varnished silk. That made the shells rigid—the parts were less likely to work loose. A disadvantage was weight. However, the shells were fast enough and suitably tippy for intramural and physical education crews to get a taste for the sport.

Stevens also had to find a coaching launch. "Until this spring (1935), we have had no coaching launch. The boys we instructed from the float. If you want a real busy afternoon, try instructing under such conditions without a coaching launch when some one hundred boys participate." One of Stevens' friends solicited the gift of a launch (the *Yellow Peril*), others donated the battery, and oarsmen installed a motor.

In just a few years Stevens saw a grass-roots program capture the unbridled enthusiasm of many hundreds of college students.

While he had driven hard to win races as an oarsman and Harvard coach, he was now seeing something more—the pulling together to build a program.

Stevens coaching from the float. Note the megaphone used to amplify his instructions. Upper two coxswains have smaller versions attached to their faces. [A-2]

Stevens recognized that he had made a dramatic philosophical shift from his earlier win-at-all-costs days. His blending of participation, competition, and innovation gave him satisfaction that exceeded the feeling of winning big-time crew races. I quote a long passage from his 1935 history to detail his personal transition and introduce the philosophy my dad was seeing when he joined Stevens.

"Perhaps you wonder what our objective is and what we hope to accomplish. The answer is very simple. This started as an experiment, although it is pretty conclusively proved to have passed the experimental stage now. Rowing has long been considered an expensive sport with no income, and in the United States, at least, it has always been conducted as a competitive sport, and participation has been confined to a comparatively small number of boys in most schools. Our objective at Oregon State College, where the sport is a 100 per cent physical education activity, is to teach the boys an appreciation of the sport. They learn a little of the historical background of rowing, considerable theory, something about the rigging of the boat, and as much practical instruction in shells as we can accomplish in two class periods per week. They are prepared to participate in the sport in later years if they desire to do so, or in the role of spectators they have a better understanding of the contests they may witness.

"They learn to play, which may sound strange to you who probably always supposed that schools of higher education exist for the one purpose of teaching boys to work. The American people do not know how to relax and play, and all work and no play certainly makes Jack American a dull boy indeed. It crowds our highways with cars going nowhere at express train speeds and fills our graveyards and hospitals to overflowing. Something has to be done about it, and physical education activities of all sorts, and our intramural sports programs at Oregon State College ... [are among] ... the solutions to this and to many other problems resulting from our high pressure, complex 'made in America' mode of living. A whole book can be written on the subject."

Stevens' agenda, however, was bigger than teaching a way to play. In the 1930s, America was worried about the dictatorships emerging in Europe and Asia. Our science and technology were vastly inferior to that of the Germans, and the Japanese were beginning to beat war drums.

"We also believe we have something to contribute to our boys that will help them maintain our American way of life. Rowing teaches self-discipline. A crew is composed of nine men who act as a unit. They are under obligation to each other to be prompt and regular in attendance. If one is late or absent, the other eight are inconvenienced, so for the first time, for some of them at least, they learn about considering the rights of others. Cooperation is a first principle in the crew, physically and psychologically, as they learn how to get along with each other. They learn a true sense of values, because the boat can only progress through the full cooperative effort of each man. No flashy ball carrier flits through holes in the line made by a hard-plugging lineman. Each man makes his own contribution and shares equally in whatever reward there may be. Defeat and victory are accepted with equal restraint and composure; to be a good loser as well as a good winner is fundamental to American democracy. Any election furnishes ample evidence of this fact.

"As for competition, we believe in it so long as it does not interfere with our main program, which allows any student physically able to participate. The competition may range from intercollegiate contests through all the various [PE] classes; in fact, we hope to see regattas where ten or a dozen eight-oared crews instead of the usual two or three from a school may sometime take part. Why exclude any boy or group of boys just because nature did not endow him with six feet two or three inches in stature and 175 or 180 pounds, or sufficient coordination to acquire the necessary skill to hold a seat in a varsity shell? We think there is more to be accomplished with the great group of average boys than with the small group of individuals who have greater natural ability."

Stevens finished his 1930s rowing history with pride, "Well, this pretty well covers our program. Without question we have started something. When one coach (Stevens) handles double the number [of boys] who row at Washington or California, where three [coaches] in each school are employed, it is something. Of course, no one knows all the answers to the problems facing humanity today. We are convinced, however, that Mother Nature has done her part to make Oregon, and the western portions in particular, the best place in the United States in which to live. ... It is part of our job here in physical education at Oregon State College to help in the correction of man's delinquencies as far as possible and thus make Oregon in fact all that Nature intended."

Stevens did not verbalize self-sufficiency: that was ingrained in the program. He provided the adult guidance. Later, my dad, as coach, built on that tradition by explicitly focusing on self-sufficiency through projects that developed both skills and the rowing program.

Chapter 8

DRLICA JOINS STEVENS

M
y dad entered Oregon State College in 1936, just as Stevens was beginning to build racing shells. My dad was a scrawny 18-year-old with wavy blonde hair and thick glasses. He wouldn't need to shave for another four years. He claimed he was six feet tall, but I never believed it, perhaps because he shrank as he aged. He weighed at most 135 pounds, which made him particularly unsuited for crew: too big to cox and too small to row. Moreover, his Portland high school athletic experience was unremarkable—he was a soccer benchwarmer who played in only one game. However, he did earn a varsity letter as the manager of the golf and tennis teams. When he walked into the Men's Gym to register for classes, Stevens was manning the PE registration table. Stevens asked my dad whether he wanted to sign up for rowing or general gym. He had to choose one or the other.

Yearbook picture of Drlica as a senior in high school, 1936.[O-51]

My dad later wrote, "I had had enough of boring general gym in high school. I didn't know what crew was, but whatever it was, it was probably better than general gym."[O-81]

Crew meant boats. Even as a child my dad was attracted to boats. At age ten he convinced his dad to help him build a metal canoe. My grandfather owned a sheet metal shop, so folding a long sheet of steel into a V shape was routine. They folded and riveted the ends to keep the "boat" from leaking and hauled it to a small lake in a Portland park. The boat floated. My grandfather lifted my dad into the "canoe", ready for the maiden voyage. As my dad knelt in the bottom, the sides collapsed inward, trapping him in the canoe. They had neglected to install cross-members (thwarts) to hold the sides apart. The lake was shallow, and my grandfather easily waded into the water and rescued my dad.[O-81]

By the time he was 15, my dad had become a more sophisticated shipwright, as his next metal boat was a sectional sailboat. It worked well in local rivers, as long as the wind was from behind. Otherwise, paddles were essential. The seams must have been tight, because his writings don't mention leaks.

My grandparents were immigrants, one from Czechoslovakia and the other from Denmark. Their strong work ethic passed down to my dad. As a young teenager, he worked several newspaper routes; years later he wrote that he was expected to buy his own clothes from paper-route money. These routes included many apartment houses located on Portland's hilly west side. He would climb the steep streets with a pack of newspapers and deposit them with building superintendents. He'd made deals with the supers: for a free paper, they'd deliver the rest to the apartments.[O-81]

As he got older, my dad worked in his father's sheet metal shop after school and on weekends. The shop fabricated gutters, heating systems, and metal furniture designed by my grandfather. To emphasize free enterprise, my dad was paid by the piece, "The faster I worked, the more I got paid."

He also recalled, "Dad wanted me to learn to be a salesman, but I never did like that job. He sent me to Eugene (100 miles away) one time to sell radiator covers. I went from door to door ... looking for building managers and owners without any prospect list."

I suspect that much of this work was to toughen him up, since from pictures I would say that my dad was a young-looking nerd. Both of his parents knew that his eyesight was poor: anyone looking at him could see that his eyes were constantly shifting from side to side. My grandparents were pushing him to gain survival skills.

My dad failed miserably with music lessons, as he couldn't read the scores. In grade school, the teachers would write test questions on a blackboard at the front of the classroom. My dad would move from seat to seat in the front row to read the questions. The other kids accepted his eccentricity, and in high school he was elected to a class office.

He couldn't see a baseball well enough to play, but tennis balls were softer; moreover, the courts were much smaller than baseball fields. As a teenager he'd sneak out to play tennis at the public courts, usually with young ladies. Since cars were not commonplace, my dad wasn't forced by peer pressure to pursue a driver's license. Indeed, he never got one (an exception was a license procured from an Army friend in Occupied Japan). He may have wondered how other kids could see well enough to play baseball, but he didn't realize how bad his eyesight was until designated 4F by his draft board. Being rejected from fighting in World War II was a big disappointment.

My dad was born with nystagmus, a condition of continual, involuntary eye movement that prevented his eyes from focusing. His brain compensated with the help of thick lenses, and he was able to see well enough to hit a nail with a hammer (he was always careful to keep his fingers out of the way). But the heavy glasses left his ears sore, and he often used a magnifying glass to read the newspaper. When coaching, he commonly used binoculars. One of my nieces recalled that he taught her how to slip into a house in the dark by finding the keyhole with one hand and slipping the key in with the other. He learned that lesson from classes for the blind taken as an older adult. Other than needing a driver, my dad managed well even into his 80s. He saw his poor vision as an inconvenience rather than a handicap.

His teenage years coincided with the Great Depression. My grandmother later stressed that I should never scrimp on food during hard times, intimating that she made sure that they had enough to eat during the Depression. I think that hard times for my dad's family meant working hard, downsizing to a one-bedroom apartment, and looking for opportunities.

In 1931, at the depth of the Depression, my grandparents saw opportunity in a ten-acre plot of cabins and campground located in the small coastal town of Bandon. Since cash was scarce, my grandfather probably traded something for the property. As my dad recalled, "It fell to my mother, my younger brother, and me to manage [the campground] during summers. Dad stayed in Portland to run his sheet metal business, while we went to the beach to manage the 18 cabins. Dad didn't come down very often, as it was about 300 miles, and Highway 101 was non-existent. The [coastal] bridges were not built yet, and the rivers were crossed by ferry. At 14 years old I was cutting wood, helping clean cabins, and clerking a grocery store. I rode my bike to town to buy groceries for us and the 'mom and sons' store, as my mother neither had a car nor drove." [O-81]

Ultimately the campground was a loss. In the fall of 1936, shifting winds directed a nearby forest fire toward Bandon. The founder of the town had brought a shrub called gorse from Ireland to remind him of the old country. This spiny, greasy plant had become popular throughout Bandon, often serving as fencing. When the gorse ignited, the entire town, including the campground, burned to the ground. The family let the property "go for taxes", which meant that the local tax authority foreclosed and sold the property.[O-81] Nevertheless, my dad's father prospered in the sheet metal business. His shop, which he built, still stands.[O-156] For many years it was the east side location of the well-known Powell's bookstore.

By the time my dad set out for college, he had a strong work ethic, a sense of self-sufficiency, and a love for boats. Shortly after signing up for PE crew, he was caught in the rowing euphoria. The University of Washington had just won the eight-oared event at the 1936 Hitler Olympics (described in *Boys in the Boat*), and at Oregon State the fastest PE crew beat the Portland Rowing Club. Stevens had his boathouse in place and was now building racing shells. My dad rowed, coxed, and did whatever was needed to get boats on the water. He soon began spending every spare minute at the boathouse.

Despite racing success, competing seemed to be incidental. Students would show up at the boathouse at about 3 p.m. Those who were interested would fill the boats on a first-come-first-served basis; others were content to work on broken boats or repair docks that were continually eroded by the river. Indeed, some students never rowed, being satisfied with repair work. There was a niche for everyone at the boathouse, even city kids who didn't know that a small, furry black and white animal is not always a kitty (the clothes of the oarsman who petted the skunk were buried in a very deep hole). Sometimes an oarsman was subjected to a practical joke, such as being convinced that the coach needed to have a board stretcher hauled from the boathouse to the dock (the mythical board stretcher was a harrow, a heavy farm implement for plowing).

My dad began as an engineering student. He managed the problem of reading small numbers on his slide rule by equipping it with a magnifier. However, he couldn't see well enough to prepare engineering blueprints (he couldn't connect some of the lines). He switched his studies to industrial arts, which in the

1930s was a popular curriculum for college students. That fit well with the rowing program, especially construction of racing shells.

Stevens couldn't keep up with so many beginners using fragile racing shells, so he relied heavily on the training barge. Each day in 1936 my dad and his fellow oarsmen would spend about 30 minutes bailing water from leaks. Then they rowed for 15 minutes and bailed for another 30 minutes. They needed a new barge. A year later Stevens, my dad, and other oarsmen built one.

Since rain filled the new training barge almost daily, they decided to construct a shed for it. The shed would be floated by long logs. About two miles downriver, on the Corvallis side, was an active log dump. Loaded log trucks pulled up to a ramp high on the steep riverbank, a small crane lifted the logs off the trucks, and the operator sent the logs rolling down the ramp. He then lifted the trailers onto the trucks for the return trip to the woods. The floating logs were assembled into large rafts for the trip downstream to sawmills.

Portion of painting showing example of a log dump.[O-122]

Stevens demonstrated how to barter: he took a couple of bottles of whiskey to the log dump and returned, via boat, with two 70-foot logs for his new shed. The resulting barge house eliminated much of the bailing.

My dad rowed, but he was too small to win a seat in a competitive boat. Instead, he became Stevens' chief assistant. As oarsmen would arrive at the railroad-depot boathouse, my dad would line up each crew and send the men down to the river. The first crews to show up would carry oars and shells to the float; Stevens would instruct them, and the last crews of the night returned the oars and shells to the boathouse. Sometimes Stevens would start the students in boats and then return to the boathouse where he and my dad would repair damaged equipment. My dad also taught rowing to newcomers and ran the towel room; in 1939 and 1940, his junior and senior years, he coached the freshman crews.[J-23]

*Drlica (left) and Stevens (with hat), 1939,
working on a racing shell.*[A-35]

My dad was also in charge of the coaching launch. Stevens had obtained the 21-foot *Yellow Peril* as a donation from fishermen in Astoria,[A-66] largely because the boat handled so poorly in the rough water at the mouth of the Columbia River. By the time the *Yellow Peril* arrived in Corvallis, its old inboard motor had stopped working. A student named Wade stepped forward to fix it, and after several months Stevens and my dad had a coaching launch. But it was always a problem.

A shed had been built at the end of the float to keep the *Yellow Peril* from filling with rainwater. To prevent her from being stolen, the boat was chained to a log supporting the shed. One day, while Stevens was organizing several crews for practice, my dad walked to the launch house to prepare the boat for coaching duty.[J-5] He stepped into the shed and saw that the *Yellow Peril* had disappeared. He assumed that she had been stolen. The locking chain was hanging in the water, and he wondered where it'd been cut. He grabbed the chain and started to pull. It didn't budge. The boat was still there, invisible in the murky water. My dad returned to the float and gave Stevens the bad news.

I don't know how they got the boat out of the water for repairs. One of the better swimmers may have put lines under the hull, and a pulley system may have been used to gradually raise the *Yellow Peril*. But that would have required making the shed strong enough to raise the boat. Somehow the leak was found and repaired.

An unreliable engine could be a serious problem in the swift springtime river—a crew in a racing shell wouldn't be strong enough to tow the *Yellow Peril* back to the float if the engine failed. On at least one occasion the motor died when the boat was close to the float, but on the far side of the river. The water rushing under the bridge was too swift for the driver and coach to paddle the boat across to the dock without drifting far downstream. My dad decided to work the boat across 300 feet of river using ropes held high on the bridge.[J-4]

The boat was heavy and difficult to handle, even when secured by several lines, each wrapped around a portion of the steel framework of the bridge. The boat was like a kite in a strong wind, whipping back and forth in the current and eddies below the bridge. In those days auto traffic was slow, so it easily edged around the oarsmen working the ropes from the roadway. Eventually my dad's crew got the *Yellow Peril* to the float. But many years later, as part of a lesson on handling ropes, he showed me scars on his left hand where a rope had pinned his hand to the bridge railing.

Portion of Van Buren Street Bridge showing how high the deck was off the water. This view is upstream with Corvallis on the right.[K-12] The old ferry slip, immediately downstream from the bridge, had been filled by the time this photo was taken. The western bridge pier shown here was a navigation problem for racing shells.

When coxswains were needed, my dad eagerly volunteered. Ironically, this is the one rowing position in which eyesight is important. While still a freshman, he took an inexperienced crew upstream from the bridge. When they were about a quarter mile above the bridge, they turned around, pulling on one side and backing on the other. Another crew came along side, and they began to race downriver. My dad's shell was in the middle of the river, well away from the bank but perfectly aligned with the western bridge pier. In the excitement of the race, he misjudged how fast they were traveling, how quickly they were approaching the pier. Soon the steel framework of the bridge loomed overhead, with the pier dead ahead and a strong current driving him into it.[J-22]

I can imagine his thoughts when he realized what was about to happen. Turn the 60-foot boat left or right? He chose port (left), pulling as hard as he could on the tiny rudder and shouting for more power from the starboard side. The bow cleared. Now pull hard on port, get the stern around.

"The men didn't know their commands well enough to execute them immediately. After I had shouted, 'PULL! PULL! PULL!

PULL!' like a maniac, they finally caught on to what I wanted. It was too late. We crumpled into the pier with a slow crunch."

My dad recorded the incident in his diary. "My first thought was that the shell had broken in the middle. It seemed to me that one half was going to go on either side of the pier. I felt kind of hazy. Thoughts of the coach flashed through my mind. The next thing I knew, the water was up around my shoulders. The coldness brought me out of the haze.

"One fellow started to swim for shore. Thoughts of [a] story about a canoeist drowning while swimming ashore whipped me into action. I ordered everyone to stay with the boat. I finally called [the swimmer] back. We were perhaps a hundred yards below the bridge before anyone had the presence of mind to get out of the boat and let her rise.

"In the meantime, [the other] crew nearly crashed into the pier on the east side of the river. They were so interested in our mishap.

"I guess Coach was kind of sore, but he didn't say much."[O-139]

From the dock Stevens saw what had happened and immediately headed onto the river in the training barge. However, a nearby tugboat came to the rescue first, and the rowers were quickly pulled out. A line was put on the largest of the boat parts, and the half-submerged shell was towed to the float. Then the river was scoured for the smaller parts. From this incident came the cry, "Save the pieces", which was prominently displayed in the rowing book my dad wrote many years later.

My dad thought he'd never live down this error, but Stevens was probably happy that everyone survived. He and my dad spent weeks splicing the shell together.[J-5] Since this accident could have happened to anyone and since my dad had concealed his vision problem, he continued to cox practice sessions.

In 1940 my dad was the Rowing Club President, which put him in charge of intercollegiate competition. The varsity crew, which was clearly distinct from the PE crews, had a good year. In a fall race against Cal, from the log dump up to the bridge (more than 2 miles), the Beavers lost by only four feet. At spring break, the crew barnstormed to Los Angeles in two cars, one of which was Stevens' old Lincoln Zephyr. In Los Angeles they lost to UCLA by a quarter length and later to Cal by a length and a half in what were probably four-mile races. The record book lists these races as losses, but simply being close was considered a victory by the Oregon State oarsmen.

Sketch in Ready All Row *(KF Drlica, a textbook for PE classes). Emphasis was placed on recovering boat parts that could be copied as replacement parts following accidents.*[1-1]

That same year (1940) my dad, as an undergraduate, pressed Langton, head of PE, to change the structure of the crew program.[J-24] The key issue was the need for more money so Stevens could hire an assistant. According to my dad's quantitative analysis, the actual time for instruction averaged about one minute per student, even when Stevens was free of boat repair. An assistant was needed to handle non-rowing chores, such as taking attendance and organizing the crews. Moreover, too much time was wasted getting from the boathouse to the river. While my dad made an impression on the PE boss, it is doubtful that Langton had more money for crew. Soon World War II reduced the need for an assistant, and decades would pass before one was hired. But my dad never gave up on having a boathouse on the water.

Long walk to the river.[O-48]

Ed Stevens had put three elements of the program in place: PE classes, a boathouse, and racing shells. He taught the oarsmen how to make a racing shell move fast, but intercollegiate racing, the fourth element, was managed by students in the Rowing Club. The Club kept that responsibility for decades until my dad, as coach, stepped in to formalize conference rowing.

Chapter 9

THE ROWING CLUB

I n the 1930s, the student-run rowing club gave Stevens free labor for his projects, and Stevens gave the Club free coaching. For my dad, the Club solidified the importance of self-sufficiency.

Rowing in the 1930s. Man in the hat on the float is probably Coach Stevens.[O-161]

The Club operated like a fraternity: elected officers guided the racing program and drove promotional efforts, including recruiting. In the 1930s, the many construction activities over-shadowed fundraising, which was needed only for a modest travel schedule. A sharp shift occurred in the 1950s when my dad, as coach, expanded intercollegiate racing. That forced the students to add fundraising to Club activities.

The actual rowing during the 1930s is poorly documented, but I can approximate the experience with my own recollections from the early 1960s. We used the same old railroad depot as a boathouse and the same old, broken-down boats. Moreover, rotten oars still broke to the glee of heavyweight oarsmen pulling on them, and water sloshed around our feet when collisions with floating debris cracked a hull.

We arrived at the boathouse at about 4 p.m., changed into gym clothes, and checked the posted lineups. Then we each grabbed an oar and carried it to the float. I had a favorite oar, one with grooves I had scratched into the handle—I thought the grooves would improve my grip in the rain. The cost was more blisters on my hands. At the float we quickly smeared Crisco on the leathers so the oars would turn smoothly in the oarlocks. Then we ran the 200 yards up the gravel path to the boathouse, pulled the assigned shell off the rack, and carried it on our shoulders to the river. We lifted the boat overhead (about 35 pounds for each of us), grabbed inner supports, and lowered the shell gently onto the swirling river, always bow upstream. Oars were fixed in the oarlocks, and by 4:30 most crews had pushed off into the brown current.

Once we cleared the float, the port side rowed a few strokes, turning us broadside in the river below the piers. Then everyone pulled for four or five strokes to send us across the river. As we slipped across the last eddy below the bridge, the current drove the bow downstream. The cox yelled for starboard oarsmen to hold their blades under the water while port oars took a couple of strokes. Soon we were pointed downstream, and within a few seconds we were underway, running with the current and whipping past the trees on the bank. We felt so powerful, eight of us pulling as a unit. I can still hear the loud thunk with every stroke as all oars came out of the water together and rolled in the oarlocks.

In the early fall, before the rain and wind cleared leaves from the trees, the mild weather and beat of oars countered hours of classroom tedium. But we were not out for a pleasure cruise: we worked on hooking the water with the blades and then getting our weight on the oar handle. Breathing was heavy but not gasping, since the pace was slower than racing speed. Arms and legs soon tired, but they didn't burn as they would in a race. It was hard, sustained work.

We usually rowed for about 30 minutes before turning back upriver. By then it was almost dark, so the bow oarsman reached around toward the bow and switched on a battery-powered running light. This flashlight-sized light showed red on port and green on starboard. At the same time, the cox reached back and switched on the white stern light. Now we were set to row in the dark as we worked against the current.

The small running lights were only to alert other boats, showing them our heading and allowing the coach to find us. We never had a light big enough to see river debris: that would've been excess weight, as the necessary batteries would have been large and heavy (about the size of a small car battery). Moreover, oarsmen saw only where they had been. The cox could look ahead, but his view was obstructed by oarsmen. Thus, we rowed blind unless a drifting tree was large enough for the cox to see in the twilight. Strict traffic patterns kept us from running into other racing shells.

White oar blades and city lights, reflected from rain clouds, were enough for me, rowing near the bow, to keep time with the stroke oar, twenty-six feet astern. The dim light was also enough for the cox to see an oar blade enter the water too early or too late. Then he would yell at the errant rower through a small director's megaphone strapped to his face. The cox could also see when a blade failed to get perfectly perpendicular to the water at the catch. That sent the oar knifing deeply into the water, causing water to run over the oar shaft like a stick being held in the water.

This unwanted drag would cause the cox to yell at me, "Number two, you're too deep!"

Pulling hard on an oar produces a tight whirlpool, which we called a puddle. The shape of the puddle reflects how effectively power is being applied. For example, pulling the oar handle down into your lap causes the blade to leave the water early, producing a weak puddle that soon dissipates. The cox would yell, "Number two, you're washing out!"

Even when the cox said nothing, I knew that everyone in the boat could see my puddle, along with the seven others. We each wanted our puddle to be visible far behind the boat. That meant pulling hard, putting a bend in the wooden oar.

Much of the time we were on our own, since the two launches and coaches were spread over five or six crews. My guess is that a coach was alongside less than half the time. In a race, crews are on their own, so part of the coaching philosophy was to let the team develop its own discipline, its own push to win. It was understood that Oregon State rowing was an exercise in collective self-improvement.

One of our tasks was to keep the boat on an even keel. On the recovery we could lean slightly to one side or the other. But when the oars were in the water, we had to feel the boat as a team and pull the oar handles a little higher or lower. These corrections had to be rapid, automatic, and together.

For boat speed we could vary two parameters: how hard we pulled and how fast we rowed (stroke rate, the number of strokes per minute). Knowing whether a particular combination was effective depended on determining how fast the boat was moving. GPS tracking had not been invented, so we found other ways to judge speed. We could certainly feel speed, because the faster the boat moved, the trickier it was to catch the water cleanly and smoothly with our oars. A more objective measure was to look at the puddles behind the boat and guess how many feet we traveled per stroke. The cox had a stopwatch for determining strokes per minute, which he would periodically call out. Thus, we could calculate feet per minute. Our goal was to exceed 1100 (12.5 mph or almost 4 football fields per minute).

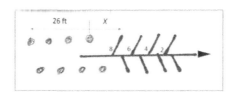

Estimating boat speed. Twenty-six feet plus x equals feet per stroke.[O-170]

In the days when crews raced three or four miles, they generally rowed at slightly more than 30 stokes per minute, but by 1960 the races had been cut to 2000 meters, the international standard. Then a stroke rate of about 34 to 36 could be maintained with good power. Elite West German crews began winning international races by rowing above 40 strokes per minute using shortened, paddle-shaped blades. We tried copying the German style with our standard oars, but we couldn't get the boats to move faster at the higher rate. At 40 strokes per minute, we had no time to get set for the catch. Moreover, finishing the stroke cleanly was difficult, because we had to rush to be ready for the next stroke. We experimented to find our own optimal stroke rate.

Coaching focused on aspects that the coxswains couldn't see, particularly how well we controlled our sliding seats and whether we were using leg muscles to drive the boat forward. The coaches also determined who would make the boat go fastest. That meant shuffling the crews and then racing to identify the best combinations. Seat races were common: eight-oared shells would race with only two persons rowing at a time. Then we would switch the pairs by climbing over each other and race again. To adjust for differences in the current, the coaches had the boats switch lanes in the river. Since we often didn't know who was being compared, we always had to pull hard.

Practices were not simply rowing a specified distance. Sometimes we would row at a low stroke rate to work on form, getting the blade in and out cleanly, training the muscles through repetition. Our bodies also had to respond instantly to small shifts in balance and to disruptions caused by waves. To prepare for races, we would practice different parts of a race: starting from a dead stop, taking a mini-sprint in the middle of a race, and raising the stroke rate at the finish despite the searing pain in arms and legs.

Coxswains steered using two thin ropes attached to a small rudder. Since the ropes were difficult to grip, especially in the rain, each line had a six-inch wooden dowel attached as a hand grip. These dowels were called knockers, because the coxswain would bang them on the side of the boat, sometimes to keep time and sometimes as a pre-arranged signal to jump up the rate for 5 strokes. Another knocker signal would call for ten extra powerful strokes, a big ten. The strategy was to move past another boat suddenly and convince the competition to give in to the pain, to slack off. Of course, coxswains got excited in a race and hoped that simply banging the knockers would make us pull harder, which it usually did. Since we often practiced next to another crew, we could tell whether sudden moves were effective. The satisfaction from suddenly shooting past another boat was worth the extra pain.

Racing starts were a routine part of practice, particularly during the spring racing season. Getting off the starting line quickly was important to me: I rowed better when I was ahead, especially when the pain in my arms, legs, and lungs seemed unbearable.

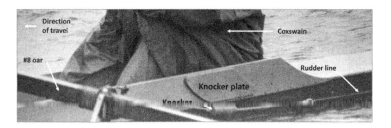

Port-side knocker shown attached to rudder line (cox is not holding the knocker). Boat is headed to the left. Note the wooden plate attached to the side of the boat where the cox pounded the knocker.[K-17a]

In races, the starts always seemed cold, wet, and full of trickery. I remember a race in Seattle in which we backed the stern of the boat up to a young man sitting in an anchored rowboat (stake boat). He held the stern of our boat while other shells backed up to their stake boats. A crafty crew came to the line last to reduce the time they'd be sitting in the bone-chilling cold. I was rowing number two that day, and I had to row against a crosswind to pull the bow around to point straight down the course. Our cox held his hand high in the air, signaling the starter that our 60-foot shell wasn't properly aligned. Other boats were having the same problem. Ideally, the starting gun would be fired only after all coxswains lowered their hands. In this case the wind was so strong that the starter gave up, firing the gun while our cox still had his hand up. We took off but had to make a costly course correction.

We weren't surprised by the premature start, and we knew nothing could be done. My dad had once complained to starter George Pocock about an unfair start. Pocock replied, "You weren't going to win anyway." We knew our position in the pecking order—we didn't need reminding. The message from my dad was that our crews must be ready to go at any time.

Many venues, including races on the Willamette River, had a drifting start. Alignment could be a problem, but it was more likely that one crew would be moving forward while others waited, drifting back to the line. As with fixed starts, each crew would try to be last on the line to avoid waiting motionless in the cold—sweat clothes were left at the dock to avoid extra weight.

A typical start on the river was in a light drizzle. I was always nervous. My oar handle was so slick that I worried about losing control and catching a crab. We'd pull up to the line, keeping straight as the bow pair paddled to keep us on the line. Soon, the opposition was also on the line, paddling gently. Then the starter would shout, "Are you ready? Ready all. Row!" The coxswains screamed and pounded their knockers. We would take a full stroke, pulling hard on the dead weight, trying to lift the boat out of the water. Then came a quick half stroke to keep the boat up, followed by a three-quarter stroke and a full stroke. That completed the four-stroke racing start, setting us up for twenty big ones, rapidly and at full pressure.

Knockers pounded out each catch, and the oarlocks thumped at every finish. We could hear the boat next to us, its cox screaming, its oars turning in the oarlocks as they came out of the water. We didn't dare look out; every stroke had to count. Then the pain set in, usually after a minute. I wondered why I was there, just as oarsmen in the 1930s must have. Only 180 more strokes to go for me; three times as many in the 1930s due to the longer races.

Steering a race was tricky in the current, and every pull on the rudder cost boat speed. The lanes were not marked by buoys, so the boats could drift together, accidentally or intentionally. We practiced with our oars only a foot away from those of another boat, always eyes in the boat. We never knew what would happen in a race, what the referee would allow. We would try to pull ahead and force the competition to row in our puddles. We didn't worry about broken oar blades.

Practice focused on synchrony and making our bodies perform automatically with maximum efficiency. Mile after mile we worked a simple mantra: firm catch, drive with the legs, hands down and out quickly. Keep the fingers loose to minimize blisters. As a port oarsman, I let my oar handle spin in my left hand, using the right to roll the blade for the catch and to feather after the left hand forced the blade out of the water.

Every stroke differed slightly, as the boat rolled a little, a wave disrupted the balance, or focus was lost for a moment. When fatigue set in, the crew got sloppy; forearms tightened, and fingers locked on the handle. Blisters became open wounds. But the puddles had to stay tight.

Near the end of practice, as we worked our way up the river below the float, another crew would invariably come alongside in the dark and rain. Our cox would pound his knockers, and the race was on: first to the float was first to the showers—losers wait. In the freezing rain.

Standard uniform for OSU coxswains that included a small director's megaphone.[K-17] *In 1962 waves washed over Charlie Carlson, and his clothing froze. He had to be lifted out of the boat.*[O-35]

Maintaining focus in the 1960s was as difficult as in the 1930s: almost impossible in a race. My first freshman race, on the Ballona Creek Channel in Los Angeles, was particularly unfocused. The racecourse comes straight off the Pacific Ocean, and on that day the breakwater at the mouth of the creek failed to block ocean swells from rolling up the course. The swells were unnerving as we pulled to the starting line; the strong onshore breeze was also new to us. And we were shaking nervous.

The opposition, UCLA, was a big-time sports school. They must be good to have such striking blue rowing shirts. The bright yellow UCLA across the chest contrasted with the orange "O" we had stenciled on the white T-shirts we'd bought at Penny's Department Store. At the dock, the UCLA oarsmen towered over us. Brian Finn, our stroke, recalled that we averaged 154 pounds, pulled up by our number seven weighing in at 204.[O-135] UCLA might have averaged 190.

The tailwind and excitement caused us to take off faster than intended, probably around 38 strokes per minute. Brian soon dropped it down to 36 or 37. I tried to concentrate, but with the wind pushing us and the high stroke rate, it seemed that I was just sliding back and forth without pulling. But my arms and legs were burning. I must have been doing something.

From my number two position I had a good view: at the 500-meter mark we were several seats ahead. We were giving the big guys a race! Our bowman, who was normally very quiet, shouted "Go". I passed it along to number three. Three was never quiet and cheered so eagerly I muttered, "Shut up and pull!" Our cox went crazy, pounding his knockers and yelling at us to pull harder, several times calling for a big ten. At the halfway mark we may have been a length ahead. The cox called for a big twenty, pull away. My forearms were locked solid, my fingers were like hooks on the oar handle. We were rowing too high to make it all the way like that, and I'd never surfed rollers with a 60-foot boat. Brian's arms burned too, but adrenalin kept him at 37.

At 1500 meters we had open water on UCLA. We went silent, no more knocking, no more shouts—make them think we're so far ahead that they can't hear us, that they can't catch us. Make them give up. But they didn't. Why didn't they tire and quit, drop back, make it easy for us? We were all watching the race. That's why both Brian and I remember winning by at least a length of open water. So much for Fred Newell's mandate, "Eyes in the boat."

In the 1930s, Oregon State crews probably had experiences similar to mine. Racing was the carrot used to attract young men to a program whose off-water activities seemed to equal or exceed the rowing effort. The oarsmen were very proud of what they'd created, with a history appearing only seven years after the first shells arrived in Corvallis.[A-49] The history mentions a detail that gives a feeling for the times: "... In 1929 the Portland Rowing Club was defeated by the winning class crew ... [that had] earned the right to compete with the U. of W. freshman crew, which they defeated by a narrow margin. That evening a water carnival was held on the river in which the two crews were illuminated with phosphorus on their blades and flashlights on their backs. Also included was a firework display and a local orchestra in the training barge."

Arthur Orr, Club President in 1935, left a detailed written record of Club activities. He coordinated the program through letters to Stevens. In one, Orr asked whether the training barge had escaped down the river; in another he requested keys to the new locks on the boathouse. He also wrote follow-up letters concerning a promised coaching launch, and he contacted the railroad to assure that the Club had a legal right-of-way to the river.[C-22] Stevens was the boss, but Orr was a close second.

Snags were an ongoing problem. Oarsmen couldn't easily remove these trees stuck to the river bottom or to bridge piers—they couldn't simply jump into a boat with an axe or two and chop up a snag, because the trees were mostly under water. Instead, the Rowing Club turned to the Army Corps of Engineers (the Corps was responsible for maintaining a channel 60 feet wide and 4 feet deep between Portland and Eugene, largely for moving log rafts to sawmills). A 1935 letter from Orr revealed prompt action by a four-man snagging party that removed a tree hung up on the bridge.[A-59, K-23] In a thank-you letter, Orr commended the workers and invited the major in charge to visit the crew facilities. Orr never missed an opportunity to build relationships.

*Undefeated OSU crew, spring of 1934. Left to right are Al Cook,
Leland Gillette, Einar Flood, Al Lubersky, Jolly Batcheller, Stan
Gregory, Al Opdenweyer, Dick Whitcomb, and Coach Stevens.
Crouching is Leonard Davis, coxswain.*[B-7d]

One of Orr's failed efforts involved a request to the college
Dean of Men. Orr wrote, "… In as much as the rowing club …
is entirely on its own feet financially and without any support
from the Associated Students, it is necessary that we arrange in
some other way our finances (specifically by incorporating and
registering as a non-profit organization)." The Dean ignored Orr's
request, using the traditional way to kill a student-sponsored idea.

Having non-profit status would have fit well with Orr's efforts
to obtain donations from the Portland elite. One of his targets for
a new racing shell was Aaron Frank, department store magnate.
Frank resisted Orr's advances:[A-59]

My dear Mr. Orr:
Your letters of July 13th and 25th have just come to my
attention.

It is news to me that I have been giving serious consideration to giving a shell to the Club. It seems to me
that the College should be able to provide some means
of financing this sport.

I should be glad to meet with you at your conve-
nience; however, you should first write to ascertain if I
will be in the city at that time.

Yours very truly,
Aaron M. Frank

Decades later (1962), Fred Sterk, then President of the Rowing
Club, thanked another Frank family member for a donation.[C-54]
Persistence was characteristic of oarsmen, as was the sense that
they held the fate of Oregon State rowing in their hands.

Orr's promotional efforts bordered on obsession. He wrote
letters to the outgoing Chancellor of Higher Education, wishing
him good luck, to the incoming Chancellor welcoming him to
his new job, to the Oregon State football coach wishing him victory in a game at UCLA, and to the Governor of Ohio seeking a
donation (Orr may have been from Ohio).

The practice of inviting politicians to crew races continued
until at least 1959 when an invitation was sent to the Governor
of Oregon. The Governor sent his regrets.[C-9] I doubt that oarsmen expected dignitaries to visit Corvallis; the likely goal was
to make Oregon State crew widely known. I don't know whether
Stevens was behind any of these activities, but he was skilled at
getting students to carry out his designs.

Orr also pushed locally. An example is seen in his written
instructions concerning the 1935 homecoming ceremonies.[C-3]
The homecoming queen was to be rowed to the dock in the
training barge by oarsmen whose attire and presentation were
carefully choreographed. Letter winners would display their
awards on sweaters; all coxswains would be dressed in white and
oarsmen in black with white socks. The President of the Rowing
Club (Orr) would be distinctively dressed. Crews would race, and
the winning crew would file up to the queen, who would present
scrolls to each. Then the losing crew would cheer.

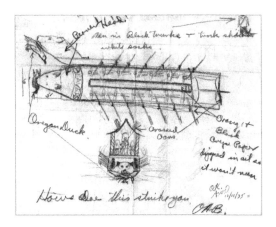

Details of training barge decorations for homecoming 1935.
Sketch by Oliver "Jolly" Batcheller (initials OAB, fifth from left in
1934 photo), approved by Arthur Orr (AWO). Note the bowhead
in which the Oregon State Beaver has a University of Oregon
Duck in its mouth. Rivalry between the two schools was intense
(a few years later, Beavers, including my dad, went to Eugene
en masse, riding on the sides and tops of cars, to fight Ducks;
many got thrown into the mill race in Eugene).[C-3]

On another occasion, Orr wrote to the President of the College, suggesting that faculty might be interested in learning to row.[A-59,C-18] "[Coach Stevens] and I will be delighted to coach you, and at hours that you can have the river to yourselves." President Peavy sent a favorable, supportive response.[C-18]

Similar letters were written by Al Cook, Orr's predecessor, and Dean Painter, who followed Orr. Rowing Club self-promotion was relentless. However, the Club overstepped when it attempted to name its new railroad-depot boathouse after its founder, Robert Young. This naming was disallowed by the State of Oregon, presumably because schools try to sell naming rights for buildings. The Club backed off[A-58,61a] and apologized to Young and Clair Langton for embarrassing them. The apology letter to Langton included profuse gratitude for his continuing support, which Langton acknowledged.[C-17]

At the end of 1935 Orr returned to the Midwest for a family emergency.[C-20] While there he took a job and never returned to Oregon. Nevertheless, Rowing Club presidents continued with the writing tradition, and their annual newsletters trace Club history. The enthusiasm, which Stevens would have attributed to the bite of the rowing bug, was evident in a portion of a summer letter my dad sent to the crew in about 1940.

"Have you any ideas for boosting the club? How about a counter sign for members meeting on the campus? How about a song? What are your ideas on intramural rowing? How about a more efficient managerial system? How about social activities of the club? Will our own bleachers be allowed and will they make any money? What can be done to get the club in the 'limelight'? … Remember, it's easier to stay a length ahead than to make up a length."[A-61]

Writing songs and poems about rowing may seem a bit silly today, but it was part of being bitten by the rowing bug, as several songs were composed decades later by members of the early women's crew.[O-63]

We are the crew team from Oregon State
We know our rowing really does rate
We'd like to get up at quarter of eight
But we have to be up at 5—no joke

We go to classes; now and again
But we are all caught up in trying to win
Our teachers all hate us but what can we say
We're OSU rowers—hey, hey

They think that we're muscle bound, crude, and obscene
But what they don't know is we're just really mean
'Cause we are the crew team from Oregon State
And we know we are first rate.

In the latter part of the 1930s, the Club arranged for the University of California to row a fall race in Corvallis, and in the spring Oregon State traveled to California. The 1940 trip to California, recalled by oarsman Mel Monroe, was probably typical.[C-49]

"I have vivid memories of our first trip to California to row Sacramento J.C. (the crew then went to Berkeley). … We went out on the launch with Coach Stevens and Ky Ebright for a mere 18-mile workout with their No. 1 team. I think they rowed around Alameda Island, and at the time the water was pretty rough. That night they put us up in some of the U. of C. fraternities. The next morning we were to get up at 4:00 a.m. to drive to UCLA. I came out of the frat where I was staying and walked into a campus security guard who thought he apprehended a second-story robber, as I had my stuff wrapped in a towel. Finally convinced him we were OK and he let me go.

"I hope someone has a picture of our 8 oars mounted on the top of Coach Stevens' Buick. I think we traveled in 2 cars, the second one furnished by Phil Ault. In Los Angeles we rowed in Ballona Creek Channel. … I think we lost by 6 feet but thought we were big stuff.

"Going down I was initiated into the pleasure of 'tree-ripened' olives. Some clown in the car extolled their virtues, so we stopped, climbed through a fence, and went out into a nearby orchard. It only took one bite to show me how very acid and bitter they were before the long blanching process made them edible.

"On the way back, we drove though the redwoods at night. I'll swear some of those trees were in the middle of the road, but we kept rolling and reached Corvallis the next afternoon. … In those days (1936-40) we didn't have money for hotels and all that frivolous stuff but depended on fraternities to put us up. At that time we were coming out of the Depression and everyone was getting by on as little as possible."

Coach Stevens' car loaded with oars, 1940. Man in the hat is likely Stevens, as he is often shown with a hat, even inside buildings.[C-7]

Although Stevens downplayed his role in competitive rowing, oarsmen, such as Mel, readily acknowledged it.

"Coach Stevens accomplished miracles with next to nothing. When he wasn't out in the launch coaching, he was in the old, converted Oregon Electric Station boathouse repairing boats so we could keep going. His good wife deserves some mention for all the things she must have put up with during the time we were considered to be a bastard outfit at best. We sold tickets to local businessmen who helped us scrape together enough to go."

1940 Oregon State crew in California. From left: Frank Seberg, Mel Monroe, Glenn Morganson, Jean Hollstein, Wilbur Fischer, Roger Johnson, Phil Ault, John Cravath, Jim Bell (cox).[C-5]

Mel added a bit more perspective when writing his recollec tions 50 years after the events. "Most people view a fully function- ing program and assume it was always thus from Day 1. Little do they know the struggles and sacrifices that were made to get it going. Often times the enemy was our own Athletic Depart- ment who couldn't bear to have anything encroaching on their fair-headed program of football, basketball, and baseball. They had the advantage of locking the gate and charging admission to enter. On the other hand, how do you charge admission to a crew race?"

The student-run Club helped Stevens find a satisfying niche. He taught what he thought was important to enthusiastic stu- dents, his program was protected by his boss, and he was assured of having a sense of accomplishment by building racing shells.

For my dad, the Rowing Club provided a community with a purpose that he quickly embraced. But college days came to an end, and World War II put a hold on the rowing program. My dad moved, temporarily, into other activities, among which was a struggle with the Communist Party that solidified his conserva- tive political outlook.[O-140]

———— Chapter 10 ————

Quiet Years

The 1940s were largely a time of retreat for rowing. Crew racing stopped during World War II, as did almost all other athletic programs, including major league baseball. Survival of the country was at stake. Gasoline was rationed for the war effort, and essential materials, such as steel and rubber, were conserved and recycled. Women built war ships, and anyone with a plot of land grew food. Young men, including my uncles, scrambled to join the military and fight.

Colleges continued to operate during the war, and Stevens taught PE rowing, mainly using rowing machines. Each machine was similar to a station in a racing shell: sliding seat, stretcher boots, and an oar handle on a swivel attached to a shock absorber for resistance.

Coach Stevens teaching rowing. Rowing machines were only for instruction, since they were not robust enough for serious rowing exercise.[A-34]

My dad and Gail Hufford, a University of Oregon graduate, married in 1940. At that point, my dad focused on school, finishing in 1941 as an industrial arts teacher. They stayed in Corvallis for a year, as my dad filled in for a junior high school shop teacher called up by the Army. Then he and my mom headed to Portland where my dad taught high school industrial arts.

Gail Hufford, 1940.[O-190]

In Portland, the family had a middle-class life: two kids and a hillside house with a four-acre vegetable garden. My mom had grown up on a farm where she had become an expert shot with a rifle (she was also on the university rifle team). That kept the varmints out of the garden. A few sheep mowed the lawn and chased me up a ladder. And the outhouse was soon replaced by indoor plumbing.

Portland had a long tradition in ship building, a crucial industry for the war effort. Like many others, my dad participated, probably during the summers when school was out. As a sheet metal mechanic, he focused on duct work in aircraft carriers.[O-81]

World War II ended in 1945, and the heroes began to come home. The inability to fight gnawed at my dad. In 1946 he saw a chance to contribute after the fact. The United States was occupying Japan, and the Army had initiated an industrial arts program. The program would give American soldiers skills that could be used when they returned home. My dad applied as a teacher, but he was initially rejected due to poor eyesight. He argued that teaching industrial arts didn't require seeing well enough to shoot a rifle. The colonel in charge eventually accepted the logic, and my dad left for Japan. My mom encouraged the move, because it would create distance from her mother-in-law who had recently moved too close.

My mom bought a car, sold the house, and with two kids moved in with an uncle on the Oregon Coast. The Army promised to ship the family and car to Japan immediately, but many months passed before marching orders were issued. Then the Army terminated my dad's teaching program. My mom, two kids, and the car were already on a troop ship in the middle of the Pacific. To avoid turning back, my dad transferred to Military Government and a posting in the northern city of Sendai.

His new task, with the help of an interpreter and a driver, was to teach democracy to 1.5 million Japanese, including 10,000 teachers. Part of his goal was to prevent the Communist Party from controlling the trade unions, especially the Teachers' Union.[O-140] He had several skirmishes with Communist students, took a severe beating in the local press, and experienced death threats (shortly after we returned to the States, the car he left in Japan was bombed). Rather than bar the Party from the Teachers' Union, which he had the power to do, my dad gave many speeches throughout the region. As a result, the Japanese teachers voted the Party out of power.

My dad didn't forget about rowing during his stay in Japan. He took movies of Japanese crews and analyzed their style. The oarsmen were much smaller than Americans and couldn't match larger crews in a stroke-for-stroke race. Instead, they rowed at a very high rate in which they accelerated the slide (seat) toward the stern immediately before the catch. That allowed them to use their legs like coiled springs. That was opposite to Stevens' style in which the slide slowed to facilitate a strong catch. My dad considered the Japanese method to be a radical form; as far as I know, he never tried to copy it.

His experience in Occupied Japan made my dad deeply anti-Communist. When he returned to the United States, he wrote a master's thesis on his work in Japan, gave anti-Communist lectures to local civic groups, and described Communist tactics to Oregon radio audiences. He developed a life-long commitment to instill democratic ideals in American youth. Part of that effort involved teaching self-sufficiency.

While my dad was in Japan, oarsmen returning from the war restarted the competitive rowing program in Corvallis.[J-23] Restarting was difficult, in part because the students were older, and their priorities had shifted away from college athletics.

An added problem was that the *Yellow Peril*, which had never been a good coaching launch, aged poorly. To solve the launch problem, the Rowing Club lobbied the Class of 1949 to gift the school a new coaching launch. A letter to the student newspaper illustrates the effort.

"Such a gift is a means for making our OSC crew one of the best on the Coast. Though you may not know it, Coach Stevens is a former Harvard coach. He knows how to produce winning teams. There is not a boy on the rowing team this year who is not working his best every day for two hours of grinding drill, even on Sunday, to do his part in becoming a winning team for Coach Stevens and the College. Our biggest handicap is our coaching launch. We have a strong team, and we have a coach we will work for. But our coaching launch is too small to keep up with our crew. And Coach has had to instruct us from the dock. … We are confident that with the College students' support, and with Stevens' expert coaching, our crews will be a credit to the school."[A-65]

Jim Wahlstrom, the Rowing Club President, and Jim Barratt, editor of the campus newspaper and later OSU Athletic Director, persuaded the Class of 1949 to donate enough money for an 18-foot inboard coaching launch. After 20 years, the rowing program finally had a dependable launch. Since Stevens would retire within a year, the new launch was expected to help recruit his replacement.

In 1950 Stevens convinced his boss, Clair Langton, that the coaching replacement must know how to fix wooden racing shells, keep the river from taking the floats, and tolerate winter rain. My dad was the ideal candidate. As Carl Bower, an assistant coach for my dad, later said, "There didn't seem to be anything he didn't know about using tools and equipment. ... He [even] knew foundry practices, how to use shrink rulers, etc. when we cast the rowlocks for the training barge and the old training shells."[O-31] This was high praise, as Bower was himself skilled at brazing and welding, skills that were needed in the early 1960s when the boathouse was replaced.

Finally, a reliable coaching launch. Left: The 49er, new coaching launch.[A-40] Right: Roof of the Oregon Electric Depot boathouse.[A-42]

By 1950 our occupation of Japan was shifting, and my dad's Military Government job was constantly changing. The Korean War had broken out, which made it dangerous for families to stay in Japan. Langton offered the rowing position to my dad, with Stevens pointing out that "The job is as bad as it has always been." My dad knew the challenges: the river, the insufficient funds, and the constant need for repairs. On the positive side, Langton was an avid supporter. My dad accepted the task of maintaining what he considered the most valuable educational program at the College.

Chapter 11

NEW MANAGEMENT

One of my dad's goals was to make intercollegiate crew a permanent part of the College. That meant providing tangible value. Winning races would help with public relations, and providing a good student experience would eventually create strong alumni support. Having a solid, independently funded infrastructure would make it easier for the College to maintain the program during times of financial stress. I doubt that my dad verbalized an overall plan, but his actions could be interpreted within a framework of program building.

His immediate problem was keeping boats on the water. As in Stevens' time, the old boats required daily repair. Since no money was available for help, boat repair was my dad's unpaid job. Fortunately, Stevens loved to work on boats: he was a regular at the boathouse until his death in 1957. The oarsmen also accepted the challenge, somehow fitting boat work in with classes and rowing practice.

My dad's teaching experience was put to good use, as the repair shop was often filled with students. His shock of blonde hair, thick glasses, and often a cigarette dangling from his mouth made him easy to spot as he moved from one repair job to the next.

My dad institutionalized some of the repair work by offering advanced crew as a PE class in which specific tasks were assigned to oarsmen. One of the easier jobs was replacing the leather on an oar. Another was replacing the metal tracks that seat wheels ran along in the racing shells. Care was required to get the alignment right. More challenging was making a sliding seat. This involved laminating (gluing) pieces of wood together, using a router and template to shape the seat, sanding and varnishing the wood, and attaching the rails and wheels.

Work on boats in the shop. Coach Drlica
is third from the right.[A-3]

The fancy contoured seat had a pair of 2-inch holes in the bottom to make it light. The contours were not deep enough to maintain contact between the rower and the seat, because during the stroke rowers would rise off the seat as they pulled an oar anchored in the water. That uses body weight and leg drive to move the boat. However, some seat contact is needed, or the rower will jump over the seat and end up sitting on the tracks, unable to take another stroke. Even if jumping off the seat didn't result in "catching a crab" or an oar handle in the back, the rower would be out of commission as he or she climbed back onto the seat. Often rowers splashed water on the seat to increase the friction. Members of the women's crews, which emerged in the 1960s, maintained seat contact by sticking tape, rolled with the sticky side out, to their shorts.

Stevens and my dad decided that the crew needed a new training barge. The old one, which they had built twenty years earlier, had sprung too many leaks to fix. Building a sixty-foot,

2000-pound boat seemed like a massive undertaking to the oarsmen, but Stevens was an expert. The group effort resulted in a beautiful V-bottomed craft, tapered at both ends for speed. This boat lasted many years, even surviving the flood of 1974 that swept it and its protective shed downriver.

Constructing a training barge. Coach Drlica is fourth from the left, wearing coveralls.[B-7]

Rowing in the training barge.[D-109] *This photo, taken in the 1960s, shows a women's PE class instructed by Coach Drlica (standing amid the rowers).*

Barge house and training barge.[A-41, A-36]

My dad's effort to build *esprit de corps* extended to social activities. Fifteen years earlier, Arthur Orr had been told by an Oregon State dean that social activities sponsored by athletic teams were strictly forbidden.[C-21] My dad tested the rule in early 1952 by encouraging the Rowing Club to socialize with the Aquabats and Sea Horses, two women's swimming groups. He obtained approval for the event, but afterward he received an administrative reprimand: he failed to return the women to their residences before closing time (in that era, college women were confined to their residences at night).

Paul Knoll, Chairman of the Student Life Committee, chastised my dad, pointing out that special permission had been given to hold an event that was limited to two hours (it was scheduled for 5:30 to 7:30, but it actually started at 7:45, well after dark). Moreover, the women were not in their houses until 10:10, which was ten minutes after closing time. The Committee admonished my dad with "In the future, plan with more care."[C-52]

My dad later wrote about the incident:[J-2] "In the spring [of 1952], the Oregon State Rowing Club sponsored [a] … co-educational picnic on the Willamette River. The spot chosen was about three miles downstream (from the boathouse where the brush and poison oak had been cleared from the tree-covered bank). The plan was to row to the picnic spot, carrying all necessary picnic goodies, firewood, shovels, and axes as well as various and assorted rowers and friends in the training barge and two motorboats.

"All went well. The campfire was warm after a dip in the cold river. The food was excellent, and the singing was melodious. Time slipped away too quickly. The 10 p.m. women's closing hour approached all too soon.

"As most rowers know, there is a difference between rowing upstream and rowing downstream. A miscalculation in the return distance, the speed of the current, the strength of the rowers, and the weight of the cargo on the upstream return trip presented increasing anxiety as the closing hour approached.

"When it became apparent that we couldn't get back in time to get the women to campus before ten o'clock, the little coaching boat, the *Molly S*, named after President Strand's wife, was put into towing service. With a top speed of about ten knots, the *Molly S* struggled slowly but steadily against the current. The closing hour approached faster than the boat would go. No one wanted to be on the Dean of Women's disciplinary list, so the women were transferred, a few at a time, to the coaching launch *49er*, for a quick trip to the crew house to scurry the women to their living groups. The only casualty was the loss of a woman's shoe as she came over the side from the barge."

No alcoholic drinks were involved, as my dad was opposed to drinking by his crews, just as Stevens had been. Thus, the reprimand was simply for being ten minutes late. Indeed, the main story concerned what happened next: getting the training barge back to the dock.

"In those years, Highway 20 near Dixon Creek was protected by a wooden riprap to keep the river from washing out the bank. As the barge passed this wooden wall, waves from the boats ricocheted off the wall, surging over the barge's bow.

"Suddenly the waves came over the top of the fifty-eight-foot boat, and all the men stood up in unison. This unified force of nearly a ton and a half swamped the boat, which had a freeboard of only nine inches.

"I was already standing in the bow. The water came in over my feet. My shoes filled up. The water covered my ankles. Boy, that water was cold! As it slowly crawled up my pants legs, I took my billfold out of my pants pocket and put it in my shirt pocket. When the icy water was in my hip pockets, I took my watch off and put it in my mouth.

"As the water seemed to be coming in over the bow, many passengers scrambled to the stern. 'Don't come back here!' shouted coxswain Bob Ertel ('53) from the stern. 'It's coming in here too!'

"Someone started to swim ashore, but either Skip (Harry) Hanna ('55) or Roy Mason ('53) swam after him and got him back to the barge. Someone else shouted, 'I can't swim!' We got that person back to the barge and everyone else out of it so the boat would rise back to the surface. It 'floated' submerged about four feet below the surface [when] we stood in it. Out of the barge, I found myself standing on a log, armpit deep in the darkness in the middle of the Willamette River. I held the barge there for a moment or two, but it pulled me off the log. The captain was down with his ship.

"There was pandemonium. Various instructions, cries and expressions created momentary confusion. Suddenly Roy and Skip started singing a hymn. All those who could, joined in. It was a spontaneous prayer.

"The two motorboats somehow got the barge to shore on the Corvallis side. They shuttled back and forth to the crew house with rescued men. Some went ashore on the Corvallis side and went home. Those that went to the crew house spent an hour or so in the showers, trying to get warm."

It was after midnight before all was secured and my dad felt that the situation was under control. However, everyone had scattered, so it was not until the next day that he was able to determine with certainty that all had returned safely.

"Ironically, Art Krueger ('53), the man who swam ashore to make the barge fast for the night, tied it to a tree covered with poison oak!"

The official report[O-30] sent to Langton was much drier, stating the names of the oarsmen, the date (May 6, 1952), and the time (10:10 pm). The cause of the accident was attributed to the "peculiar conditions of the river at this point." Total losses were one kerosene lantern and one wristwatch. The report did mention that female personnel had been shuttled to the dock to lighten the load, but it did not specify why female personnel were involved.

My dad was impressed by how well the women handled the pressure of getting back to their dorms. Maybe they were tough enough to row. At the time, college-age women were viewed as being so delicate that they had to be locked up at night for their own protection. A few were serious individual athletes, but competitive, cut-throat teams were actively discouraged by American society.

That fall (1952) my dad persuaded the Sea Horses and Aquabats to try rowing in a "fun-type" competition. Since the women had no rowing experience, a pair of varsity oarsmen served as coxswains. The men could handle the training aspect and protect the shells from being broken on the bridge. Those two crews marked the beginning of women's rowing at Oregon State.

Seahorses, 1953.[D-130]

The rowing bug does not discriminate on the basis of gender, and within three years sororities and other living groups began rowing competitively on an intramural basis. To obtain practice time, women began sneaking out of their living groups at 5 a.m., an hour before college rules allowed.[J-25] This infraction leaked to the Dean of Women, and everyone involved, including my dad, was called onto the carpet.

My dad initially saw women's crew as a way to vastly increase rowing visibility on campus (described in a 1958 article for the *Rowing News*).[D-115,D-122] At first he didn't appreciate that young women could be bitten by the rowing bug, that they would want to be pulling an oar before dawn, often in the fog and rain.

However, he soon realized how wrong he was: "... The impact upon campus of nearly two hundred girls actively interested in rowing is phenomenal."[J-19]

Sorority crew, 1955.[D-131]

By the 1960s he was applying the self-sufficiency philosophy to young women, and in 1964 he built a new shower facility designed for women rowers.

The College took notice of the rowing philosophy, and in 1952 the alumni office asked Stevens to put his thoughts in writing,[A-46] presumably for subsequent publication. I quote portions of Stevens' long letter because they allow us to see where my dad agreed and disagreed with Stevens.

"Well, I put this off as long as I could because I hate to write letters. ... As I told you, rowing at Oregon State is a PE activity. Period. Sure, we race with half a dozen other schools, but informally only. We row races under the rowing club organization. ... The boys handle their own finances, schedule races, help maintain their equipment, and build floats. ... In all the years I have been at OSC, the relationship between the rowing setup and the Athletic Association is the best it has ever been, and everyone is happy.

"The unbelievable fact is that we do not want conference rowing for several reasons. Not that we are against intercollegiate athletics. We are all for them, for the other fellow, not for us, thank you. ... To start with, conference rowing cost Washington 40,000 bucks last year. ... We do not have that kind of money. ... But that is not all the story. We do not think that rowing a few races a year is worth that amount of money. Washington has a crew house that cost 320,000 berries. Guess what our setup cost. But before the War more men rowed throughout the year at OSC than did at Washington."

Although my dad strongly agreed with Stevens about instilling a do-it-yourself philosophy, he was not part of the "We do not want conference rowing". By 1957 he had helped organize a West Coast rowing "conference". For eighteen years, he coached the intercollegiate crew as a volunteer, finally getting part of his salary from the Athletic Department in 1968.

Stevens continued, "If we start the fall term with 50 men, we are likely to finish with 50 men except for the few who always drop out. We do not <u>cut</u> the squad, because we are interested in rowing for any and all boys who want it.

"No one breathes down our neck and says win that crew race or else. In order to compete in conference meets, we would have to row a couple of hours every day, 6 days a week. I do not mean paddle. I mean row like hell with the coach driving like a slave driver, 10 or 12 miles a day. His job is to produce a winning crew, but the boy who is after an education? How much education do you think a boy feels like absorbing after that kind of workout under such a program?

"Three or four varsity crews line up every day, and all the time they are out, they race and fight each other. Competition between crews. Competition for seats in the first boat between individuals and for what? A [varsity] letter and the glory of being a big shot for a little while? Well, it isn't worth it to most of us, so we are not having any. All work and no fun, just grind. ... If the crew is really serious about it, they drive pretty hard for the time they are on the water. ... They are on their own responsibility to live up to a reasonable training code.

"Once in a while OSC might show up with a crew good enough to compete with the big boys. What's wrong with knocking their ears down as long as we don't have to live up to such heights all the time? Who gives a damn whether we do it informally or not?"

By "big boys" Stevens meant winners of big-time races. Here he was not exaggerating. In the 1950s and 1960s, the annual competition included Cal and Washington, perennial international powers, and the University of British Columbia, which routinely represented Canada at the Olympic Games. Other name competition came from Stanford, UCLA, and the University of Southern California, schools Oregon State could beat. Occasionally races were won from British Columbia.

"And because most fellows really enjoy participating in the sport, they come back for more. … The first time he appears in class at the boathouse, he learns that crew is one place where he is not going to get something for nothing. He is going to pay his way regardless of what [President Franklin] Roosevelt's New Deal leads him to believe. He is on his way to learning the hard way that things worth having must be paid for.

"Care and maintenance of equipment. Mind you, none of this is compulsory. Suggestions yes. No one gets pushed by the coach. Technique of rowing? Heck yes. Rowing machines, barge, shells, lectures, demonstrations, slides, and motion pictures. Even a big mirror in the launch at times so a crew man can see for himself what he looks like."

By mirror, Stevens meant a pair of mirrors, each about 3 or 4 feet square, fixed at a 90-degree angle to reflect the image even if it were not straight on. For this exercise, the coaching launch would be only a few feet from your oar blade, and you could look out of the boat and see how well, or poorly, you were using your leg muscles to drive the boat forward. At the same time, you could watch the blade and see whether you were making a nice, tight puddle and whether you were getting the blade out cleanly at the finish of the stroke.

Stevens continued, "… What I mean to say, we are trying to expose these kids to a cross section of life from which they can acquire a background of experience that will help them to live a useful, happy life and at the same time learn some of the basic values in this old world. … In our own small way, we are trying to make an atmosphere here at the crew house that will in some measure point the way. Life on this toad stool is becoming longer and more complicated. We are learning more about more things, but if democracy is to succeed, we must not look only at the little simple things of life. We still have to live with our neighbors."

My dad agreed with Stevens that the rowing program was a character-building activity, and they published articles showing how Oregon State rowing was an exercise in democracy.[A-3,C-67] But he realized that maintaining Stevens' program through unpaid overtime work and student help would not make rowing a permanent part of the College. He knew that programs could easily be cut by institutions—shortly after he arrived in Japan, the Army suddenly terminated his teaching job. He had to find ways to institutionalize rowing at the College.

One avenue was real estate. Except for the boathouse, the land along the river was part of a large farm owned by the Beach family. In 1952, my dad, with Stevens' help, convinced Nellie Beach to sell her 200-acre farm to the College. The farm was largely corn fields located next to the river in its flood plain; a farmhouse and large barn were situated on high ground between the boathouse and the river. The crew didn't need 200 acres, but if the coaches could convince the College to build a golf course, students and faculty would flock to the river. That would increase the visibility of the adjacent rowing program. Moreover, if the College had a popular investment, it could not easily walk away. Neither Stevens nor my dad played golf.

Another solidifying move was to start conference rowing. If rowing expanded to include many schools and became organized, the College might be too embarrassed to pull out. Stevens could downplay winning, since he'd already won races, both as an oarsman and a coach. My dad had not. Winning races was the key to making rowing a regular varsity sport with funding from the Athletic Department.

Although my dad occasionally brought visiting coaches home for dinner (without alerting my mom), he never talked about rowing at home. Thus, I was surprised when Joe Michalek, Rowing Club President in the late 1950s, recalled, decades later, that my dad's goal was to have a crew row in the prestigious Henley Royal Regatta in England. To obtain an invitation and the necessary financial support, he had to beat Washington's first boat.

Carl Bower, assistant coach and oarsman.[K-12]

My dad knew he couldn't compete with the financial and man-power depth of the Washington rowing program. Moreover, he had to depend on oarsmen taking the initiative to win, since there weren't enough hours in the day for him to be a slave driver and also maintain the overall program. Consequently, he began to look for technical ways to make his crews more competitive, often with the aid of Carl Bower.

Carl was a lightweight oarsman in the late 1950s who took time out from college to serve in the Army. He returned in the early 1960s, rowing and becoming my dad's primary assistant.

A classic rowing problem was finding a quantitative way to evaluate oarsmen. Rowing machines had been available for many years, but they either provided too little resistance, as was the case with Stevens' machines, or the recovery portion of the stroke was unnatural, as when a weight was attached to the oar handle by a rope and pulley.

According to Carl, my dad was working on land-based evaluation concepts long before the current rowing machines came into training use. Carl recalled, "For example, in 1962 and 1963 we used a dock-mounted rowing machine with a full oar to pull in the river. We measured overall power for one complete sweep, timing on the catch, and negative energy from getting the oar out of the water. The oar had a strain gauge that would change the length of a wire when the oar was flexed. The stretch of the wire was recorded on paper through a linkage with an old version of the cylinder barograph used in meteorology (the flexing of the oar was transformed into a vertical pen movement on a rotating drum). The behavior of the oar was recorded from the catch through the entire pull-through. We actually got measurements: large guys had more impressive power curves. Modern strain-gage technology would have gone a long way toward getting a power curve that we could integrate and use to select the strongest oarsmen.

"Since the river moved slower than a racing shell, we cut the oar blades down to simulate actual rowing. The next step would have been to factor in frictional effects due to oarsmen of different weights causing the shell to ride lower or higher in the water."O-31

By the late 1970s others had solved the rowing machine problem with a flywheel design. The resulting machines, called ergometers, became a major tool for training and weeding out physically weak candidates. Indeed, ergometer racing became a sport of its own[O-82] as well as a popular piece of equipment for every gym in the country.

Hull design was another development project. John Campbell designed a shell that had less drag than the commercial Pocock shells (the Campbell boat had less wetted surface area; when towed at eleven miles per hour, resistance from the Campbell boat was twelve percent lower[A-73]). In the 1950s, Stevens and my dad built an eight-oared Campbell shell (the *White Whale*) that was fast. However, the shell was tippy, a property we blamed on the boat rather than on our lack of skill. We could have learned to row the *Whale*, but the outriggers and oarlocks needed refinement. The boat didn't feel right. Lack of time prevented optimization, and the opportunity to win races with a new hull design was shelved when the Rowing Club earned enough money to buy brand-new Pocock shells.

I also recall an idea, developed in the mid-1960s, in which friction-reducing polymers would be added to the water ahead of a racing shell. The Navy had been experimenting with these materials to give ships a sudden burst of speed when under attack (after torpedoes had been launched). Suppliers were found,[A-74,75,78] but success would have given a crew such an advantage that the strategy would soon be outlawed. Use of the polymers would also create water pollution. Thus, the polymer program was also shelved. But my dad was ready in case other crews tried it. I imagine he had someone check opponents' racing shells to be certain that no tubes were sticking out of the bow to dispense friction-reducing agents.

When computers became powerful enough, my dad turned to optimizing boat parts. In a collaboration with local computer scientists, he sought to personalize each rowing position. Leg, arm, and trunk length were used to determine optimal oar length and oarlock position. It's likely that this effort was ahead of its time, since the experimental test of the adjustments, namely boat speed, was difficult to measure in a tightly controlled way. But he did apply the methods to lightweight crews that, in the late 1960s, were Pacific Coast champions for several years (those oarsmen also gained considerable experience in small boats, making it uncertain that boat optimization contributed to their success).

While my dad was the driver of innovation, his general approach was to create ways for students to exercise ingenuity. His presence was noticeable, but once a project was started, he stepped back and started another one. On the water, he would point out principles, and then the crews were expected to implement them on their own. During the 1950s and 1960s, this approach was seen as empowering students to think for themselves. In the late 1970s, however, rowers, both men and women, saw this style as lack of guidance.

In retrospect, my dad accepted Stevens' core values. Both felt that they were strengthening the country during a period (1931-1980) when we were under almost constant threat of war. First was World War II, then the Korean War, and soon after, the threats came from the Soviet Union. The awareness extended to grade-school children: we practiced duck-and-cover drills in case the Russians attacked us. In my dreams I saw Russian bombers flying in low over the Pacific Ocean, headed for us. In addition, China claimed it would overwhelm the United States by 1972. War threats kept the coaches focused on teaching self-sufficiency and teamwork.

Varsity-level rowing was where my dad differed with Stevens. PE classes provided financial continuity, but my dad was uncertain how long that would last. Thus, he looked for opportunities to institutionalize the rowing program: he brought women into the fold, expanded the rowing campus, and began a competitive program that would merit support from the Athletic Department.

Each of his efforts was influenced by the river. Rain seemed almost constant from late fall to early spring, transforming the river into an unstoppable force. In flood, the water was a deeper brown, swept quickly past the docks, and carried off structures that my dad thought were tied down firmly. Eddies created by the bridge piers were unsettling; launching and landing shells was trickier than usual. Standing waves below the bridge, although small compared to white-water rivers, were enough to worry scullers. The river seemed like a wild horse that could be ridden, but only with difficulty and danger.

Chapter 12

New Coach and the River

Stevens and my dad viewed the river differently. For Stevens, the river was a part of Nature that would occasionally flood and inconvenience him. He didn't teach PE classes during the winter when most floods occurred. Like other citizens of Corvallis, his home was inland, protected from floods. For my dad, the river was always on his mind: in the summer he prepared for floods, and when they came in the winter, he was there protecting the docks. Moreover, to win races my dad had to have his crews on the water throughout the school year. He knew that anyone who fell in the winter river risked hypothermia, but he accepted that risk as part of crew.

Communities along the river also worried about floods. Town employees would take water-level readings, often several times a day. By sharing information with other towns, they could accurately predict when a flood would crest and how high the water would get.[K-21] A twenty-four-hour notice gave farmers time to move their tractors to high ground, alerted police to roads that should be closed, and told my dad when his docks would be threatened. Then the water would recede, and the cleanup would begin.

Since the east side of the river at Corvallis, the boathouse side, is in the flood plain, year after year flood waters would rush over fields and highways. Low spots in the roads were known, and concrete spillways were built far into the brush to halt erosion. But the water could not be stopped.

Clean-up after a flood. Right panel shows Coach Drlica (left) with life jacket, worn before the barges were in place as boathouses. Drlica thought the life jackets would be dangerous if he fell in and got sucked under a barge.[O-151]

The winter of 1952 was typical, as the two-lane highway headed east out of Corvallis, over the bridge and past the boat-house, flooded at least 16 times. A pilot car was posted to guide vehicles through the low spots, but when the water got a foot deep, the road was closed.[K-21] In some places the current across the highway was fast enough to sweep a small car into a roadside berry patch. That's where my dad ended up when he offered to ferry a stranded motorist across a swift part in the rainy darkness of early evening. The two headed across the low spot in a small, aluminum skiff powered by an outboard motor. Soon the boat was washed off the road, down a small embankment, and up against blackberry vines.

How do you get out of berry vines when rushing water threatens to capsize your boat, vines tangle your propeller, and your passenger is screaming?

My dad always carried canoe paddles for such emergencies. By paddling in the ditch at the edge of the berry vines, parallel to the road, he could move the boat to a break in the brush line. There the current would push him out into a calm, flooded field.

But first he had to get his weight onto the downstream (berry vine) side to avoid flipping the boat, since the boat would have been broadside to the current rushing over the edge of the road. He also had to shut off the outboard motor and push the engine compartment down into the boat: that would raise the prop out of the water and release the entangling vines. Then paddle and push against the vines. This strategy was successful.

In the main river channel, debris was the problem. Flood waters cleared fields and riverbanks of refuse left by farmers and loggers from summer operations. The river also undercut trees along the bank, adding them to the flotsam streaming past the crew docks. Some of the trees were so large that their limbs and roots dragged along the river bottom.[K-23]

The drifting logs and stumps were dangerous to thin, wooden racing shells, especially because rowing practice continued well into the rainy, evening darkness. Moreover, scullers faced backwards without a cox to look for danger. Scullers would turn their heads to glance around, but seeing dead ahead is difficult (looking ahead is similar to peeking over your shoulder while driving a car as you quickly check the blind spot before changing lanes). The glance has to be quick, because turning to look in the middle of a stroke is destabilizing, especially when crossing an eddy line. We rowed blind most of the time.

We should have been afraid of the river, but we weren't. We all knew that hypothermia would set in quickly if we fell in—there really was danger. Indeed, my dad had a collection of medical articles on cold-water effects, and his own textbook insisted that rowers stay with the boat in case of accident: it would take too long to pick up nine scattered rowers. But my dad seemed to be unafraid, and the twenty-something brains of the rowers ignored the warnings. My daily focus was on the time required to get back to the dock after practicing downriver. We never carried flotation devices.

The flow of logs and stumps made the river most dangerous when rising. Once flood waters crested, much of the debris got trapped in the shoreline brush as the water level fell. A crucial issue was whether the water was rising or falling at the moment crews were to launch. Reports from town officials along the river helped in the determination, but more immediate results were obtained by looking across the river at water level: if the river showed a bulge near the far bank, it was rising (that bank was the outside of a large bend, so centrifugal force would put more water there).

My dad also worried about water speed, especially when novice crews were on the water: how far down the river should he let them go? To make that judgement, he built a water wheel that spun faster as the water rose. Once the river topped the eastern bank and flooded the fields, the current slowed.

Half-sunken, water-logged trees sometimes got stuck in the river. These snags were a constant danger, especially in the dark and especially near the bridge piers—eddies immediately downstream from the piers created an upstream current that could pull a shell onto a snag. Eddies were particularly strong when the water was high. A typical snag hooked to a bridge pier was an old, leafless tree with many sharp, pointed branches. The trunk would often extend more than fifty feet downstream, usually in the eddy below the pier..

In 1951, an inexperienced PE crew was rowing immediately downstream from the bridge in the *Beaver*, one of the original eight-oared shells donated by Cal coach Ky Ebright. The cox, heading upstream, got too close to a pier. The boat was caught in the eddy—the shell was pulled upstream onto the fork of a snag hung up on the pier.[J-5,J-22,O-42] The cox yelled for his crew to back water. They tried, but pushing an oar backward is much less powerful than pulling on an oar. They were stuck on the snag. By some miracle the pointed branches had not breached the hull.

"Stay with the boat" had been drummed into rowers, so I doubt that any of the crew seriously considered swimming the 100 feet to the dock. Moreover, the icy current was swift and intimidating.

"IN NO CASE LEAVE THE SHELL"!

From Ready All Row *by KF Drlica.*[1-1]

My dad had just helped the crew launch and was still on the float. He saw what happened and shouted for the crew to sit still, "Don't puncture the hull!"

The coaching launch had already gone out with another crew, so my dad had to quickly come up with another solution. He knew that oarsmen were still at the boathouse preparing to carry a shell to the river. He ran up to the boathouse, which at the time was the equivalent of two football fields from the river. There he rounded up a dozen oarsmen. They grabbed oars, raced back to the float, and pulled the training barge out of its shed. The oarsmen and my dad jumped in, locked in their oars, and pushed off. The fifteen-year-old barge moved slowly upriver, barely a match for the current. But after several minutes of hard work, the rescue team reached the *Beaver* and its motionless crew.

Details are absent, but my dad would have been kneeling in the bow where he could keep the barge from smashing the *Beaver* as the barge eased up to the port side of the coxswain's seat. As my dad grabbed the shell, the cox would have reached out with his left hand and grabbed the barge. An oarsman in the barge would have scrambled to the bow and also grabbed the *Beaver*, probably the number eight outrigger. Other oarsmen in the barge would have paddled gently to maintain the barge's position, as it was partly in the current and partly in the eddy. Once the *Beaver* was held tightly, the cox would have climbed out and onto the barge, being careful to not rock the shell and risk a puncture.

Then the challenge was to get the oarsmen out. Number eight would have pulled in his oar, resting it on the gunnels, out of the water. Then he would have leaned as far as possible toward the stern, reaching for the sides of the shell. Once he grabbed the boat, he could put his weight on his arms. In the meantime, his feet would have come out of the stretcher boots. He would have placed one foot on each of the gunnels, raising his rear end high in the air. That would have put him in position to "walk" on all fours to the coxswain's seat. There he would transfer to the barge. One by one the oarsmen moved to the barge, staring at the swirling brown water only two feet below their faces.

According to my dad, the boat lifted off the snag as soon as the weight left the shell. The current grabbed the boat, driving it into the snag's branches, ripping holes in the skin. The *Beaver* quickly filled with water. Meanwhile, the barge rowed back to the float, and the foundered racing shell drifted downstream.

Jim Monroe, who lived across the river in a houseboat, saw what was happening. He jumped into his "pumpkin-seed" speed boat and raced across the river to the foundered shell. He tied a line to one of the outriggers and tried to pull the half-submerged *Beaver* back to the crew float. Jim's tiny boat, which was little more than a motorized surfboard, could barely move the waterlogged shell. After fighting the current for about ten minutes, he gave up and towed the shell to the riverbank on the boathouse side. Since the river level was near the top of the bank, Jim could pull up to a tree where he secured the shell.

Because the *Beaver* was tied on the boathouse side of the river, oarsmen could fight their way through the brush on the riverbank to reach the boat. They recovered the oars and then stretched a quarter-mile-long cable from the shell to the float. Half a dozen oarsmen on the float grabbed the free end of the cable and walked it up the dock, pulling the submerged racing shell. They then got a new grip on the cable at the downstream end of the dock and repeated the process.[J-22]

*Race program photo of "Pumpkin-seed" hydroplane. These boats
were popular on the river during the 1950s.*[O-171a] *A racing club,
called the Aquathusiasts, teamed with the Rowing Club to host
annual race days during the 1950s (in 1957 the club hosted a
national championship outboard motorboat race).*

By the time the *Beaver* reached the dock, little was worth
saving: maybe outriggers, stretcher boots, and seat tracks. Water
was drained out as the shell was lifted out of the river, and the
boat was carried to slings on the bank where the useful parts were
salvaged. A funeral pyre was built, and the *Beaver* met her end.
In the process, the bow was found crammed full of glue mixed
with sawdust, explaining why the boat always seemed so heavy.[J-14]

A different type of problem was to keep crew property from
being swept away by the river. During one of the floods of the
1950s, a faculty friend named Salisbury brought his motorboat
over to the crew float, probably out of curiosity. By the time
Salisbury arrived, my dad had already removed the coaching
launches from their small shed, the single-story launch house
built on logs. Salisbury tied his boat to the launch house and
climbed onto the roof to get a better view. The flow of debris
made the view captivating, somewhat like being on the second
floor of a mid-Manhattan restaurant watching taxis travel down
Lexington Avenue. Sitting on the sloped metal roof added a small
sense of danger.

Launch house similar to the one ridden by Salisbury.[G-20a]

My dad didn't remember why, but somehow the launch house broke loose from its mooring on the bank. Salisbury was soon in mid-river. He still had his boat tied to the house and decided to enjoy the ride, to pretend that he was Huckleberry Finn. Salisbury finally got tired when he reached Albany, about 15 miles downstream. He climbed into his boat and abandoned the launch house to the whims of the river. For my dad, building a new shed was easier than chasing after the house and trying to tow it back against the strong current.

Another flood incident (1956) began with an urgent, early-morning phone call.[J-7,9] The river had taken the Aquathusiasts' "log-raft" clubhouse (the Aquathusiasts were motorboat racing enthusiasts). In the winter, my dad was the only person on the river with immediate access to a boat. He was also a member of the Coast Guard Auxiliary. Presumably he'd know what to do if he could find the clubhouse.

Aquathusiasts' boathouse located on the Corvallis side of the Willamette River immediately upstream from the present boat ramp.[D-109]

He would have jumped into our maroon 1950 Studebaker and driven to the boathouse on back streets, hoping that his lack of a driver's license wouldn't be noticed. Then he would have quickly thrown heavy rope into the *49er*, unlocked the chain tying the boat to the launch house, and checked to make sure the fuel tank was full. The engine in the relatively new boat probably started on the first try. After casting off lines holding the boat to the building, he would have backed out of the launch house, shifted to forward gear, and powered into a starboard turn that took him into the churning, flooding river. Soon the dock was far astern. By steering from a standing position, his view of the river was unobstructed by the windshield.

My dad must have been alone, since his sparce notes don't mention anyone joining him. The single-story clubhouse had a big head start, but it might get hung up in the brush along the banks. It should have been easy to see by scanning the bank with binoculars, but rain on his glasses may have been a problem. Moreover, my dad's scanning was intermittent, because he had to dodge drifting trees.

Coach Drlica.[K-15]

He reached Albany without finding the house. He began to worry, since he didn't have much fuel left and he didn't know how much he'd need to get back against the current. He continued searching for several more miles before giving up and heading back upstream. Then, between Albany and Corvallis, he spotted the clubhouse up a slough. I don't know how he missed it on the way down. Perhaps the slough angled upriver, hiding the building from a boat moving quickly downstream.

Details are missing, but I imagine that he found a spot on the clubhouse to tie the *49er*. Then he would have pulled out his heavy rope, found a strong point on the clubhouse for tying the rope, and made his way to the bank where he tied the rope to a tree.

By the time my dad finished tying off the clubhouse, daylight was gone. He had spent all day in the search, and now he had to get home in the dark. The river was full of stumps and logs, and the swift current would have made progress slow. He would have tried to stay close to a riverbank to minimize the current, especially since his gas tank must have been approaching empty. But in flood, the riverbank is little more than a row of trees with water on both sides. He wrote that he had trouble distinguishing the main channel from flooded fields. He also mentioned many fences in the fields. He had a spotlight on the boat, so seeing fence posts was not a problem. But how do you get a propeller-driven boat over wire fences without becoming entangled? His terse account ended with three words: "Difficulty getting back." He almost never acknowledged difficulty.[1-9]

I didn't realize until I read the rowing archive that my dad had a first-responder mentality: he was always available if persons were in danger or if buildings of value needed to be chased down. Indeed, his boats always seemed to be prepared with extra ropes and a spotlight for working in the dark.

High water was not always a negative. In 1955 my dad and Stevens built an 18-person training barge. They faced the problem of hauling the 1-ton vessel 600 feet from the boathouse to the river. When a flood brought the water to within a hundred

feet of the boathouse door, my dad got over-eager and decided
to launch before he had all fittings in the boat. He gathered 30 or
40 oarsmen, picked up the unfinished, 60-foot boat, and walked
it to the icy water. The launching worked, but had he waited a
month for even higher water, he could have launched from the
boathouse door. The wait would have allowed him to finish the
boat in the warmth of the boathouse.[K-21]

Preparing to launch a new training barge.[K-11]

Launching a barge was simple compared to launching a float.
In 1947 Ed Stevens had acquired huge logs to support a floating
boathouse. The logs had been placed on high ground near the highway approach to the bridge. By 1961 they were no longer needed for
a boathouse, and my dad decided to use them for a float. Rumors
had been circulating that a new bridge would pass through the
logs, and my dad was concerned that he might lose them. When
an exceptionally high water came along (November, 1961), my
dad decided to move the logs, which he had built into a raft, to
the main channel about a hundred yards away. There he would tie
the raft to trees, build a deck on it, and use it for launching shells.

Volunteers eagerly stepped forward for the challenge. According to a newspaper account, five men (my dad, Ed Lee, Harold
Legard, Botond Eross, and J.R. Goerke) began moving the 18- by
52-foot dock at 6 p.m., finally finishing the move nine hours
later.[O-43]

They must have performed the night-time move by attaching the float to trees along the route and "walking" the float into position, using several motorboats to guide the large raft. For much of the next day the crew fought, successfully, to keep the logs in place, not knowing which trees would hold the cabled logs or whether attachment points on the raft were strong enough. Goerke fell in the river three times and was treated for exposure at the local hospital.

My dad occasionally sought help. Federal authorities controlled the Willamette River and were responsible for removing snags. He followed the *Beaver* incident with a request for the Corp of Engineers to remove snags and dredge the river upstream from the bridge. He generally avoided having crews row above the bridge due to snags, which were almost continuous along the eastern bank. However, his racecourse ran up there. Moreover, he wanted better access to the Marys River, a small tributary flowing into the Willamette from the west at what was then the southern edge of Corvallis. He intended to increase river activities there—his overall plan was to popularize the rowing program by getting more people on the river. The Corps resisted working that far upriver.

The Corps did occasionally dredge the river. In the 1950s they employed a pipeline dredge and built a rock wall along the Corvallis side of the river. Jim Monroe was reluctant to move his houseboat during the dredging; he became a local folk hero by claiming that his house was buried under river rock when he refused to move.[K-23] Resistance to government bureaucracy was standard practice in Oregon. For example, my dad planted a wooden tombstone on his front lawn when the City of Corvallis forced him to pay for a sewer connection. The monument read, "Here lies $1500, buried as a result of annexation."

The snag requests continued into the late 1960s, especially as interest in College canoe classes grew (canoes would travel a mile upstream from the boathouse to the Marys River for a peaceful paddle up this quiet little tributary). In 1969 my dad again asked the Corps to extend snagging upstream to the Marys River.[K-25] The response was typically bureaucratic, "Every effort will be made to remove snags within our authorization when the overall number of snags makes the work economical." More pressure would be required for removal of major snags, but my dad handled those close to the docks.[K-37]

In the mid-1960s, flood-control dams were built in the mountains, giving my dad a new option—on race days, when he really needed the river to be debris-free, he would ask the Corps of Engineers to slow the release of water from one of the main dams in the Cascades. By planning a few days ahead, he could decrease the chance that rowers would have to dodge a large tree cruising down the racecourse. Such requests were not extraordinary and usually met with a favorable response.

The river clearly defined Oregon State rowing. For members of the crew, the river posed challenges we could meet more easily than beating Washington in a race. For my dad, the events seemed to be routine parts of the job. His apparent fearlessness caused the rest of us to be less cautious than was warranted. The routine nature of the river anecdotes kept most from becoming public knowledge: many I discovered only by reading the archive. In contrast, my dad was eager to publicize race results and fund-raising projects. Indeed, gaining recognition was an ongoing activity of Oregon State crew.

--------- *Chapter 13* ---------

RECOGNITION

I n the 1920s, the Rowing Club easily obtained general recognition, as crew was a major sport in pre-television America. Indeed, many newspaper articles document the early days in Corvallis. However, gaining personal recognition comparable to that afforded football and basketball players took many years. The effort began in 1934 as a request for the College to award a block O with crossed oars for men who participated in at least two intercollegiate races.[A-62] According to the Club, the men, nine of whom qualified, were "entitled to such awards because their activity is beneficial to the school, to the student body, and to themselves." The College denied the request: it didn't sanction awards for physical education activities such as rowing, fencing, and wrestling. The Rowing Club needed to break free from its perceived connection with the Physical Education Department.

Al Cook tried again a year later. His additional argument was "There are more men turning out for crew than any other sport on this campus, crew has proven itself a ... sport by development on its own initiative, we have brought to Oregon State College recognition and publicity from the entire country, and we have brought to Oregon State College a new sport." Cook was successful: approval for a varsity letter six inches high was issued in May 1935.

By 1939, my dad, as Rowing Club President, was pushing for more.[A-62] To give the Oregon State program free labor, he suggested a system of student managers, with the incentive a varsity block award. To the eighteen awards then approved for crew, he wanted to add five for managers who would drive coaching launches, repair broken boats, and in general keep the program running. The University of California had eleven managers plus full-time employees repairing boats. My dad wrote, "At Oregon State the coach does all of this for an oarsman turnout that is larger than at either Cal or Washington." His request was probably denied, but managers did eventually receive varsity letters.

After World War II, the Rowing Club effort shifted toward raising the status of the rowing award. At the top of the prestige pyramid was the Varsity O, a club for real athletes, such as football and basketball letter winners. While Varsity O perks were invisible to our classmates (free passes to College sporting events and a wool blanket with a large O in its center), the oarsmen felt that acceptance into the Varsity O would move rowing into the big leagues.

In a long 1948 letter, Carl Clogstrom, a former Rowing Club President, pointed out that each term more than 100 men turn out for crew; it's becoming a sport of major importance.[A-64] The denial letter stated, "The sport is being carried on too informally at other colleges to make an organized intercollegiate program possible. Also, to carry the program here would involve more funds than are available at present. ... Since the school does not recognize crew as a major sport, the Varsity O cannot admit your members into our organization."[A-62] The Varsity O idea was dead until rowing was brought into the Athletic Department.

Jim Wahlstrom, Ed Stevens, Irene Stevens (Ed's second wife), and Carl Clogstrom circa 1949.[A-38]

If not Varsity O, perhaps the puny six-inch letter could be enlarged to eight inches, thereby matching those awarded to football players. After another decade, the Rowing Club argued, "We have a year-round training program with races in the fall and spring. We represent Oregon State College when we race. An eight inch 'O' would ... give us equal prestige with the other schools we race ... it would be recognition of the time, work, and money put into the crew program by those participating members." To avoid pushing too hard, the Club agreed to retain crossed oars on the letter and words indicating lightweight or JV if appropriate (JV or junior varsity is the second boat, the backup team). By the early 1960s, the rowing letter was an eight-inch "O". Rowing was becoming a real sport at Oregon State—oarsmen could in good conscience check the box "Athlete in Training" on medical questionnaires.

Varsity letter for crew, early 1960s. This 8-inch, bright orange block "O" contained identifying insignia (crossed oars) that was absent for sports sponsored by the Athletic Department.[C-1]

The Rowing Club's collective push for recognition reflected its members' individual struggles for position in mid-twentieth century college life. My own sensitivity to dominance hierarchy serves as a 1960s example. In a town where winter rain seemed to fall 98% of the time, umbrellas were an important status symbol. Everyone had an umbrella, but only members of a prestigious fraternity carried an extra-large, black one. I would have carried that umbrella even if the weather were only foggy.

But I wasn't invited to join the club; my umbrella had to be the standard size.

If I couldn't get near the top of the pecking order, at least I'd conceal being at the bottom. That position was reserved for first-year male students, the Rooks. They were easily recognized by the small beanie, the Rook Lid,[O-188] that they were forced to wear by their living groups. This bright green cap with its orange bill, top button, and letter "O" had been a freshman tradition for decades. I don't recall the punishment for being caught without your Rook Lid, but it was likely the application of a fraternity paddle. I lived at home my freshman year and easily avoided wearing my Rook Lid.

Oregon State College Rook Lid.
Photo from Hansonhats.com.[O-188]

Much better than the large, black umbrella was the varsity letter, the orange O that could be worn only on a special letterman's sweater or jacket. The black letterman jackets with yellowish leather sleeves were distinguished by the absence of orange trim—similar jackets could be bought by anyone at the college bookstore, but those all had orange trim.

I bought a jacket with orange trim for my freshman rowing award, a five-inch, orange 64 with an oar through it. I ran home and immediately sewed the 64 onto the jacket. The weather never got too hot to wear that jacket.

I'm sure my behavior bordered on braggadocio. For example, after a freshman race at Stanford, several of us drove to Santa Cruz and paraded up and down the boardwalk wearing the racing shirts we'd won (rowing tradition is to bet shirts). We wore the Stanford shirts all the way home and around campus for at least a week. Eventually we smelled the sweat and began looking forward to the next race and a chance to get a different trophy shirt.

I thought that if I worked hard enough, I could get in the varsity boat. In those days, our team didn't have many big guys who would have a natural advantage over me. Throughout the summer I lifted weights, and several of us fixed old single sculls so we could row on the river. As the miles mounted, my oar blades started coming out of the water cleanly, and they stayed off the water as I reached for each stroke. These were focused miles: a hundred strokes working on finishing smoothly, another hundred on power, a third hundred on raising the stroke rate, and so on—everything I could think of to make the boat go faster. I was so focused that I came within inches of ramming a log raft, head-on at full power. Only an emergency stop, a sudden driving of oars under water, saved the old wooden shell.

I don't know whether I received any benefit from the varsity letter. But I did wear out the jacket, and I kept my eight-inch "O" for fifty years.

The personal impact of the varsity letter was probably greater for women rowers than for men. The women had fought hard to overcome the cheerleader stereotype. They deserved recognition as athletes. By the mid-1970s they were racing the same clubs and schools as the men, but no precedence existed for women being awarded letters.

Astrid Hancock, the women's coach, recalled, "Back in the 60's and 70's none of the women's sports received varsity letters, although [in] some years women's crew received a small, three-inch orange "O" with a diagonal oar, probably purchased from the men's crew resources. I remember a woman who coxed for four years and married a wrestler. He got a large letter that dwarfed hers. She was not happy. Male rowers were also getting a jacket for their large block "O". In 1975, Fred Mann, interim coach, gave out some of the large six- or eight-inch "O's" to the women with CREW written on the bottom; some women got stripes related to the number of years of rowing. I don't think that Coach Drlica continued this in 1976 and 1977."[D-4a,O-112]

Astrid continued, "In late 2013 I realized that 2014 would represent 50 years of women's rowing. I thought that it would be fun to have a reunion and commemoration at the annual Rowing Club banquet. I collected email addresses for special invitations to women rowers of the early days. I considered having block letter awards, but I was told that I couldn't make post-facto awards. Then, two weeks before the banquet, Bob Poole, an oarsman of the 1960s who was on an OSU administrative committee, [managed for] … the women [to] receive varsity letters. Fourteen women, representing every year from 1964 to 1977, had agreed to attend, so I knew how many letters and the number of stripes I needed. The women were overwhelmed with their awards, as was I when a new shell with my name on it was displayed. I doubt that there was a dry eye in the hall." [O-112]

Display of awards by women rowers. In 2014, varsity letters and certificates were presented to women's crews of the 1960s and 1970s.[D-102] Astrid is holding flowers. The women obtained letter-winner jackets from the Athletic Department, sewed on the letters, and proudly wore them to campus activities. [O-112]

Awarding varsity letters, even if they came from the Rowing Club rather than the University, would have fostered the development of women's crew. However, obtaining University approval for varsity letters would have been difficult, just as it had been for men's crew. Even after the Athletic Department sponsored women's crew, University approval was doubtful, because society did not consider women equal to men in most activities. For example, my younger sister Dianne recalled, "During my interview for vet school, one of the doctors on the committee stood up, pounded his fist on the table, and said that women had no business in vet school. If I liked animals, I should go into animal science."

Since varsity awards would mean little if our classmates were unaware of rowing, the Club needed publicity beyond simply wearing an orange "O" on a jacket. Good publicity might also help us convince our classmates to row: we needed to develop more team depth to compete with Cal and Washington. Recruiting in the 1960s was far more difficult than in the 1930s, since television-friendly sports had displaced competitive rowing. The thousands of fans of the pre-war era had disappeared; newspaper reporters rarely made it down to the boathouse. Thus, the Club constantly looked for ways to advertise rowing.

One effort involved a small billboard. The main campus of Oregon State contained a large, central square surrounded by classroom buildings. Foot traffic between classes was heavy on the paved sidewalks that crisscrossed the grassy quadrangle. The center of the quad was perfect for a billboard. In the early 1960s we painted 4 x 8 sheets of plywood with announcements of upcoming crew races and then planted them in the middle of the quad for several days before each race. We didn't consider obtaining permission from University administrators, and they chose to ignore our sign. We were the only advertisers. Moreover, we always removed the sign after a few days to update it for the next race. The billboard didn't increase the number of spectators, but

we convinced ourselves that we were raising the general awareness of rowing. That might pay off later in unanticipated ways.
    Although the coaches supplied paint and plywood, I don't
recall any guidance. The sign was probably not their idea. Nor did
they seem to care about varsity letters and individual prestige: I
found no evidence that Stevens or my dad, as coach, lobbied for
more and larger varsity letters other than for managers. Instead,
they spread the rowing bug by focusing on intramural rowing. For
example, in the late 1930s, Oregon State had enough male students
with rowing experience for a men's eight-oared program in which
living groups competed. Interest in rowing declined after World
War II, but the program was maintained by using four-oared
shells. In 1952, my dad introduced rowing to women. He had no
idea that rowing would be so appealing to young women or that
women rowers would eventually outnumber men by two to one
in the United States. What began as a publicity stunt quickly grew
into serious competition among sororities and other living groups.
    The women's intramural season was short: four or five weeks
in the autumn before high water. Varsity oarsmen coached and
coxed the crews at early morning practices. When two crews
came abreast, a mad dash followed, accompanied by a flurry of
shouting by the men.
    My dad didn't mention that women's intramural rowing
was for publicity. We thought that the goal was to have fun.
Indeed, sharing rowing with a young lady was such a draw that
one summer I was up at sunrise to double scull with a former
high school classmate. Her parents didn't want to be disturbed
so early; consequently, she would spend the night in a sleeping
bag on her lawn. I drove by at about 6 a.m., and we sculled for
an hour or so five days a week.
    My dad eventually found that intramural rowing was too
expensive: the PE rowing budget couldn't support the repairs
needed for the intramural programs. The men's intramural program was stopped in the early 1960s; women's intramural rowing

was halted after the 1967 season. Langton had been replaced as head of the Men's and Women's PE Departments, and a budgetary feud developed between my dad and the new head: the PE budget for crew had been cut by 50%. Since it had not been increased since 1952, the amount of money for crew was a quarter of the 1950s level. According to my dad, conditions "forced" him to halt women's intramural rowing despite being ordered by his boss to keep it going.[D-35,O-28] By that time the heavy-weight men's crew was sponsored by the Athletic Department, and the women's intercollegiate team appeared to be self-sustaining. My dad wasn't going to be bullied into more volunteer work by a pencil-pushing administrator.

Although oarsmen shouldered much of the effort to gain recognition, lobbying College presidents was largely up to Stevens and my dad. In an example from 1953, my dad "updated" President Strand on progress with the future golf course and included unidentified materials about rowing. Strand responded, "Although you men work under considerable handicap, the struggle for your existence seems to have resulted in a spirit that probably could be generated in no other way."[C-36] By the 1970s that spirit had produced a small campus.

——— *Chapter 14* ———

THE ROWING CAMPUS

Although my dad was hired in 1950 to teach PE rowing, he was not going to be just another physical education instructor. He saw his appointment as a base for building a first-class rowing program.[G-13] By 1970 key elements were in place.

A central feature of his plan was a new crew house, either on the water or close to it. Ever mindful of government surplus, he initially hoped to obtain an ex-Army building from Camp Adair, a World War II training facility located about 10 miles north of Corvallis. He envisioned tearing apart a building and reconstructing it on the river. Another priority was a rowing tank. These tanks typically have a set of rowing stations positioned around a trough of water. The tank would serve for practice during periods of high water, which could last a week or more. My dad had detailed drawings for a tank and special oars Stevens had obtained from Harvard. A third idea was to build and sell racing shells. He was convinced that rowing would grow explosively on the West Coast, which would create a market for shells and make his program financially self-sufficient.

These dreams were not idle fancy, as one of the projects was realized: a boathouse from military surplus. But the Rowing Club failed to get a rowing tank as a class gift from the College[G-14], and Stevens' death in 1957, plus my dad's increased responsibilities, kept the boat-building enterprise from developing. Nevertheless, other opportunities were found and exploited.

My dad subscribed to Stevens' 1930s salvaging philosophy, which some might call scrounging. For example, he obtained an old, gray pickup truck from Navy surplus specifically for salvaging. Since he couldn't see well enough to drive legally, he and Carl Bower would make trips to the University dump. There they found old pipe, angle iron, and serviceable lumber to haul back for boathouse construction projects.[O-31] My job was to pull the rusted nails from the lumber to make it useful.

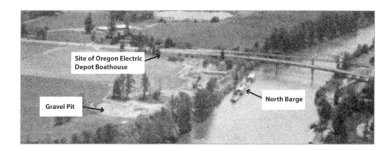

Rowing campus, aerial views, circa 1970.[K-1, G-10] *Top: View from the north; river flows from top to bottom. Bottom: View from the east; river flows from left to right. The Beach farmhouse and the Oregon Electric Depot boathouse were demolished in 1963 to make room for the new Harrison Street bridge.*

When the Beach farm was acquired in 1952, one of the immediate benefits was access to the large barn situated on high ground between the boathouse and the river. The barn was more than 60 feet long, long enough to allow storage for new eight-oared racing shells. The hayloft, which was reached by an internal staircase, was converted into a small gymnasium.

The main floor of the barn had housed horse stalls that still contained harnesses. Some of the stalls were cleaned and outfitted with weightlifting equipment. My dad fabricated dumbbell-style weights from pairs of empty food cans of various sizes. He filled the cans with concrete and connected pairs with a piece of iron pipe to serve as a hand grip. Then he painted the weights silver to look official and printed the weight on the ends of the cans. Other horse stalls were opened and rebuilt into a classroom, complete with a tiered floor and blackboard. The basement was used to store canoes and miscellaneous motorboats. Obtaining the barn was a major advance, as it allowed off-water training to be taken seriously.

In the summer between my junior and senior high school years, I worked at the boathouse. One of my chores was to install adjustable sit-up boards along the walls of the barn's hayloft.[G-21,J-23] I also prepared the floor of the loft for 18 rowing machines. That meant a thorough cleaning to remove cobwebs and residual straw. Then I applied several coats of linseed oil to the floor. The room was so large that I painted somewhat randomly to overcome the monotony. Lack of attention put me in a corner with painted floor on every side. The only solution was to back out of the corner and paint over my footprints. When I got outside, dirt stuck to the oil on my shoes, ruining them for anything but boathouse work.

Progress along one front was countered by annual floods that took away docks and floating sheds that housed launches and the training barge. These mishaps were expected. An unexpected one occurred in 1955 when a fire burned part of the boathouse. Apparently, flammable gases accumulated in the boiler used to generate hot water for showers. An explosion and fire followed.

Fortunately, the fire broke out during daylight hours, and neighbors quickly called the fire department. Damage was confined to the rear of the building with no loss of racing shells.[O-44] The fire was mentioned only in an archival news clipping, never at home or at the boathouse. I suspect that it embarrassed my dad, since the cause was probably a substandard, do-it-yourself hot water system carried over from the Stevens' era.

Off-water training. Left: Beach barn[G-44]. Right: Rowing machines and sit-up boards in the barn, circa 1960. Although the rowing machines contained shock absorbers, they were designed for technique, not endurance training.[G-12] Sit-up boards are in the background.[G-21]

Newspaper photo of fire at the boathouse, 1955.[O-44]

In late 1960 or early 1961, my dad happened to be chatting with the commander of the college naval ROTC unit, Captain Richard Shafer.[J-23] Shafer had been a submarine commander and was still well connected with the Navy. As Shafer was walking out of my dad's campus office, my dad asked, in an off-handed way, whether the Navy had a surplus barge that could be used as a boathouse. Shafer said he'd check, and a week later he called with news that the Tongue Point Naval Yard in Astoria had surplus. Maybe there was a suitable ammunition barge. My dad would need to hurry, because the surplus would soon be towed to Bremerton, Washington for storage.

Shafer requisitioned a driver and truck to take my dad to Astoria at the mouth of the Columbia River. Although my dad thought it was a long-shot, he went on the 150-mile trip. Along the way he stopped at Oregon City, a small town immediately south of Portland, to measure the locks where the Willamette River flows over a fall. As he recalled, the locks were 34 feet 7 inches wide and about 200 feet long. Those dimensions defined the maximum size for any vessel he might bring home.

Newspaper photo of Richard Shafer.[G-22]

When my dad reached the naval yard, he could hardly believe his eyes—scrounger's heaven.

"There were all kinds of stuff up for grabs. We took a truck-load of stuff: cable, pulleys, flood lights, (and more)."

Moreover, there were two ammunition barges, not just the one he hoped for. These barges, called lighters, were roughly 100 feet long with a deck about eight feet above the water line, low enough for a ramp with a reasonable pitch to reach a float only a few inches off the water. The bow and the stern of the barges were slanted to reduce drag, making roughly 45-degree angles with the water. Both barges had single-story, metal buildings, perfect for storing racing shells. And the barges were only 34 feet wide: they could pass through the Oregon City locks with several inches to spare.[G-9]

My dad immediately submitted a request for both surplus barges.[G-4] He then raced home to get Langton, who was still head of the PE Department, to take them. Langton agreed, provided my dad could get the barges upriver at no cost. Then began multiple letters to the Navy,[G-4] including an April 1961 request for release of the ships for live storage of racing shells and canoes. Within a week the Navy responded that the vessels were "… in excess to the needs of the Columbia River Group". To allow time for a decision about the release of the barges, the Navy delayed the scheduled tow to Bremerton for a few weeks. My dad got Oregon Senator Wayne Morse involved, and by mid-May the Commandant of the Thirteenth Naval District sent a one-line release statement: "There is no current or anticipated need for the YFN314 or the YRL6 (barge names) in the Thirteenth Naval District." Additional permissions were needed for tools the Navy left on board, such as hoists, vices, and drill presses.

One of my dad's PE colleagues, Norm Martinson, had a brother-in-law who ran a river towing service. Martinson talked him into bringing the barges to Portland for no charge. The rest of the trip from Portland cost about $1,000. The source of that money may have been E.C. Sammons, the long-time friend of Stevens, rowing supporter, and in 1961 a bank president. Fred Newell, after seeing the barges in Portland (November, 1961), advised my dad to contact Sammons.[A-53] The rowing archive does not reveal the source of the $1,000.

The trip upriver was slow, as the barges sat at Oregon City for two months. Eventually they reached Corvallis where they were tied to trees on the eastern bank of the Willamette. They were huge.

"I had not appreciated how big they were when they were next to much larger ships in the naval yard," my dad later said. "I now had two big ships, each as big as a barn. We were not ready for them."

Barges tied to the bank soon after arriving in Corvallis. In the background are the Quonset hut and the barn. The Oregon Electric Depot, seen only as a bright line, is in the distance on the far left. Widow-maker cottonwood trees line the bank.[G-19]

My dad had little trouble pulling the barges into place, as a 16-ft runabout with a 35 hp outboard motor had sufficient power. A barge was placed at each end of a 100-foot float, and ramps were built, largely under the direction of Carl Bower. Piling had to be driven into the river to hold the barges properly; my dad couldn't risk tying the barges to trees, since floods routinely uprooted riverside trees. The piling had to be tall enough to survive a flood as high as the one of 1927; however, it didn't need to be extraordinarily strong, because the barges offered little resistance to the river.

The installation of piling (1963) did cost the University money, but now the school had, in my dad's view, two beautiful ships. The value of these vessels was difficult to assess, because no market existed. However, in about 1985 similar barges sold for $40,000. The rowing campus had a capital asset that gave the program a feeling of permanence. Unfortunately, the buildings on the barges would eventually require maintenance, which became a problem that threatened the entire rowing program.

Carl Bower welded racks for storing eight-oared racing shells. No longer would it be necessary to carry shells 200 yards from the Oregon Electric Depot boathouse to the water. Moreover, one barge was already outfitted as a workshop.

I remember walking through the doorway, stepping over the raised threshold characteristic of ships. On the left was an enclosed coaches' office that was roughly 12 feet square. On the right was a screened cage roughly the size of the office. It was used for storing valuables. Beyond these two structures was a large room that was outfitted with tools: a table saw, band saw, chop saw, planer, lathe, drill press, chain hoist, and many others I've now forgotten. In the center was a long, narrow boat stand used for racing shells needing repair, and at the far end were sliding doors that opened onto a ramp that led to a downstream float. Carl Bower had cut a large rectangular hole in the steel deck about midway along the river bank side, and he then constructed a staircase to a huge storage space below decks. The upstream barge contained racks along the walls for storage of racing shells. That barge lacked an office and storage cage, thereby allowing more shells to fit. The two barges were perfect for the rowing program.

Carl Bower brazing components to a barge circa 1963.[C-26]

As with Stevens and his boathouse, managing the release, shipment, and mooring of the barges was the task of the rowing coach. My dad became tied emotionally to the barges; future disputes with University administrators became personal issues.

Planning had been required for the construction of floats and the sheds that kept rain out of the coaching launches and training barge. The decks of the floats had to be only a few inches off the water: the outriggers and oars of racing shells had to easily pass over a deck. The floats also had to support a crowd of people without slipping under water.

Securing barges on the river. Left: Driving piling, circa 1963. Right: Piling securing the north barge. Photo on the right was taken when the river was flooding.[G-25.J-23]

Once the floats and sheds were built, they had to be protected from floods and kept from sinking. After a few years, the large logs used for support became water-logged. My dad was faced with either replacing the logs, which would mean reconstructing the floats, or finding a way to raise the deck. His solution was to install empty oil drums for flotation. We screwed a steel pipe about three feet long into the side hole (bunghole) of a drum, partially filled the drum with water, and capped the pipe. Then we forced the drum in between logs such that the end of the pipe stuck out above the water. One of us, usually me as the junior member of the team, got in the water and pushed the drum under one of the logs and into place between two logs, constantly fighting the current. When the pipe became visible, Carl would grab it and pull it until the barrel was in place, parallel to the logs and the surface of the river. Then the pipe was uncapped, water was pumped out of the drum, and the pipe was recapped. The same strategy was used to float a new barge house without using logs. We must have installed 20 to 30 barrels one summer.

Construction of barge-house and flotation using oil barrels. Left: Barrel waiting for installation;[G-29] Right: Partially submerged barrel being forced into place.[G-32]

Eventually the oil barrels rusted, leaked, and dragged the floats and barge house under water. That required continued maintenance. However, in the late 1960s the logs and barrels were replaced with styrofoam blocks obtained as a gift from the Dow Chemical Company. These blocks would support a float forever or until a flood took the entire construct (that did happen; even an aerial search failed to locate the float).

Styrofoam blocks to support the floats.[G-17,G-26, G-27]

The ramps from the land to the floats posed a different problem. They were normally out of the water and required no flotation. But during floods, the ramps had to be tied down and floated. Empty fuel tanks from military aircraft served as floats for ramps.

Ramp from the riverbank to the float showing two pontoons (arrow) hanging from the ramp, out of the water.[G-20]

Pontoons shown under a portion of a ramp that was moved out of position due to a flood in 1965. The pontoons were originally airplane fuel tanks obtained as military surplus.[G-20a]

Land transportation also had to be improved. In the late 1950s, the Rowing Club purchased two new eight-oared shells, and the need to haul them to other racing venues became apparent. Racing shells are somewhat like shoes: you are more comfortable in your own. Moreover, borrowed boats were not always as good as those other crews were rowing. My dad designed a boat trailer, had the design approved by College engineers, and obtained financial support from the Benton Lions Club. He then had it constructed by inmates at the state prison.

*Shell trailer. Trailer that had space under the oars
for a small coaching launch.[G-11]*

Next came the problem of storing the trailer, as the winter
rain would soon lead to rust and structural weakness. The answer
was the garage of the Hickman house (the caretaker's lodging for
the Beach farm). To accommodate the long trailer, the garage was
extended. In the late 1960s a pickup truck ran off the highway and
tore into the garage, illustrating the unpredictable maintenance
costs for the University.

*Hickman garage accident.[G-33] The garage had been extended to
act as a storage facility for the shell trailer. A pickup truck ran
off the highway and into the Hickman garage. Photo date is
unknown, probably after 1965.*

The acquisition of small boats from the Portland Rowing
Club and the growing canoeing program created another storage

problem. This one was solved by moving a Quonset hut from the main Oregon State campus to the river. These metal World War II buildings were designed by the military to be torn down quickly, moved, and rebuilt. For decades, Oregon State College had used Quonset huts as temporary buildings; by 1960, some were no longer needed. My dad arranged to have one transferred to the rowing program. In 1961 the Physical Plant poured a foundation. Then, during two years of weekend work, oarsmen assembled the large hut, built the floor, constructed ramps, and made racks for shells and canoes.[H-2] This new facility eventually added to the maintenance problems of the PE Department.

Dave Prodehl and the author hammering nails attaching the metal sheets. Circa 1962.[C-2]

It seemed that something was always happening at the boat-house. For example, during construction of the Quonset hut, a freak windstorm traveled north up the Willamette Valley. At about 2 p.m. on Columbus Day, 1962, my dad heard radio reports of the oncoming storm. That gave him about two hours to prepare for winds up to 80 mph. Many metal sheets, destined to be siding on the Quonset hut, were still piled on the ground. Those sheets would be lethal if picked up and hurled by the wind. My dad and oars-men arriving early for practice frantically moved the sheets under the barn for safe storage, beating the wind by only a few minutes.

Nothing could be done to protect the fragile cottonwood trees along the river. The wind broke off limbs, and one whole tree crashed into the Van Buren Street Bridge. By 5:30 the storm had passed,[G-3,J-15] but traffic over the bridge was halted for several days.

Small boats house (Quonset hut). Left to right:
Larry Birke, John Hamstreet, Fred Sterk.[G-16]

The Navy barges and the Quonset hut eliminated the need for the Oregon Electric Depot boathouse. That was fortunate, because in 1963 the Highway Department spanned the river with an additional bridge whose approach passed through the boathouse. The building contained a full boat-building shop—oarsmen saved everything, including racks for holding shells and oars.

Oarsmen salvaging everything from the Oregon Electric Depot, 1963;[G-28, G-30] Lower photo shows Cameron Brown moving racks for shell storage.

Demolition of boathouse.[G-31]

Somehow my dad was able to keep the money from the sale of the Oregon Electric Depot in the rowing program: it was used to build a new locker room, which was named after Ed Stevens. My dad designed the building to eventually serve women's crew after another wing was built for men (no urinals were installed).[J-8]

Salvaging the shower/locker room facility from the Oregon Electric Depot. Arrows: The Hickman house was for the caretaker of the Beach farm; the Hickman garage was expanded to store the racing shell trailer; the shower/dressing room was moved about 100 yards toward the river.[G-18]

Since a period existed between demolition of the old Oregon Electric Depot and construction of the new locker room, the old locker and drying-room portion was cut off the boathouse and moved next to the garage of the Beach farmhouse.[J-23] The Beach house had been razed for the new bridge, but the well remained as a source of water. Dave Prodehl, an oarsman at the time and later a women's coach, performed the plumbing work. This small locker room, with three shower heads, served well—we had never known anything better—for a year or so until the new locker room was completed. Then the salvaged shower/locker room was used on a temporary basis for the women's intercollegiate crew. It remained temporary for decades.

Although the women's locker room was functional, it was very primitive compared to the men's facilities. When Title IX legislation (1972) required equal treatment for male and female athletes, University administrators sought to eliminate superior men's facilities rather than build equivalent ones for women. That created an outcry. Administrators then realized that their problems would disappear if crew were simply eliminated. My dad later said that having a women's locker room on a temporary basis was one of his biggest mistakes, because it gave administrators a tangible reason for shutting down the entire crew program.

Maintenance eventually became a problem with the buildings on the barges. The roofs leaked, perhaps in part from sanding that was done by the Physical Plant prior to painting. Local kids, diving from the roofs to the river, also contributed to leaks that were ruining the interior insulation. My dad thought that the leaks should be fixed before more damage occurred. The University administration resisted—salvaging and volunteerism provide no money for maintenance.[G-8]

My dad saw no issue with the hulls of the barges. During the procurement process, Navy personnel told him that the hulls had been refurbished recently for storage at Bremerton. Navy experience with mothballed ships in the Sacramento River showed that no problem was expected. If a leak developed, an unlikely occurrence, it could be repaired easily from the inside—that's what was done with ships at sea. In contrast, University officials maintained that the barges must be dry-docked, their bottoms sanded and painted, and only then could the roofs be repaired. Such faulty reasoning led to vastly inflated maintenance estimates. My dad challenged the underlying motivation. He began to suspect dishonesty, but as far as I can tell, he didn't develop those ideas beyond notes to himself.

Stevens and my dad had built the campus by actively seeking free materials, buildings, and labor. The low initial costs made it difficult for University administrators to say no. However, this tactic made few friends among top administrators, since they were aware of maintenance costs. Moreover, they felt forced to go along with my dad's plans, which probably made some of their opposition personal. Indeed, my dad was proud when he forced a University vice president to put money into crew by obtaining barges that required the installation of piling.

Although the floats and barges were held by piling, the river continued to be a threat throughout the 1960s and 1970s. Dams in the mountains reduced the danger, but winter surges were powerful enough to snap cables holding ramps to the docks, and uprooted trees would scrape the sheet metal siding off the launch house. Moreover, river accidents could be life-threatening, as spring floods from melting snow were icy. But for my dad, the challenge of the river was more or less routine.

Chapter 15 ───

MORE RIVER

When the river was high, I'd carry my oars to the float and stare at the brown, swirling flow. Did I really want to be sculling a narrow, tippy boat on water having such power? I wasn't afraid, but I should have been: the water was snow melt. Instead, I focused on the rain that would make my oar handles slick and on the cross currents that would keep me from getting an even pull on both sides. I'd have to be alert, just as I was yesterday and the day before.

My dad had to be alert for a different reason. He had expanded the rowing campus in the early 1960s, and he now had even more for the river to take. All-night vigils with pike poles were required to fend off the logs, whole trees, and parts of barns cruising downstream. Tug boats could be called to pull trees out from under a float or one of the barges,[K-23] but that cost money and was to be avoided.

The eastern pier of the old Van Buren Street bridge was a danger that could be anticipated: we could see when the pier had collected stumps and debris that would break loose as enormous tangles of branches, roots, and miscellaneous pieces of wood. When a pile broke free, some of it could lodge under a barge or shear off parts of the sheds used to store coaching launches.[K-23]

As the water rose, the river's edge shifted outward, making the floats inaccessible from land in what had become a much wider, faster river. To reach the floats during a flood, my dad had a small rowboat loaded with pike poles, a sledge hammer, axes, saws, spikes, rope, and cable.[K-21] He also had a peavy, the stout, hooked pole used to roll logs. He was ready. But he couldn't control the timing. According to Carl Bower, the floods always seemed to come on Thanksgiving or Christmas Eve when most of the oarsmen had left school to visit families. That left only Carl and me to help my dad protect the floats and launch house.

My mom was stoic about the river. She grew up on a river almost in her backyard. As a child she rode a riverboat to school. When the river flooded, the children crossed the flooded fields to the boat landing by walking on a series of planks attached to the tops of fence posts. It seemed like business as usual when, after dinner, my dad and I announced that we were on our way to the boathouse to protect the docks.

But my sister Karen felt the danger. "Sitting up at night after bedtime and crying and staring out my window, praying that he would be OK at the boathouse and come home safely … these were nights of rain and storm, and I had heard that he would be on the dock collecting logs or saving the dock from logs."

I was five years older than Karen and actively participating with my dad; for me it was adventure and what guys did.

My mom was more concerned with my dad's cigarette smoking. That was more dangerous than a flood. My dad claimed that smoking tobacco helped him stay alert through the night. He initially relied on cigarettes, but the incessant rain extinguished them before they were half-smoked. He switched to a pipe that could be turned upside down.

He failed to convince anyone that his smoking was acceptable, as revealed in one of Carl Bower's recollections: "One summer we had a log tied to the dock. Coach was out walking on the large log, and it rolled. In the drink he went. We all cheered when he pulled out his pack of cigarettes, thinking they were lost forever. But he carefully plucked the nasty, soaked cigarettes out of the pack and laid them on a log to dry in the sun so he could enjoy them later."[O-3]

Sculling in the flood water of 1964. In the background is the Hickman garage with its extension that housed the shell trailer. The flood completely covered the fields near the rowing campus.[K-9]

A 1964 flood is still remembered,[K-29] although the water didn't reach the middle of Corvallis as it had in late 1920s. The few flood-control dams were overwhelmed when a rain-filled warm front dropped the snowpack in the Cascades from 72 to 24 inches in two days. Nearly 30 state highways were rendered impassable, six bridges were washed out, and towns were flooded. Oarsmen got the rare pleasure of sculling peacefully over flooded farmland with no current to fight.

Example of debris, flood of 1965. Photo taken from a float shows ramp to the float in disarray; building on left is Stevens Crewhouse; Quonset hut is on the right. Flooded field is shown in the background.[K-7]

High water. Left: Barn that housed weight-lifting equipment (1965); viewed from a Navy barge used as a boathouse.[K-3] Right: Beach farmhouse in undated photo.[O-119a] This house was razed in 1963 when the Harrison Street Bridge was built.

Even as late as 1974, floods seemed routine,[O-40] although by then flood-control dams in the Cascades suppressed the surges. That year, on a January night, the training barge and its sheltering shed broke loose. Both were located about 2½ miles downstream, hung up in the brush. The shed had completely collapsed and was too flimsy to recover. I imagine that the lumber and metal roof were salvaged, but the shed was certainly not dragged back to the dock. The training barge was recovered undamaged.[K-21]

Training barge house and barge taken by flood in 1974. Left. Collapsed barge house. Center. Stern of the barge under the collapsed house (person steering the barge would stand inside the semicircle formed by the pieces of pipe).[K-13,K-14,] Right. Additional view of the barge house.[K-30]

A few years later the training barge ran into a floating tree. As my dad reported, "… about 3 p.m. … a tree drifting down the river lodged against an outrigger of the training barge causing … several hundred dollars damage to the side of the barge and to the rudder, which was torn off but retrieved."[K-27]

Despite such incidents, we generally felt safe while rowing, because we were skimming over the surface. I thought that being in the water was far more dangerous, as moving water can be very powerful.[K-28] To my dad, being in the river was just part of the job. Several dunkings occurred when he was walking on logs: they would roll unexpectedly, leaving him time only to catch his breath. Walking off the ends of floats was routine, since there were no guard rails. Being soaked by rain was also routine, even with rubberized coats and hats. My dad once recorded changing clothes seven times in a day.

"Where'd you go?" asked a young woman in one of my dad's PE classes as they stood on the float. He had suddenly disappeared for a few moments. They were landing inexperienced crews, and he was waving instructions as the incoming crews fought the wind and current. He stepped off the edge of the float but was out of the water so fast that his billfold didn't get wet. The day was clear and sunny; the woman asked, "How'd you get soaked? Not good for your business suit."

My dad sometimes misjudged the speed of the current when pushing logs around. One day, while walking on a log, he was on the wrong side of his pike pole when he stabbed another log. He was slowly pried off his log and into the river. That day he was wearing his usual uniform, coveralls with pockets full of nails, hammer hanging from his belt. Such weights must have made it difficult to reach the surface.

He frequently lost tools in the river, with the biggest problem arising when his keys dropped in—then he lost access to motorboats, buildings, everything. He and his helpers would stab a pike pole into the river bottom and then dive down the pole to retrieve the keys (these spiked poles were 10-12 feet long and usually reached the bottom easily).

My dad never dove in high water, making it necessary to enlist help from divers with tanks, usually swimming instructors from the PE Department. Often the keys were found about 15 to 20 feet downstream from where he dropped them. Visibility was sometimes less than a foot in the silt-laden river, but the swift current washed away the mud on the river bottom. That left a gravel surface to grope along while searching for keys and tools.

The summer current was slow enough for my dad to dive for keys without using a pike pole for guidance. One day he decided to try a face mask, thinking that it would improve his visibility. The current pulled him under the float. When he tried to reach the surface, he was confronted with a maze of submerged logs. He remembered that the logs paralleled the bank, so he knew which way to head as panic began to set in. But the combination of poor eyesight and an unfamiliar mask caused him to misjudge the location of the surface. After a big gulp of water, rather than air, he gave up diving upstream from a float and never again tried a mask.

A serious incident occurred when the occupants of a coaching launch were sucked under the north (downstream) boathouse barge. The deck of the barge, which was about 8 feet above the float, was reached by a ramp, leaving a gap of 10 to 15 feet between the end of the float and the barge. Often coaching launches were tied under the ramp to be out of rain and traffic; reaching this moorage was not difficult, as long as the launch had power.

During a regatta in 1974, a women's coach, Karen Bluel, was driving a 14-foot, open aluminum coaching launch. She, along with cox Mary Werner, two race officials, and a photographer, approached the float as usual, just upstream from the barge. As she nudged the boat into the gap above the barge, the boat's motor died. The launch quickly jammed sideways into the angle between the river and the slanted bow of the barge. The boat and passengers were trapped by the cold, rapid current of early spring.

One of the passengers stood to fend off the steel barge. The boat listed upstream, a violation of the cardinal rule of small boats—always lean downstream. The current caught the edge of the boat. Over it went, and all five, plus the boat, disappeared instantly under the 100-foot barge. Two quickly popped out and were rescued at a lower float. Eventually the other three surfaced, and all were safe. But the boat didn't come up for three weeks. When it did, rowers on the dock saw it, and a salvage crew quickly recovered the boat.

Prow of barge where several persons were sucked under water. The upper part of the ramp is where Astrid Hancock accidentally stepped off into the river.[G-25]

Nobody timed how long the capsize victims were in the water, but my dad knew it was at least 45 seconds, since that's how long logs took to bump their way from one end to the other when under the barge. That's a long time to hold your breath when you suddenly plunge into ice water.

The barge and river also gave a scare to Astrid Hancock, the women's crew coach and canoeing instructor.[K-23]

"I was standing on the ramp going from the dock to the lower barge giving a safety talk and telling the students about the motorboat incident—lost my balance and fell in. Yes, I was petrified, as the water sucks in under the barge there. The students thought I had fallen in on purpose, that I was giving them a lesson in getting someone out—not so!"

Astrid was a strong swimmer, but she must have fought the current furiously to get back to the float, as safety devices, such as ring buoys attached to ropes, were not kept handy.

Fortunately, Astrid's canoeing students generally had few problems with the river, although in at least one instance they capsized a canoe that went under the dock. The students saved themselves, but the canoe sank and disappeared. About three weeks later a farmer found it far downstream and returned it intact.

My dad tried to educate the rowers about the danger of the river by forming a club he called the Helldivers. He hoped his students would learn from example and history. To become a member of the club, one of two criteria had to be met: 1) be thrown completely out of a shell as a result of a crab (failure to get the oar out of the water; beginning scullers were ineligible); or 2) in some accidental or stupid manner become completely submerged.[K-18,K-24] From 1953 to 1971 eight crew members were inducted due to crabs. At least four times entire boats tipped over at the dock, leading to multiple, simultaneous inductions into the club (incidents with pair-oared shells were excluded because these boats capsized so often). Capsizing was usually due to failure to properly lock oars into the oarlocks, since during the push-off, unlocked oars will pop out and leave no support for the shell. That even occurred with fully loaded eight-oared shells.[K-18,K-24]

In one example, my sister Karen and another woman rower, heavily dressed in sweat clothes, were too short to easily reach the oarlocks on the river side of a pair-oared shell. They lost their balance as they were trying to lock in the oars, and the shell capsized. The wet sweat clothes prevented them from easily climbing back onto the float. As they clung to the float with one hand and the boat with the other, they wondered why men on the dock didn't help them out. "You're the coach's daughter. We thought you knew what you were doing."

Preparing to launch a racing shell, 1972. Left: Rower tightening the keeper bar to hold her oar in the oarlock. Too much lean before the oar is locked could cause the shell to capsize (right foot is almost off the float). With her left foot she is stepping on wood framing, not the bottom of the boat. The white tape (arrow) on her shorts was used to keep her from jumping off the seat during the stroke.[O-33] *Right: Women's crew pushing off the dock against the current.*[O-32]

In other instances, four different oarsmen walked off a dock or ramp, and several rowers stepped on a rotten part of the float and plunged waist-deep into the river. Another rower tried to avoid getting his feet wet while working on a submerged portion of the launch-house. He noticed a rope suspended from a rafter and thought he could swing himself across the wet spot. The hemp rope was rotten. It broke, and he went swimming. In 1961, coxswain Fred Smith liked to sit on the raised, back edge of his seat to get a better view; he got tossed out by a strong racing start. Of course, the five persons who went under the barge, mentioned above, were inducted.[K-18] My dad went in so often I think he stopped counting; he was not listed as a club member.

University administrators eventually became concerned with liability issues, thinking that the number of coaching launches was insufficient to assure student safety. But they didn't consider the danger at the dock, as they probably never knew about the incidents recorded in the archive.

Newspaper reporting did occasionally alert University officials to a river danger. According to one report, a canoe carrying two local men and a two-year-old toddler collided with a partially submerged tree in the middle of the river about a mile upstream from Corvallis (see map in Front Matter).[K-19]

Astrid remembered that tree. She often took her canoe classes past it; indeed, she had been there only a week or so before the trio was stranded. She later mentioned that several miles upstream from the tree the river split off a side channel to the west, to the left of canoes traveling downstream. This side channel, called the middle channel on some maps, rejoined the river immediately above the tree. Water pouring from the middle channel into the main channel created swirling whirlpools and drove debris into the tree. The result was a huge pile of branches, some of which were more than four feet above the water. The pile resembled a giant beaver construct. The re-entry of the middle channel would drive a canoe into the tree if the paddlers were not exceptionally alert and able to handle the swirling cross-currents.[O-90]

Astrid had warned her canoe class that the tree must be avoided at all costs. If they went to the left, the current would tend to force the canoes into the tree; if they went right, shallows could be tricky. Either way, they would need to paddle hard to get by, using all the skills they had learned in class. Astrid didn't remember which way her students went, but they got a thrill; even Astrid was on high alert when she passed the tree.

As the two paddlers and toddler came around a sharp bend in the main channel, they were surprised by the tree. Ripples in the river revealed fast water. A quick decision was needed: go left or right? As they picked up speed, all focus was on the tree in mid-stream. Did they not see the middle channel pouring water in at an angle from the left? Suddenly they were in a swirling mess, out of control. The tree was unavoidable.

There was little to do but hang on as the aluminum canoe crashed into the tree and tipped sharply upstream. Water would have poured in with such force that the men could do nothing but get the child onto the tree and yell at him to hold tight. The gear and broken canoe went downriver as the men climbed onto the tree and sat, wet and shivering. The current around the tree was too fast, and the river was too deep for the stranded trio to risk wading or swimming the 200 feet to shore.

On the bank to the west was the local water treatment plant. Occasionally a treatment employee walked into view, and the men on the tree shouted and waved. Eventually they attracted attention, but water-treatment personnel had no boat for a rescue. Moreover, the Sheriff's boat was out of the water. The solution was to call Coach Drlica.

My dad later wrote,[O-83] "One afternoon in 1973 I received a phone call at the crew house; … two men and a child were stranded in a tree in the middle of the Willamette River. … Would it be possible for me to see if I could rescue them? The reason: no emergency boats were kept ready to go on the Willamette River near Corvallis. … The only operational boats on the Willamette were those used for coaching crew teams.

"Normally the crew never went above Marys River, as the water was too shallow and turbulent for good practice; hence, I was unfamiliar with operating a motorboat above that point. But I had run the river from Peoria (an upstream town) with my canoeing classes a number of times so was aware of the river's treacheries.

"Running jet boats in shallow water with no propeller was okay, but to take a propeller-driven boat was hazardous, as the water was fast as well as shallow. It was quite easy to lose a propeller and thus lose complete control of the boat and the whole rescue operation."

After hanging up the phone, my dad would have quickly walked out of his office on the north barge and down the ramp to the float where his 14-foot aluminum coaching boat was docked. The boat would have been gassed up for rowing practice later in the day, but he would have double-checked for fuel, life jackets, paddles, and extra shear pins in case he ran into rocks on the river bottom (a shear pin is a weak bolt that connects the propeller to the drive shaft; if the propeller strikes a rock, the pin will break and prevent damage to the motor). He probably threw a blanket into the boat. He was all business.

Astrid was on the dock, and she briefed my dad on conditions around the tree. The water was fast and too deep to touch bottom. He'd have no problem nosing into the tree, but it could be shallow off to the east (left, if headed upstream), so be careful. She knew he didn't see well and might need help. But he was determined to go alone—he'd need room in the boat to hold anyone he could rescue. She'd wait on the dock until he got back in case he ran into trouble. Then Astrid alerted him to the hard part—getting across the shallows just above the Marys River. That's where he might shear a pin. The people on the tree would be wet and very cold. He'd better hurry.[O-90]

My dad cranked up the outboard and headed upriver, under the bridges, past the mouth of Marys River, around a sharp turn to the left, across the shallows, and then a sharp turn to the right. The tree was obvious, stuck in the middle of a spring-time river.

"It was precarious going, picking my way through shallow spots without shearing a pin. I knew I had to be even more careful than usual, as I had to get to the people. I couldn't take a chance on a breakdown. That would really leave them stranded."

His steering wheel was on the port (left) side of the boat and a spinning brodie knob was attached to the wheel to allow the driver to quickly rotate the wheel with one hand. The throttle was a lever on the far left, next to another lever for shifting between forward, neutral, and reverse. My dad would have inched his boat up to the tree from downstream, moving his left hand from throttle to shift lever as he creeped up to the tree. The cross currents and eddies from the tree pushed his little boat back and forth, but he put the right side next to the tree for the men to grab.

"... I was able to maneuver in close to the old tree in the middle of the river. I found two men and a small child about two years old perched in the tree. ... Fortunately, the child was wearing a life jacket, but the two men were not.

"I was able to get close enough for one of the men to get into the coaching boat. He then helped the other man and child into the boat. As I recall, I then took them to the treatment plant where an ambulance crew and other emergency people were waiting.

"These folks had been in the tree for about two hours before someone at the treatment plant saw them. ... The water was cold. There was danger of hypothermia. To the best of my knowledge, all survived, but the canoe and gear were lost."

University President MacVicar read the newspaper report and sent my dad a commendation letter.[K-22] He probably didn't know that University canoe classes routinely passed that tree.

Trees in the river were always a problem, and sometimes those on the bank caused worry. The river was bordered by cottonwood trees, some of which were 80 to 100 feet tall. They were called widow-makers by loggers—the wood was weak, and occasionally large pieces fell. My dad was not a logger and failed to appreciate the danger until a chunk fell, narrowly missing him as he walked down a ramp to the float. After repairing the ramp, he chopped down most of the trees near the docks. He also cautioned crews to stay away from the riverbanks during windstorms. But the bank was where the slow water was, so we didn't pay attention when rowing upstream.

It was difficult for students to row, build the program, fight the river, and also do well in college classes. Thus, the river took a toll on the racing record, as a high drop-out rate caused the crews to lack the depth and experience needed to beat Cal and Washington. In the late 1950's my dad saw a way to quickly increase rowing expertise and perhaps increase rower retention.

Fred Newell, Stevens' assistant at Harvard and member of the Portland Rowing Club, offered my dad a fleet of single and double sculls plus two old four-oared shells. These "small" boats were much less stable than the large, eight-oared shells, and many of us enjoyed the challenge they posed. Learning to row singles and doubles would raise the skill level faster than many miles in eights. My dad knew that allowing rowers to spread along the river was potentially dangerous, but he couldn't resist Fred's offer.

——— *Chapter 16* ———

SMALL BOATS

In 1959, Fred Newell, then 73 years old, was still sculling a single in Portland. However, few others in his Portland club were rowing, and most of their shells hadn't touched water in many years.[J-22] Newell offered Oregon State nine small boats. [A-54] Never to turn down anything free, my dad eagerly accepted the shells, even though he knew that major repairs were needed. He'd read that single scullers are self-starters: they don't need seven other rowers in the boat to push hard. That might help make selection of fast crews easier. Simply place the good scullers together in an eight-oared shell (this vision led to three consecutive West Coast lightweight championships in the late 1960s and early 1970s).

The old wooden shells from Newell were in various states of disrepair. All were so dried out and cracked that they quickly filled with water. Moreover, the old parts were brittle. To make the boats river-ready, Carl Bower, Steve Mitchell, Bob Janz, and I spent summer evenings replacing broken parts. The thick, cracked varnish on the hulls was unsightly, but it yielded to several rounds of paint remover. We scraped off large clots of partially liquified varnish with a putty knife and then used sandpaper to reveal the unique beauty of wood planking. Many cracks also became obvious.

In the past, Ed Stevens had covered his old boats with muslin and added varnish to keep out water.[J-23] We went for more modern water-proofing by covering our hulls with fiberglass.[A-56]

We began with a roll of loosely woven glass cloth. Cutting the cloth into strips with scissors was straightforward, but fine strands of glass got into our clothes and our made our skin mildly itchy. Nevertheless, we soon had enough strips to cover the hull of an old shell. We set the glass cloth aside, mixed a small amount of catalyst with fiberglass resin, and opened all windows and doors to allow the chemical smell to escape. Then we quickly painted the clear liquid onto the hull, slipped on rubber gloves, and covered the hull with strips of glass cloth that we patted into the resin. When we painted on more resin, the glass cloth became invisible. Usually two of us worked together, because we had only 15 minutes to complete the job before polymerization thickened the activated resin.

In about an hour the resin formed a firm coating; after a day it was hard as glass. To get a smooth surface, we sanded the boats and then applied another coat of activated resin. Our product was as clear as glass; we were pleased with how the wood grain showed through. The invisible glass fibers made our coating rigid.

Refurbishing an old boat was addictive. I liken it to repairing a large model airplane. In both cases, the vehicles are built for lightness; the parts are very thin, with strength coming from how they fit together. The thin parts were an issue with the old racing shells, since much of the internal bracing was weak or broken. Even when parts were intact, the old glue joints no longer held. New glue didn't work, because the wood was so hardened with age that we couldn't get our glue to soak in. We had to replace most of the internal framework: we removed the pieces one by one, copied them, and carefully installed the new parts.

The outriggers were intact, and even though the 1920s-era metal tubing was more flexible than desired, we decided to use the original outriggers. Replacing them didn't seem worth the effort. But we did replace all the heavy, clunky seats. In contrast, the brass oarlocks were perfect; these works of art polished nicely once we got the grease off.

Bye Bye Daddy was the name Carl Bower gave the double he worked on, because he'd return to the boathouse every evening after putting his two young children to bed. My dad helped some, but he started the work and then stepped aside. In the process we all learned lessons. For example, Steve Mitchell discovered exothermic chemical reactions when he used fiberglass to replace a broken stern section of a single shell. He asked my dad how to make a mold for the replacement part. My dad gave Steve a piece of waxed stencil paper (used for making multiple copies of documents) and told him to wrap the paper tightly around the end of a boat that was intact. Then place fiberglass and resin on top of the waxed paper. When the resin hardened, the fiberglass could be pulled off the boat, the paper removed, and the resulting mold used to fashion a new fiberglass stern section for the broken boat.

My dad recalled, "When I came back up from the river later, Steve was excited. The catalyst and the resin reacted with the paraffin in the stencil paper and nearly burned up the boat, at least it got hot enough for Steve to think it might."[1-4]

After the internal structure was rebuilt, we tested the boats on the river. No leaks. But when we rowed the shells, they flexed so much that the fiberglass separated from the wood. Our elegant wooden boats developed large white splotches.

I wanted a perfect boat, so I decided to build a single from scratch. I planned to use thin cedar planking for the hull. My dad had some old cedar boards and a wood planer that quickly thinned the boards to about 1/8th of an inch. I built the internal framing for the cedar planks and carefully bent the cedar using a steam iron and wet towels. Rubber bands made from automobile inner tubes held the wood in place as I glued the planks to the internal framing. I wasn't sure the glue would hold, so I hammered small brass nails every inch along the seams of the twenty-six-foot boat.

The first side was perfect. The cedar planking curved smoothly as it dried. Boat building seemed easy. I repeated the process for the second side, hammering hundreds of nails. I went home that night thinking I had a racing shell. When I returned the next day, I discovered a six-foot-long split in the second side. I thought I might re-steam the wood, force the crack shut, and hold it with glue. My dad discouraged me. "We just learned that old, dry cedar cracks. If it cracked once, it'll crack again. You'll be buying a batch of troubles."

I pulled the nails from the cracked side and then used the blade of a utility knife to pry the split cedar planking off the internal structure. I scraped all remaining glue off the interior framework so I could start over with that side. Since I had no access to fresh cedar, I used what was available: 1/8-inch plywood. The steaming, gluing, and nailing were flawless. I finished the internal structure, made a seat using a router to copy a commercial seat, and varnished the hull. The boat was not pretty: cedar on one half, Douglas fir plywood on the other. The real test would be on the water.

The shell didn't leak, but it listed sharply toward the heavier plywood side. To row the *Dribble*, as Dennis Searcy called it, we had to place weights on the cedar-side outrigger for balance. Then we found that the boat wouldn't go straight until we twisted the metal fin attached near the stern. I had built a heavy practice shell for beginners. But I was ready to try again.

My second attempt was based on John Campbell's design for eight-oared shells. Campbell was the naval architect who had designed racing shells for Ed Stevens, the Oregon State rowing coach in the 1930s and 1940s. Stevens and my dad had built a Campbell-designed eight-oared shell, the *White Whale*. The boat had a smaller wetted surface area and less drag than commercial shells, as noted in an earlier chapter. I thought I could build an exceptionally fast single by scaling down Campbell's eight-oared dimensions. I found Campbell's blueprints and calculated that my one-person shell should be 24 feet long, three feet shorter than commercial singles. I could easily match that hull length by splicing together three eight-foot sheets of 3/32-inch, two-ply cherry plywood. My challenge was to join three pieces of very thin plywood into a single piece. How do you get a strong glue joint with such thin pieces? The 1962 solution was to carefully shave the overlapping edges and then use a heated, experimental glue press at the Forest Products Department of the University. Another rower and I then carried the 4 by 24-foot piece of plywood the two miles to the boathouse.

I probably spent a hundred hours completing the boat. The hull never leaked, but the boat sat too low in the water. I had made it too small for racing in waves, even when they were tiny.

Building and testing a single scull. Left: The author is attaching thin planking to a wooden framework.[C-23] *Right: Test cruise on the river.*[C-32]

My dad needed at least a dozen singles to meet student demand, so he decided to make fiberglass boats. In the 1950s, he had covered the hulls of five racing shells with fiberglass, built fiberglass parts for racing shells, and constructed a fiberglass motorboat.[A-76] Building a one-person racing shell should be straightforward.

My dad used a commercial wooden racing shell to construct a fiberglass mold. He then painted chemical mold release in the mold and added a layer of glass cloth. This he followed with glass matting, another layer of glass cloth, and finally activated resin that permeated the glass layers. In a few hours the resin hardened, and the next day my dad popped the new racing shell hull from the mold. Adding the wooden internal structure was routine, and by 1968 my dad had rowers turning out fiberglass singles.

Fiberglass boats. Left: Motorboat built by Coach Drlica in the late 1950s.[O-186a] *Right: Coach Drlica preparing a mold for a fiberglass shell.*[C-33] *Coveralls were his usual work clothing.*

Rowing the small boats gave us a sense of accomplishment, even though we didn't go very fast. We could feel our own contribution to moving the boats, and simply staying upright was a challenge in a river full of cross currents. Moreover, getting the 1960s-era oars in and out of the water cleanly was difficult. Consequently, we needed many miles of practice. We even rowed in the winter, when the current was swift and the water dangerously cold. Drifting debris added to the challenge, especially since much of it was barely visible for rowers facing backwards. I was particularly concerned with snags, the dead trees stuck in the riverbed: running into one could quickly sink a wooden racing shell.

The premier crew races were at the Olympic Games. The seven categories were for men only: single sculls, double sculls, pair-oared with cox (two persons each with one long, sweep oar), pair-oared without cox, four-oared with cox, four-oared without cox, and eight-oared. We had boats for all events except the pair-oared races. To create a pair-oared shell, my dad cut out the middle section of an old eight-oared shell, retaining the number one rowing position in the bow portion and the number eight position in the stern. After carefully matching the bow and stern portions, he spliced the ends together with internal bracing. A fiberglass covering sealed the joint. He sacrificed two old eight-oared boats to add two working, pair-oared shells to his collection.

Snag at low water on a sunny day.[O-153] *When the water level rose, the tips of snags could be below the surface and invisible.*

Pair-oared shells seemed precarious to me, since they were rowed with only two oars and I would have to trust the other rower not to catch a crab (failing to get an oar out of the water cleanly). A crab could cause the boat to tip over, because the crab itself would tend to pull the boat down on that side. Nevertheless, these boats were wide enough for oarsmen to think they could balance the shell without the oars.

Overconfidence led rowers of a pair-oared shell to attempt an exchange of oars while in midstream. I suspect they'd been in a hurry to leave the dock and had locked their oars into the wrong sides of the boat (the blades were symmetrical, unlike the modern hatchet-shaped blades). They flipped over a mile or so downriver. They swam the boat to the riverbank, pulled it into the brush, and ran for the boathouse. One oarsman lost his way while running through the fields in the dark, but after an hour he came to Highway 34 and followed it to the boathouse. The other oarsman ended up in a blackberry patch and had to fight his way out. Neither had shoes, since shoes were always left at the dock before stepping into a racing shell.

I had a similar experience while double sculling. One rainy night Terry Parker and I were struggling to get our double scull back to the boathouse. I was teaching him how to scull, and we had pushed off the float into a swift, February river. We had paused at the float for a few minutes, wondering whether the river was too fast for us, but I'd had no trouble the day before. Moreover, we didn't see much drifting debris to worry about. Off we went.

Our push had been upstream, and with a few port-side strokes we were soon midstream, scooting across tricky eddies before turning downstream. The current grabbed us, and within a few minutes the dock was out of sight. We sculled smoothly, together and with good power. Perhaps too smoothly, as we turned around farther downstream than we should have.

The sun set as we began working our way upstream, now several miles below the boathouse. It soon became apparent that I had misjudged the current. Each stroke seemed to move us only a few feet relative to the trees on the bank. We had gone only a half a land-mile before a light drizzle soaked us.

I was sculling in the bow; it was my job to watch for debris. I felt that we needed every advantage I could squeeze out of the river, so we were hugging the bank on our right, keeping about 25 feet out to avoid the many snags stuck along the bank. I must have been looking over my right shoulder for a snag when the weight shift gave us a pair of port-side crabs. Over we went. The cold water instantly sucked the air from our lungs. We soon came to the surface and grabbed the boat, choking on river water. As was customary, rowers never wore life jackets; the boat was our flotation device.

My first thought was to save the seats—they were the only items not fixed to the boat, as the oars were locked in the oarlocks and the stretcher boots were bolted in place. The seats were still on their tracks: we wouldn't have to search for parts.

As the current whipped us past the shoreline bushes, it was clear that we had to get out of the water before we crashed into a snag and broke the boat. Moreover, every second in the water meant that getting home was becoming more difficult—and the cold water was beginning to stiffen our muscles.

The shell had rolled upright after dumping us, but we couldn't climb back in without damaging the fragile wooden boat. Terry didn't argue when I shouted to swim the boat to the riverbank.

I don't remember how long it took us to side-stroke the shell to the bank, probably only a few minutes. We were lucky and found a spot about ten feet wide that was free of brush. Terry climbed out and carefully lifted the bow out of the water and set it on the bank. He quickly freed the oars while I struggled to gain a foothold in about three feet of swift water. He lifted the bow, and at the same time I lifted the stern, turning the boat over and emptying the water.

Launching the shell from the bank would be difficult with so much brush in the way, and we were beginning to shiver. I suggested that we leave the boat and run back to the boathouse. There must be a farmer's field on the other side of the trees and bushes lining the river. Since we'd gone around a bend, that field would offer a short-cut to the boathouse.

Terry agreed.

I knew that the brushy tree line along the river was usually thirty to fifty feet wide, not far in daylight. But the trees blocked the weak light reflected from rain clouds. We wouldn't be able to find an animal track through the brush and berry vines. Moreover, our shoes were back at the dock. The socks issued by the PE Department were always loose, and I'd lost one in the river. I don't remember whether Terry had his.

We had to go directly to the field. If we accidentally paralleled the river, we might never get out of the brush. We put our backs to the river and stepped gingerly over fallen branches, occasionally running into an unseen tree. Scratches were ignored. Since it was winter, poison oak was also ignored, but our tender feet suffered until the cold numbed them.

It took us ten minutes to emerge from the tree line. The field was mud and corn stubble mixed with little stones. The light rain had little dampening effect on us, as we were already soaked. No light was visible, but we knew the boathouse was somewhere off to the right. Our numb feet ignored the stones and stubble as we ran for a hot shower. The boiler was working that day, and I still wince when recalling the prickling pain as feeling returned to my feet.

I don't remember collecting the shell. Carl Bower must have taken a launch downriver with several oarsmen and found the boat with a spotlight. They would have picked up the boat, loaded it onto the launch, and driven it back to the boathouse.

Terry and I didn't consider whether anyone knew where we were. In those days, kids ran free; college students were even freer. I'm not surprised that the archive contains no record of the incident. In retrospect, I wonder why my dad let us scull, unsupervised, under those conditions. But at age eighteen or nineteen, I saw no danger.

Occasionally mishaps reached the local press. One case involved Jim Carruthers, a strong oarsman whose picture appears often in varsity crews of the late 1950s and early 1960s.[C-31] Jim owned his own single, and in April 1963 he decided to scull from Salem to Portland (50 miles by road, perhaps twice as far by river), or maybe it was from Salem upriver to Corvallis—accounts differ. He made news under the headline "Rower Strikes Bottom".

The article read: "Carruthers started from Wheatland Ferry about 6:15 a.m. rowing steadily for about 2 hours in his single sculling racing shell. He encountered water he estimated at about 10 miles per hour. … Shortly after 8 o'clock he struck a rock in midstream, puncturing his port bow. He managed to beach the shell on a small island, and then he waded up to his neck to the mainland. P.G. Blake, a former oarsman in 1939, whose ranch was nearby, rendered aid with his boat to rescue the racing craft. Ironically, Blake's outboard motor wouldn't work, and Carruthers got more workout by having to row both Blake and his boat to the scene of the accident. Asked if he would be willing to try it again, he said, 'It was a harrowing experience, but I would try it again in a heavier boat.'[C-48]

Jim Carruthers. Left, 1961.[C-25] Right, 2001.[C-4] Jim took physical fitness very seriously, and in later years he was well known for his intense workouts (for example, at age 60 he routinely jogged on an Oregon beach dragging a heavy, 30-foot ship's chain).[C-56]

The Carruthers family was also involved in one of my accidents. By way of background, the usual way rowers push off from a dock is to put one foot in the boat on the bracing aft of the sliding seat, use one hand to grip the oar (or both sculling oars, which are long enough to overlap), and place the other hand on the edge of the boat for stability. Then give a firm push with the foot still resting on the dock.

After the push, the rower is left crouching with weight on one leg; that leg lowers the rower to the seat as the foot from the dock moves into a stretcher boot. When the dock is on a lake, even a mediocre push is good enough for the oars to clear the dock; on the river a serious push is required.

Since the river current was always changing, there were times when the current tended to push a shell back into the dock. Then the foot push needed to be very strong or bystanders had to help by pushing the oar blades.

Being in the crouching, one-legged position was precarious in a single or double shell, so we would often sit in the boat and use one arm to push strongly upstream and out into the current. That usually worked, and at worst we would drift back to the float and try again.

While examining my dad's notes, I discovered that drifting back to the float was not the worst-case scenario. Jim Carruthers' father had donated a double scull to the rowing program, and in 1962 my dad had written him an apology:[K-26] "... I have been trying to get a chance to write to you since we had an accident with the double you sent down. ... My two best scullers, one of which was my own son, had your scull out early one morning and were unable to get away from the dock properly against the current. The center of the shell got caught on the [upstream] corner of the dock, and before they could get it back alongside, one of the sculls (oars) got caught in the water and turned it (the boat) under the dock. The shell was broken in half and the gunnel with the outriggers was torn loose. I'm afraid the boat is not repairable, although we have been able to salvage everything but one seat and one track. We will be able to rebuild it or make a single out of it. ... I am sorry that we had trouble with the shell."

Eben Carruthers, who was a strong supporter of rowing, responded[K-26] "... Please do not have any concern over the loss of the double. ... I was often wondering why such accidents did not happen more often in the swift current you have to contend with."

I have no recollection of the incident. To ruin a racing shell is a major sin worthy of memory suppression.

Although my dad was aware of the cold-water dangers, he seemed to have confidence in his rowers' ability to get out of the water safely. For him, the worrisome problems came from non-rowers. Kids on the bank threw rocks at the coaching launch,[K-28] and motorboats ran through racing shells.[K-33] In Corvallis, water skiers were always a problem.[K-34] For example, in the early 1960s, a skier went on one side of the single Steve Mitchell was sculling, and the tow boat went on the other. The tow rope caught Mitchell in the chest and lifted him out of the shell.[J-22]

I was on the river every day during the water ski season, so it was inevitable that I would have an encounter with a ski boat. Mine came in August, 1962.[K-20] The day was warm, and a half-dozen ski boats were in view. I was sculling downstream about half a mile below the boathouse, keeping close to the bank on the Corvallis side to avoid skiers. No traffic pattern had been agreed upon: racing shells kept left to avoid congestion at the float where landing had to be upstream; skiers tended to keep right, conforming with highway traffic rules. The river was wide enough for everyone, but I was always alert when skiers were on the water.

I noticed that the sound of a ski boat failed to decrease as it passed me heading downstream on the other side of the river. I glanced over my left shoulder and saw it making a U-turn toward me. It skidded around the turn, slipping into a collision course. The gray hull filled my field of vision; all I could do was hold both oars tightly, blades flat on the water. The side of the boat hit my starboard oar, snapping off the blade as spray drenched me. I leaned onto my intact blade and managed to remain upright as the wake hit me, but I was helpless.

The motorboat, which had no identification number, took off. Another boat soon came to my rescue. I couldn't simply climb out of the single, so I tipped myself into the river. One of the rescue crew grabbed an outrigger while I scrambled over the side of the motorboat. Together we were able to remove the oars from the oarlocks, lift the shell out of the water, and hold it upside down across the stern portion of the motorboat.

The boat that hit me was driven by a 13-year-old boy; the lookout was his sister, age 10, and the water skier was their father. The boy finally came back, alone, before I reached the crew dock. The shell and I transferred to his boat, and we worked our way back to the dock. I'm sure I blistered his ears with advice about towing a water skier.

My dad did not seem concerned by the danger, and I was back on the water the next day. However, I did call the state police, who investigated. Water accidents were uncommon, and local prosecutors had little experience identifying the appropriate charge. The case was dismissed.[J-22]

Jeff Young and Skip Spiering 1968.[O-1] *While in a pair-oared shell, they were struck by a drunken power boat driver. Neither was injured.*[J-22]

Our racecourse ran upstream along the eastern edge of Corvallis where the river is straight for a little more than a mile. The two bridges marked the half-way point. The start and finish were marked by pairs of fixed, painted posts on the bank. During high water, the finish line was moved downstream to account for faster current.

My dad faced challenges marking lanes for racing. The river current prevented him from keeping lane-marker floats in place, so in early years he stretched cables across the river to hang lane markers. These cables posed a problem for low-flying airplanes (occasionally "wannabe" stunt pilots would fly under the old bridge). Luckily, no incident occurred with aircraft before the cable system was replaced by range markers (painted 4 x 8 plywood sheets) mounted on the bridges. These markers were aligned with other plywood sheets placed on the riverbank far upstream at a bend in the river. For sculling, we aligned markers on the bank behind us where the river made another bend.

Corvallis racecourse. The two bridges mark 1000 meters.[C-2a] Generally only two lanes were used for 2000-meter races. For relative location see map in Front Matter.

Opposing coaches doubted the fairness of my dad's racing lanes. He demonstrated lane equality by running his motorboat up the course at a constant throttle setting and measuring the time in each lane. The lanes were identical if the crews stayed in them. But the lanes were not equal at every spot. To avoid being demoralized when a competitor hit slack water and pulled ahead, we needed to know where each lane would encounter slower current. When our boat was in slack water, we would pour on the power for 15 to 20 strokes, hoping to demoralize the opposition.

Interior of repair shop portion of Oregon Electric Depot boathouse. Coaches Drlica and Dick Erickson (University of Washington) discussing the racecourse.[K-16]

I recall a single-sculls race in the 1960s in which my opponent, Bob Janz, knew the course as well as I did.[O-39] We gently paddled to the starting line, staying in the center of the river where the current was the same for both lanes. Janz was on my left; the referee was in his launch farther to our left.

Bob Janz, circa 1965.[C-28]

The referee's boat idled on the starting line, which was defined by alignment of two painted poles on the bank. When we drifted across the line, the referee quickly called out "Are you ready? Ready all!" and then fired his starting gun. We were off, and the referee dropped back to follow us. His driver moved the launch back and forth between the lanes as the referee yelled at us through his megaphone to keep us on course.

In a single, getting a good first stroke from a dead stop is difficult: pressure on each oar must be exactly the same. My first stroke was poor, even though I was taking only a half stroke to get started. My port oar barely grabbed water. Janz quickly got a boat-length lead. To maintain concentration, I started counting strokes. Over and over, I reminded myself to focus on the legs, make them feel the pressure while adjusting for current differences on the two oars. And get the hands out of my lap quickly to keep the stroke rate up. By a count of 50 I had caught up, but my arms were aching, as were my lungs. Blow out, then let the lungs fill.

As we approached the first bridge, I passed into the tail end of a bridge-pier eddy, quickly picking up a boat length over Janz. But within a few strokes I had to get back into the main stream to squeeze between the bridge piers. As I crossed the eddy line, my boat skidded, and I briefly lost balance. My starboard oar caught more current than the port, giving me a small crab. That was all it took for Janz to pull even as we hit the fast water between the bridge piers. I raised my stroke rate and pulled as hard as I could, hoping he would fade. I got a half a length on him, but he didn't quit. Instead, the extra exertion wore me down. My mind drifted, and I stopped counting strokes. I must have slacked off for a few strokes, enough to get some composure. I glanced to my right and saw the 1500-meter pole on the bank. Only 60 or 70 strokes left, ignore the pain for a couple of minutes. Count out those last strokes.

Janz made what a newspaper account called "a tremendous sprint."[O-39] I don't remember the finish, but somehow I crossed the line first. It's hard to know whether I had a current advantage at the end, since even on straight stretches the river bounces back and forth off the banks. Overall, the race was fair—we had

stayed in our lanes. I felt a bit of pride, largely because Bob Janz
was a skilled opponent and because I kept going even when I
was exhausted.

*Racing on the river. Left: The challenge of the two bridges.
Rowers are facing away from the bridges as they approach the
piers.[K-1] The racecourse ran through the center span of the first
bridge and the right-hand span of the second (see arrow). Right.
Two singles, marked by arrows, approaching the first bridge,
followed by referee's launch. Single on the right has a small
lead.[C-2] This photo shows the 1966 race described in the text.*

Lanes in crew races are rarely fair. Those on the river were
often as fair as ones on still water. Usually, wind and waves are the
problem. I recall a race in late 1965 in Long Beach, California that
was run despite a very strong crosswind. The more exposed sculler,
who was on my left, decided to even up the race by starting early,
at the beginning of a three-count starting command. He knew
he wouldn't be called back. When I saw him leave the line, I also
started early. Reed Adler, a strong sculler from the Long Beach
club, was in the protected lane on my right. He waited for the gun.

I quickly caught the boat that jumped the gun, since the
waves were worse for him. But at about 500 meters Adler passed
me. I may have crowded him a bit, since he was so close to the
bank that I could see his port oar digging dirt as he passed me.
Nobody complained about fairness, because races in the wind

were almost always unfair. Sometimes the winner was determined when race lanes were assigned.

Occasionally conditions were so unfair that we would have protested had we understood what had happened. Dennis Searcy recalled such a situation in a 1963 eight-oared race on the Stanford racecourse in Redwood City.[0-94]

"The last time I talked with your dad, he was still angry about a race we lost to Stanford [because he saw us quit in the middle of the race]. Even after fifty-five years the race is still fresh in my mind. Near the end of the race, at about 1500 meters, I blacked out, couldn't see. I was rowing by feel. I thought that if I pass out completely, I'll catch a crab and get thrown out of the boat. So, I stopped pulling. Apparently so did the rest of our boat, because we stopped, almost dead in the water. That's what your dad saw. After about ten seconds, I could see again and started to pull hard. After another ten seconds the boat picked up speed, [and we finished the race]. The Stanford boat was not following the course, heading about a quarter mile off to starboard ... I had little confidence in our cox, and I assumed that it was our boat that was off course, not Stanford's. But Stanford was off course, and not by accident. Next to the racecourse was a huge limestone kiln associated with a nearby concrete plant. The kiln was spewing out CO_2. Since CO_2 gas is denser than air, it flowed out over the water as a low-lying cloud. The Stanford boat apparently knew about this and avoided it, while we rowed right into the cloud of CO_2. We were poisoned by it. ... This explanation just came to me recently, so I never got to tell your dad."

Usually, we knew when we might encounter a problem, and in one case I was able to do something about it. I guessed that the 1966 Western Sprint Championships would be extremely windy. The racecourse was inside Vallejo's Mare Island Strait where the wind heading inland up the Sacramento River was notorious. That meant waves. Bow and stern sections of racing shells are covered and sealed, but the cockpits are open. To deal with serious waves, singles have an angled board at the stern of the cockpit that allows water in the boat to slosh out with each hard stroke—if you can stay upright.

Dennis Searcy, circa 1963.[F-9]

I could increase the odds for staying upright in my single by reducing how far I would reach for each stroke. As you slide toward the stern and reach to take a stroke, you assume a crouched, finely balanced position: if a wave catches your oar blade and pulls it down, you cannot easily compensate to avoid capsizing. Problems with waves are easier to deal with near the end of the stroke because the oars are in the water, your legs are flat, and your body is in a more stable, upright position. I reasoned that I could get a long stroke without reaching so far by moving my oarlocks six inches toward the bow. That would make removing the oars from the water more difficult, because the handles would overlap in my lap, but I'd be less likely to tip over at the catch.

The outrigger positions were fixed to the boat, but I could attach a narrow, six-inch metal plate to the end of each outrigger pointing toward the bow. Since each oarlock had a pair of threaded bolts sticking out the bottom, I could remove the nuts, pull the oarlocks out of their attachments to the outriggers, and bolt my plates to the outriggers. Holes in the plates near the bow end would allow reattachment of the oarlocks closer to the bow.

When I arrived at the racecourse, the wind was so strong that it blew the stake boats off their moorings.[O-76] These small rowboats, which each held a person who would grip the stern of a racing shell to assure an even start, had been anchored along the starting line. They were removed from the course, because the waves were so high: whitecaps were visible all along the course.

Before it was time to launch, I pulled out my wrench, attached a metal plate to each outrigger, and moved my oarlocks toward the bow. At the time, I was rowing for Lake Merritt Rowing Club. When my dad saw me moving my oarlocks, he realized that I was creating an advantage over his sculler, but I wasn't violating any rules. He didn't say much, but I felt that I was now an outsider.

By the time I reached the starting line, the water in my boat was up to my ankles, probably six inches deep. Turning to line up meant taking waves broadside. I couldn't row a rolling shell, but somehow I got turned, as did the competition. Five or six boats were lined up and sent off into the wind.

Once the race started, I tried to slosh the water out by pulling hard. It seemed hopeless, as the waves kept breaking over my outriggers and into the boat. Water covered the stern deck, and waves over the bow hit me in the back. Every pull was heavy against the headwind, to say nothing of the weight of water I was carrying. I had raised my outriggers half an inch to help my oar blades clear the waves on the recovery, but it was not enough. As I reached for each stroke, the waves banged the oars, forcing me to grip the handles so tightly that my forearms tightened solid. I had no chance to think about form, as keeping upright required full attention.

Soon the knuckles of my right hand bled from the scraping of the starboard, overlapping oar handle. Reaching for strokes was such a struggle that I cut the reach in half. The puddles my blades were leaving in the water showed that I was moving only two meters on each stroke: the race would require a thousand strokes with no rest possible.

After about 500 meters I noticed that one of my competitors had dropped back, and the referee's boat had pulled next to him: he'd tipped over. A few minutes later another boat capsized. The referee was fully occupied and no longer yelling at me to stay in my lane. Nevertheless, the remaining boats went more-or-less straight. Eventually a couple of us made it to the finish. Somehow, I got there first.

Barry Hilt, one of my team-mates at Oregon State, recalled a different solution for waves. Barry wrote, "I'm not sure if it was in Long Beach where we rowed, as that part is a blur, but the experience is still vivid, even after 50 years—when you and I beat the Pan American gold-medal doubles crew in rough water. I chuckle recalling how we taped linoleum [strips] to the gunnel [and flat across the outriggers] to keep the water from filling the cockpit. The other guys were much bigger, and while we kinda skipped over the waves, they plowed through them, taking on a ton of water. One of the guys was pretty insistent that we violated regatta rules with the linoleum splash board, but I think we got their shirts anyway."[O-114, O-166a]

By 1966, my dad was allowing twenty-four boats of various sizes to spread along three miles of river at Corvallis. He had confidence in his students' ability to handle the river, but he felt he was providing boats for participants who were sometimes unreliable and careless with the delicate equipment.

He had arranged for members of the crews to obtain PE credit for rowing the small boats. As with other college classes, the students expected materials to be ready for them when they arrived. When a few rowers grumbled about boats not being ready, the sense of entitlement annoyed my dad. These kids were acting like spoiled brats. They didn't appreciate the volunteer effort that provided them the extraordinary opportunity to scull a one-person racing shell.

Barry Hilt, 1965.[C-27]

My dad didn't exert the authority associated with drill sergeants and football coaches. Consequently, oarsmen were never shy about grumbling to him. Indeed, they grumbled more to him than to each other. He often responded with a sarcastic remark. Nevertheless, when pushed he could be direct, "This is the way it is going to be."

To make his instructions unambiguous, my dad distributed a seven-page, typewritten document.[C-60] At the end of the term we will have the Little Olympics Regatta … you'll have to accumulate points in a four, the pairs, double, single, and the whole ball of wax to be the overall school champion. … It will take a week or two to run it off—run races every day of every kind so I'll probably base your (PE) grade on how you stack up. As a matter of fact, I think this is the most objective way to grade you. … It doesn't enter into my having to think about it. … The only way I could do it subjectively is to go out there and referee it and screw (sabotage) you on the starting line. I'm not going to do that. It's going to be a little hard-nosed proposition."

My dad was frustrated with the wrong oars being used and with boats being left on the dock rather than put away. From his perspective, not all the rowers were hitting their marks. On top of that, they were complaining.

"It is almost an impossibility to see that every boat is taken care of every time. If you go out and the rigger falls off, it is because you did not tighten up the nuts; that's your fault. You've got to maintain the boat, see that everything is tight. If there's something wrong with it, write it down, tell us about it, I'll file it, and you fix it. By the time I get around to finding it in the file, it has probably fallen off [if you didn't fix it]."

Despite the equipment and scheduling glitches, the overall enthusiasm was high. In the early days, scullers sought their own external competition. For example, Botond Eross and I had the naïve idea of training for the Olympic Games. We thought that skill might overcome lack of size and muscle (I doubt that Botond weighed more than 155 lbs, and I certainly didn't). In the summer of 1963 we practiced every day, mostly in double sculls, using an old Portland Rowing Club boat we had rebuilt. Since we didn't have an accurately measured 2000-meter course, our times didn't tell us in whether we were any good. As a reality test, I asked Ted Nash in Seattle for a practice race (Nash won an Olympic gold medal in 1960, a bronze in 1964; he later became a legendary coach at the University of Pennsylvania). Nash agreed. If we could beat him, we could begin to think seriously about sculling.

Botond and I tied our antique sculling oars to the top of his tiny European car, and we drove the five hours to Seattle. After a few hours of sleep sitting in his car, we appeared at the Lake Washington boathouse. Nash put us in a brand-new double that was solid: the outriggers didn't flex with every stroke. Indeed, everything worked smoothly, unlike the old, rickety boat we were rowing in Corvallis. Nash and Bill Flint, his rowing partner that day, interrupted their normal practice session to paddle up the 2000-meter course, staying a length or so ahead without working up a sweat. We rowed as hard as we could, but one look at

Nash's biceps made it clear that we should spend our effort on other rowing activities. His consideration for runts, who would never get close to the Olympics without a ticket, was an attitude typical of the times.

Left: Newspaper photo of Botond Eross holding a coxswain's megaphone, 1961.[O-41] An OSU mathematics scholarship is named after him. Right: Ted Nash, Olympic gold medal winner, 1960.[O-146]

My dad realized that his scullers needed organized racing. To meet this need and a similar need by the new women's crew, he initiated an annual regatta in Corvallis. From 1964 to 1997, the largest racing event on the West Coast was the Corvallis Regatta.[C-11,C-12,C-13,C-55] At the time, many new rowing programs were emerging in Oakland, Portland, and Seattle. The central location of Corvallis was important, because travel funds were scarce (for some crews, fundraising was as important as rowing practice).[J-25]

To make the trip to Corvallis worthwhile, the regatta provided as many races as possible (during some years there were hundreds of participants rowing in more than 50 races).[J-25] Races were available for high schools, colleges, men, women, seniors, lightweights, and heavyweights. The scope was unique in the United States.[J-23] The press even showed up, which I found remarkable.

Crew facilities during Corvallis regatta.[C-65a]
River flows from right to left.

The 1964 regatta was noteworthy because it hosted a heated rivalry between the Lake Merritt (Oakland) and Lake Washington (Seattle) Rowing Clubs. The two clubs were fueled in part by former Cal and Washington oarsmen continuing their intense competition of college days. Moreover, 1964 was an Olympic year, and both clubs were vying for a US entry in the four-oared event. Local interest was spurred by a former Oregon State oarsman, Joe Michalek, rowing for Lake Merritt. The Lake Washington crew, with Ted Nash, won the race and went on to earn a medal in Tokyo.

Overall, the small boats program gave many young men and women manual skills and the opportunity to actively solidify rowing at Oregon State. The program was also critical for the budding women's crew. Always short of money, the women could participate in many races at the Corvallis Regatta without having a large team or traveling. Moreover, my dad had inadvertently built an alumni base that would become an important lobbying force a decade later when University administrators attempted to eliminate crew. And by promoting more races, he increased the need for rower fundraising.

---------- *Chapter 17* ----------

FUNDRAISING

O regon college students had little money for extracurricular activities, and their Depression-era parents were tight with funds. Obtaining loans for equipment was out of the question. Fundraising was essential. My dad actively encouraged it, and crew members accepted the chores.

For the first thirty years, student fundraising focused on travel. A turning point came in the fall of 1956 when the parents of oarsman Mike Zahorski created a memorial fund following Mike's death from an auto accident. His parents wrote to my dad that they had collected about $1,000. Would that be enough for a new racing shell?[C-64] My dad responded that the amount was about half of what was needed, but the Rowing Club would raise the remainder.

The chance to have a brand-new shell mobilized the Club. A committee collected the names of everyone who had rowed at Oregon State, in any capacity, since 1929. Another committee connected addresses with the names by pressuring the alumni office, and still another organized a request for donations. Despite the effort, money came in very slowly. After a year, the Zahorski family began to wonder whether their memorial would do more than collect interest. They suggested that the Rowing Club use the money for "… whatever is the greatest need at this time."

My dad responded, "There are many other things we need, but none … stimulates action more than the hope of a new shell." He also shared how matching the donation fit with his core philosophy, "I sometimes forget that these students ... are still boys. It is part of my job to try to make well-rounded, reliable, self-sufficient men out of some of them. As anxious as we are to get a new shell and as important as it is to us, I also feel that it is equally important that the students accept certain responsibilities in helping to obtain it and to learn from the process."

With more time we earned the money, and in May 1958, George Pocock, the revered Seattle racing-shell builder, delivered the *Zahorski*.

I remember what a treat it was to row that shell: our old boats were often twisted, causing number 2 to be down on port and number 7 to be down on starboard. How do you untwist a 60-foot racing shell? Do rowers in the bow lean to starboard and those in the stern lean to port? We tried adjusting the outriggers to compensate, but nothing seemed to work.

The purchase of the *Zahorski* allowed the *Orange Owl*, one of the original shells from Cal, to be retired after almost 35 years on the Willamette. In 1961, to honor the *Owl's* long service, its bow was cut off and mounted on a boathouse wall.[O-42]

Newspaper photo of Paul Hemrich (left) and J.R. Goerke (right) removing the bow of the Orange Owl.[O-42]

In 2018 the *Zahorski*, which had been retired for many years, was placed on a state surplus list as a rowboat. A farmer bought her, thinking he would use the rowboat for fishing. When the *Zahorski* arrived at his farm, the farmer must have wondered how he would fish from a tippy, 60-foot rowboat. Kirk Hutchinson, a former oarsman and coach in the 1970s, learned of the farmer's predicament and offered to take the boat. Kirk now has her historical records and has been bringing the *Zahorski* back to rowing condition. Eventually local old-timers, still feeling the rowing bug bite, will be able to row a wooden boat on the Willamette.

Newsletters following the *Zahorski* effort document the times. For example, the 1959 newsletter from Paul Hemrich described part of the current inventory, which included three old shells still in use (each had been donated by the University of Washington after many years of service).[C-68] One had been renamed the *Wet Noodle* due to its flexible twists and turns. Another, the *Beaver II*, was a bit tighter, as my dad had put fiberglass on the outside to hold it together. Hemrich wrote, "Many ribs and internal structures have dry rotted and were returning to the dust from which they came." The third boat, the *Salmon King*, was jinxed. "It ran into two buoys on Lake Washington, was smashed up in our shops when an airplane wing dropped on it, and it has run into a snag on the Van Buren Street Bridge." Hemrich concluded ruefully, "This boat is excellent for racing around corners, but hardly suitable for a straight course."

Paul Hemrich, Rowing Club President 1961.[C-1]

Why was an airplane wing in the boathouse? My guess is that Paul meant a fuel tank normally attached to a fighter jet wing. My dad obtained these metal pods from military surplus to float ramps leading to the docks. During high water, the ramps needed flotation. Why a fuel tank dropped on a racing shell remains a mystery.

The new racing shell encouraged us to intensify contacts with alumni. In the early 1960s I composed a brochure containing photos of oarsmen working at off-water projects, such as building the Quonset hut and outfitting the barn. The theme was that we were willing to work, but we couldn't support the program by ourselves. I think we obtained enough money for only a few oars. However, our mailing list improved considerably, and the brochure made us feel like we were accomplishing something.

My dad wanted his students to experience working with the local business community. One strategy was for the Rowing Club to distribute free notebook dividers to Oregon State students during class registration. In pre-computer days, tables were set up in a gym with sign-up sheets for each class. Long lines of students created a ready audience for advertising. Since class notes were taken by hand and often organized in three-ring binders, notebook dividers were handy items. Oarsmen sold ads in the dividers to local businesses, designed the ads, and handled the printing and distribution. I helped distribute the dividers as I tried to recruit heavy-weight oarsmen from the long lines of students. But I strictly avoided selling ads.

Another strategy was to paint house numbers on street curbs. This idea probably came from an oarsman seeing a friend making easy money. We prepared number templates, and for each house on a block we painted the number curbside (these numbers allowed visitors to easily identify house addresses). Then a note seeking a donation to the Rowing Club was left on the door of each house. I don't remember ever asking for permission to paint a number.

Soliciting by mail, circa 1963. From left, Fred Sterk, Gary Ray, Bill Ruzicka, and Ed Stryker.[C-24] Each wore PE clothing at the boathouse, since varsity oarsmen took Advanced Crew as a PE class. In this photo they are functioning as members of the Rowing Club.

Notebook divider given to students at registration.[C-15]

Distributing notebook dividers and painting house numbers generated good will with the community, because the older generation appreciated students who were willing to work. Painting house numbers is now a cottage industry that some police departments consider a scam.

Painting house numbers on curbs followed by requests for donations. Don Pearson (left) and Gary Ray (right), circa 1962.[C-6]

Not all projects were successful. One failed effort was a personal-service auction sponsored in 1961 by the Benton Lions Club.[O-41] Thirty varsity oarsmen and my dad were listed as having various skills. Among these were dish washer, black-jack dealer, translator of Russian, buggy whip maker, and expert on getting another to work efficiently. Pictures of the oarsmen appeared in a local newspaper for an auction scheduled to occur in front of a downtown movie theater. The outcome was not recorded, but my recollection is that the citizens of Corvallis needed no help with such tasks.

My dad also made it known among his colleagues that the crew was always looking for ways to earn money. An opportunity arose in the early 1960s when the University football team attracted more fans than the stadium seats could hold. The Athletic Department needed help moving a 5,000-seat set of bleachers from the track facility to the football stadium. For several weekends we trekked to the campus with wrenches to disassemble, move, and reassemble the bleachers. We saw this as a great opportunity, since ways to make hundreds of dollars were scarce. The cost to us was reduced time for studying and socializing on campus.

Other campus groups saw the success of the Rowing Club and began pestering local merchants and alumni for support.

The merchants were overwhelmed, and the alumni wanted to know why the school wasn't supporting these sports.[J-4] My dad used the community pressure to convince the University to set up a recreational sports program funded by a token amount of travel money. Then students would work more on sports and less on Corvallis merchants. He drafted a charter, and in 1963 his boss, Clair Langton, sold it to University administrators, thereby creating funds for Recreational Sports.[J-23]

The Rowing Club was a charter member of Recreational Sports, but the level of support was small (in 1964 it was $1,800 toward a $6,000 travel budget); thus, fundraising remained important. But my dad had finally accessed University funds for the competitive team. After thirteen years he had gotten his foot in the door—he was beginning to institutionalize intercollegiate rowing at Oregon State.

My dad didn't want his access to University funds diluted by "fly-by-night" sports teams, so he added a rule that a club team had to exist for at least three years to be considered for financial support. This rule soon created a big problem for crew. When the Athletic Department took in rowing, only the heavyweight crew was covered. Heavyweight rowers thought that all expenses would be paid by the Athletic Department, and they abandoned the rowing club concept: they refused to elect officers for several years.[J-21] That official end to the Oregon State Rowing Club must have shaken my dad, as the Club was the vehicle for delivering his core message about democracy and self-sufficiency. It also meant no money from the Recreational Sports Program.

The lightweight crew was excluded from both the Athletic Department and the Recreational Sports Program. The lightweights formed a new rowing club, but according to the rules, the lightweights had to wait three years to become eligible for funding. Oarsman Bruce Chapin kept the program together, and in the process the team won several West Coast championships.[J-22]

Bruce Chapin M-16

In the mid-1970s, jog-a-thons became popular. Runners obtained sponsors who would contribute defined amounts multiplied by the number of laps the runner would complete around a regulation 440-yard track. By the mid-1970s, the Rowing Club had been reconstituted, and in the 1976-77 season members ran in a jog-a-thon to purchase a new eight-oared shell. In 1977 or 1978 the Club raised enough to supplement the salary of a women's coach and to send both a women's four and a men's four to national championship regattas (the men's four won).

My dad, then 60 years old and considered elderly, was talked into running in the jog-a-thon. In a letter to potential sponsors, he wrote, "… People who pledged two years ago got smarter this last time, and the amount pledged on the 'old man' dropped from $30 per lap to $13.40, or $268.80 for the 20 laps he made … he may still be able to make 15 to 20 laps. … He has been seen out in the early morning hours running (walking?) the dog."

In a thank-you letter (February 1979), he related that the crew grossed $6,000. "Personally, I was challenged to get into a little better shape and ran the dog a little more than usual. At 16 laps around the track, I was still going strong, thinking that I would surprise those who pledged on me. I really felt rather sorry … that I was going to run more this time than last, especially for those who pledged large amounts. At 17 laps my left knee started complaining. … My brain told my knee to keep going, but my knee told my brain to slow down. After walking a bit, I finished at 22 laps. I didn't hurt for so many days after this time, thanks to the 'intensive pre-season training.'"

The women's crews participated with the men's crews, but they also had their own fund raisers. In 1975 they held a row-a-thon with a University of Oregon team, racing upstream from Corvallis to Eugene (about 50 miles by river).[D-136] In that same year they earned money by distributing telephone books and working as security for a PAC-8 wrestling tournament in Gill Coliseum.

My dad was proud of the extra effort by his women's crew but had little patience with other sports teams seeking a handout. For example, in December, 1977, Judy Loosley, Chairperson of the Women's Intercollegiate Athletic Board, asked the Men's Athletic Department to transfer $250 from women's rowing to the women's field hockey team, a non-sponsored group (by then the waterfront sports were covered in part by the Men's Athletic Department). The response from Jerry Ward, the Athletic Department Business Manager, was no, because budgets for men's and women's rowing had been merged into a waterfront program. The transfer from one women's program to another couldn't be done. Moreover, he emphatically pointed out that participants in crew conduct fundraising activities to supplement University funds.[D-161] My dad had provided Ward with a snarky draft response to Loosley: "The easiest way to get money is to dip into someone else's pocket, but if this is not feasible and the situation is really serious, then perhaps some imagination and initiative would generate some money-raising ideas."

My dad also tended to be sarcastic with his own crews, especially when they grumbled about fundraising. An example is seen in a letter-to-the-editor written by oarsman Kent Atwood.[C-14,C-35] In the late 1970s, the crew earned money for new boats and oars by cleaning the basketball arena after games.

"Naturally, people with any decency go to remote corners of Gill Coliseum to puke, thus being as considerate as possible to their friends and fellow attendants. Of course, this means climbing wearying stairs to reach the stuff with a putrid, dripping mop [still] full of brightly colored vomit [from a mess just cleaned]. The crew team cleans the Coliseum after basketball games and concerts. We do this for a fee paid by the University, which helps to complete our budget. Our coach tells us it 'builds character'.

"I can think of many things I would rather do in the late nights and early morning than develop my character. But we suffer it for the love of our sport.

"Yet as the clock in Gill [Coliseum] approaches 3 a.m., I usually begin to question my faith while stumbling up yet another set of stairs, dripping mop in hand. At that point in time, I fail to see in my mind the justice of the situation. It escapes me entirely. But another of our coach's inspiring quotes comes to mind, 'Rowing is so special that you people have the privilege of paying to participate.'"[C-14]

Atwood went on to invite football players to join this character-building exercise.

As pressures on my dad increased during the 1970s and students in general became more outspoken, his responses to complaints often lacked empathy. He expected more commitment. Moreover, he believed that fundraising taught self-sufficiency in ways not covered in classrooms. It was important.

In contrast, car travel to races had little educational value. Moreover, car travel using twenty-year-old drivers was inherently dangerous before freeways, seat belts, and rumble strips. In addition, communication among the vehicles was impossible, as only comic-strip hero Dick Tracy had a mobile phone. Nevertheless, travel was an important part of the crew experience for both men and women rowers of the mid-20th century.

Chapter 18 ---

ROAD TRIPS

U ntil the end of the 1960s, travel for crew races was by auto, generally in cars supplied by parents of rowers. By paying only for fuel, which sometimes got as low as 21 cents per gallon, the Rowing Club could support travel for about 30 people (varsity, junior varsity, and freshman crews). Oars were carried on car tops, boats were always borrowed, and hotels were rarely used. The team made annual trips north to Vancouver, B.C. (400 miles) and south to San Diego (1,000 miles). Shorter trips were made to Seattle, San Francisco, and Los Angeles. As a point of reference, the University-funded sports teams tended to focus on "Northern Division" competitors in Oregon, Washington, and Idaho. Rowing and football were outliers.

Although my dad took river hazards in stride, he saw road trips as seriously dangerous, partly due to traffic statistics. For example, 1963 traffic deaths per capita were twice those in 2017. The death toll was so bad that radios routinely reported the numbers for holiday weekends. But to win races, we needed to race. That meant travel using drivers my dad knew had a propensity to race. I relate a few thoughts and recollections about driving cars in the 1960s as a context for his anxiety.

Danger came from several factors. One was rarely having a yellow line painted along the outer edge of a road. That made night driving a challenge, especially in the darkness of Central Oregon. More important was driver immaturity. My friends and I all rushed to the motor vehicle department on our sixteenth birthdays to get licenses: we craved the open road with the large, powerful cars of the day. Vehicles were so wide that the front seats easily fit three adults. Three or four hundred horsepower was not unusual. Even the family station wagon was a muscle car by today's standards.

In addition to being immature drivers, some of us were risk takers. At least one had a summer job as a smoke jumper, parachuting into forest fires. Two others became fighter pilots in Viet Nam. And we were all hypercompetitive. We even told gas station attendants that we were in a road race so we could get our tanks filled quickly and beat the other cars.

Muscle was needed for passing. Roads in Oregon generally had only two lanes, and we always seemed to be following a slow car that was begging to be passed. Our cars had a passing gear—when we stomped on the gas, the cars would leap forward and quickly whip around at least two or three others before an oncoming car or truck forced us back into our lane. Even so, passing was not for the weak of heart, especially in the dark when we couldn't see whether the road ahead had a bend or rise. Of course, we each thought we had great passing skills, and we were eager to demonstrate them.

Passing a loaded log truck. ⁰⁻¹⁶³ᵇ

Occasionally we tried to pass a truck that would accelerate to establish dominance. I was probably the most cautious driver on the team, but even so, I had a truck experience. I was driving the family's eight-cylinder Plymouth down a winding road in the Coast Range west of Corvallis when a loaded log truck got in my way. The top-heavy truck was taking the hairpin turns carefully. Even with my passing gear there wasn't enough room to get around. I hung back a few car-lengths, knowing that a straight stretch lay ahead. As we came out of our last turn, which was to the left, I cut inside and quickly got even with the 60-foot logs. But the remaining down grade allowed the truck to pick up speed rapidly, preventing me from passing. The log truck was trying to force me back. Ahead was a rise that neither of us could see over: the truck was playing chicken. I vividly remember the speedometer dial pointing to 90 mph—I'd never driven that fast. The Plymouth sounded like it still had power, so I went for the pass, not knowing what was on the other side of the rise. I was not going to be chicken. The road turned out to be free of traffic.

In spite of the inherent dangers, crew trips north were generally uneventful unless a car stopped for a tour of the Olympia Brewery. That could make a crew three hours late for practice.[J-12] Travelling south from Corvallis was more challenging. Before Interstate 5 was completed, the route through the Siskiyou Mountains (south of Ashland) was difficult. There the two-lane road was slow as heavy trucks crept up the steep, twisting grade. They rarely pulled into turnouts, and passing seemed very risky, even when the road was clear of snow.

My dad, being aware of his drivers and road conditions, usually had the crews bypass the Siskiyou's by traveling east from Eugene, over the Cascades into Central Oregon. The route south to Klamath Falls was on two-lane roads that required passing, but the roads tended to be flat and straight. They were also lightly traveled in the middle of the night (we generally started trips on Thursday evening and drove at night to have time for a Friday row on the racecourses prior to a Saturday race). From Klamath Falls we went either to Weed and the San Francisco Bay Area along

US-99 or east of the Sierra Nevada Range along US-395 to Los Angeles and San Diego. From my perspective, finding fuel in the middle of the night was the main problem.

Decades later my dad wrote, "... There were several methods of car travel. One ... was to gather everybody together at a central meeting place before leaving, check all drivers to see that they knew where they were going, which route they were supposed to take, and what their license plate numbers were. The drivers were cautioned that all speeding tickets were the responsibility of the driver, and the Rowing Club would pay no ticket. Then turn them loose to see who can arrive first."[J-12]

I think this method was abandoned early on, as my dad tried to increase safety by having rendezvous points along the way: for most people it would make no sense to drive fast if you had to sit and wait "in the middle of nowhere."

My dad detailed a typical experience.[J-12] "On one occasion, six private cars were taken to Stanford. The coach elected to ride in Mike Oxborrow's Hillman Sunbeam (smaller than the present compact cars but larger than an Austin) as far as Chemult where he would transfer to Mike's dad's new Thunderbird (Chemult was little more than a gas station along Highway 97 in Central Oregon). This little car was very nearly without a muffler, but everyone was getting used to the noise by the time the water hose to the heater broke, spraying the coach with antifreeze. Our first unscheduled stop was for thirty minutes in Junction City, twenty-two miles from Corvallis.

"At Chemult the first three cars to arrive passed the time in snowball fights, in drinking pop and coffee, and eating pie. ... The coach transferred to the T-bird and all cars were gassed up. We merrily took off, down the road for Klamath Falls. Twenty miles down the road, the coach in the follow car (last in line) came upon Jim York's car, whose windshield was held together with scotch tape, alongside the road, out of gas.

"In his best (profane) Sawtooth Mountain (Idaho) logger language, 'Big Jim' York[O-53] swore up and down. ... He claimed he'd told the attendant at Chemult to fill his tank. The T-bird made the forty-mile round trip to Chemult in thirty minutes, including time required to chew on the attendant, rummage … for a one-gallon can, pump gas into the can, and pay an additional fifty-cent deposit on the can. With a gallon of gas in his tank, York returned to Chemult for more gas. By the time he got back to Chemult, he had cooled down. He nevertheless proceeded to tell the attendant in words of seven syllables, of which he was quite capable, being a four-pointer (top student) in science, that it was a hell of a note to send a man out into the middle of the night in 25-degree weather with only a gallon of gas, knowing there was no station open before Klamath Falls, eighty miles away.

"Between Klamath Falls and Weed, in the middle of both the night and the sagebrush, the coach's tail car came upon one of the cars with a blowout and no jack. Still bringing up the rear, the coach pulled into Redding (California) about daybreak with the greeting from freshman Chuck Emerick,[O-53] 'Coach, I didn't screw up. Where have you been? We've been waiting for you for two hours.'"

My dad didn't have an intimidating presence, and oarsmen, least of all Chuck, were never shy about expressing their opinions, in this case as banter.

My dad also tried having the cars travel in caravan, since he thought that would control the inevitable racing. Occasionally enough money was raised to use State of Oregon cars, which were required to be driven in caravan. But the caravan idea was hardly an improvement.

According to Carl Bower, my dad was "… very agitated on every trip, because it's tough to keep six or seven cars … together. Invariably, the cops would catch the last car speeding as it tried to catch up. The last car could not keep up on the old parts of Highway 395 from the Los Angeles area—three would pass a truck, and the others would get stuck; one by one we would eventually pass. Then the first car would think it was behind and drive like hell to catch up. In the meantime, the group that had stayed together would be following the coach to the Reno Police Department, asking if they had any info on the missing car. The missing car got back to Corvallis three hours before the convoy." O-31

Every trip seemed to have a memory. Often they were minor incidents, but even after six decades they had not disappeared. For example, Carl recalled, "On one trip, the car I was in ran out of gas and coasted down an off-ramp out of Medford into a gas station. On another trip we were in Medford and were pulled over by the police. We were all instructed to get out of the car and were spread-eagled. Seems there had been a robbery, and our car fit the description."

After races we were turned loose for a few hours of sightseeing. My dad seemed to think that the free time would help bond the crews. California was an exotic place for many of us, and Tijuana was a different world. Carl's recollection skirted around our visits to Mexican bars, "The year of the Western Sprints in San Diego, as I recall, the varsity went to Mexico and the rookies went to Disneyland. Something in the Mexican beverages depleted the size of the common bladder, and one varsity car pulled off the highway, just past China Lake. The rest of the convoy went roaring over an overpass and we never saw the car again."

I was on that trip to Mexico. To a kid from Oregon, the crowded streets of Tijuana were overwhelming, and dimly lit bars were a novelty. I spent most of the time gawking. I was afraid I might lose my wallet in Mexico, so I left it in the car we parked in San Diego. When we returned to the border, I couldn't prove I was a US citizen. The border guard decided to brow-beat me. According to him, I was required by law to carry my draft card (these were days when student anti-war protesters burned draft cards). He pulled out his handcuffs and prepared to throw me in a holding cell. Perhaps as a pre-arranged skit, a fellow officer stepped in and convinced my antagonist to let me come home if I promised to always carry my draft card. I readily promised. I think they had a good laugh.

Fortunately, no serious accident occurred on road trips, but in 1979 the lightweight crew's sectional shell blew off the van carrying it. Bouncing along the freeway caused severe damage. Ironically, this boat had been christened the *Karl F. Drlica*. The boat couldn't be brought back to racing fitness; moreover, the mishap was judged to be human error, so insurance wouldn't cover the loss. According to a news report, the crew was planning to take out a loan from the OSU Foundation, since a new boat was needed for the upcoming racing season.[N-10,C-42] After 50 years, Oregon State Rowing had become credit-worthy.

I think that my dad endured road trips because he saw them as necessary for building a successful program. He always hoped that fundraising would provide enough money for the team to travel by bus or train, and indeed I recall a rather boring train trip to Los Angeles. I only remember being unable to shower after the race and smelling the consequences all the way home. For us, road trips were adventures to be remembered for years. For my dad, it was like herding cats.

As Oregon State men's crews of the mid-1960s were raising money, rowing small boats, and traveling by car to intercollegiate races, a shift began in American culture: women were demanding status. As a part of that shift, women's rowing programs were springing up along the West Coast. My dad saw this as an opportunity to expand his intercollegiate rowing program to women, since he had already gained a foothold with intramural crew. For this next step he needed someone to drive the program. That person was Astrid Hancock.

——— *Chapter 19* ———

ASTRID

Although American women had rowed recreationally since the late 1800s, serious, competitive rowing didn't take hold until the 1960s. Even then, rowing-to-win was socially unacceptable for women (physical educators sought to protect women from win-at-all-cost team competition). The crews of the 1960s threw off that protective attitude, paving the way for the explosive growth in women's rowing following passage of Title IX (this Federal law prohibits gender-based discrimination at schools and educational programs accepting Federal funds; for athletics, that meant equal resources for male and female teams).

The 1960s women's rowing effort emerged in Philadelphia and three centers on the West Coast, one of which was Corvallis. The Corvallis center was driven by Astrid Hancock and my dad—they struggled to obtain support from an institution that shielded young women from "over-exertion" and locked them up at night.

Astrid came from a rowing family. Her uncle, Calle Froensdal, dominated Norwegian single sculling for a decade: he was national champion in 1938, 1939, 1946, 1947, and 1948 (no rowing during war years). He was selected as the Norwegian single-sculls entry in the cancelled 1940 Olympics, and he placed second to Jack Kelly at the 1947 Henley Royal Regatta.[D-51,O-90] Thus, Astrid, although growing up in the United States, knew about rowing.

She began pulling an oar as a teenager at a girls' summer camp.[D-4a] "For ten years I spent two months each summer at

Camp Mudjekeewis[O-85] in Center Lovell, Maine. The camp was situated on the wooded shore of Kezar Lake, a narrow, 10-mile-long body of water tucked into the hills of northern New England. The lake was perfect for young water enthusiasts."

The camp's special attraction was an eight-oared shell, a hand-me-down from Wellesley College. This all-female school had taught rowing for many years as a low-key, physical education activity; the school seemed to have a special connection with Camp Mudjekeewis.

Astrid recalled, "During winter months the shell was stored in a wooden boathouse that doubled in the summer as a crafts center and refuge on rainy days. For the summer season, the forty-two-foot, wide-bodied training shell was moved outside and placed in a cradle located on an inclined portion of the lake shore.[O-84] The cradle held the boat via canvas straps; by cranking rollers we lowered the boat onto the water. We then disconnected the supporting canvas and guided the shell to a nearby dock that extended out into the lake. There we loaded in the oars, eight campers, and a cox.

"Rowing was a privilege reserved for the older campers—we had to be at least fourteen to row. I loved water sports, especially canoeing, and I couldn't wait to be old enough to row. But getting water time was a challenge the year I turned fourteen. We had to sign up for practices and even for particular positions in the boat. Competing with the older girls was hard, and I got in the boat only a few times. I was also at a disadvantage, as that year I was at camp for just a month, half the usual time. I was disappointed when I didn't make one of the teams that raced against the clock.

"The next year was better: I was taller and more assertive; I got on a team. Our supervising counselor had taken a rowing class at Wellesley, so she could show us how to get in the boat, how to hold the oar, and basic parts of the stroke. She turned us loose on the lake but kept tabs on us using a small aluminum motorboat. The shell tipped a lot, and we caught plenty of crabs. But we pulled hard; I felt a new connection with my Uncle Calle.

Camp Mudjekeewis, circa 1950. Top: Boathouse and dock.[O-84]
Bottom: Two canoes tied together for float night.[O-84a]

"At the end of the summer we had a 'float night'. First was a
parade of canoes including two tied together with wooden planks.
These two canoes supported a mural that illustrated a well-known
poem or story. The parade was followed by crew races. Three
crews were selected—green, gray, and white. They went out, one
at a time, and rowed over a timed course. As the crews rowed to
the starting line, they were judged on slow form; on the return
they were judged on racing time and racing form. The winning
crew was announced, and after dark, that crew returned to the
water so each rower could leave a lighted candle on the lake.

"The counselor in charge of rowing presented awards at an
end-of-season banquet. The awards, which included a badge,
were termed varsity and junior varsity. I made junior varsity in
1950 and varsity in 1951. Later I was a counselor for two years and
able to continue rowing, probably for six weeks each summer.[O-84]

Our crews were never very good, but it was satisfying to feel us getting better with each practice.

"By today's standards, my rowing experience was low key and a bit flowery. Society was happy with women rowing for exercise. But many of us really wanted to win, and we were willing to sweat. I learned in the early 1950s that competitive team sports were not just for boys—at least when no boys were around."

As an aside, Astrid's early rowing experience was probably quite intense for the times, as women's rowing was not taken seriously by American society for another quarter century (1976 Olympic Games).

"After graduating from Mount Holyoke College and obtaining a Master's degree in physical education from the University of Wisconsin, I was hired to teach at Wellesley College. I'd had no opportunity to row in college, but we did have canoe races. For the solo races, the sitting position was standard, but I discovered that I could go much faster when kneeling and even faster when I used a standing lunge. Winning by innovation had its own special appeal. I guess I made an impact, since after graduating I was invited back to Mount Holyoke to judge canoe races.[O-90]

Wide-bodied training shells waiting on the Wellesley dock for the next rowing class.[O-84b] Rowing was for exercise, not for intercollegiate competition.

"At Wellesley I taught rowing based on my teenage years at camp. As one of five rowing instructors, I was the newbie and had a lot to learn. The Wellesley students rowed on Lake Waban, which was partially owned by the College. Harvard had donated four old barge shells, training boats that were shorter, wider, and heavier than racing shells. The boats were kept on the water all fall and spring to service the many physical education classes, fall intramural competition, and spring class races (the latter had been popular since 1920). The classes raced at a celebration called Tree Day, a traditional day in which each sophomore class, dating back to 1879, planted a tree on campus. For the rowing competition, the teams were scored on finish time, rowing form, and racing form. As with Camp Mudjekeewis, Wellesley had a float night. Part of my job, along with teaching canoeing and other classes, was to assure that all rowing events happened.

"Some of the students took racing seriously, but rowing was just exercise for most. It was fun to win as long as a certain decorum was maintained. We had no thought of training to race other schools, even if there were someone to race.

"Wellesley was a leader in women's rowing, but only within the long tradition of 'civilized' rowing for women. In the beginning, the late 1800s, crew was more about singing than rowing. The crews would row from the boathouse to the cove at the other end of Lake Waban in full-length skirts. They sang and then rowed back to the boathouse. To recruit new members, they advertised how rowing produced an erect carriage, finely poised head, full chest, well placed shoulders, strength of back and chest, and deep breathing.

Women's crew at Wellesley College, late 1800s.[O-97]

"By 1960 rowing had changed somewhat, as skirts were no longer worn, and crews were not selected for singing ability. But my recollection of Wellesley rowing is captured by the question, 'Who doesn't want to get out on the lake on a lovely day?'

"During my last year at Wellesley, heavy wet snow fell on the boathouse. The roof collapsed. That was when I saw the rowing bug exert itself. At least two of the boats were salvaged, and rowing continued. Moreover, the students had felt the magic of the racing shell and wanted the full program back. They mounted a major letter-writing campaign that pressured the College administration into building a new boathouse long enough for standard-length racing shells.[D-4a]

Wellesley crew facilities. Upper: docks with the debris of the collapsed boathouse, 1962.[O-127] Lower: New boathouse. [O-126]

"After three years at Wellesley, I wanted a larger taste of the old country. I applied for a Fulbright Scholarship to study in Norway, and when I got it, I headed for the University of Oslo and the State Gymnastic School. I'd visited Norway many times, but this time I tried to stick with Norwegians, as my goal was to really learn the language. Of course, my relatives wanted to practice their English. Uncle Calle, the single sculler, was the youngest of ten in my mother's family. I had a meal or two at his house, but we didn't talk much about rowing. World War II had not been a good time for them, so they probably didn't want to talk about those days. He continued to row every day until he passed away at age 85.

"After a year I knew I had to get on with my life. I now had a very diverse background in physical education—I could teach almost anything. I searched through a catalogue of U.S. universities, applied to several, and winnowed the final choice to two: the University of New Hampshire and Oregon State. Being an Easterner, I felt that if I didn't take a job in the West, I'd never get west. So ...

"I arrived in Corvallis in the fall of 1963 as an Instructor in the Women's Physical Education Department. I'd been told that I'd teach swimming, tennis, and fundamentals of movement [required of all first-year women students]. But I was unaware of canoeing classes and didn't even know that Corvallis was located on a river. I'd been looking for ski country."[D-4a]

Soon after Astrid settled in, Susie O'Shea, the intramural advisor, happily handed over supervision of intramural women's crew. Varsity oarsmen did all the coaching as coxswains, because the women often had no rowing experience. Boat maintenance was my dad's problem. So, Astrid thought she would simply need to assure that everything went smoothly.

Astrid recalled, "Little did I know what I was in for—more than a hundred young women, five days a week, four weeks, 6-8 a.m. at the river in the dark, fog, rain, and bone-chilling COLD—running home to warm up, shower, and change clothes before teaching at 9 a.m. at the Women's Building. Dr. Eva Seen was the Head of the Women's PE Department, and she didn't allow faculty or students to wear pants into the building: it had to be skirts or dresses (once in the building we changed into PE clothes).

"The women students weren't allowed to leave their living groups before 6 a.m., so they made a mad dash to the river—walk, run, bike—none of the women had cars in the early days. You wanted to be the first to get a boat so you could get back home and shower before 8 a.m. classes and again get dressed appropriately and look nice!

Astrid Hancock, first Oregon State women's rowing coach, 1971.[D-90]

"It took two teams of women plus the two male coxswains and me to haul the heavy barge shells (Stevens' plywood shells) out of the Navy barge and down the ramp to the dock. And sometimes the four-oared shells were up the hill in the Quonset hut, which seemed very far from the water. The hardest part was lifting the heavy shells over our heads to set them on the water.

"Some of the oarsmen, acting as coaches-coxswains, had cars, picking up the women at 6 a.m. so they could get to the boathouse quickly. Each team was allowed only two water practices per week for the four weeks; the season ended with a Saturday competition in fours and eights. Trophies were awarded, and the winning coxes were, of course, thrown into the icy river, much to the glee of the rowers! This ancient tradition of rowing had to be maintained.

Winning cox, women's intramurals, 1964.[O-132]

"In my earlier experiences, we rowed on lakes. So, coming to OSU and learning how to take off and land with the current was a major challenge, with more than one accident. And navigating the bridge piers was anxiety-producing, especially when the second bridge was built the year after I arrived."

Astrid's navigation anxiety, especially when the current drove shells toward the bridge piers, was shared by the coxswains. Suzi Wong recalled, "I know the bridge piers are really, really spread out and the shells are really, really skinny, but with those long oars, and as the cox, it was scary to go between the piers. It always seemed like we only had a couple of feet to spare. … Visiting crews, trying to come into our dock … [were not] used to the current; they'd get swept past the dock and would have to circle around."[O-172]

While Astrid oversaw the women's participation, the Rowing Club supervised the male coxswains and the boats. One year I volunteered to handle the Club portion. That year we lacked enough willing oarsmen to coach each of the women's crews, so I had to find a way to get more coxswains. I cajoled several oarsmen into early morning coaching, but I was still short one coxswain. I took on the task of coaching two crews. That worked until the crews discovered what I was doing. Both teams quit. I thought I was being a good citizen; they had a different view.

My 1962 report adds perspective to Astrid's account: "Approximately 150 girls turned out for women's intramural rowing, representing eleven eights and thirteen fours. ... In every capacity there were too many girls for the facilities. Due to a lack of coxswains, freshmen were used. ... Much time was wasted because of the lack of equipment. This was further complicated by the fact that the Rooks (first-year oarsmen) didn't know what they were doing. The equipment was broken and not repaired due to inexperience. ... Do not use freshmen for coxswains."[D-156]

For the young women of the 1960s, rowing was their first serious compete-to-win athletic experience—Oregon high schools had limited them to cheering for male teams. Now they were sliding back and forth in a tippy boat, sitting only a few inches above a swirling river cold enough to be dangerous. A guy was yelling at them to pull harder, treating them like real athletes. Blisters were popping up on their hands, and the killer instinct was palpable. Women's intramural crew was not a social exercise.

Astrid, my dad, and I each felt the intensity of women rowing to win. Astrid was only nine years older than the students, and she identified with the competitive drive. Decades later she wrote,[O-90] "I guess I was competitive myself. In high school I went out for a sport every season: field hockey, basketball, softball. I was the pitcher for the softball team. We got points for sports, and the top female athlete received a silver ID bracelet. I won it by one point over my rival, but it was touch and go ... she was also my rival for President of the French Club, which she won by one vote. And yes, I did vote for myself in that election and in many others.

"At summer camp we got badges for different things, and I wanted all the badges I could get. The "Dip" badge was for getting out of bed, jumping into a swimsuit, running down to the dock, and plunging into the lake. That was a tough badge. If you missed a day, you didn't get the badge. Even after sixty years I remember how cold August mornings can be in Maine. Other badges were for tennis or riding every day, a free swim every afternoon, and compiling 100 miles of hiking. I especially wanted the "paddle" award, which was based on accumulated points for swimming races, canoe races, and I don't remember what else. I won the paddle many times. Yes, I fell in the very competitive category."

In Corvallis, Astrid sensed something new—women rowing to win as a team. She had just come from a women's college environment where rowing was for exercise; no men were around to pass judgement. In Oregon, young men and women were in the same boat, on the same team in the predawn fog and rain, striving to win as a team. Rowing was about winning, not about exercise.

Rowing was also distinctive because all other PE activities were segregated. Astrid recalled, "Rowing was probably the only sport where the men and women interacted—and men coxing women's intramural crews had been going on for a long time. Coach Drlica really encouraged the interaction."

My dad's perspective on women's rowing probably differed from Astrid's. He focused on the numbers—he'd been expanding his campus, and a large increase in participants would support his arguments for more money; it would help solidify rowing at the University.

I was participating as one of the coxswains for the pleasure of a race and perhaps bragging rights (fifty years later Carl Bower reminded me that his crews won the women's intramural championship two years in a row). I was surprised by the competitive intensity of the women rowers, by the grimaces on their faces as they pulled on the oars. This intensity was new to me, as my high school had no female athletic team that I knew about.

For my dad, the next step was to form a women's intercollegiate team. He had designed the new locker-room/shower facility for women, but he was already over-extended. Perhaps he could get Astrid to run the program. He saw her as a kindred spirit and one of the few women in the country with rowing knowledge.[D-4a,D-45] For him it was a blessing that she had come to Corvallis. Indeed, she had a unique set of credentials: she had rowed in crew races and taught rowing to young women. Moreover, at Wellesley College she had seen the power of grassroots fundraising. In retrospect, her position as a PE instructor at Oregon State was a crucial stabilizing factor, because it provided a connection between women's crew and the University. For other colleges, that institutional bond didn't develop for another decade.

In the spring of 1964 Astrid was new at her PE job and had a full teaching load. My dad knew she didn't have time to take on another responsibility. Nevertheless, he asked whether she'd start a competitive team. Astrid said yes.

Decades later I asked Astrid why she took on the extra work. "It was in my blood; I loved being on the water. And I was down at the docks for canoeing classes anyway. At first, I could just stay down at the docks for the crew, since it practiced right after my canoe classes. Plus, Coach Drlica was persuasive."[O-90]

According to Astrid, my dad worked hard to engage her in the project, making sure she had a voice at the National Women's Rowing Association (NWRA) constitutional convention (1966). That year he also dragged several women rowers and Astrid to the first NWRA regatta in Seattle.

The year before Astrid arrived in Corvallis (1962-63), the University listed eleven interest groups for women's sports. Astrid's arrival made rowing number twelve. That official recognition, plus the continuity provided by Astrid and my dad, were critical differences between the Oregon State crew and the University of California team I coached two years later.

Astrid later wrote,[O-90] "Since crew was a new group, I may have done it on a volunteer basis the first year. After that I was allowed a release of one teaching class to coach. That first year was hard, as I had to get my bearings in my new teaching job. And at times I was sure I'd bitten off more than I could chew. Coach Drlica taught the initial women's PE rowing class, as I sat in to learn his style. He also thought that canoeing would bring more people to the river (some years before he had bought twelve used canoes and rebuilt them).[J-8] Canoeing classes, which were up to me, plus coaching the crew, tied me to the river.

"Canoeing had its challenges. My classes were generally early in the afternoon, before the crews got on the water. Invariably a few canoeists, knowing they were the last canoe class of the day, would go farther up the Marys River than I instructed. That made them late getting back—no fun trying to land canoes in a current with shells on the dock.

"I would have the first class of the day bring the canoes down from the barn, and the students would leave the boats on the dock for the second class. Occasionally a few students in the second class failed to show up. Then I had to scurry around to find a way to get the extra canoes back to the barn—they were too heavy for me to carry by myself, especially up ramps made slick by rain. And occasionally beginners would tip over a canoe. Fortunately, such mishaps occurred at the dock where I could easily help.

"Due to scheduling, there was a break between my canoeing classes. I was often alone with canoeing—Coach Drlica wasn't there—I would sit in my car to warm up between classes or go use the heater in his office. We had many cold and rainy days. Needless to say, I was tired after canoe classes, but I enjoyed being at the river.

"My first year (1964) included the initial Corvallis Invitational Regatta. I think Coach Drlica started this regatta to boost my team. We could race without having to raise travel money. This regatta became an annual event that lasted many years as a main regatta on the West Coast. Attendance by rowers and spectators was huge, and eventually the regatta became a two-day affair. This really promoted rowing at OSU and on the West Coast.

"I was amazed that twenty young women showed up for competitive crew that first year. We fielded a heavyweight eight, lightweight four, and heavyweight four in the Corvallis Regatta.

"I didn't want to push too hard, so practice that spring was light: on the water two days per week for two hours each. I left physical training up to the women, although some testing was done. They were to work on sit-ups, push-ups, a quarter-mile run around a corn field, and wrist rolls (an agonizing exercise in which a thin rope, attached to a weighted can, is rolled onto a stick using outstretched arms). I'm not sure when we got an ergometer—in the late 70's—but there was only one.[D-4a]

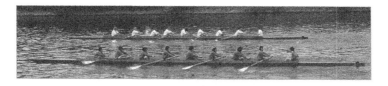

OSU women's eight-oared crew (near side) at the 1964 Corvallis Regatta.[O-109] In some years as many as 500 seats were filled in over 70 races.[J-1]

"Although some of the women had rowed in the intramural program for four years, others had only one season in boats. Our inexperienced crews were pitted against veteran teams from Lake Merritt and Lake Washington. But we were happy to be in races, and our eight-oared crew did beat Seattle's Green Lake Rowing Club.

"I found it hard to recruit women in the 60's, because almost everyone majored in education, home economics, or physical education. These were the professions open to women in those days. They required student teaching during the senior year, most often spring term. We lost a lot of women from time conflicts. The men's rowing program didn't have that problem, since few men focused on teaching as a career. At Oregon State, the men tended to be in science or engineering.

"The next season, 1964-65, was even tougher than the first. I could get only six women to race. That wouldn't be enough to sustain the program, since we had to raise funds in addition to rowing in the fog and rain. I thought our program would fold. That would cause the PE Department to withdraw its offer to let me coach the crew.

"Coach Drlica also worried. He'd been pushing hard to build up the facilities, and a strong women's crew would solidify his effort. The intramural program was strong, but it required a much smaller commitment from the women. Had we done something wrong? Had I pushed too hard or not hard enough? Had second-wave feminism (women's lib, a critique of male-dominated institutions) not yet reached Corvallis?

OSU women's crew, 1964. Left to right: Jan Liesegang, Sherry Smith, Barb Olson, Judy Kamphenborg, and Ellen Nakada (cox).[D-104]

"I felt obligated to keep the program going for my crew of six; however, the river didn't make it easy. I had access to a fourteen-foot aluminum outboard motorboat, but I had no driver and sometimes no megaphone. Once I got the crews on the water, I'd unlock the boat, check the gas, and make sure I had extra shear pins. I couldn't afford to get stuck downriver with no power if my propeller hit something and a shear pin broke. The boat did have a paddle, so I knew that I could make it to the bank. But then what?

"Usually the motor started easily, but when it didn't, the coaching had to come from the coxswain, as I was stuck at the dock. On the water I needed three hands to stay close enough to see the crew through the fog: one hand on the steering wheel, constantly adjusting to variations in the current; one on the throttle arm, also adjusting for current; and one to hold the megaphone. By the end of the workout, I was just as tired as the rowers.

"The fall intramural program had exposed a hundred young women to rowing, and the men were supportive. But training to race other schools was more intense than the short intramural season. My crew of six had been rowing for three or four years in intramurals as well as during the previous spring in PE class. They knew what they were doing. But I began to think that society wasn't ready to let large numbers of young women work so hard.

"At Mom's Weekend (1965) my problem became immediate: I could put together only one four-oared crew—we had nobody for a demonstration race. The team couldn't show women's rowing to parents visiting campus. Somehow, I had to support our team. And Coach Drlica didn't want to miss the public relations opportunity.

Mom's Weekend race, 1965. The "pseudo" women's crew.[D-108, D-154]
Members of the pseudo crew were Gary DeVoe, Frank Nelson, Jim Keefer, and Dan Patterson.

"We solved the problem by forming a crew of male managers and coxswains to race our women. The men had all taken a PE class in rowing, so they knew how to get into a shell and which end of the oar to put in the water. The guys were very enthusiastic,

borrowing skirts and wigs to play their part. I don't remember
who won. It didn't matter. I needed my crew to feel part of the
rowing community, to keep going another year.

"I was relieved when the number of rowers bounced up to thirteen the next year (1965-66), the same year that crews on the West
Coast began to organize. Coach Drlica pushed for my women's
crew to become an official part of the Rowing Club. Official affili-
ation was important, as that year Oregon State became a charter
member of the National Women's Rowing Association. The crew
still had no funding, and I had to return the NWRA request for $20
dues with a note saying that the team had no money. When Coach
Drlica heard that I declined to pay dues, he covered them—he felt
that a charter member shouldn't shirk on dues.

"In April of 1966 the team made its first road trip, travelling
to Oakland for races against Mills College, Cal Women's Crew,
and Holy Names High School. That was a big boost: the women
realized that they were being taken seriously. A few weeks later,
we had three sculling and two four-oared entries in the Corvallis
Regatta. The program was beginning to look sustainable, even
without financial help from the University.

"The small boats program was especially important to us,
because the national regatta took place in early summer when
most of our team was starting summer jobs. Even with a small
team I could field entries."

Indeed, Astrid needed only one rower: Janet Schoenborn.
With special dispensation from the Dean of Women, Janet was
able to leave her dormitory at 5 a.m., an hour early, to get enough
practice time before classes. Since she sculled a single, she could
also be on the water after classes without needing partners. The
men began to notice her work ethic. When a vacancy occurred
during men's practice, my dad put Janet in a four-oared shell with
men. She must have been swept up by the surges of power, as
each stroke drove the boat faster than she could have imagined;
the loud thunk from oars turning simultaneously in the oarlocks

would have driven home the one-ness of the crew. Astrid could count on Janet to race.

Janet Schoenborn, 1967.[D-141] *She had to obtain special permission from the Dean of Women to leave her dorm before 6 a.m. for practice on the river. The archaic practice of a women's curfew was abandoned a few years later.*

Astrid later recalled, "In June of 1966, Coach Drlica hauled me and two rowers (Janet and Marcia Morley) off to Seattle for the First NWRA Regatta. We slept on the floor of Ollie Rieflin's house (Lake Washington Rowing Club; nobody had any money, and it was common practice for host teams to house the visitors; it was also common to use boats from the host team, often determined by lottery). Since we were a charter member of the NWRA, of course we had to have some entries."

Seven teams rowed in this first NWRA regatta: the four charter members plus Green Lake Rowing Club, Mills College, and Cal Women's Crew. Attendance by the Philadelphia Girls Rowing Club made this the first sanctioned regatta involving East and West Coast teams. Lake Washington and Green Lake supplied the shells, but every crew brought its own oars.

The boats were assembled in slings at the edge of Green Lake, a small fresh-water body in Seattle. Once the shells were assigned, each crew scrambled to adjust oarlock height by placing thin metal shims between each outrigger and the side of the shell where bolts attached the riggers to the boat. Meanwhile, coaches and coxswains met with referees to learn the local rules. Then officials from Lake Washington herded the nervous crews onto the water amid shouts of encouragement and pleas to avoid catching crabs. It was a real national regatta.

Astrid recalled, "We all felt very proud. We had really started something. Marcia took a third in the open wherry, a short, wide, single-sculling boat. Janet took a third in light-weight singles, but she was disqualified in the lightweight singles dash for getting out of her lane. Janet was second in mixed doubles with a gal from Cal (Julie Shew, who years later, at age 64, set her East Coast club record of 2,700 miles in a single year; she was headed for 3,000 when, sad to say, she died in rough water on an 18-mile row.)[D-113]

"The second national regatta was held in Oakland. This time the rowers stayed in the Mills College dorms and had some money for meals. Among the memorable events was trying to get one rower to lose two pounds so we could enter a lightweight four (no rower over 125 pounds). At first, I tried sweating her on a run. When that didn't work, I tried a sauna. All that did was give her a cold. We didn't enter the lightweight four event. But Denise Jolly did set a national record for the heavyweight wherry, and we took third or fourth in the open single, open single dash, lightweight single, and lightweight single dash. We were beginning to feel competitive.

"The yearly national regatta rotated among Seattle (Green Lake), Oakland (Lake Merritt), and Philadelphia. In the early years we could attend only the West Coast meets, as we were able to cut costs by sleeping in homes of crew members. However, in 1975 five students raised $3500 by writing to foundations, associations, and athletic directors for support. They flew to Princeton with Coach Fred Mann, who arranged for their oars to be transported. By then there were more than forty-five teams attending the regatta. Oregon State placed second in the open pair and seventh in the open four."

Race program photo of Oregon State crew, 1967. Left to right, bottom row: Ellen Nakada, Denise Jolly, Jane Lorenzen, Erika Bessmer. Top row: Janet Schoenbom, Kathy Severns, Mary Holst. [D-1]

Recollections from the young women provide additional perspective.[O-63,D-4a] A common memory was rowing in early morning rain and fog, needing a break for hand warming. Another was reaching the boathouse by bicycle in the pre-dawn rain, with emphasis on rain. A third was rushing back to campus to change clothes to look decent for 8 a.m. classes that were often slept through. Or missing the class, as recalled by Suzi Wong, "One quarter, for some reason I signed up for a soils class that started at 8 a.m. In theory, I could do practice, go home and change, and make it to class, but in reality, most of the time I was too cold because as the cox I didn't work up much of a sweat. I'd take too long of a shower and usually missed the soils class."[O-172]

Although the women used the men's racing shells, as a team they had to pay for travel and buy their own oars (oars tended to break). Personal money was in short supply, which meant fundraisers—selling programs at football games, cleaning the football stadium after games, selling concessions at football and basketball games. Later, in the 70's, they delivered telephone books, painted house numbers on street curbs, cleaned up at the docks after floods, and held several row-a-thons to Salem[D-139] or Albany. They also participated with the men in jog-a-thons.

My dad was pleased with the development of self-sufficiency, and he soon had the women picking up manual skills by repairing damaged oars. They also sanded and varnished racing shells. They even built a wooden boat carrier to mount on top of a van to carry a sectional eight-oared racing shell.[D-4a]

Occasionally the women simply needed to show up to earn money. Astrid recalled, "The highlight for fundraising occurred in June 1969 when *Playboy* magazine came to campus and took photos. They had men in stylish clothes standing on the ramp to the lower barge looking out at a four-oared shell of women and some canoers. I had to rustle up some people at the last minute, which was not easy before cell phones. One of the rowers said she came down in curlers, perhaps to protest the *Playboy* philosophy. The team got $100, which was a big help to our budget."[O-90] Astrid was probably the first pregnant woman to appear in *Playboy*.[O-160]

Intramural rowing was an important recruiting activity for women's crew. Astrid's leadership was recognized by the PE Department, and after her first year she was charged with running all of the women's intramural programs. In 1967 a budgetary feud between the new head of Physical Education and my dad halted intramural rowing. Astrid was extremely disappointed,[O-90] as she lost a way to spread rowing to more than a hundred women each year. I suspect that my dad made a unilateral decision, since Astrid didn't know the underlying reasons. My dad tended to adopt a military attitude toward decision making—it was his job and didn't require consultation.

In 1968 the women's crew joined the Recreational Sports Program and received a few thousand dollars toward travel. According to the funding rules, the women still had to buy their own equipment. As expected, they treated their oars like personal items, taking pride in painting them to differ from the men's oars. By 1969 the women had raised enough money to purchase their first boat—the *Heather*. This four-oared shell, which was designed for women, was smaller and much lighter than shells built for 200-lb men.[D-4a]

After 1966, eight or nine women turned out for the team each year until spring 1972 when the number climbed to 16. Oregon State had an impact at regattas even with small teams: Astrid had the team enter as many events as possible. A particular rower might row in both four-oared and eight-oared races; scullers would row in both sweep (one long oar per person) and sculling (two shorter oars per person) categories.

Passage of Title IX (1972) was a turning point. The women wanted to practice daily, both in the fall and spring. Astrid was pleased with the competitive spirit, but daily practice didn't work well with her teaching schedule. Student coaches were enlisted to facilitate daily practices, while Astrid continued to supervise practices two or three days a week. She also organized home meets.

One of the student coaches was Dave Prodehl. He had rowed at Oregon State during the mid-1960s and had participated in much of the rowing campus construction. Dave coached from a single, as was common, since coaching launches were in short supply.

Coaches Drlica (left) and Prodehl (right).[D-100]

Astrid recalled an event that tested Dave's patience. "The 1960s and early 1970s were transition years in which traditional society still had a strong pull on young women. That sometimes made coaching women challenging. I remember one time when Dave wanted the gals to go back out for another practice row, but two of them said they had to get home and wash their hair and set it. Dave and I were unhappy with that attitude. But such events were very rare, and the women really pushed us and themselves for more rowing time."[O-90]

OSU women's crew, 1971 (bottom to top: Carol Paight, Robin Symank, Donna Bestwick, Carol Schmitt, Ellen Kinnunen, Monica Circle, Cheryl Gray, Becky Lynch.[O-16] The women are sitting on the ramp where Astrid accidentally stepped off into the river.

Departmental responsibilities after 1972 prevented Astrid from travelling with the team (she was responsible for children's Saturday swim and gymnastics lessons that enrolled more than 300 for each sport).[O-90] Nevertheless, Astrid continued as the official crew advisor until 1977, fighting for varsity status. In 2022 she was inducted into the Oregon State Sports Hall of Fame.

Astrid had grown the women's program from one away-meet spring term in 1966 to three in 1971. By the 1974-75 season the women's team listed thirty members. That season they rowed in three fall and eight spring away-meets: that was comparable to the men's schedule. Her early efforts were complemented at other West Coast centers, thereby providing the racing competition needed to build Oregon State women's rowing. One of those centers involved a crew I helped start at the University of California in Berkeley.

--------- *Chapter 20* ---------

WOMEN'S CREW
BEYOND OREGON

I graduated from college in 1964 and remained in Corvallis for another year to scull. At the same time, I took additional college classes not normally included in an entomology curriculum. In the fall of 1965, I drove to Berkeley to begin graduate school. My crewcut made me look like the innocent I was, one who had just rolled in from a small valley town in Oregon.

The author, Berkeley 1965[O-59]

My first stop was Oakland's Lake Merritt Rowing Club, since I needed safe storage for the homemade single scull tied to the top of my '57 Chevy. The black and white car had been a gift from my grandmother, as the power from its eight cylinders had become too much for her. I improvised some seat belts and added a pull-up sign for the back window that said "Tailgater".

The sign was not well received when I flipped it up on California drivers; I soon stopped using it.

Lake Merritt, Oakland, California. Longest dimension is 1000 m, long enough for women's races of the 1960s and 1970s.[O-54]

I shortened my daily research effort to allow time for sculling. After a few trips to the lake, I noticed young women rowing; I soon found myself in the middle of the women's liberation movement, rowing division. Since women's interclub competitive rowing started two years before I arrived, I need to provide a context for my experiences.

Although men's rowing had been a popular sport since the late 1800s, women's rowing was informal, limited to a few venues where the focus was on exercise. Early sites were at Wellesley College (1875) and ZLAC (San Diego, 1891). The Philadelphia Girls Rowing Club (founded 1938) is a modern pioneer with a rich historical record.[D-50,O-86a] These early groups generally competed internally; organized interclub racing was uncommon: serious, competitive women's rowing in the United States was non-existent. That was not by accident. For years the Philadelphia women fought unsuccessfully for recognition by oars*men*. Women's Lib generated a male backlash that included armed intimidation, boarding up the women's restroom, and stealing boat parts (seats and stretcher boots).[O-86a] The male-only attitude came from the top levels of the sport: in the early 1960s, an executive of the national rowing organization ordered Olympic gold medal winner Ted Nash to stop encouraging women's crew.[O-86a]

I was unaware of this animosity, having come from a West-Coast environment that supported women's competitive rowing. Moreover, in Corvallis I had taught female friends to scull in a double; we even traveled to Oakland for a mixed double sculls race.

Women's rowing in Oakland was driven by Ed Lickiss, a former Cal oarsman and sculler in the early 1940s. His successful electrical contracting business gave him extra time to coach several women's crews that included a sizable contingent from Mills College. They raced against the Lake Washington Rowing Club, the Philadelphia Girls Rowing Club, and by 1964, Oregon State.

Lake Merritt women's rowing. Left: Race program photo of Coach Ed Lickiss, an early leader in women's rowing, 1967.[D-1] Right: Lake Merritt crew, composed largely of Mills College students.[D-92]

Two years before I arrived, Lickiss, Nash, and Philadelphia's Joan Iverson met informally after a regatta in Oakland to discuss women's rowing. They decided that it was time to form a national organization (National Women's Rowing Association, NWRA) to promote competitive rowing.[D-88] Thus, the young women I saw rowing on Lake Merritt were serious competitors.

Ed's teams shared the lake with a new group from Berkeley coached by Art Sachs, a former Cornell oarsman. Art recruited young women from a university campus where street activity was almost constant. For example, within a week after my arrival, I watched 10,000 students and activists march down Telegraph Avenue to Oakland, protesting the Viet Nam War. Windows were broken along the way, and the Bank of America branch soon bricked up its windows. Art competed for attention with the theater atmosphere of Berkeley.

The street corner where Telegraph Avenue ended at Bancroft Way was a Berkeley hot spot. This T-shaped intersection borders Sproul Plaza, an open, paved area partially shaded by low, leafy trees. About two hundred feet into the campus are the broad steps of Berkeley's Sproul Hall where, in the fall of 1964, Mario Savio initiated the Free Speech Movement. By 1965, the Sproul Hall steps were where many protested the Viet Nam War by burning their draft cards.

My bike route to campus took me to Telegraph and Bancroft where I often paused for a few minutes to join the crowd of the day. The preaching of Holy Hubert generally attracted twenty to thirty hecklers. Hubert was a small, red faced, red-haired evangelist who stood on a low wall at the edge of campus, haranguing hippies about the dangers of Hell. Whenever challenged, which was often, his retort was, "Bless your dirty little hearts".[O-93]

Hubert's wall also served student leaders as they stirred up small knots of sympathizers, seemingly looking for unattainable concessions from the University. These spokesmen for the Students for a Democratic Society would have been labeled communist agitators by my dad. After they gathered a crowd, they'd shift their forum to the steps of Sproul Hall. If the speakers were inspiring, they captured the attention of hundreds of students and on-lookers. They could raise the numbers into the low thousands with pre-rally publicity. That publicity would also result in hundreds of blue-coated, baton-wielding police assembling in nearby parking garages, ready for crowd control. The "Blue Meanies" were eager to punish the "Commies." A deep political chasm existed between the young liberals and the old conservatives. The scene could get tense, even for a by-stander like me. One day I was a bit late to campus, reaching Sproul Plaza at about noon. The daily fog was burning off, and a modest-sized rally was beginning. I easily walked my bike through the crowd of long-haired students and began pushing my way up the hill to the Virus Lab. I noticed twenty or thirty police in front of me, forming a blue line. I was not surprised, as police were common at rallies. I kept moving, making my way through a gap in the line. After a minute or so, I stopped to look back. The police had trapped the crowd. That seemed interesting, but I continued on. I was late, and that day's work would probably take all night. Within a few minutes I heard helicopters. Their presence was also common; I didn't pay much attention. The rally seemed like many other rallies.

I reached the Lab, put on my lab coat, and began chopping tobacco leaves to isolate chloroplasts and extract their DNA molecules. Within about fifteen minutes, tear gas drifted through the open windows. Gas canisters had been dropped from helicopters to teach the un-American Commies a lesson. That was unusual, but not rare. I quickly closed the windows and continued to work. The next day I discovered what I had missed: television footage showed police running after students, grabbing the long hair of young women, and clubbing them to the ground.

I escaped the Berkeley milieu by sculling on Lake Merritt several days a week. I imagine that Art Sachs hoped to find women students who also needed the break offered by rowing. He ran an ad in the student newspaper that captured the imagination of a dozen women who soon joined him on Lake Merritt.[O-180]

After about a month, I drifted past the boathouse and saw Art on the dock instructing his group of young women. I recognized him from a race we had in Corvallis when he was sculling for the Lake Washington Rowing Club. I landed my boat and offered coaching assistance. Art accepted my offer.

Art had moved from Seattle to Berkeley in the fall of 1965 to attend optometry school, leaving behind a girlfriend (Judy DeVries) who also rowed for Lake Washington. Thus, Art had a personal interest in women's crew.

Art Sachs and Judy DeVries at their Berkeley wedding, 1967.[D-129]

Among Art's followers was Carol Simpson, then in her first year at college. At five-foot seven or eight, she was among the taller of the team members. Carol later recalled, "In grade school I was timid on a bike and scooter (after a downhill mishap), and a loner prone to wandering. Sometimes I'd get lost, but never when I was walking to school carrying my double-belled euphonium, nearly as big as I was, wishing someone would give me a ride. I was never cheerleader material in high school, not overly athletic.

Carol Simpson, 1969.[O-62a]

"Coming to Cal was an entirely new opportunity to explore in all directions. I came to Art's practice one day out of mild curiosity and a hankering for tall men. It was raining, and we ran laps in a gymnasium, shoes squeaking on the floor. I didn't like it a lot. Soon we got to the boathouse; that was better."

At the Lake Merritt boathouse the neophytes began in four-oared racing shells, since no training equipment was available for beginners. As Carol recalled, "We probably began with a demonstration: someone who knew, probably Art, showed us how to get into a racing shell without stepping through the bottom. We faced the stern of the boat. Then one foot to the stern of the seat between the tracks, bend the knee, and place your butt on the seat. Then feet into the stretchers. All the while one hand on an oar and the other on the side of the boat. I'm sure we all practiced the move until we were smooth.

Cal Women's Crew at Lake Merritt boathouse.[O-62]

"When four of us were in the [four-oared] boat, Art, standing on the dock, told us that we each had a number, one through four, counting from the bow. He pointed at us, one by one, to make sure we each knew our number. I was number two. Then he grabbed my oar blade, told me to hold on tight, and pushed us out into the lake. We glided away until all oars were free to dip into the water. We sat there, balancing the boat with our four oars. From the dock Art yelled for numbers one and two to row while numbers three and four were to keep their oars on the water for stability. Slide forward, gingerly until we realized that numbers three and four could indeed keep us from tipping over. I pushed the oar forward, let my knees bend, turned the oar with my hands to bring the blade perpendicular to the water, and raised up to put the oar in and pull. 'Drop your hands and feather (turn the blade parallel to the water),' Art yelled. I did, and the oar came out. A stroke!

"We took a few more strokes and then stopped, letting our oars skim the water surface. It was time for numbers three and four to row. Eventually all four of us pulled at the same time, very slowly but together. At first, I felt like I was pulling the boat by myself. But after maybe thirty minutes we actually seemed to be moving the boat together, although with considerable tipping from side to side. I was concentrating so hard that it wasn't until we stopped that I noticed Art alongside in a single. He had been yelling at us the whole time, but I hadn't heard a word."

Art, whose days as a lightweight had long passed, had a disheveled manner, wearing T-shirts that always seemed stretched out and tennis shoes that were charitably described as broken down (one of us, probably me, held his shoes together with duct tape).[O-91] Art was intense, all business and all about winning races. He believed that women athletes wanted to win, and he had his crew sweat in days when most young women "glowed" during exercise.[D-37] The crew felt his commitment, and they responded.

The Lake Merritt environment was more competitive than collegial. The Cal women, being new, were at the bottom of the pecking order.[O-91] Art and rowing club founder Ed Lickiss frequently crossed swords, especially over tools Art borrowed.

I tried to keep some distance, but I soon found myself pushing our crew with the mantra "Beat Mills and Lickiss".

According to Carol, "I don't remember that Art so much yelled at us as had to yell to be heard from the launch (or his single). He was our seeing-eye dog, keeping us focused, charting a course we knew nothing about, always toward a sustained 1000-meter race. He drove us, often harder than we wanted to be driven, and was driven himself. It was always clear that he wanted us to be good at rowing, and there didn't seem to be a lot of his ego in that, although he did have a personality.

"With every workout, we'd get to the boathouse and follow the program. At first, struggle with the simple, yet tricky business of feathering the blade, with dropping the oar in at the catch, and getting it out cleanly at the release. Over and over, always working at that simple drill, and covering the miles as we went. Finding whole-body engagement as both enjoyable and tiring, learning to work while tired and keep on working. Rhythmic, repetitive, soundscape of oars, in and out of the water, coach urging and suggesting and, well, coaching. Days, weeks, months: it's what you do. Everything else is playing a supporting role for rowing.

"Spring break came, and we were able to have twice-a-day workouts. Rowing became our reality; the intensity deepened our love for being in the boat and on the water, where we felt so alive.

"Running in the hills and stairs in the Cal stadium was how I discovered that I had stamina and a love for physical exertion. That applied to being in the boat and, as it happened, to everything else of importance in my life.

"Training was novel and intense and supervised. Motivation felt partly externally provided, even though something in me rose to the requirements and demands and wanted to be good. From the runs in the hills, I realized that I could go farther and longer than I had set out; I realized that limits were often just ideas.

"In spite of Art's motto, 'We row to race, and we race to win', I didn't really like racing or race day with its extra pressure. Because we were clearly underdogs, even in the small-pond, newly-hatched arena of competitive women's rowing, winning wasn't my assumption or expectation. But rowing a race did take everything and then some out of me/us. Perhaps rowing with Ilene (Wagner) in the pair that first year at the nationals on Green Lake (Seattle) was my initial taste of wanting to win and thinking it was possible."

Ilene Wagner began rowing a few months after Carol, also out of curiosity. Together they made a good pair (they placed second in the pair-without-cox event in the 1966 national championship regatta; in 1967 they were only a deck-length (12 feet) out of first).

After that first year of rowing, Carol spent the summer in Los Angeles. She recalled, "Getting into a wherry (a wide-bodied, one-person shell) in Long Beach during the summer of '66 was simply out of curiosity, for pleasure, a way to get out of the house during the break from school. I walked into the old boathouse and asked if I could take a boat out. The guys said sure and helped me launch it. ... Some of those men, unbeknownst to me, had been on our '64 Olympic team.

"Sculling the wherry seemed to improve my skills: I remember Art saying so in the fall. He had me race in singles or wherries in Corvallis that fall, and I remember him saying something like 'She muscled her way through', so I had figured out something about fighting a current and, in the process, coming in ahead of an opponent."

It's likely that many in the crew experienced new-found stamina. Ilene recalled, "I discovered that I could keep going even after I was dead tired." This was a common realization, as a recollection from an Oregon State woman from that era was similar: "I learned so much about ... hard work and grit, perseverance."

Race program photo of Cal Women's Crew 1967. Left to right: Chris Rakestraw, Pat Savercool, Ilene Wagner, Carol Simpson; middle: cox Sydney Smith.[D-1]

Art and I treated his women's crew just as we would have treated male athletes: we knew no other way. We emphasized after-practice running, sit-ups, push-ups, and sets of supine pull-ups (a broom handle was set across a pair of chairs as a pull-up bar). Carol later recalled that there were only two excuses for missing practice: you were dying or someone in your family was dying.[O-180] I was surprised that young women lacking athletic experience could be pushed so hard.

Cal Women's Crew after practice at Aquatic Park.[O-147]

None of us realized that we, along with Astrid, other West Coast crews, and the Philadelphia Girls Rowing Club, were pioneering an emerging concept: teams of women racing to win. Within six years the concept had entered mainstream American consciousness, as Betty Harragan wrote that participation in team sports by boys, but not by girls, was part of why men were much more successful than women in business (*Games Your Mother Never Taught You*, 1971). A year later, federal legislation mandated that women's and men's sports receive equal support.

True to the spirit of beginning rowing programs, Art's crew raised travel money any way it could. For example, one woman arranged mortuary tours for which we were each paid a dollar. While this may seem like a paltry sum, gasoline for a round trip to Corvallis cost only $20.

Art's own fundraising was more standard: paper recycling. I vividly remember late-night visits to Berkeley computer labs looking for used punch cards to sell as expensive wastepaper. In the 1960s, computer centers used thousands of punch cards and threw them away every day. Art and I entered computer rooms as if we belonged, working our way past graduate students to the garbage cans. There we found piles of cards, usually as individual pieces about three inches wide and eight inches long. We separated the cards from dead cigarette butts and half-full cups of stale coffee before tossing them into the cardboard boxes we carried. We cheered when we found a boxed set of used cards that had been dumped intact. And we never passed up a dumpster outside the centers as we foraged for cards.

On a good night we filled the trunk of my Chevy and drove the cards to Aquatic Park in Berkeley where Art had built a shed[O-91] (Art hoped to eventually relocate his crew to this lagoon next to the I-80 freeway). After a few weeks of night-time collections, Art would borrow a pickup truck from a local construction company, move the cards to a recycling center in East Oakland, and sell them, probably for a few cents a pound.[D-37]

We didn't seek permission from the University to rummage through garbage cans. Who would we ask? I never thought about the campus police coming after us as I drove my car through dark alleys to reach the computer centers. After all, we were performing a free service, and both Art and I were registered Berkeley students.

Art didn't socialize with crew members; he was a serious coach with a girlfriend in Seattle. But he was approachable, as the women would joke with him about what they ate on race day. Art had strict rules about eating lightly, and Carol and other rowers would casually discuss their fictional breakfasts of bacon and multiple pancakes soaked in maple syrup.[O-91]

I deferred to Art. During the first year, I was clearly an assistant who was more concerned with his own sculling. Most of our conversations were about rowing, although he occasionally had relationship advice, since he was the experienced one from the East Coast. I felt that my major contribution to the team was moral support and my car, as I transported the crew from the Berkeley campus to the boathouse every day (Art's beat-up car seemed unreliable, and none of the rowers had a car). I also traveled with the team to Corvallis and Seattle, mainly because the crew needed my car. Sometimes we deviated from the direct route to drive the twisty McKenzie Pass in the Cascades. It seemed that nobody was in a hurry to get back to studying.

While Art was striving to beat Ed Lickiss and Mills College, another intense rivalry developed between the women's crews from Lake Washington and Lake Merritt (Mills College usually rowed as Lake Merritt Rowing Club). The intensity increased when a Lake Merritt crew traveled to Philadelphia, beat the Philadelphia crew, and then claimed to be national women's champion. The Seattle group disputed the claim, saying that the race wasn't a sanctioned regatta. They then proposed to host a championship regatta in the spring of 1966, with a follow-up regatta in Oakland in 1967.[D-1] Oregon State and the Cal Women's Crew provided additional competition in these regattas.

To bring order to women's rowing and provide sanctioned regattas, Art and my dad organized a constitutional convention in Corvallis (February, 1966).[O-90] Ted Nash had been the spokesman for the women at the men's national rowing association, and he prepared many parts of the women's constitution.[J-17] Racing categories, weight limitations, and regatta sites were among the issues raised.[D-44,D-114] Agreement was readily reached. The group then decided that all officers of the National Women's Rowing Association would be women: the time had come for men to step back.

The immediate outcome was addition of an annual championship regatta to our schedule. In 1966 that meant an extra trip to Seattle; in 1967 we rowed at home in Oakland. The crew fit the extended seasons into their schedule of final exams, graduations, and weddings, as if the races were routine.

Art's program was completely voluntary and unsanctioned. He tried repeatedly to get the University of California to acknowledge his crew, but the women's sports program rebuffed every effort, even though the rowers were Cal students. We suspected that the men's rowing program lobbied against Art. Many of the men rowing at Cal felt that the women were not serious athletes. In their opinion, jokes aimed at the women's crew reflected poorly on their own program. Perhaps newspaper headlines contributed to the sentiment. For example, after a regatta in which Art's crews won one race and lost another, the headline in the student newspaper read "Golden Bras Split." We wrote the articles but had no control over the headlines.

Since Art's crew didn't share equipment, facilities, or water with the Cal men, we generally ignored them. Perhaps their attitude drove Art a little harder, giving him a "We'll show them" attitude.

In retrospect, we were fortunate that the University didn't try to stop us. I imagine that a rogue sports program was a small irritation compared to the massive student unrest the school was experiencing. We may have received some help from Jim Lemmon, the Cal varsity coach in 1966. Carol recalled that he sent some freshmen to Lake Merritt to race the women in four-oared shells. Her main recollection was the intense anger she felt when her boat didn't move faster against the men.

In 1967 Lemmon was promoted to Athletic Director and replaced by a young coach who had no love for women's rowing. The new coach invited two women rowers to join him in his coaching launch to observe a practice. He was recalled saying something like, "So now that you see how it really is, you'll stop, right?" Some men felt that women degraded the grand sport of rowing.[O-86a]

During the mid-1960s, San Francisco Bay was in danger of being filled. To call attention to the Bay, Berkeley activists encouraged water activities at or near the waterfront. In the fall of 1965, activists helped Art tack a boat shed onto the Rod and Gun Club building at Aquatic Park, a narrow, mile-long lagoon adjacent to the I-80 freeway in Berkeley. I designed a small dock that was built next to the shed.[O-37] In November, 1965 shells were hauled from Lake Merritt to Aquatic Park for races between Mills College and Art's crews.[O-37] The shells were then returned to Oakland. Art had to base his operations at Lake Merritt until a real boathouse could be built at Aquatic Park.

After two years of friction between Art and Ed Lickiss, it was time for us to move. The Berkeley activists, Cal Women's Crew, and former Cal oarsmen raised enough money to establish the Berkeley Rowing Club; by late 1967 a boathouse and dock had been built at Aquatic Park, making it feasible for us to row there.

In the summer of 1967, Ilene and I married, as did Art and Judy DeVries. At the same time, Art completed school and took an optometry job in Eastern Washington. Ilene and I decided to keep the crew going at Aquatic Park.

Rowing wedding, 1967. Cal crew holding oars. Julia Shew, who later set her club distance record, is shown in the lower left.[O-169]

The Berkeley Rowing Club, which served as an umbrella group for the women's crew, leased racing shells from Conn Findlay, a rowing icon. Findlay won four Olympic medals, including two gold medals rowing a pair with cox.[D-143a] He also coached the Stanford crew and in the mid-1960s realized that rowing at many schools was held back by lack of funds to buy racing shells. He purchased shells, mainly fours and eights, and then leased them to beginning programs.[N-12] Since the shells were new, maintenance problems were generally minor compared to those experienced by Ed Stevens in Corvallis.

Dedication ceremony for the Berkeley Rowing Club boathouse, March 1968.[O-62]

The afternoon wind at Aquatic Park invariably whipped up little waves, and the adjacent freeway produced an incessant drone. But unlike the river in Corvallis, Aquatic Park was free of floating debris: we didn't hesitate to row our wooden shells in the dark. We still had to avoid running onto the bank, but not having to think about the current was a relief. We could focus more closely on the fine parts of rowing and sculling. Moreover, we could rest without drifting backward.

Shortly after the Cal Women's Crew moved to Aquatic Park, Berkeley High School started rowing there. The new Cal men's coach began complaining that women's rowing was interfering with the Berkeley High School crew (the Cal men's crew rowed several miles away on the Oakland-Alameda estuary). I assumed that the coach intended for the high school to eventually send experienced oarsmen to his program. That would give him a legitimate interest in Aquatic Park, but I couldn't let misinformation circulate.

To make sure that nothing was misunderstood, I wrote a letter to the Cal coach.[D-33] I pointed out that no scheduling conflict existed. Moreover, the women were easier on the equipment, having never run shells onto the dock (high schoolers had done that twice). The half-dozen women also contributed much more financial support to the rowing club than the 30 high school oarsmen. I also emphasized that there would have been no rowing for Berkeley High School if the women's crew hadn't helped get a boathouse and dock built. I finished by pointing out that at the Corvallis Regatta, the Cal Women became crowd favorites, and the public address announcer "…stressed that they were from Berkeley, not just California. This was in a land where Berkeley student and dirty hippie are synonymous." In the open four-oared event, Cal beat six other teams, including Lake Washington and Mills College. I later learned that Ilene had talked with the announcer to make sure Berkeley got credit.

Ilene Wagner at Aquatic Park, Berkeley, 1969.[O-80]

I received no response from the Cal coach, we continued to row, and I heard no more complaints.

Art had given up on University sponsorship, as informality was working. No money meant no bureaucracy. Ilene and I ignored the University, but we were careful to avoid using its name. The original Cal Women's Crew lasted four years. We traveled by car to races in Seattle and Corvallis. Many races were won, some were lost. Unlike my dad, neither Art nor I sought to teach our crews self-sufficiency: we simply wanted to win races.

The small field of women's crew provided winning opportunities unavailable to Art and me in men's rowing. We pushed our rowers harder than the competition, but without browbeating. We expected conditioning to make up for the lack of experience. Often it did. I don't know how many parents knew that their daughters were real athletes who were winning races (Carol's dad and Ilene's parents were the only crew parents I met).

In 1969 Ilene and I moved on, but Carol couldn't stop rowing. Two years earlier the Philadelphia Girls Rowing Club had traveled to Europe and opened the door for American women to compete internationally.[O-86a] By 1969 the Lake Washington Rowing Club was training for the European Rowing Championships, and Carol set off for Seattle.

Berkeley Rowing Club boathouse (1969) with Cal Women's Crew.
Bow: Alexis Lumsden; 2: unidentified; 3: Kathy Dietrich; stroke:
Carol Simpson; sitting; unidentified; standing: the author.[O-62]
The boathouse is still in active use by the Berkeley Paddling
and Rowing Club.

She later recalled, "In the summer of '69 I began as a spare for the LWRC (Lake Washington) eight that went to Klagenfurt. I very much wanted to get into that boat, worked my butt off, and made it a day or two before the event. Dick Erickson was coaching us, generously (Erickson was the Washington men's varsity coach). We came in seventh out of seven eights—the organizers added a lane so we could row with the other six boats in the final. Even though last, we didn't disgrace ourselves: we rowed the race to the end in relatively good form."

Carol returned to Long Beach where she became a founding member of the sculling group. The small club was extraordinary: many of the elite, male Olympic scullers were training there, and they seemed to have no issue with women wanting to row. Carol later described these times.[O-91,D-65]

"For a while I was the only woman rowing at the Long Beach boathouse. One day early in 1970, Melinda Collis paddled up to the dock in her kayak and asked if I would teach her to row. She was a natural athlete. Her father had been an Olympic paddler without an Olympics (Helsinki, 1940), and she had been on the water in small boats all her life. We practiced together in a double that spring, and on a whim went to the 1970 nationals along with Karen McCloskey, who had shown up at the boathouse and been taught to scull by Melinda. Karen entered the novice wherry (a wide-bodied, one-person shell), and Melinda and I were second in the lightweight double. Melinda and Karen returned to Long Beach, college, and rowing. I went back to northern California, moving to San Francisco to take up post-college life as a computer programmer, with my own little apartment on Russian Hill.

"In the fall of 1970 Joan Lind showed up at the boathouse. Melinda got her into a wherry and taught her the fundamentals of sculling. Tom McKibbon, interested in coaching women and looking for a partner for Karen, invited Joan to train seriously and aim for the next nationals. They were a strong duo and came in a close second in the heavy double at Old Lyme, Connecticut in 1971.

"In December of that year Melinda got married at her parents' house on Marine Stadium in Long Beach, which is where I met Joan for the first time. She and Karen had been training hard and were aiming to win the doubles event at the 1972 nationals in Seattle. Melinda's new husband would be at sea on a Navy ship for six months or so; she was feeling the itch to train and suggested that I quit my job, move back to Long Beach, and train with them to make a quad. I returned to my life in San Francisco thinking 'Certainly not'. The three of them were younger, all still students, living at home. I had a full-time job and was (I thought) a 'Grown-up'. Rowing was behind me.

"When I went into work the following Monday, I looked around and the decision made itself. The caption in my mind was 'For this I'm not going to go row?' I gave notice immediately; best impulsive decision I ever made. I piled my paltry possessions in my car and drove south. My dad still lived in the family home in southern California, within driving distance of Long Beach, so I moved in. A former employer of my sister gave me a job at his donut shop, midnight to 6 a.m., which gave me unencumbered training hours. A week or so later I flew back up to San Francisco for some kind of event and made the 500-mile return trip south on my bicycle to inspire myself and mark the adventure.

"We four showed up at the boathouse every day and trained alone or with one another in wherries, singles, and doubles. Tom spent time with us, even though he and John Van Blom were training for the double at the 1972 Olympics in Munich. Karen and Joan were the premier duo, but Melinda and I were determined to meet the challenge. Knowing that our quad would need a cox'n, we recruited a 12-year-old we had seen in a rowboat on the water, and her parents agreed to let us take Nancy to the Nationals with us [without training].

"About a week before we left for Seattle, I pulled something in my back and was in extreme pain, couldn't easily get out of bed or tie my shoes, and certainly could not get into a boat. Great: I've quit my job for this rowing adventure and now, at the final hour, I won't be able to.

"When we got to Seattle, local rowers had donated boats for the events. A doctor who had donated a single and also had access to the UW Sports Medicine Department arranged for me to get some treatment and some relief.

"Our first time together in a quad was at the nationals. Nancy needed sandbags to make minimum weight. We asked her to steer straight and let us know when we passed a certain tree along the course to signal our final sprint. We were completely thrilled to come in first.

"Karen and Joan won the double event decisively. They were likely two of the best oarswomen at that regatta.

"The single was a bit of an afterthought, something we had entered without specifying who'd actually row. Joan stepped back and I stepped in, thinking to use the race to warm up for the quad later that day. I was rowing along when mid-race I realized that there were four boats behind me. When I turned around to check for the fifth boat, I saw it was in my lane. I got angry and put on some speed to swerve around her. At the end of the race I rowed over to the judges to protest the lane violation. They told me to wait, the race was too close to call. After checking the photos, they told me that I'd won. No need to protest.

"Long Beach [Rowing Club] won all heavy-weight sculling events in 1972, and Jane Loomis, who'd joined us in the spring, came in first in the novice wherry by a margin of more than a minute.

"We returned to Long Beach and trained even harder for the Women's European Championships to be held in East Germany at the end of the summer. Melinda stepped away to be with her husband, and Gail Pierson of the Cambridge Boat Club, the second-place single sculler [at the Nationals], joined our boat. She provided essential organizing skills for actually getting us to Europe, including recruiting Jody McPhillips as cox'n and bringing along her good friend Sy Cromwell as coach (Cromwell was an Olympic sculler). Our quad did win a club event in Hannover prior to the championships in Brandenburg. At the championships, in a field of about eleven entries, we came in 8th. We were much impressed with the size, speed, and skill of the other teams, many of them from communist-bloc countries and well-supported by the state. We'd paid our own airfare and wore shirts made by Karen's mother.

"I could see this as a graceful exit, just ahead of the increased interest and competition that were sure to come with the first-ever Olympic women's rowing events in Montreal in 1976. Joan saw the Olympics as a challenge and goal for herself, to row against the best in the world and to join their ranks. She did indeed. I contributed by serving on the Women's Rowing Olympic Committee (1972-1976).[O-91]

Coxed quad, 1972, European regatta in Hannover, West Germany.
Gail Pierson, bow; Karen McCloskey, two; Joan Lind, three; Carol
Simpson, stroke.[D-63]

"For me, and I think for other women, the fact that rowing
was something of a blank slate was a big part of the appeal. I was
a general-purpose tomboy growing up, with no particular sport
excellence, and rowing gave me an opportunity and a sense that
I could be good at something. And it is beautiful and elegant
and introspective."

The group, started by Carol and world-class male scullers,
such as Tom McKibbon and John Van Blom, created a supportive,
competitive environment in which talent could grow.

According to Carol, "And then there was Tom, who so deeply
and honorably took on the sacred task of coaching. ... The hard
work and serious training examples were all around for emu-
lation, but the skill and artistry of sculling were revered and
transmitted and personalized by Tom. He deserves way more
credit in the annals of rowing than he gets."

McKibbon also thought highly of Carol, as he was quoted
saying that she was an incredible athlete.[O-89]

Joan Lind emerged as a premier sculler. At the time, Soviet
Bloc countries focused heavily on women's rowing, enhancing
performance through extensive doping. In 1975, Joan lost to
the champion East German single sculler by fifteen seconds,

which was far out of the running. But she came back in the 1976 Olympics, the first year that women's rowing was included. Joan engaged in a stroke-for-stroke battle with the East German, missing gold by a deck length despite drawing the windy, outside lane. Her spectacular race solved one of the problems for women's rowing: male rowers began to take their U.S. women colleagues seriously.

The Cal Women's Crew, although lasting only four years, added numbers to my dad's effort to solidify rowing. More crews meant more awareness of rowing by the administrators he needed to convince. For Astrid's early crews, Cal provided quality competition and a sense that they were not alone in the effort to convince administrators that women rowed to win, not just for exercise. Indeed, the distinguishing feature of Cal crews was the intensity: when the crew was tired, Art pushed harder.

The absence of administrative support and the many distractions of Berkeley made it difficult to build the Cal crew beyond one four-oared team. In Corvallis, Astrid and my dad provided continuity, but the transformation of young women from spectators to competitors may have been a greater leap in Corvallis, because Oregon was so quiet, so conservative.

Corvallis did have one protest large enough for my dad to anticipate problems. Fred Milton, a star African-American football player, refused to shave his mustache and goatee at the command of Coach Dee Andros. Thousands of persons marched in protest on each side of the issue. Milton transferred to Utah State where he played football and graduated; he was later inducted into the Oregon Sports Hall of Fame.[O-92] What would my dad do if oarsmen showed up with beards?

When I visited Corvallis, my dad would invariably introduce me to his friends as his "hippie son from Berkeley", perhaps to cover his embarrassment. He prepared for beards by compiling sketches of acceptable deportment by oarsmen.

My dad certainly wouldn't have a beard problem with women rowers. Instead, he got into trouble over gender integration. He had no problem with men coxing women's intramural crews, since those races were local events: in-house competition. But for intercollegiate races, rules against mixing the genders were in place. For him, changing rules required a democratic process. He made national news by taking a strict, unbending position on whether to race a University of Oregon crew coxed by a woman.

———— *Chapter 21* ————

STANDING FIRM

At the end of 1971, my dad received a letter from Victoria Brown, first-year student at the University of Oregon. The University had initiated men's rowing as a club sport, but the school still lacked a women's team. When Ms. Brown expressed an interest in rowing, she was told that NCAA rules prohibited women from competing in men's sports. She asked her coach, Don Costello, for advice, and he suggested that she contact my dad and other West Coast coaches. She wrote, "I meet all requirements for coxswain except the most obvious and (I assume) the most important: I am a girl. Mr. Costello, however, has no objections to me being coxswain, nor does the team itself. Please, Mr. Derlich [*sic*], give me every possible consideration. I am not seeking publicity or glory for myself or for any group; I merely want to coxswain, and no girl's crew team exists at present."[D-23]

Although only 35 miles upstream (south) from Corvallis and just as wet, people at the University of Oregon had expressed little interest in rowing, perhaps because suitable water was fifteen miles away. Occasionally an ex-oarsman would show up in Eugene and try to get a club program started, but even with my dad's help not much happened until 1971.[N-8] Don Costello, a former oarsman at the University of California, restarted the program, and he decided to have Victoria Brown cox his varsity boat.[O-137]

Participants in the gender equity debate. Left: Newspaper photo of Victoria Brown,[D-27] University of Oregon varsity cox. Right: Advertising brochure photo of Karl Drlica,[D-90] Oregon State University coach and "Male chauvinist pig."

Several years earlier (1967), the Western Crew Coaches Association, in response to a similar coxswain situation with the University of California at Irvine, had voted against collegiate racing when women were mixed in the boats.[D-10,D-12,D-14] In a long letter to Ms. Brown, my dad described that decision and indicated that members of the Western Crew Coaches Association would abide by that ruling.[D-12] He then suggested additional contacts and alternatives. One was that she start a women's crew. He wrote, "… [Y]ou will probably be able to realize more success in this direction. But these are changing times—who knows?"

My dad was caught in a no-win situation. He had been encouraging women's rowing for almost two decades, both locally and nationally. In Corvallis he and Astrid had brought women's crew to a sustainable level. Their women rowers had a sense of self-sufficiency that would give them even odds in the fight he knew was coming—when Title IX was passed, and soon it would be, Oregon State University wouldn't give in easily to the women's demand for equal resources.

On the other hand, he was President of the Western Crew Coaches Association (he was also a founding member).[J-8] He needed to support the 1967 vote against mixing men and women in boats. Perhaps more important was his firm belief that rules should be changed in a democratic fashion by vote. He had spent four years in Occupied Japan fighting for this principle.[O-140]

A female coxswain was not really an issue in terms of racing. Rowing at the University of Oregon was still in the beginning stages, and University crews were unlikely to match Oregon State, regardless of who was steering the boat. In late March 1972, my dad upheld the principle of "change by vote"—he refused to allow his crews to race the University of Oregon because a female (Victoria Brown) was coxswain of their varsity boat. Public outrage followed.

A letter from a female Ph.D. student in the Zoology Department at OSU captured the sentiment, writing to my dad that his behavior was unbecoming of a person who professes to value sportsmanship. She then reiterated the popular refrain that women should not be barred from a position if they can do as good a job as a man. Her conclusion was that my dad's attitude bordered on being outdated or worse, male chauvinist.[D-17] The assertion of male chauvinism was reiterated by George Pasero, Sports Editor for the *Oregon Journal*,[D-10] and equal opportunity was pushed in a letter from a mother of three who couldn't see why a female should be banned from a male-dominated sport in which there is no physical contact.[D-24]

Some letters were a bit more caustic. One referred to a photo in a California newspaper, writing, "This picture is from Monday's *San Francisco Chronicle*. What is it with you, Coach? Don't you know Congress just passed (March 1972) an Equal Rights Amendment to the Constitution? And that your own state will soon be ratifying that amendment? Get with it, Coach. Become a leader instead of remaining a moss-back (a large sluggish fish or an extremely old-fashioned person)."[D-13]

Another writer thought that my dad's move was just to win a race. After quoting a newspaper article reporting that my dad's crew won a race against the University of Oregon, the writer questioned that conclusion. He was going to reserve judgement until the next time my dad's crew faced Vicky Brown, asking whether my dad was man enough to let a woman compete.[D-26]

The Oregon State student newspaper joined the fray with a short poem and a cartoon (*Daily Barometer* April 6, 1972; orange was an Oregon State color, green represented the University of Oregon):[D-57]

> Row, row, row.
> See the orange boat go.
> The orange boat goes fast.
> Boys are in the orange boat.
>
> Row, row, row.
> See the green boat go.
> Boys are in the green boat.
> A girl is in the green boat too.
>
> The orange boat will not play
> With the green boat.
> The green boat should not
> Have a girl in it.
> The rules say so.
>
> The rules say boys and girls do not mix.
> Coach says boys and girls do not mix.
> Coach makes the rules.
> All good boys do what Coach says.
>
> Ellen T. Drake,
> Unclassified graduate student [D-57,O-179]

Hey! They can't do that! I mean, what if they would win?!

Daily Barometer *April 6, 1972.*[O-38]

My dad replied to the letters, emphasizing that women had been rowing at Oregon State for many years and that he was one of the strongest supporters of women's crew.[D-17,D-24] In his mind, the controversy was unrelated to women's rowing, since he was actively promoting it and had been for decades.

My dad pointed out to Pasero that the issue had been resolved internally months earlier: the Oregon coach and Ms. Brown had been told that the Western Crew Coaches Association had ruled against female coxswains in male crews. As with his responses to the other critical letters, my dad reminded Pasero that a strong feature of our society is rule of law, that undermining that principle sends the wrong message to our young people (that was the establishment mantra during student confrontations in Berkeley and at Kent State).[D-10]

My dad also explained the underlying logic to Pasero. "Why, then, you ask, is it that experienced crew coaches are not eager to have females on the crew? Crew is probably one of the most psychological team sports and certainly renowned as one of the most grueling and exacting. Every member of the team must have confidence in every other member. Two team members interested in the same girl (not at all connected with crew) leads to jealousies and team problems. A man who worries about his

girlfriend while on a trip or while at practice has problems. ...
A girl on the team naturally becomes interested in one or more
of these strapping young men (Why not at this age?). But when
two [oars]men get interested in her, what happens?"[D-10]

I couldn't find a response from Pasero, but a few years later
he strongly supported an award for my dad from the Oregon
Sportswriters Association.[M-2]

The Athletic Directors at Oregon State and the University of
Oregon got involved, with Jim Barratt of OSU pointing out that
the PAC-8 Conference, of which both schools were members,
had affirmed that competition was for males only.[D-28,D-49] The
University of Oregon argued that the "rule" was simply a minute
from a coaches' meeting, not an official rule. Barratt then wrote
to the Oregon Athletic Director, challenging the University to an
exhibition race: the loser would treat the winner to a steak dinner.

Don Costello, the Oregon coach sent the official response:
"We feel that your attitude in this challenge is one of condescen-
sion and disrespect—toward Vicky and our entire team."[D-28]

Since the coaches' association had a provision for mail-in
balloting, my dad told Costello how to obtain a vote (Feb. 9,
1972;[D-14]). Costello then wrote a letter (March 3, 1972) to West
Coast crew coaches concerning Victoria Brown and the relevant
rules.[D-21] He asked whether they would race his crew.

Costello's poll of coaches shows mixed reactions.[D-15] A
response from Loyola University was that men's rowing is for
men.[D-29] In another, a strong supporter of women's rowing wrote,
"I have read your letter with great pleasure—you have done some
good research. As you know, Vicky wrote to me last summer
about this situation and I did _not_ discourage her. Unlike most
of the coaches on the Coast, I am not afraid of girls and enjoy
having them around. They are easy to coach and smell good. Our
best cox'ns are girls—more intelligent, better voice penetration,
and able to move a crew well. Also, no weight problems."[D-20] But
he finished his letter by declining to race unless all of the schools

were willing to change the rules. Dick Erickson, the University of Washington coach, wrote that his crew would not compete in such a situation.[D-16,O-137]

The University of Oregon and Victoria Brown did have several races that year.[O-137] Their view was that the NCAA had no rule against mixed competition—the issue was that simple.[O-137]

The controversy ended abruptly when Erickson, the Washington coach, used a female cox in a men's crew. Apparently, he had a change of heart. My dad felt that Erickson had undercut him, since the Washington coach didn't bother to inform anyone of his decision, much less try to reach a consensus.

In an attempt to avoid future conflict, my dad suggested to the National Association of Amateur Oarsmen that a clear ruling was required (April 1, 1972).[D-19] At about the same time (late April), a Federal judge in Michigan ruled that high schools couldn't exclude girls from boys' teams, even in contact sports such as football.[D-25] According to my dad's recollections in 2002, the eligibility rule concerning women coxing men's crews soon died a natural death,[D-18] and by 1979 a news photo showed Barbara Bosch coxing an Oregon State varsity crew.[D-11]

Barbara Bosch, coxing an OSU varsity eight, 1979.[D-11]

Although my dad was constantly seeking publicity for the rowing program, he probably backed into the female cox incident. Once it started, there was no way he would cave to pressure—he stubbornly stuck by his principles. I doubt that he enjoyed being beaten up by the press, but he had endured similar criticism in Occupied Japan. He later said that public criticism was part of the job, and he acknowledged that Victoria Brown did more to put Oregon State rowing on the map than twenty years of his publicity efforts. For example, *The Christian Science Monitor* and *Sports Illustrated* reported on the "girl cox". *Sports Illustrated*, which almost never had articles on rowing, focused its story on the "Male Chauvinist Pig."[D-27]

The public was paying attention to gender inequalities, but women's rowing struggled to be taken seriously during the 1960s and early 1970s. Despite having a national organization and championship regattas, the idea prevailed that women rowed for fun and exercise rather than to win. Even as late as 1969 a Seattle newspaper, reporting on a women's regatta, quoted a Washington oarsman as exclaiming, "You'd think they never got tired ... They all jump out of the shell smiling and giggling."[D-125]

Another issue was a national protectionist policy. In 1971 the head of Women's Physical Education at Oregon State stated the policy to her staff.[D-159] "The Division of Girls' and Women's Sports in the United States, in an attempt to keep competition good for women, recreational and educational, and not become cutthroat or winning for the sake of winning, has established the policy that all girls' and women's sports competitive teams in schools and colleges must be sponsored by the Women's Physical Education Department (not an Athletic Department). We must coach the teams, see that they are appropriately chaperoned, adequate rest between games which are correctly officiated, have had recent physical exams, etc., etc. As head of the Department of Physical Education for Women, I must sign for our teams for every tournament or match they enter, signifying that all of these conditions have been met."

This policy shows why Art Sachs had no chance for official recognition, even at the progressive University of California, Berkeley—Art's philosophy of rowing to win directly opposed the prevailing standard. Additional resources would have been needed by the school to bring Art into compliance. In Corvallis, women's rowing already had a bona fide PE advisor, Astrid Hancock. Moreover, my dad was on the PE faculty. Thus, Oregon State could, in principle, satisfy the policy requirements. However, the policy was largely ignored in Corvallis.

A few months after the Victoria Brown incident, Federal Title IX legislation was passed (June 1972). This anti-discrimination legislation was widely interpreted as a sports-equity law: any institution accepting Federal funds must provide male and female athletic teams with equal resources (equipment, travel funds, etc.). The law was taken seriously, because failure of colleges and universities to comply could mean loss of essential funding for scientific research.

Administrators at many schools lacked sufficient funds to suddenly double the size of athletic programs, especially those involving non-income-producing sports such as rowing. Moreover, Oregon State administrators didn't believe that women should or would want to compete at the varsity level, despite the efforts of Astrid and her crews. Thus, the issue was not only about money. The intensity of the administrative resistance is emphasized by legal action being required to bring the University into general compliance with Title IX. The women and my dad would not wait for court decisions in their push for varsity status.

——— *Chapter 22* ———

WOMEN GO VARSITY

P articipation in women's rowing exploded when schools began complying with Title IX.[D-66] The national regatta increased from seven teams in 1966 to 32 in 1974; colleges and universities, except for Oregon State, poured money into women's rowing. The difference among schools was striking. For example, Radcliffe's rowing budget was $42,000 compared to OSU's $1,500. At the 1974 national championship regatta, which was held in Oakland, every team except Oregon State, Washington, and Oregon brought their own racing shells.[O-164] The top three finishers brought along new fiberglass boats made especially for women (these shells were about 80 pounds lighter than the wooden boats used by OSU). Nevertheless, out of more than 30 organizations, OSU took fourth in the heavyweight eight, third place in the quad, and fifth in the wherry. In the heavyweight eight, Oregon State beat 14 other crews, including all West Coast crews.[O-164,O-166] University administrators were being forced to reconsider the concept that women didn't want to compete at the varsity level.

By 1977, the national championship regatta program listed 45 teams and 475 rowers in 24 events.[D-4a] Rowing had changed from the elitist, spectator sport of the 1930s to a participatory sport.

My dad was upset that a charter member of the National Women's Rowing Association was not seriously supported by his university. He knew that Title IX would eventually force action, since Oregon State University depended heavily on federal funds for its extensive oceanography program. He thought he could ride the Title IX wave and push administrators for more money. But he needed to push carefully, because the administration knew that one solution to the Title IX rowing problem was to eliminate both men's and women's crews.

The University response to Title IX was weak. In 1972, an eighteen-member committee was tasked with solving the problem but with little money. The committee began by creating a new department—Women's Intercollegiate Athletics (WIA)—to fund women's sports. Administrative organization charts showed the WIA being parallel to the Men's Athletic Department. Perhaps the parallel nature of the two departments on an organization chart would be seen as a good-faith effort toward gender equity— without a serious investment of funds.

By 1972, the men's heavyweight varsity crew had been sponsored by the Men's Athletic Department for several years, while the women's and the lightweight men's teams were club sports. The two clubs received a few thousand dollars each for travel from Recreational Sports, but fundraising was needed for equipment and most of the travel. PE crew, which was separate from the intercollegiate teams, paid for much of the rowing maintenance costs. Intramural rowing had been a voluntary effort by the Rowing Club with supervision by Astrid and boat maintenance by my dad. The new head of PE refused to allocate money to fix broken boats and oars; thus, my dad had halted intramural rowing five years earlier. Within this context, the underfunded WIA invited women's crew to join.

Astrid and her crew knew that money from the WIA might reduce their need for fundraising. However, they feared that joining the WIA would restrict their racing competition to colleges and universities. That would be a death sentence, because in 1972 almost all available opponents came from non-university organizations. Moreover, Astrid was concerned about the use of men's equipment by the women. No other women's sport was doing this. Her program could not survive if the women had to buy their own boats, and she knew that the WIA couldn't afford to buy new racing shells (as in earlier years, one eight-oared racing shell cost about the same as a moderately priced automobile). Astrid also realized that the program needed a paid coach, which the WIA could not afford. She tried to get a commitment from the WIA that these issues would be taken care of, but she failed. Thus, women's crew declined the invitation: the money did not outweigh potential restrictions.

Astrid probably didn't consider boathouse maintenance, since my dad took care of that. For decades the PE Department had covered routine costs, such as boat repair and rebuilding docks after floods. But Clair Langton, the long-time supporter of rowing, had been replaced in 1964 by James Long, who sought to shift physical education money away from crew.[F-1]

Long had an impressive resume. He had been a star athlete at Missouri Valley College, earning 15 varsity letters in four major sports.[O-19] He then moved to Northwestern University for a master's degree and to the University of North Carolina for a doctorate and a Master's in Public Health. He taught and coached at the high school level, served as head of physical rehabilitation at a Navy hospital, and was on the faculty of Wake Forest College. He eventually became an administrator as Director and Professor of Physical Education and Athletics at the Universities of Toledo and New Hampshire. Long seemed perfect for the Oregon State job, but not for rowing. He repeatedly claimed that rowing was straining his departmental budget, and he used that claim to argue against University support for women's rowing.[D-48, D-149]

By 1974, women's rowing on the West Coast had grown enough for the OSU team to no longer worry about finding collegiate competition. They applied to join the WIA, but Dean Long, as an external voice, pointed out that there were insufficient motorboats and coaches for each crew to be properly supervised.[D-48,D-121] Moreover, the WIA could not meet the financial requirements projected by Long; women's rowing was refused entry. Funding had to come largely from the crew members themselves. That year Oregon State was one of the top four teams in the country.

*James Long, refuting allegations that he
doesn't like the crew program.*[D-98]

Long was sharply criticized in the OSU student newspaper. In his defense he stated, "It sounds as if I am opposed to crew and am uncooperative. Actually, I am not, but the questions and problems should be worked out in advance."[O-25]

Working in advance with bureaucratic committees was not how my dad operated. He initiated grassroots efforts that then forced administrators to give in. That didn't win administrative friends. By 1974 he had been at loggerheads with Long for seven years. Their power struggle was personal, and women's crew was in the middle.

Dean Long continued to seek reimbursement for rowing from other sources. In a February 1975 letter to the Recreational Sports Program, the source of the small amount of travel money allocated to women's crew, he asked that money from women's crew be transferred to PE to cover some of his expenses.[D-43] As part of his argument he included a long list of items that my dad had submitted for maintenance support. Long claimed that most of the items were impossible for him to fund. His request was denied: Recreational Sports Program rules prohibited use of the funds for maintenance.

That year women's crew again requested admission into Women's Intercollegiate Athletics. This time the WIA Board refused to even listen to crew representatives, "... it would be to no avail."[D-42] The WIA didn't have enough money to sponsor another sport, especially one that had the high maintenance costs claimed by Long.

At about the same time, women rowers met with Dean Long and University President Robert MacVicar to press for a new locker room.[G-6] My dad had built the Stevens Crewhouse (1964) to house women's showers and dressing room, but the men's crew was using it. The women wanted access. They had been using the remnants of the Oregon Electric Depot for a decade, and the facilities for men and women were clearly unequal. That violated Title IX. MacVicar countered by threatening to shut down the entire crew program. According to a report written by my dad, the women dropped their demands.[G-6]

Oregon State University crew locker rooms. Left: Stevens crewhouse 1964. Right: Women's dressing room circa 1965. The building was salvaged from the original crew house (built 1934) and moved next to the barn. According to Astrid, the women's dressing room looked better from the outside than the inside.[D-96,D-155] Ironically, by the late 1980s the women preferred the old dressing room.

University administrators neglected to carefully study the rowing operation, which led to several missteps. One directly involved women's shower facilities. My dad wrote, "President MacVicar appointed a top-level administrative committee to solve the ... maintenance problem. ... The biggest fiasco came in the fall of 1976 when this top-drawer committee ordered the plumbers to remove the showers in the men's dressing room to lower the men's facility to the level of the women's dressing room." [D-115] But the women had showers.

The shower story was bizarre enough to gain coverage by the local Corvallis newspaper. Roy Gault wrote, "Certainly the cost of operating already existing showers is not great. The rationale for removing the showers from both the men's and the women's locker rooms escapes me. The men are willing to submit to reverse discrimination [by giving] the women the better building for the sake of having showers. Apparently, the game is a political one to stimulate student and alumni support for the crew program. In the meantime, the students have been without showers." [O-4]

The comment about a political game sounded like something my dad would say. I suspect that he inspired the article to generate alumni support. Indeed, Gault's quote from Milosh Popovich, a member of the central administration of the University, fit with getting alumni support: "I know we'll have Oregon State crew alumni from all over the nation writing to us". [O-4]

Popovich was a powerful member of the administration. He had obtained degrees in engineering from Oregon State in 1939 and 1941, followed by appointment in the Department of Mechanical Engineering in 1945. Four years later he began a rapid climb up the academic ladder, first as Chairman of the Department and soon after as Assistant Dean. By 1959, he had been appointed Dean of Administration, a title later changed to Vice-President. [O-177] My dad mentioned to me, proudly, that in the early 1960s he forced money out of Popovich for the piling that held the Navy barges. I doubt that Popovich was a supporter of crew.

*Newspaper photo of Coach Drlica standing
where the showers used to be.*[O-20]

On November 4 the student newspaper reported that the showers were being turned back on.[F-7a]

Gault also revealed the administrative attitude regarding budgets in a quote from Popovitch: "I'm afraid ... that it (crew) is going to have to get used to operating on a shoestring budget."

In my opinion, fifty years on a shoestring was long enough to get used to it. As far as I could determine, no administrator other than Langton, who was no longer in charge, visited the crew facilities to accurately assess the issues until after the shower episode.[F-7a]

When the student newspaper asked whether anyone contacted Affirmative Action concerning the original decision to remove the showers, it was told by James Long, "We don't check anything like that in advance. ... We wouldn't want to encourage a discrimination case."[F-7a]

Anticipating future outcomes was not a characteristic of OSU administrators, at least for their rowing program.

During the previous season, 1975, the women's crew was strong, winning the Northwest Regional Regatta in the open eight, open coxed four, and open pair without cox. The program was gaining increasing national respect, but more importantly, the rowing bug had bitten Judy Kitzman.

Judy Kitzman, 1975, repairing an oar.[D-111]

Judy first rowed in a PE class in the spring of 1973; in 1974 she joined the competitive team. That year, she was a member of the eight-oared crew that placed fourth at the Nationals; by 1975 she rowed wherever she was needed: varsity eight, senior eight, row-a-thon to Salem, lightweight eight, and pair-oar.[D-46a] During 1976 and 1977 she was the student coach (fund-raising efforts provided financial support for her in 1977). She was exceptionally serious about coaching, later saying that she performed "… a lot of research into coaching, rowing technique, rigging, etc., plus attending coaching clinics."[D-46a]

Judy fought for her team. In a memo to my dad regarding poor coverage of women's crew by a Beaver Crew Association (BCA) newsletter, she wrote, "Why is it, then, that 90% (at least) of this last BCA newsletter was concerned with MEN'S VARSITY CREW? … The main purpose of the newsletter was to promote the upcoming jog-a-thon … and the letter implied all monies received … would go for a new (varsity) shell. It did not mention that the lightweights and women were participating, with the agreement that their pledges would go to support their respective programs (Judy wanted to be sure that money from supporters of women's and lightweight crews wouldn't go to the heavyweight varsity program) ... I wonder how many alums realize that the women purchased 10 new oars last year through earned money projects; that they had to raise $2,650 by working at registration, schedule distribution, wrestling tournaments, phone book distribution, soliciting row-a-thon pledges, etc., just to support our basic program ... that Rec Sports crews (women's and lightweight teams receiving money from Recreational Sports Program) were kicked out of the crew facilities ... that the women finally have some rowers who have come to OSU from other crews ..."[D-89]

Site for weight training. The Beach barn housed ergometers, muscle-building equipment, and a classroom.[D-95] Canoes and other boats were stored in the basement.

In another memo she complained, "Of our two [weight-training] circuits attempted, both have been interrupted by the men coming in and moving the weights, taking over equipment, and starting their own circuit, which creates so much noise that the women cannot hear the timer. The men further interrupt a set, timed circuit by showing off and making distracting comments. How are the women supposed to take this seriously when no one else takes them seriously?"[D-87]

The women were fighting two battles, one against the University administration and one to gain respect from the men's team. A decade was not enough time for cultural biases to change; Judy was determined to accelerate the change.

"It would be appreciated by the oarswomen if they were referred to by the head crew coach as women, not girls. It's ironic that we are a group of men and girls. Let's be fair. If you insist on calling them 'girls', you may wish to call the men 'boys'. I am getting to be more and more of a feminist as time goes on, thanks to sexist 'jokes' and being treated as an idiot because I belong (and proudly) to the female sex! (I can imagine the snicker as you read over this ... take me seriously please.) As a passing note: one reason I have never bothered to socialize with the men while at the docks is that I have been appalled all too often by the physical abuse the women receive as <u>serious</u> athletes."[D-68]

In the same memo Judy wrote, "... I heard no plans by [Coach] Hutchinson as to what the women are to do at Dads' Weekend events other than just be there and look cute. We would like to know before the date arrives. Will we be rowing or pouring coffee and serving donuts?"

At the time, all crews were practicing in the afternoon. Judy thought that shifting her practices to mornings would solve many of the logistical problems. She wrote, "I know that you want to keep all working together, but I think this [separation] would help more than hurt our 'group continuity'."[D-68]

Then the men's crews decided that they wanted to row in the mornings.

My dad was concerned about group unity. He thought that having the men and women in a structurally integrated program was the best way to educate the men—they would see how hard the women were working. Moreover, a unified program would allow rowing to speak to the University with a stronger voice.

The women rejected his approach. They wanted to move forward on their own; they repeatedly boycotted informational group meetings. This resistance to team unity annoyed my dad, and it required extra work from him when he was fully engaged in battles with the administration.

Judy recognized that gaining power meant taking responsibility. With respect to practicing in the morning, she wrote, "I would be responsible to see that everything is in order for the afternoon practices, i.e., facilities locked up, boats in order, etc. There would be no safety problems because I have always been very careful about adequate supervision and intend to be just as responsible regarding safety in the morning."[D-87]

She diplomatically finished the memo by saying that her classes would soon be over and she would begin working on the next regatta. Being responsible was important to my dad, since the men's coaches didn't always do their part. The women began practicing in the mornings.

Meanwhile, the women continued to apply pressure to University administrators for official recognition and financial support. Four women spearheaded the effort, with Judy as the official conduit.[D-47a,D-82] They prepared comparisons between the men's and women's rowing programs to leverage Title IX into action.[D-85] The committee also produced a broader comparison of Men's Intercollegiate Athletics with the underfunded women's programs. The data spoke, although not with the hoped effect: University administrators repeatedly threatened to eliminate all intercollegiate rowing.

How hard should the women push? Relationships are the key, and the other side couldn't be treated as the enemy. The women rowers needed my dad on their side, at least to maintain what they already had.[D47a] Also, having an older-generation advocate was important for advancing with older-generation, mostly male, decision makers.

My dad kept no personal notes on struggles over women's crew, and he didn't share his thoughts. When I visited him during the 1970s, he mentioned only that he was having problems with his boss in the PE Department (James Long). His almost constant conflict with Long and other administrators is well documented through memos and newspaper accounts, but he may have stepped into the women's situation only at crucial junctures.

Although my dad opposed having a woman on a men's team until the rules were changed, it is likely that he never wavered from seeking varsity status for women's crew. However, he wanted a unified program,[F-16] and the women wanted to be separate. This ideological difference may be why one woman rower recalled that my dad seemed gruff, to only tolerate the women's program.[D-47a] Moreover, during difficult negotiations he probably wore several hats. It's unlikely that there was a serious breach, since Judy would not write, "I will not tell you what I have been doing regarding Rec Sports crew programs, because I have a gut feeling it will not be to our advantage."[D-67] If she were really being secretive, she wouldn't reveal that she was. I think she wanted a two-pronged approach from independent perspectives, or perhaps she was protecting my dad's job in case her attack was more than administrators could bear.

In 1976, Astrid was still the official advisor for women's crew, and in January she again requested that women's rowing enter Women's Intercollegiate Athletics.[D-38] She reiterated that even after repeated attempts she'd been unable to get a decision from the WIA regarding restrictions on competition. In the meantime, the University of Washington women's crew had been accepted by their athletic department while still maintaining an association with the National Women's Rowing Association and noncollegiate teams. Thus, much of the anxiety regarding potential restrictions on racing had dissipated. But Judy's team needed a salaried coach to keep pace with the competition, and that was not allowed with money from the Recreational Sports Program. The crew looked to the WIA for coaching money. Astrid's request was again denied due to lack of funds.[D-41]

Among the issues behind the rejection was the fear, raised year after year by Dean Long, that sponsorship of women's crew would financially break Women's Intercollegiate Athletics. For example, he rightly emphasized that the temporary locker room, which had been used for more than a decade, would not withstand Title IX scrutiny. But his assertion that the WIA would have to cover the cost of a new locker room had no merit. The crews handled the problem, initially by the men and women alternating buildings. This was the type of problem solving my dad liked to see among crew members. In the 1990s, the women actually preferred the old locker room once it was painted—it was warmer, and by staying in the old locker room they got a new eight-oared shell from money raised by the men.[F-9a]

The situation at Oregon State was not unique. Across the country women rowers were struggling with their male counterparts for recognition and with university administrators for full enforcement of Title IX. Some went to extreme lengths to get their voices heard. A notable example occurred at Yale where women were denied shower facilities. The women rowers wrote "Title IX" on their bodies with marking pens, stripped to reveal the markings, and appeared naked before administrators and newspaper reporters.[F-3] They got their showers.

Although the Yale incident was widely publicized (*New York Times*, March 4, 1976), the strength of the women's movement was not appreciated by upper management at Oregon State, as the University created a rowing crisis later that spring. The Recreational Sports Program repeated that their travel funds could not be used for coaching, facilities, maintenance, or related costs. Dean James Long reiterated that crew maintenance was very costly, even without building a new locker room. According to him, the women's crew would require a budget of $9,800 (the actual budget for 1976 was $1,900 from Recreational Sports; by including money earned by the women, the women's crew had a surplus that year). Among Long's superfluous budget items were costs for a tractor to mow weeds along the river bank.[D-84]

Long would not allow the PE Department to cover his projected maintenance costs, and Recreational Sports was not allowed to. Competitive rowing appeared to be unsustainable, at least for women and lightweight men, the two teams receiving funds from Recreational Sports (at the time, the heavyweight varsity was sponsored by the Men's Athletic Department). Don

Sanderson, the head of the Physical Recreation Board, which governed Recreational Sports, decided to eliminate rowing for women and lightweight men. There was no point in throwing money into doomed programs.

Sanderson sent letters to my dad and Judy (June 1, 1976) stating that the two rowing programs should prepare to vacate the Stevens Crewhouse and dock area by the end of the month.[D-120] Moreover, the equipment owned by the two crews would be moved to storage under the football stadium, three miles from the river.

Judy and her crew must have been furious.

On June 11, Judy informed Pearl Gray, Director of Affirmative Action, that Sanderson had based his decision on Long's vastly inflated cost estimates. For example, Recreational Sports was not allowed to pay coaching salaries, yet, according to Judy, Dean Long had included part of my dad's salary in his budget estimate. Moreover, the effort of Clay Poole, who helped with boat maintenance, was estimated by Long to cost more than $1,000. Judy pointed out that in the previous year it was $74 (the women owned only one shell at the time, and it was so new it required no maintenance). And women's crew was to be charged for a portion of my dad's office, which was not used by women's crew.[D-73]

That same day Judy sent a letter to student members of the Physical Recreation Board, Sanderson, and other University officials.[D-74,D-69] As a result of the budget estimate submitted by Long, Sanderson would be moving the oars and racing shells, purchased by the women, not the University, miles from the river. Even if the women could build another float and find a place for it on the river, they'd need to truck their shells to the river every day. She called for an evaluation of Long's budget estimate.

The only rapid solution was to get Long to recant. On June 14 Judy asked him to re-examine his numbers: "It is my assertion that the crew facilities' maintenance and related costs report is inaccurate. As the women's coach, I am aware of the actual costs. ... And they are far below what would be our share of the costs ... cited in your report."[D-119] She then told Long that he needed to tell Sanderson what the actual and realistic costs and expenditures were for her crew.

At that point my dad came out of the background. His June 17, 1976 letter suggested that Long had been careless in his efforts to terminate crew:[D-84]

"... Your figure of an average yearly cost of $1,932 for services and supplies is a figure with which I cannot agree for several reasons. You yourself have said that it is impossible to give me an accurate accounting of the costs because you have 56 sports to account for and cannot separate them, but you can somehow single out crew. ... Although I have requested a detailed accounting for charges against crew, these have never been supplied. Consequently, I do not know about hidden charges, but my accounting of expenditures, which I have made for facilities upkeep and PE crew, as well as some expenditures for canoeing, appear to approximate the following ... yearly, last 5 years ... average expenditure for 5 years—$512.69 (not $1,932).

"... It should be made clear that much of the equipment that you list is primarily for use in the maintenance of the golf program. Equipment such as tractor, mowers, trucks, trailer, and many other groundskeeper tools represent capital investment that would not be necessary for the crew area simply because it would be cheaper to hire the equipment and labor for the three or four times a year that such work is necessary.

"... MIA (Men's Intercollegiate Athletics) equipment is being used for the PE program as well as for Rec Sports. The 'What's yours is mine and what's mine is my own' attitude and the increasing shortage of MIA funds is causing some serious rifts in the rowing program.

"... $25,000 for the renovation of the Stevens Crewhouse probably will be necessary eventually to comply with Title IX,

... but such a renovation is not necessary for the continuance of the rowing program next year.

"... $6,250 for ventilated lockers will not be needed until the building is renovated, and this is not likely to take place soon or at all. Certainly, these lockers are not needed to continue the rowing program next year.

"... Barge roofs and other routine repairs that are preventative maintenance are just good common sense and cheaper in the long run, but they are not essential to the continuance of the rowing program next year. The barges need painting, but the powers that be thought it was more important to pave a road than to paint the barges when painting money was available.

"... $6,000 additional money needed to complete a building that would replace two former buildings is desirable, but not necessary to continue the program. There has been no motorboat boathouse for five years, and we have improvised by mooring boats under ramps ... pumping of the training barge during the past winter indicates that we could get along without this [barge house] too, if it is a factor in discontinuing the program.

"... [crew] has ... requested for purchase over a three-year period ... replacement of oars and shells. These are items that are needed for the operation of the PE program and not for the team programs (the teams purchase their own equipment from fund-raising efforts)."

Dean Long would not back down. Rather than justify or correct his budget, he responded to Judy (June 25) by pointing out that he had omitted a number of expenses, such as electricity and custodial services; thus, reviewing his budget would make it even higher. Moreover, his own program of PE classes and intramural sports was so extensive that it "will not allow us to give anything but minimal support to the Willamette River programs (canoeing and crew)."[D-76] I imagine that Long's letter was like pouring gasoline on a fire.

Vanessa Rennewitz, President of the Women's Rowing Club,

kept up the pressure with a letter to OSU President MacVicar copied to state legislators (July 6).[D-77] She reiterated the essence of Sanderson's decision and emphasized that crew members raise much of the funds for the program, that the crews are nationally competitive, and that the student athletes are committed to continuing the program. She then asked that funds be found for maintenance, for what administrators would call overhead. I imagine that she wanted to show the older generation that these students, women no less, were willing to work just as hard, if not harder, than the legislators themselves had when they were young.

My dad then tried to turn the conflict around in a July 24 memo to Sanderson, who was directly responsible for the expulsion of crews from the boathouse, and to Charlotte Lambert, Chair of the PE Department (subordinate to James Long).[D-78] My dad proposed that equipment purchased by the crew teams through outside fund-raising efforts be rented to PE for class crews. That would replace the long-standing policy in which the PE Department used these boats for free. The rental fees could be used to cover overhead. There was no response, and the crisis dragged through the summer.

In an October letter written to the women's crew, Judy summarized the situation:[D-32a] "Having no other immediate choice, we complied [with Sanderson] and moved our 2-year-old sectional eight (*Drlica*), *the Heather*, and our 28 sweep oars. ... Needless to say, we worked continuously throughout the summer trying to resolve our predicament. Many letters were written to rally support. On the Corvallis home front, I exhausted every avenue I could think of, or had been advised to check out. To make a very long story short, it was a most frustrating summer for Women's Crew. It was as if the rug were being pulled out from under us ... not a good feeling after all the long hours of practice and sincere, dedicated efforts you and all the others connected with Women's Crew at OSU have so thanklessly given!

"Until a few days before school started, I didn't know exactly what we were going to do as far as practicing as a team! We were not to store our equipment at the docks nor were we to use the facilities to row out of. Well, thank goodness, we finally saw some action from the University administration."

The administration had formed a new committee to study the Willamette Riverfront Area. The committee needed until the following June to come to a final decision. Until that time, the crews were allowed to move their equipment back and row as usual.

Judy and my dad saw Long's behavior as personal; the "errors" were deliberate misstatements. Student perspective was summarized several years later (1984) in a report based on interviews: "Some would say, with hindsight, that, by listing charges for PE activities and classes as part of the Women's and Men's Lightweight Crew budget, the Physical Education Department would be defraying its costs…" [D-3a]

Judy's campaign[D-80] produced many letters supporting OSU women's rowing. These outside voices pushed a consistent, three-part message to the OSU administration. The women had proved themselves to be one of the top crews in regional and national competition; of all the collegiate institutions in the country that sponsor competitive women's rowing, OSU had been active the longest; and the OSU rowers were willing to work to keep crew alive.[D-83]

The women's crew negotiators (Judy, Sue Jack, Joan Foster, and Sue Taylor) applied again for admission to Women's Intercollegiate Athletics. Among the accomplishments they listed were a second-place finish in the pair-oared category (1975) and placing a member in tryouts for the national team (Kate Gribskov attended the national training camp in the summer of 1975; she made the first cut but not the second). [D-85,D-134] The 25-page packet included listings of other colleges with rowing programs, budgets, and equipment inventories. Moreover, the group made it clear that rowing was head-and-shoulders above other OSU women's "recreational activities" and merited substantial support.

The WIA was not a serious vehicle for satisfying Title IX: it was unable to meet the financial needs of its existing programs, even without considering women's crew. For example, it had to eliminate support for the field hockey team,[D-135] possibly the group with the largest budget, and the WIA considered cutting swimming.[D-81] The field hockey team was visibly upset, as it had been in existence since 1938 and had been the first team to compete off campus. Women's Athletic Director Sylvia Moore felt that the hockey team had been done a disservice,[D-135] but the funds were gone.

Several months later (spring 1977), the WIA mysteriously accepted women's crew.[D-81] Did the Riverfront Committee examine Dean Long's budgets? Had women's crew made it obvious that the University never intended to comply fully with Title IX? Could alumni support have swayed the administration? The field hockey team was understandably outraged over the acceptance of rowing. But it lacked Title IX leverage, because no men's field hockey program existed.

After several more months, the women's and the men's lightweight crews suddenly entered Men's Intercollegiate Athletics. Varsity status had been won, with rowing becoming the first women's sport to be supported by the Men's Athletic Department.

My dad had achieved a goal he had proposed two years earlier: a joint program.[F-16] The idea worked because University administrators saw that they could shift the rowing part of their Title IX problem to my dad. With a single budget for the waterfront program, my dad would have to assure that the women were afforded equal treatment. Let him split the same budget into more parts; let him deal with the women rowers.

In retrospect, gaining varsity status required winning races, years of pressure from the women, and careful bookkeeping by my dad to refute Dean Long's inflated budgets. Title IX prevented administrators from ignoring Judy Kitzman and her team. Decades later, a crowdfunding campaign gathered enough money for the women's crew to purchase a new eight-oared racing shell that was christened the *Judy Kitzman.*[D-62] Astrid recalled, "... Before she passed away in 2017 at age 65, Judy saw her boat compete at the PAC-12 regatta in Sacramento. Judy was our hero."[D-4a]

My dad was happy to have a single rowing budget, since that brought all of the teams together for what he wanted to teach: fending for yourself. Of course, the heavyweight men were not pleased about sharing resources, especially since many didn't consider their women colleagues to be serious athletes. Women's rowing had become an Olympic sport, but that was not felt locally. The Oregon State women needed to win some big races to gain respect.

---------- *Chapter 23* ----------

RALPH

S oon after women's crew joined the Men's Athletic Department, Judy Kitzman entered graduate school at the University of Oregon. The vacancy she left was difficult to fill, in part because the job didn't pay enough to attract a person to Oregon State. My dad usually had to obtain assistant coaches from among persons who, for other reasons, were already in Corvallis.

Although Judy had moved to Eugene, she was keeping track of her Corvallis crew. She became angry when friends mentioned that the Men's Athletic Department wasn't providing enough support for the team. The women were rowing without a regular coach. She hadn't spent four years building a crew to have administrators let it fail. She sent an impassioned letter to OSU President MacVicar (November, 1977)[D-86] and a call to the college newspaper for a women's coach.[D-137] At the end of her hand-written letter she wrote, "I'm on the verge of giving up full-time grad studies at the UO to return to OSU to coach. I am _very_ concerned."

Although the turmoil was brief, the women were concerned: no coach had been assigned to the team. The void was being filled by experienced male rowers who had recently graduated, but the women were feeling discouraged—until Ralph showed up. The women were sitting on the ramp to a barge when Ralph Mathison skipped down the ramp from the riverbank, exclaiming, "Hi, I'm Feather J. Blueberry! I'm your new coach!'"[D-126]

Coach Ralph Mathison, 1975.[D-112]

Ralph was what my dad would have called a hippie: long beard, tinted glasses, and a headband. Otherwise, he looked like a typical heavyweight oarsman, tall and muscular. Ralph had been my dad's assistant several years earlier when he established himself as an outstanding coach. Ralph could move women's crew to a higher level, and perhaps my dad could influence Ralph's appearance.

Ralph began rowing in Corvallis as an undergraduate in the late 1960s and was a member of the first Oregon State crew to compete at the Intercollegiate Rowing Championship Regatta in Syracuse, New York. Although the crew did not win, Ralph was bitten by the rowing bug.

Ralph's son provided background in an interview with Erik Dresser in *row2k*.[D-124] "My father Ralph ... graduated from OSU [in 1971], the first in his family to graduate from college. In the spring of 1971, he took the bus and hitchhiked from Oregon to Rochester, NY and slept on the doorstep of then national team coach Allen Rosenberg. When Rosenberg left the next morning, my father stood up and said, 'I came here from Oregon. I want to row for you.' And he did."

Under Rosenberg, Ralph rowed in the senior eight that won the men's national championship in New York City. "Ralph went on back to Oregon to coach at Oregon State ... sending old 'Super 8' tapes of his oarsmen to Coach Rosenberg for advice. Coach Rosenberg would review the tapes and then call or write to Ralph with his advice."

As recalled by Kirk Hutchinson,[O-90,O-113] "Ralph coached the lightweight men in 1972 and 1973. He did a great job! After the '73 season, Ralph worked a bunch of odd jobs and traveled to Australia. He returned in '75, working with Kate Gribskov and Jan Brown, who placed second in the open pair at the national championships.

"In '76 the lightweight men didn't have a real coach, and from the Monday after the Corvallis Regatta he coached the lightweight men's team, which I was on, through the Western Sprints. He slept on the couch at our apartment during this time."

According to Kirk, Ralph was a student of rowing and a brilliant coach; he knew how to advance the style of stroke taught by my dad to a championship level. Indeed, he had rowed on a national championship crew and been an assistant coach for the national team.[O-152] Moreover, Ralph was consumed with finding ways to make racing shells go fast. In addition to training rowers, he would modify oarlock location to maximize the power applied by each rower. That meant late nights at the boathouse working on the boats (one night he was spotted at three in the morning[D-153]).

Since neither Ralph nor Kirk had much money, they looked for earning opportunities. One was construction of a logging road in the mountains. Another was an excursion to Eastern Oregon where they entered the wild-horse-riding event at the Pendleton Roundup, a major cowboy rodeo. When Ralph got bucked off, he stayed down, lying in the dirt. The rodeo announcer noted, "It looks like we have a dead hippie out there,"[O-152] and an ambulance was called to take him to the local hospital. Ralph soon recovered, and in the fall of 1977 my dad hired him to coach the women's crews. Although my dad respected Ralph, the two didn't always agree. The main dis-agreement concerned Ralph's appearance.[D-116] My dad thought that Ralph should be more presentable, more in line with my dad's conservative standards.

My dad wrote, "I told him that, as a member of the academic staff, he should be cleaned up when he was on the campus and [when] representing the University on trips. He said that we were not paying him enough and that the A.D. (Athletic Director) should furnish some clothing. ... Somewhere in the conversation I said that he looked pretty grubby when he came to the Athletic Department. He said he wasn't going to change clothes just to come here when he was coming off a job where he was working on a house." My dad was dispensing unsolicited advice that failed to work on his own son. Although my dad didn't write about his motivation for commenting on Ralph's appearance, I believe he thought Ralph had a bright future as a coach if he looked the part.

Hippies according to Coach Drlica. Left: Newspaper photo of Ralph at an old-timers race, 1976.[D-147] Right: The author at an academic job in 1977.[D-117]

The assistant coaches never earned much from their coaching stipend and usually had to have side jobs (even as head coach, my dad had to work one summer for a building contractor to make ends meet). I imagine that Ralph may have been using his side-job appearance to emphasize the need for more pay, since that's what I'd have done.

Ralph and my dad also disagreed about molding the rowing program into one big team. Ralph wanted his crew to be separate, to develop its own *esprit de corps*. As in previous years, the women boycotted joint meetings.

By the fall of 1979 Ralph sensed that he could put together a fast team if he had some help. He talked Kirk into assisting, providing financial help from his personal funds. Kirk coached the lightweight women, giving local competition to Ralph's heavyweights.[O-152]

According to rowing standards, half of Ralph's women's crew was short (5 feet 6 inches and below) and light (under 140 lbs).[D-150] He knew that his small crew couldn't go stroke-for-stroke against heavier competition: under the usual racing conditions, the extra power of the opponents would carry their boats farther between strokes. But he believed that a 1000-meter race, the Olympic distance for women, was short enough to sprint the whole way. His philosophy was to apply full pressure at a very high stroke rate. That required convincing his crew that they could endure pain for 1000 meters. Get in front and stay there. Being ahead would help with the pain.

Ralph pushed his crews to get strong enough for this long sprint.[O-152] For example, he enforced eight-mile runs, which was unusual at the time (he gave up on twenty-six mile runs when he realized that they were unproductive). In practice, the women would row many 500-meter pieces at a high stroke rate and often against each other in four-oared shells. By mixing the lineups, Ralph could determine which rowers made the boat move fastest.

Racing starts were stressed. As in any sprint, getting a fast start is important. During the three-command start, the women would have their oars in the water, ready to pull. At the second part of the command, they would begin a gentle pull that didn't immediately move the boat. But it gave them an edge when the gun fired.[O-152] Ralph wanted to get in front quickly.

The women were confident that Ralph would produce a fast boat. One woman recalled, "Ralph was a ridiculously eccentric person. ... We loved him dearly, but [he was] a free thinker. And I think he's really the [only] person who could take a motley crew like that ... and say, 'OK, we'll try for this [national championship]'."[O-79] Moreover, the women may have wanted to prove that they deserved varsity status: they were the only female team in the Men's Athletic Department.

1978 lightweight four. Left to right: Becky Stephenson, Juanita Heiman, Sally Goodwin, Kate Engel, and cox Lettie Richardson.[D-142]>

Early success in the 1980 season led to talk of competing at the National Championships in Oak Ridge, Tennessee. Since the travel budget didn't include funds for the Nationals, additional money had to be found. As a sign of acceptance, the Men's Athletic Department agreed to pay for travel if the women's crew placed first or second in the PAC-10 regatta. They finished second to a big, strong Cal crew.[O-79]

That year national champions were determined for three classes: college, senior, and elite (members of the national team had to race in the elite category; college teams could race in all three). Cal won the collegiate championship; Oregon State won the other two.

The blog interview with Ralph's son (quoted above) had two appended comments that summarize the Oak Ridge races.[D-124] In one, John Davis reported: "In 1980, a lot of the women's races were 1000 m. Ralph's crew rowed so high (43-44 SPM) and so hard that they went out to massive leads on the opposition and clung on for dear life. Ralph had it all planned out. He didn't have that much raw talent, and several were lightweights up against powerful Cal and Wisco crews, but they were crazy tenacious.

"The [Women's] Collegiate Nationals finals were on [Thursday]. A great Cal crew won the Varsity eight, taking down OSU, which [at one point] led by at least a length of open water. But on Sunday, at the NWRA, with the college crews hanging around, OSU managed to take an even bigger lead and hung on to win. Considering the short distance and the fact that one could see the whole thing unfold, it was really something to watch OSU go out to these massive leads while the pack struggled to catch up."

Another commenter, identified as OSU80, wrote, "Yes indeed! Oak Ridge made a postcard of the start of the 1980 women's eight-oared championship race, about four strokes in, OSU had nearly 3/4 of a length and just kept building. Crazy high and crazy fast. And they hung on!"

Ralph gave his own version in a newspaper article.[D-128] He was clearly pleased with the identical crew winning the senior eight (not restricted to colleges) and elite eight. Ralph said that doing the difficult is easy; it's the impossible that requires our best. He felt that their wins were an incredible accomplishment, especially since the two races were only 1½ hours apart and the day was hot.

1980 National Champs. Left image, left to right: Holly Godard, Lise Hubbe, Judy Davidson, Carol Deeming, Connie Johnston, Nancy Tuttle, Becky Stephenson, Ann Hinman, Lynn Nishida. Right image: Ann Hinman, Lynn Nishida (cox).[D-118]

Ralph, about to be thrown into the lake by his crew, Nationals, 1980. (left to right): unidentified, Ann Hinman (facing), Bene Schlueniger, Ralph Mathison, Judy Davidson, Sue Honcharski, and Cheryl Griffin.[D-118]

Ralph entered the elite eight event to get another shot at Cal, which had won the collegiate finals a few days before in a disputed race. Cal won by about five feet, but Ralph thought that an improper finish line had cost his crew fourteen feet. The officials did not overturn the result.[O-79] In the rematch, Cal came in third.

Ralph was also pleased with the overall team score: Oregon State (76.5 points) placed second to Pioneer Valley Rowing Association (78.5 points), a composite of several colleges from Hadley, Massachusetts. This was a tribute to Oregon State, since members of its numerically small team rowed in multiple events.[D-39]

Ralph used his national championships to lobby for more equality between men's and women's crews, especially regarding equal pay for coaches. Although Title IX had been in effect for almost a decade, for a man to espouse equal pay for executives was a radical idea. In his letter of resignation (July 1980), we see that he also espoused some of the same philosophy that characterized work done by Stevens and my dad. Ralph wrote, "I would not have coached for the meager salary I received if I did not believe that I had a positive influence on the athletes I have worked with and that they are better people because of their rowing experience."[D- 160]

Women's rowing had become institutionalized, but Oregon State University continued to resist full compliance with Title IX. In January 1980, an administrative complaint (similar to a lawsuit) was filed by several students. The University responded, and in April the parties began negotiating a settlement. In July they agreed to a five-year development plan to attain gender equity in intercollegiate athletics.[D-158]

For the University to be forced into compliance with Title IX illustrates the intense resistance faced by Astrid Hancock, Judy Kitzman, and my dad. It's ironic that University resistance was so strong against a pioneer in intercollegiate women's rowing— Oregon State led the way, not Washington, Cal, or Harvard. Mills College had an early crew, but it often rowed as Lake Merritt Rowing Club. The University of California crew of Art Sachs, which came two years after Oregon State, was never allowed to use the words "University of" and was lost to history until remembered fifty years later by the Cal Women's Crew History Project.

Ralph Mathison's pair of same-day national championships put pride in the women's rowing program—the men began to take their women colleagues seriously, and they stopped begrudging the women a share of the rowing budget. In 2020 Ralph Mathison and his 1980 crew were inducted into Oregon State Sports Hall of Fame (Ralph was honored posthumously, as he passed away in 1997 at age 48). He had made it clear that women in Corvallis were rowing to win.

Throughout the 1970s, as women were gaining varsity status, my dad fought to preserve the overall rowing program against active administrative opposition. To describe these struggles, the narrative jumps back from 1980 to the late 1960s.

---- *Chapter 24* ----

STRUGGLES

A
fter winning a four-oared national championship, my dad mentioned to me, "I guess I can retire now." But he wasn't serious—Oregon State rowing was in a survival struggle with University administrators, and my dad needed to keep fighting.

The crew lost its patron when Clair Langton left the PE Department in 1964. He was replaced by James Long. For my dad, the shift from Langton to Long was striking. At the beginning of each year, Langton had provided a budget for the rowing coaches to manage. If the budget were inadequate, which it always was, the crew would make up the difference by scrounging and volunteerism. In contrast, my dad thought that Long needed to control everything, he "… kept track of paperclips and rubber bands and was afraid to let anyone have any freedom."[F-2]

Long made it clear that he was redistributing funds in the PE Department, with the waterfront program having low priority.[D-76,F-1] Within two years, Long's budget cuts made it almost impossible for my dad to keep enough boats on the water for all the programs he was running. He decided to cut the very popular women's intramural rowing program.[J-23] Perhaps Long would restore some of the crew budget when he realized how serious the situation was. My dad understood that the intramural program was an important source of new recruits for the women's team, but it was the one aspect of rowing that Long might care about.

Long responded by ordering my dad to keep the intramurals running but without more money.[F-2] My dad refused: he was not bluffing. He would not ask varsity oarsmen to run a volunteer program that was eating up resources needed for them.

Money was not the only factor, as Long had been treating my dad like "just another PE instructor", not as someone who had built and run a large, nationally recognized PE and varsity program.[F-5] Disrespecting my dad was not the way to increase his volunteerism.

At the same time (1967), the heavyweight varsity crew, as the premier rowing category, entered the Athletic Department. Within a year, Long sought to get part of my dad's salary and rent for the rowing facilities from the Athletic Department. That seemed reasonable to my dad, but negotiations were difficult, because Long had created an adversarial situation. One of his ploys was a failed attempt to get University President MacVicar to stop giving athletes PE credit for participating in intercollegiate sports.[O-6a] Then he challenged the practice of Athletic Department coaches receiving PE teaching credit.[F-32] My dad was not the only one struggling with James Long.

Long also attempted to recover crew maintenance costs from the lightweight rowing program, just as he had tried with women's crew. Neither the lightweight nor the women's crew had been brought into the Athletic Department at the time (early 1970s), but they did receive a small travel allowance from Recreational Sports. Long failed again to overturn rules that prohibited spending on maintenance.

Passage of Title IX exacerbated the financial problems. In 1974, PAC-8 officials worked to divert more funds to women's sports. They sent a confidential memo to athletic directors advising them to save money by shifting maintenance expenses to other parts of universities, such as physical education departments.[F-45] That gave the Athletic Department a mandate to resist Long's efforts to transfer his rowing expenses.

The PAC-8 advisory also recommended eliminating spring break travel and travel to California. Both were central to the rowing program, as competition would otherwise be limited to Washington. My dad would have to work around these travel restrictions by fundraising efforts. That would cause the rowers to grumble: they wanted to spend more time on training. Somebody else should keep the program going for them.

As the threats to the rowing program mounted, my dad decided, in the fall of 1974, to take a year of sabbatical leave in Mississippi where he would work on a doctoral degree. He'd been trying for years to get promoted to full professor, and he thought that the advanced degree would help. His earlier degree efforts had been blocked by failure to master the German language. By 1974, the language requirement had been abandoned, so it was time to try again, even though his boss was unlikely to support promotion. In deciding to take leave, my dad probably felt that women's crew had become self-sustaining, and he was confident that Fred Mann, a championship rower at Washington, would be an effective interim coach in Corvallis. But sabbatical leave meant that my dad had to handle conflicts with James Long from a distance.

In September 1974, as my dad was leaving, Long made what seemed to be a reasonable request: please list items that need attention at the crew facility. My dad naively thought that something might get done, so he prepared a comprehensive list. Leaking roofs were the main issue, and he wrote, "Since the Physical Plant painted the roof on the Quonset hut, it has really leaked. The sand blasting blew all of the solder out of the nail holes. I personally soldered these up when we built the hut, so I know it did not leak. But the PP (Physical Plant) will deny this."[F-38]

There is no doubt that my dad did the soldering himself, as I have a clear image of him on the curved roof of the Quonset hut, wearing a white tee-shirt and baggy coveralls, on his knees and elbows, plying a soldering iron in his right hand and a roll of solder in his left as he meticulously soldered the hundreds of nails I had helped pound in.

In late November, Long sent a memo to OSU President MacVicar that began, "The problems associated with the Willamette River Complex are numerous and fraught with danger. One of the most serious is the constantly increasing costs. For example, restoration costs alone since January 1972 have totaled $23,989. Every flood brings on additional losses. It is my belief that funds for capital outlay and maintenance costs have been most inadequate.

"Much of the actual labor and capital outlay have been furnished by Karl Drlica and past crew members through a great deal of dedicated efforts. They have gone far beyond regular hours and expenditure of energy. These efforts and dedicated hours of labor are no longer to be expected. The school's maintenance staff and student labor do not have the time nor resources for meeting many of the needs. The Women's Varsity Sports and lightweight (Men's Junior Varsity) have moved on the scene requesting the use of more boats, more oars, more maintenance, and other necessities. In turn, more pressure is brought to bear for equipment, and maintenance problems are compounded and the vicious circle continues."[F-37]

OSU President Robert W. MacVicar, ca. 1970.[O-21a]

While MacVicar probably failed to notice Long's inaccuracies (lightweight was not junior varsity), they were a constant feature of Long's battle with my dad. For example, he misrepresented equipment needs, as competitive crew equipment had always been purchased by the rowers, not the University. And almost 30 years of history indicate that extra effort by rowers could be expected.

Long's memo continued, "I would suggest that we consider carefully whether or not Oregon State University wishes to continue the Crew activities (Varsity, Physical Education Instruction and Recreation) on the river. If so, funds should be made available for the essential facilities, equipment and personnel. This is such a vulnerable and dangerous area that we cannot afford to take chances with young men's and young women's lives in approved sport activities. We need to be sure that no negligence charges can be lodged against us for lack of proper leadership, equipment, facilities, and other safety features."

The liability issue was real. Stevens and my dad had been lucky that no crew member drowned or died from hypothermia. Indeed, I was in dangerous situations many times.

Long then listed changes needed to keep this too successful, grass-roots program going. One was building a new women's locker room. The list was followed by an alternative that included discontinuing crew and selling the equipment, including my dad's beloved barges. Perhaps the canoeing program could continue if it moved to an abandoned gravel pit downriver from the boathouse.

Long's alternative was likely to appeal to MacVicar, as he was known to be very tight monetarily.[O-2] However, he was also an experienced administrator. He had started as an agricultural biochemist at Oklahoma State, but early in his career he moved into administration, subsequently becoming the chancellor of Southern Illinois University. By 1974, he had been President of Oregon State for only four years, but he was on his way to overseeing striking growth: during his fourteen year tenure, the school added 23 new buildings, its budget tripled, and its faculty expanded by 27%.[O-178] How he would handle the crew problem was unclear.

My dad felt outflanked by Long. In a mass mailing to oarsmen, he wrote, "While I was home at Christmas, Dr. James Long ... showed me a letter that he had sent to President Robert MacVicar recommending that the rowing program be closed down and that all of the equipment be sold or disposed of. ... This really disturbs me. I don't know how to handle this, but I really think that the safest thing to do is to show a position of strength. ... We just can't let a simple stroke of the pen wipe out 50 years of building a program with national stature. But I am on the inside, and if you understand at all the hierarchy of a university, practically voiceless."[F-19]

Fred Mann, the interim coach, alerted key crew alumni that massive action was needed to save rowing.[F-22] Karl Brandt, a former varsity cox and freshman crew coach, quickly responded. He stressed to President MacVicar that the rowing program had been built largely by volunteer effort, donations, and non-University funds. Crew at OSU had not survived by chance, and those former oarsmen were now alumni who should be heard. Brandt closed with "I further suggest that you replace the Dr. Long's [as administrators]." [F-21] Long was not replaced.[O-19]

Coach Fred Mann, 1975.[D110a]

Tim Hayden, an impassioned oarsman of the late 1950s, coach of my freshman crew, and later a driving force in high school rowing in Klamath Falls, reached MacVicar by telephone following a discussion with Long. Tim summarized the conversation for my dad.[F-20]

"I didn't pull any punches and told Dr. MacVicar that Long was a very biased man. ... I emphasized my point with his erroneous claim that it was too dangerous to row ... Long wanted to sell all the equipment and put in a canoeing program in a small gravel pit [that would have the same problems]. I stated that this shows Long's basic ignorance and his basic, complete misunderstanding ... of rowing. ... I also stated that Long morally had no right to destroy 50 years of labor. ... I mention[ed] the golf course idea to MacVicar as something you had cherished and fought for years to obtain. ... I hit a good point here, as MacVicar is very unhappy that the golf course [has] not happened. ... [He could] get a successful crew team and a golf course."

Key crew alumni. Left: Tim Hayden[F-28a]. Right: Mike Oxborrow[G-12]

On March 3, 1975, the University student newspaper announced that rowing would be eliminated due to lack of funds, effective in the 1976-77 season.[F-12] That would solve the maintenance problems and the Title IX issue with women's crew, since equality would be achieved by elimination.

That same month, Mann mounted a letter-writing campaign using the large alumni mailing list the Rowing Club had been compiling for two decades. Mike Oxborrow, President of the Beaver Crew Association, which had taken over fundraising from the Rowing Club, distributed, as samples, the letter to MacVicar written by Brandt and one that I wrote.[O-18]

Three days later, the women's crews from Oregon State and the University of Oregon rowed from Corvallis to Salem, the state capital, to publicize the problem and raise money.[D-133] The press release noted that the women distributed phone books, acted as security at athletic events, and tore down condemned buildings to obtain funds for travel and boats.

My dad was very pleased with the initiative taken by the women's crews, as he wrote to crew supporters in Klamath Falls: "Here you see an example of what we try to teach our young people in crew—to have initiative, drive, enthusiasm, persistence, and a will to do things for themselves, not always with a hand out to government. This is a sign that I have been able to get my point across."[F-24]

Letters to MacVicar from rowing supporters included checks made out to Oregon State Rowing, testimonials from the parents of crew members, and many letters from past oarsmen. For example, Dennis Searcy wrote, "… I believe that I can speak for the thousands of alumni, both men and women, who would never forgive OSU if the crew program were terminated."[O-22]

The letter from Eldred Halsey captures the spirit.[F-17] Halsey had been on the crew in 1929, which he documented by including an October budget that showed his $2 dues to the Rowing Club out of a total budget of $32. Part of his letter read, "… It is obvious to me that somebody is maliciously attempting to destroy the crew program which many others have been building up for 50 years. It is wrong to destroy the good works of others. Whoever would do this is not a trustworthy part of the University. … It (crew) has helped me for 47 years, and I now again enjoy the sport as a member of the Station L Rowing Club in Portland."

From Mississippi my dad sent a five-page letter to the Oregon State Athletic Board,[F-16] "... The Board has been challenged by President MacVicar to keep out of the red (debt). So far, the answers I have seen have been self-defeating in proposing to cut budgets and ... programs, although this may be necessary on an interim basis. Programs that have taken years to build, like civilizations, when abandoned are soon reclaimed by the jungle. This short-range planning seems designed to take care of necessity but not to provide for the future."

He also reminded the Board that student interest in rowing was strong. "The crew program has more participants on the whole than most other intercollegiate sports except football, but these are diversified under the headings of heavyweight varsity, lightweight varsity, women's crew, and P.E. The [rowing] program runs all year long, and in the first three intercollegiate [crew] programs, the turnout ranges from 40 to 60 people."

My dad sensed that MacVicar was testing the strength of rowing. He told my dad that he had never experienced such enthusiasm and loyalty to a program from writers who had participated 25 years earlier.[J-21] My dad perceived elimination of crew as gamesmanship, as he wrote at the time, "After having talked with the old man (MacVicar), I would suspect that he is playing the game of threatening to cut out a program ... to stir up enough controversy so that he will be forced to support the program. I believe he wants enough to be stirred up ... that irate people will take it to the legislature and get things straightened out."[F-23]

Things got straightened out, and Oregon State rowing avoided elimination.

At about the same time (October 1975), University administrators halted the towel service at the boathouse.[F-1,F-4,F-5] Compared to eliminating the entire rowing program, the towel episode seems trivial. But nothing is trivial in power struggles.

Since the 1930s, the PE Department had supplied gym clothing and towels to rowing participants so they needn't carry wet clothes back to campus. Stevens had built a drying room at the boathouse, and a paid student or other employee exchanged dry clothes for wet ones and assured that inventories were maintained. Dean James Long had taken over the exchange service in 1965, having Robert Printz, his administrative assistant, handle the work-study students who managed clothing distribution and inventories.

Michael Rollins, 1975.[L-6]

In November 1975 Michael Rollins, a reporter for the *Barometer* and coxswain of a national championship crew, wrote that Dean Long gave three reasons for eliminating the towel service: 1) maintenance of crew equipment was more important than gym suit service—the PE Department could not do both; 2) all PE classes should be treated equally—canoeing and women's crew did not have towel service, in violation of Title IX; and 3) a need for tighter control of the gym suit distribution. Robert Printz then asserted that a greater loss and theft of gym clothes occurred at the crewhouse than at the Men's Gym (on the main campus). According to Rollins, "Both (Long and Printz) felt a work-study student is incapable of operating the service at the crew facility."[F-4]

Students were insulted. A student newspaper editorial called on Long to reinstate the gym suit service (the student senate had unanimously passed such a resolution). And Long was chastised for "Twisting the meaning of Title IX."[F-8]

My dad had provided data to the press: from 1950 to 1965 the PE Department gained 134 towels, 48 sox, 10 sweatshirts, 7 sweatpants, 44 supporters, 51 gym shirts, and 52 gym pants.[F-13] Those numbers allowed student editors to speak with some authority: "During the years when Drlica was in charge of the towel room personnel, there was actually a gain in equipment for the PE Department in terms of surplus towels, sweats, jocks and the like. In the past ten years, the PE Department lost money at the docks due to lost towels, sweats, etc. Long blames it on incompetent work-study people. Drlica blames it on poor management. We agree with Drlica."[F-7a]

Other students attacked Long through the letters-to-the-editor column of the student newspaper.[F-13,F-7a,F-14] For example, "In the last few weeks our apartment has taken on the odor and appearance of a locker room. This is particularly disturbing at dinner time. … Perhaps if Dr. Long ate his dinner tonight while smelling a sweaty sock, he could grasp what we are experiencing."

My dad was well versed in the power of the press, as Communist agitators had used it against him in Occupied Japan. He kept the controversy going by providing interviews for the student newspaper. In a December 9, 1975 piece he accused Long of not being transparent with the PE Department budget, that Long's claims of not having enough money for crew were unfounded.[F-1;F-7a] Then, according to the article, Long stated that "He (Long) is merely trying to redistribute funds more evenly throughout the Department. Crew has the highest per capita expenditure of any physical education class." The article concluded with my dad stoking the fire, "Drlica suggested that Long's pattern of actions is a typical bureaucratic principle about not caring for the student, as long as it's easy for the administration. It's more convenient for

200 students to carry gym clothes from the campus to the docks than it is for the administration to hire a student."[F-1]

Not to be outdone, Long clarified his position with an interview in the student newspaper.[D-98] The caption under his photo states, "Refuting allegations that he doesn't like the crew program and that he's carrying Title IX too far, James Long, Dean of Health and Physical Education, explains why gym suit service to the crew docks was canceled." In the article Long denied that he holds a "grudge against crew" as charged previously in an editorial. He also denied that Title IX entered into his original decision, but he had stated that Title IX was a main reason for shutting down the service.[F-1] According to him, "The reasons are distorted and misleading."

Long tried to rein in my dad:[O-7] "The article in the *Barometer* on Wednesday, November 12, 1975, had some statements and 'quotes' that were hard to believe would come from a responsible faculty member in the Department of Physical Education. Surely, they were misquotes or misinterpretations. It is expected that when problems occur in programs and services, that these problems are to be worked out within the Department and School, with minimal involvement, if any, of outside parties."

I doubt that my dad tried very hard, or at all, to negotiate with Long. I found no note on conversations in an archive containing notes on much less important issues.

Long's assertion that it was difficult to find a reliable work-study student brought Benton County Sheriff John Dolan into the fray. In a letter to MacVicar, he wrote, "Comments made concerning student labor used to assist in the gym clothing program certainly are not in line with my experience with student interns ... who are given considerable responsibility in making decisions that affect persons' lives."[F-18]

It turns out that Dolan rowed in intramural crews for three years, and, as he stated to Fred Mann in 1975, he had "assisted Karl in some scrounging."[F-34] Dolan previously invited Mann to contact him "if any problems came up, since marine law enforcement problems are, of course, part of my official responsibility to resolve."

Jack Dolan, Benton County's longest serving sheriff. In 1974 he was named Oregon Sheriff of the Year. [O-134]

My dad was a legally blind Deputy Sheriff in addition to his other duties.

The deciding factor may have been a legal issue overlooked by Long. Students were being charged a fee to help offset the cost of the gym suit service:[O-6] "... The fee of $5 is to offset costs not normal to Physical Education classes. Expensive rowing shells must be properly maintained and gym suit equipment must be checked out in an off-campus setting which requires greater expense."[F-15] The towel service at the crew house was restored and expanded to include women.[F-3]

The clothing issue seemed to be just a minor gambit until I re-read Rollins' initial article.[F-4] Three sentences jumped out: "Long said his decision was not made overnight. It was many months in planning, and he often consulted with Milosh Popovich, Dean of Administration. He carefully considered all the alternatives and consequences." Since Popovich was a close associate of President

MacVicar and in charge of University finances,[O-177] the Central Administration of the University seems to have been involved in creating the towel service fiasco. Over the years my dad had ruffled a lot of feathers.

The grassroots support from alumni and students, plus the ongoing effort by the women's crew, gave my dad the sense that he had sufficient momentum to push forward on the unequal shower facilities. Maybe he could get new building out of the University.

In a memo to President MacVicar [F-44] he wrote, "Other opinions being to the contrary, it is my opinion that it is the intention of both Title IX and HB2131 that equality is intended to mean that persons being discriminated against are to be raised to the level of the more privileged. I do not believe that it is the intent of the law to downgrade those with the advantage. Such action of downgrading might be considered 'Fair in form but discriminatory in operation.'" He then recommended that the men's locker room building be expanded to accommodate women and comply with Title IX (my dad had designed the building to have two wings, one for men and one for women).

He also pushed on the Athletic Board, which had to work on the "problem of crew". In a May 1976 meeting, my dad detailed Long's many budgetary errors. He also emphasized the ability of the rowing program to provide for itself.[F-33] Such lobbying may have helped bring the women's and lightweight men's crews into the Men's Athletic Department a year later. However, two weeks after my dad met with the Athletic Board, both the women and lightweights were kicked off the docks by a different administrative body (Physical Recreation), largely in response to Long's budgets—if you cannot afford a sport, get rid of it.

By 1977, the problem of crew had been festering for more than three years. Strong student and alumni support kept the University from eliminating the program, and in the background my dad had been arguing that the intercollegiate crews should be combined into a waterfront program with a single budget.[J-21]

In the spring of that year, in what seemed to be a sudden move, rowing became the first fully integrated sport in the Athletic Department.

At the same time, Oregon State crew was being noticed on the racecourse. A 1977 letter from Dick Erickson, coach at the University of Washington, to the OSU Athletic Director, had a particularly noteworthy phrase:[N-7] "... OSU has a real crew this year." This comment derived from Oregon State beating the top Washington boat in Corvallis and losing by only half a second in Seattle (a boat length is about 3 seconds on still water).

Nevertheless, the struggle over who should pay for upkeep at the river continued.[G-6] Perhaps to keep up the pressure, my dad sent a series of memos to Long, requesting that maintenance be carried out (June 1978). Whether my dad really expected to get University help with maintenance is unclear. He, Stevens, and countless rowers had created the problems, and in principle, they could fix them. Painting a locker room would take less than a day by a crew of rowers; fixing rotten floorboards in the women's dressing room might take couple of weekends. Poison oak and brush removal should have been trivial for Oregon youth. Perhaps my dad realized that he could no longer mobilize the rowers to handle maintenance issues. Crews were winning races, and they resisted spending time on program maintenance,[H-32] even key activities such as organizing races. Their job was to win races, not make sure they occurred. Times had changed.

Long responded a month later. According to him, his PE program does not use, nor does it intend to use, the locker rooms. He pointed out that the crew/canoe facilities have always been given the lowest priority for capital outlays, although he declined to present budgets to support the statement. The locker rooms should be transferred to the Athletic Department. As for maintenance of the barges and leaky roofs, special fees should be levied and used as my dad saw fit. Other maintenance should come from maintenance crews from the Athletic and PE Departments, perhaps using work-study student labor.

My dad seemed to be gradually wearing Long down, but the almost daily struggle with the PE Department kept my dad on edge. For example, four days after Long's letter, my dad confronted an administrator in the PE Department. My dad was concerned about a reduction in the number of PE rowing classes. This was another way to erode the crew program.[O-5] According to my dad's notes, the administrator responded that there had been no change during the last seven years. But my dad had the numbers: "... The class offerings in PE have been reduced from 18 to 12, or a reduction by one third, as shown in the ... Schedule of Classes."

The administrator tried to sidestep by asserting that my dad couldn't teach all of those classes, that he (the administrator) would only approve someone who was a PE major, and none was available. My dad pointed out that there were already three qualified persons in the Department. Moreover, my dad had two recent PE graduates, one being Coach Kitzman, who would be happy to teach. The other was Kate Gribskov, who at the time was trying out for the U.S. national team. In addition, he asserted that being a PE major was not a valid criterion.

My dad noted, "... You seem to be imbued with the idea that crew is expensive, but you admit that you have never seen the budget or figures. You simply have accepted the word of someone else, which does not necessarily make it true. ... Furthermore, the constant repetition of erroneous statements eventually makes the person stating them believe that they are true. Pretty soon he has others believing the same thing and even defending the position without in fact knowing for sure that they are true." The last sentence is a universal truth called "The Big Lie". My dad first learned this truth from Communist agitators in Occupied Japan, a truth that was subsequently reinforced by Mao in China.

Meanwhile, the number of West Coast institutions sponsoring rowing had grown to 25. The PAC-10 schools (eight sponsored rowing, thus PAC-8) created their own championship regatta, which institutionalized Oregon State rowing. By 1979 my dad was applying for NCAA status.[F-40] PE classes in rowing could be halted easily by the University, but withdrawal of the competitive team from athletic conferences would be more difficult.

By 1980 Oregon State crews had won a pair of national championships in both men's and women's rowing, two oarsmen made Pan-Am and Olympic teams, and one rowed on the US lightweight team. My dad had received a merit award from the Oregon Sportswriters and Sportscasters Association (1977) along with general acknowledgement in the press. Moreover, pressure for raising travel funds had relaxed as the Athletic Department made a sizeable contribution. However, my dad could not relax, because he was losing his battle to keep the Navy barges.

Coach Drlica multitasking, 1977.[O-72]

The barges were important to him, because they provided a boathouse on the water. He had argued as early as 1940 that carrying boats from a shore facility was a waste of time. Moreover, it was difficult for women's crews, especially for PE classes. He thought that carrying boats was a disincentive to participation. His arguments fell on deaf ears.[F-41]

He felt that University administrators had a hidden agenda, since estimates of maintenance costs were highly inflated. He recalled that the Navy person responsible for transferring the barges to the University said that a leak in the hull was unlikely. If one should develop, it would be a simple matter to weld a plate over the spot from the inside. "He further described what to look for should one care to send divers under a barge to actually inspect the bottom. He said it would be fairly simple to take the barges ashore in Corvallis rather than taking them to Portland for drydocking."[F-41] My dad's recommendation to obtain a second opinion before selling the barges was ignored.

My dad could have stopped requesting maintenance support if he had realized that the barges were the Achilles heel of the rowing program. They gave administrators a reason to think about terminating PE crew even if they weren't in a personal battle with my dad. However, leaky roofs did need to be fixed; it is doubtful that my dad could get the rowers of the late 1970s to take on the task, since they were focused on training to win races. He didn't want to do it all himself. Thus, he asked the University for help.

His fundamental problem was that the property had been obtained by salvaging and volunteerism. That was the tradition Ed Stevens had established decades earlier. Without funds for maintenance, my dad's rowing campus was vulnerable to University budgets. He later wrote, "It may have been the wrong way to do things."[G-6] As with Shakespeare's King Lear, my dad discovered the problem too late. But it's doubtful that much would have been accomplished if he had tried to build the program through standard channels that carried overhead.

Although the barges were perfect for the rowing program, they were not essential. They could be sold, and the resulting money used to build a new boathouse on land. He could live with that if it made the rowing program more stable financially. More problematic for him was the unrest among his crews.

──── *Chapter 25* ────

KICKED UPSTAIRS

By the late 1970s, OSU rowing was showing visible change. Pressure from Dean Long lessened as he approached retirement in 1980, and the Athletic Department provided funds for all intercollegiate crews, at least in part. Moreover, Oregon State rowers were winning seats in national crews. When these oarsmen returned to Oregon after competing internationally, their ideas about rowing technique clashed with my dad's. My dad thought that his rowing style was the best for winning collegiate races with inexperienced athletes, even if it might not be what was used at the international level with very experienced rowers. The experienced oarsmen thought he was old fashioned and needed to change or retire.

Younger Oregon State oarsmen realized that they would improve their chances for getting on a national team by learning the international style early in their rowing careers. Rowing style involves training muscles to behave in a particular way time after time, trying to squeeze a half-inch more run out of every stroke. Changing style requires retraining muscles. Thus, the advocates for change had a ready audience. Moreover, at the time the national coach was Harry Parker, one of the most revered coaches in American rowing history. His rowing style was proven to win races.

In early 1979, oarsmen wrote letters-to-the-editor of the Oregon State student newspaper, charging my dad with coaching incompetence. In particular, two championship rowers criticized his workouts, the style of rowing, his empathy toward his teams, and his general understanding of physical training.[H-59]

National champion men's crews. Upper: 1975 IRA champions in four with cox. Left to right: Cox Mike Rollins, Robert Zagunis, David Nealey, Tom Dover, and Craig Ambrosen. They set the course record. Lower: 1977 IRA champions in four without cox. Left to right: Steve Kelley, Gary Bohlin, Coach Karl Drlica, Tom Woodman, Tom Sissul, and IRA Chairperson. Zagunis also rowed in the 1976 Olympic Games; Woodman was on the 1980 Olympic team.[L-3,L-6]

The intensity of the conflict is captured by vitriolic comments in a February letter:[H-47] "... Workouts under Drilica's [sic] direction are made up on the spot, with no overall plan or goals, and without regard to the rower's needs. He also teaches a style that everyone else in the country dropped some two decades ago. The program is used only to satisfy his own egotistical goals, which are distant from the oarsmen's, and since few people can put up with his nonsense for very long, crew suffers the highest turnover rate of the OSU sports. ... When a coach knows less about the sport than the oarsmen and is strangling their efforts to achieve, perhaps it is time to ask him to retire—before the program dies!"

A second letter (March 2, 1979) finished slightly differently: "Rather than continue in a negative vein, I would like to offer a positive alternative. Since it appears crew will become the eighth varsity sport for Men's Intercollegiate Athletics, the Athletic Department should be encouraged to hire a full-time assistant with a current knowledge of rowing, whose sole duty would be to plan workouts and do the actual on-the-water coaching. Then Coach Drlica could continue to devote his energy to the administration of the program, which he feels is more important than the actual rowing." [H-16]

Of course, without a program there would be no rowing. Only three years earlier, the University announced that it was eliminating crew even though it had been part of the Athletic Department for almost a decade. [F-12,F19]

Alumni came to my dad's defense with responses such as, "Any athlete worth his salt should eventually, in some form or another, exceed his coach's talents and knowledge. At least I would hope so! To then come back on the man who, in many ways and by his own hands and long hours, for 28 years and against lousy odds and poor support, provided you the opportunity to represent the U.S., OSU, and yourself in the World Championships, that's what's known as biting the hand that fed you." [F-8]

My dad admitted that the letters upset him, but after a month he became more philosophical. He fell back on the adage, "... If the team loses, the coach did it. If the team wins, the players did it." [H-59]

As in his disputes with James Long, my dad rebutted the two oarsmen through interviews in the student newspaper. For example, he asked, "How did they get to be national champs? Everything was available to them here. They had the opportunity to be successful." [H-59]

The oarsmen wanted more than opportunity. The 1970s produced a generation of student-athlete that demanded more attention, more supervision. Indeed, one rower even faulted my dad for not giving more compliments.[H-30] That reinforced my dad's view that parents had dispensed compliments so freely that children failed to develop an internal sense of accomplishment.

My dad also disputed that he taught an antiquated style by pointing out that he uses the method of Karl Adam, which he learned by attending numerous clinics led by Adam.[H-59] Adam revolutionized rowing in the early 1960s with several innovations that included interval training, modified oars, elevated stroke rate, and rigging racing shells to put two adjacent positions on the same side of the boat.[O-162] My dad modified the method to suit collegiate conditions in Oregon.

One issue was raising the stroke rate, perhaps from 36-38 strokes per minute to above 40, in a way that would actually increase boat speed. Boat speed is a product of strokes per minute times feet per stroke; keeping all oars together with good power is more difficult at high stroke rates. A lower stroke rate gives the rower a short rest on each stroke and more time to get set for a good catch. With 2000 meter-races, which were roughly six-minute sprints, an elite crew could maintain a high rate without falling apart. But my dad discovered in the early 1960s that his college crews, using standard oars and heavy wooden boats, had slower times using the high stroke rates.

A second issue was the rower's demand for more empathy. Empathy is generally not in a coach's job description, as illustrated by Oregon State football coach Dee Andros: he dismissed a star player for sporting a beard.[O-92] Like many driven persons, my dad was probably not very empathetic. Nor was he tactful, as seen in his response to a request for crew funds by the field hockey team, "… Perhaps some imagination and initiative would generate some money-raising ideas."[D-161]

Indeed, my dad may not have understood the meaning of empathy, as he seems to have missed a rower's point when he responded to a lack of empathy with, "Personalities don't enter into it. If a person makes a boat go faster, he races. Sometimes you cannot be very sympathetic." [H-9]

The center of his response, however, revealed a generational divide, "The crew is a miniature democracy, … and the heart of it is the students. There is always the risk in giving them too much responsibility; they will assume they know everything." [H-59]

That wasn't what the students wanted to hear. They wanted him to change.

Newspaper photo of Coach Drlica driving coaching launch, 1980.[H-12]

His notes illustrate that he did listen to crew members. Concerning a conversation with a team leader, he wrote, "We discussed the team's inability to follow directions and to get the stroke count up. He countered that they did not have the technique and must have the technique before putting the stroke up. … He pointed out the other things, like raising money, that the team was doing. I said they were not alone. Other teams did similar things. Baseball, golf. He thought that I was inadequate at teaching and coaching the team."[H-32]

By early March 1980, Portland newspapers began reporting on rowing unrest.[H-59] According to one oarsman, without my dad coaching, Oregon State rowing would have died many times. But the team felt that they weren't going anywhere. The team was not growing and being properly utilized under my dad.[H-28]

A member of the women's crew and President of the Rowing Club said that a major complaint was that my dad was not spending enough time on the water with the crews.[H-59] My dad responded, "They want someone on the water with them every minute of the day telling them to do something. ... They should be solving some of these problems for themselves. College is supposed to be a learning process. ... The history of Oregon State rowing has been do-it-yourself. If you don't do it yourself, it's not gonna get done. ... In my opinion, and others, it is not necessary for the coach to be alongside a crew constantly continually talking. ... Continual dependence on the coach is a carryover from the lower schools and ... in some respects it shows an inability to develop leadership within the group."[H-59] He felt that the rowers were experienced enough to not need his constant attention.

A third complaint, perhaps more important than water time, was a lack of communication. According to the rowers, my dad wouldn't listen. His notes show that he did listen, but his perspective was that they were wrong, "The objective of the rowing program as intercollegiate teams, and winning intercollegiate goals, must be kept in mind. And whether or not the goal is to subjugate all collegiate team members to the goals of national team membership for the less than one percent of the team [must be kept in mind]. ... To sacrifice the style that seems to produce reasonably good crews using people who have little athletic experience and practically no high school experience [and allows them] to compete against crews with far greater resources, and do well, is an accomplishment in itself."

My dad had experienced situations in Occupied Japan in which a few agitators could sway a crowd that he then had to deal with. Was this a similar situation? He tried to find out by composing and distributing a questionnaire asking a series of pertinent questions, such as how well was practice time used, how well was the coach prepared, and should the style of rowing at OSU be changed?[H-4] He even asked whether his eyesight affected his coaching. Tabulation of the results indicated a broad spectrum of opinions.

Nevertheless, my dad altered his rowing style to get the stroke rate up. One modification, which he wrote into his text-book, was to shorten the stroke at the end of the pull-through: instead of pulling the oar all the way to the chest, the pull was stopped two to three inches early. That would eliminate the tendency to lay back at the end of the stroke. In addition, once the pull is complete, the hands must get out of the lap quickly, and full body reach should occur by the time the seat has moved half-way down the track toward the stern of the boat.[H-31] There would be no extra reaching just before the catch.

In 2018 Kirk Hutchinson provided some insight into the crew situation. After completing his coaching stint at Oregon State, Kirk taught school for more than thirty years. During that time, he saw a new generation with new ideas emerging every ten years or so. My dad didn't seem to adjust to such rapid change. In the 1970s, society changed suddenly. Everyone seemed to have power except the bosses. Thus, it is not surprising that Ed Lickiss in Oakland was caught in a similar situation and had a view similar to my dad's.[H-15]

When my dad listened, it was through an old-fashioned set of standards. Moreover, he was certain that he was right. When I asked Kirk whether my dad had become a curmudgeon, Kirk paused for a moment and then answered, "Yes." A negotiated solution would be difficult to find.

Oarsmen met with Athletic Director Andros and demanded an on-the-water coach to supplement my dad, and several peti-tions were sent to Andros.[H-13] It appears that two separate issues were being combined and perhaps confused. One was the general need for a dedicated men's coach to provide more coaching atten-tion. The second was specific, that my dad was not satisfying their needs. Andros released a statement that their biggest complaint was about my dad's eyesight; their question was whether he could still coach effectively.[H-1] Indeed, my dad was legally blind—that's why he rode his bicycle in the freezing rain even though the family had two cars. Had his sight have gotten worse?

Newspaper photo of OSU Athletic Director Dee Andros coxing a crew. Andros was an avid supporter of rowing.[F-6]

My dad was not good at sharing problems with staff. Even Astrid learned of major decisions after the fact. Moreover, my dad didn't view the rowers as adult partners in a difficult enterprise, one that went far beyond pulling on an oar. Once the situation became adversarial, he probably didn't meet with the students to describe the situation in detail, to ask them for help, or to take more responsibility. The students knew that he was focused on preserving the rowing program,[H-16] but as he became increasingly entrenched in his position, they became firmer in a stand my dad thought reflected immaturity and selfishness.

The crew was probably unaware of how thinly my dad had been stretched. He wrote, "Among the problems that were encountered last year was the resignation, just before school started, of one of the coaches (Kelly Moore). ... He had done no recruiting or planning during the summer. I was in a very precarious position because of the number of people rowing and the various levels of accomplishment. I thought it was necessary to coach the experienced people in the morning and the beginning oarsmen in the afternoon because of the shortage of coaching help. I tried to do both jobs, with the varsity at 6:00 a.m. and the freshmen at 4:00 p.m. This then made it necessary for me to get up at about 4:30 in the morning to be at the crewhouse prior to the team's arrival and to coach the varsity, run over and get a little breakfast and get my mail and then return back to the crew house to teach the PE classes until noon or after, [and then] do a little paperwork, maintenance, and planning. ... By the time I got home in the evening for supper, it was 7:30 or 8:00 o'clock, and it was then time to go to bed.[H-2a]

"No one offered to pay me for doing all of these jobs, ... and I really got mostly condemnation. In retrospect, I should have said sorry, it's an impossibility to do this. ... A few student leaders began to criticize what I was doing, and I felt that it was physically impossible to do all of it. I did conduct a survey and found only a few of the more vociferous people were dissatisfied. They were leading the rest of the group, but in a strike situation, and as in most strike situations, very few students had the intestinal fortitude to stand up for their convictions and were led by the more outspoken people."[H-4,H-39]

My dad had faced public criticism before, and he probably could have survived this revolt: winning crews gave him Athletic Department support, and turnover of college students would make their collective memory short. Moreover, James Long was due to retire. But my dad's top-down management style had become ineffective, and his incompatible goals had collided: he could not emphasize self-sufficiency and also institutionalize intercollegiate rowing with its requirement for winning races. The latter was prevailing. Was it time to quit?

His view focused on finances. "... Eventually the [waterfront program] grew too big to be sustained by student, instructor, and limited Department effort. The program grew to encompass both men's and women's intercollegiate crew teams, co-educational physical education crew classes, intramural rowing, co-educational physical education canoeing classes, and a golf driving range for beginning and intermediate golf classes (my dad secured an adjacent golf course to keep the University invested at the river). The need for more money in times of both growth and inflation (13.5% in 1980) overtook the program.[G-6]

"In earlier times, under different social conditions, it was possible with fewer athletes to also be a fund raiser, accountant, architect and planner, boat builder and designer, maintenance man, supply clerk, and general roustabout. The expanding program and pressure for excellence require either an expansion or a cut-back. It is not possible to stay where it is."[G-6]

To my dad, expansion meant hiring full-time coaches for both the men's and women's crews plus a rowing coordinator to handle the budgets and maintain the facilities. The crisis with the oarsmen might be solved if he gave up on-the-water coaching and focused on PE classes and keeping the overall program going. But to him that would be the same as quitting.

My dad's decision seems to have emerged from a conversation with Ralph Mathison, the very successful women's coach. According to my dad's notes, Ralph participated fully in off-the-water chores, and it was clear that my dad respected Ralph despite unsuccessful efforts to change Ralph's appearance. The notes concluded with "These were not his exact words, but the implications were that I should resign from the actual coaching."[H-42a] My dad was tired, and Ralph's vote of no-confidence pushed him over the edge. Three years before retirement age my dad became an off-the-water administrator.

At one level, the decision felt bad: he often said to me that he had been "kicked upstairs", a term commonly applied to losing coaches who become athletic directors. However, newspapers described the move as a logical expansion of the rowing program, as did leaders of the crew. At my dad's request he retained the title of head coach, saying, "I've served my apprenticeship and had my fanny wet out there all these years in the miserable cold weather."[H-59] But in practical terms his career was over.

─────── *Chapter 26* ───────

THE AFTERMATH

My dad gave a farewell address to the Athletic Board (June 11, 1980) in which he criticized the Board and reviewed his achievements.[H-40]

"It appears to me that people on this Board are afraid to say to the students, 'If you want something, you have to earn it.' It is a little difficult to maintain morale on men's teams when the newspapers carry demands by women's teams for new traveling bags and $15 a day per diem when the crew team hasn't had any new clothing since 1968 and furnishes all of its own sweat gear, including its own towels. The crew team itself earns enough money during the year to pay for almost half of the travel budget and to occasionally buy a new racing shell.

"The athletic programs espouse a handout philosophy seeking athletes and begging them to come to our university, whereas, in my opinion, student-athletes should be seeking to come to this university as a privilege. As you know, I do not believe in the scholarship program for athletes on the basis of their athletic ability. It simply turns into a procedure of buying their services, but the Department is caught in that very unfortunate bind."

He also expressed bitterness over the general lack of support "... But the straw that broke the camel's back, so far as I'm concerned, was when this Board hired a women's volleyball coach on a twelve-month, full-time basis ... while at the same time, the men's coaches are working on a part-time basis and teaching other classes in physical education. ...[A]fter 36 years, I now realize that it is futile and no longer worth my effort to continue with the crew program. ... I anticipate that [continuing would] be like hitting my thumb with a hammer because it's going to feel so good when I stop.

"In conclusion, I would like to remark that I think that over the past thirty years as rowing coach at Oregon State, and six years prior to World War II, that I accomplished the goals that I set out for myself. ... I have been elected to the National Board of Directors, made a National Referee ... and become a national authority and author in rowing. I think that I have established crew on a somewhat permanent basis at OSU. In addition to that, I [helped] start rowing [programs] at Oregon, Hawaii, Lewis & Clark, Reed, Station L (Portland), University of Santa Barbara, and University of California at Santa Barbara. I also helped [with] the women's crew at the University of California at Berkeley and helped establish the National Women's Rowing Association. Now it is time for me to set some new goals ... and challenges for myself."

My dad did not mention his less quantifiable legacy, the contribution he made to young men and women becoming self-sufficient. Testimonials were numerous, such as one from Jim Carruthers, "Coach Drlica was number one. Without crew I would have most likely dropped out [of college] and not graduated."[O-34]

I'm sure that Stevens and my dad enjoyed winning races; they were proud of the teams. For example, in his address to the Athletic Board my dad said, "I next call your attention to the 1980 crew summary ... the men's ... teams won all of their (regular season) races. They placed third in the PAC-10 championships behind Washington and California in the heavyweight varsity and the lightweight varsity and fourth in the freshman group. ... In the women's races we also placed high, in the first three positions and in first place in many of the races [two national championships]. ... [Previously] one of our men rowed on the U.S. Olympic team at Montreal in 1976 and another rowed in Denmark and Norway for the lightweight team. Another man is presently on the American Olympic team and has won gold medals in Pan American events last year and gold medals in the National Championships.[O-63] ... This is an accomplishment that few other teams in the Athletic Department have attained."[H-2a]

The next problem was hiring a new on-the-water coach. Kelly Moore, who had helped coach during the previous year, was one of the applicants. Moore had rowed for four years at the University of California, Berkeley, and in 1971 he was the national collegiate pair-oared champion. He then coached the Cal lightweight crew (a club sport) for three years and Berkeley High School for a year before his year at Oregon State.[H-8] Steve Adler also applied. Adler was a former Long Beach oarsman and coach who had also coached at Oregon State.

My dad favored Adler, since Moore had written, "... While I understand and am sympathetic with many of the problems you face in trying to run the program, so many of them are made worse by your own attitudes and methods."[H-7]

Moore was also quoted in the press as saying, "The problems on the team started a few years back as the team became more competitive. Better athletes were in the program, and their motivation was national championship. Before that, crew had been a participatory sport. I think Karl Drlica has had trouble making the transition from that kind of activity sport to a competitive program."[H-28]

But the problem was deeper than confrontational statements. My dad felt that Moore was unprepared to lead a program that had many critical funding problems and complex university issues, although his "rapport with the oarsmen was excellent."[H-11]

A ten-person committee split on the two, and my dad sided with Adler as a tie-breaker.[H-1] Then Adler withdrew for "personal reasons," leaving the crew without an on-the-water replacement.

The rowers presented a boycott ultimatum to Athletic Department officials, stating that they would not row. A student, Sam Western, reported that the oarsmen were threatened with elimination of the sport. To that, Athletic Director Andros responded, "No, we didn't do that. It would seem that if they are not willing to row for the coach, they're the ones dropping the sport, not us."[H-1]

The Portland Oregonian reported that Adler had declined the coaching job for personal reasons but returned after a week to take the job and end an oarsmen boycott (Adler couldn't find a supplementary job in Corvallis and needed more money). The Beaver Crew Association anticipated the salary issue and got the Athletic Department to match their $2,400 donation to increase the coach's salary.[H-10]

By the time fall practice started, the turmoil had disappeared. In a letter to me (October 30, 1980),[H-24] my dad wrote, "I am not doing anything with the crew now except some administrative work on the facilities. The new Dean is pretty good and has made room for me in PE, which I appreciate. I am teaching classes and going home for supper. I think that things are going to be good here and will get some support. I don't take any work with me at night. Things are quite different."

My dad continued to oversee the facilities for another three years as a bureaucrat responsible for securing the equipment. In 1975 he had learned a difficult lesson about loaning racing shells. While he was on sabbatical leave in Mississippi, a brand-new pair-oared shell had been loaned to oarsmen from Lewis & Clark College in Portland. The boat was then stored at the Station L Rowing Club where a fire burned the boat, almost beyond recognition.[H-55a] Station L insurance was insufficient, and nobody stepped up to assure future good will. [H-55] My dad stopped loaning boats. Thus, when a request to borrow boats for summer practice came in 1982,[H-45] he refused. He pointed out that he was not officially employed by the University in summers and could not assume the responsibility.[H-45a]

He also had difficulty convincing some of the young coaches that liability issues affected many persons above them at the University—for legal reasons the coaches could not take responsibility for non-University personnel using the facilities.[O-27] The problem even extended to oarsmen who had purchased their own singles and were storing them at the boathouse. Where could they go with 26-foot boats when they were kicked off the crew facilities?

The rowing bug was still biting people, making them want to row. But as the rowing program solidified, rules, regulations, and cautious administrators seemed to impede efforts to get on the water. Times had changed.

At the same time, my dad turned to a new career as a conservative politician. He had tinkered with politics previously through an unsuccessful run for Mayor of Corvallis (1970; he came in second in a field of thirteen). In 1982 he was elected to a four-year term as a member of the local Board of Education.

My sister Dianne, who lived in Corvallis at the time, wrote that he had become less stressed and irritable at home. He remained steadfast in his beliefs, seeing himself as honorable, experienced, and with the obligation to try to do the right thing. He had many friends; both Dianne and I had people approach us to say how much they admired and respected our dad. This sentiment extended to Oregon State University as he was inducted into the OSU Sports Hall of Fame in 1991.

He also began to write, publishing a memoir about Occupied Japan.[O-140] In addition, he began a history of Oregon State crew,[J-13] just as Ed Stevens had done forty-five years earlier.[A-44] He started by collating race records, which I thought was a waste of time: nobody would be interested. However, the records do make a nice appendix in the archive. He passed away before he could do much more.

In the end, he felt that he had completed his task of putting Oregon State rowing on firm footing. In the process he had provided young men and women a college experience that would serve them well in life.

Surprisingly, he never promoted rowing at home other than inviting me to try a single. Nevertheless, three of his four children rowed in PE classes. Two of his grandchildren rowed in high school, and two turned out for the Oregon State team (my niece Kaitlyn, rowed competitively for four years). My sister Karen recalled, Dad never encouraged or discouraged them as to whether to row. I don't recall it ever coming up in conversations with him. He was quiet about it, and now I know why. His belief system was more than competition and accolades: it was personal growth, self-awareness, and making decisions independently of others. This quality each of my kids has, whether I like it or not."

Oregon State rowing is strong. Although Washington and Cal are still the crews to beat, Oregon Staters are being invited to row on U.S. national teams. The program is firmly a part of the University, with the OSU Athletic Department handling the finances for both men's and women's crews. On the rowing website, the team listed three men's coaches, four women's coaches, a financial administrator, and a rigger to handle boat repair. The crews travel to West Coast regattas by van and bus—no longer does the first car in a caravan speed to catch the last one. Travel east is by air. Both crews have new dressing rooms with hot showers, restroom facilities, and towels—plus washing machines and driers.

Racing shells on the Willamette River. The boats are pointed upstream about 1½ miles down-river from the docks.[K-5]

The river remains a great place to row: no ice in the winter, and none of the waves that plague large bodies of water. Flood-control dams in the mountains have muted the high waters, although occasionally the dams cannot hold it all back.

The years of struggle for campus recognition have been successful. Both men's and women's rowing are represented on the Board of Directors of Varsity OSU, the successor to the Varsity O letterman's club. Rowing is an accepted sport now.

The boathouse barges have been gone for decades, replaced by a large metal shed on the bank next to a covered rowing tank. The barn is still used, now filled with more than 100 Concept-type ergometers distributed throughout the two main floors. Under the barn are singles, and seventeen pair-oared shells are now available. Thus, opportunities for OSU rowers to participate in small-boat rowing still exist. Noticeably gone are the old women's locker room, the Quonset hut, and the trailer-storage garage. Also gone are PE classes for the masses. Now fall PE rowing is offered only to screen for rowing talent. Some of the trees Stevens planted are still alive, but only one hemlock remains from the six I planted in the 1960s.

Racing is different. Crews routinely row the body of a race at 39-40 strokes per minute, much faster than the 34 to 36 of the old days. Bob Poole, who stroked Oregon State crews in the 1960s and still races, thinks that equipment improvements help get the rate up. Bob related, "The boats are lighter, as are the oars. When I stroked at Oregon State, I would pray before each race that I could hold onto the oar and feather for the complete race due to the lactic acid that developed in my forearms from the heavy oars with thickly greased leather collars. Our oars are now so much lighter, and with blade design they are shorter and more conducive to higher rates."[O-111] The effort seems to be more like hooking the spokes of a bicycle wheel to spin it with your fingers than to bend the oar on each stroke.

Races are now held at Dexter Reservoir (near Eugene) and Vancouver Lake (near Portland). Gone are attempts to draw spectators to races at the river. The larger venues allow for multi-crew regattas—more competition at one time reduces travel. The Willamette River current no longer complicates the race lanes, but practice on the river can still be tricky: in 2014 an 8-oared shell broke apart on a bridge pier.

Oregon State Crewhouse.[O-50] *This photo was taken during a Corvallis Regatta when racing still occurred on the river.*

As maintenance problems diminished and the Athletic Department covered key expenses, the mission of the Rowing Club shifted almost entirely to fundraising, a task also taken on by the Beaver Crew Association. The two merged to form the Beaver Rowing Club. The mix of students and alumni produced a strong organization with a mandate that includes producing fast boats, retaining student athletes, and building connections among athletes, parents, and alumni. Oregon State University has held one-day, school-wide fundraisers for a variety of activities. In one, men's and women's rowing ranked first and second, with rowing having almost four times the number of donors as the third place finisher.[O-57] Rowing alumni still care.

An important addition is a separate Corvallis Rowing Club (https://www.corvallisrowingclub.org). Founded in 1993, this organization solved the problem of ex-collegiate rowers getting on the water. The Club, which has about fifty members, contracts with Oregon State Rowing for access to the crew facilities: floats, dressing room, racing shell storage, rowing tank, and weight training setup. Classes in rowing and sponsorship of masters racing are among Club activities. Moreover, through a contribution to OSU, Club members can obtain storage for personal single sculls.

Racecourse on Dexter Reservoir.[O-136]

When I walked out on the old Van Buren Street Bridge, I noticed five coaching launches tied to the float. That should be enough to keep tabs on the crews—no more running barefoot through muddy fields after tipping over downstream. The ramp to the float had railings to keep rowers from inadvertently stepping into the river (in the old days, railings were themselves a hazard, because the ends of the fragile wooden shells would bang into them during transport to the float, a consequence that was worse than someone stepping into the river). Snags still populate the eastern riverbank, clearly visible in the low water of autumn. But the most noticeable feature of the river was its current. Seeing the swirling eddies downstream from the bridges made me uneasy when I thought about a shell slipping and sliding across them. I can understand how, almost one hundred years ago, College officials, and even Fred Newell, Ed Stevens' assistant at Harvard, had doubts about a rowing program on this river.

LIFE-SAVING RESCUE

In 2018, as a result of working on *Bitten* and re-living ancient rowing history, I joined the Berkeley Paddling and Rowing Club. I found that I could still keep a single upright. The hatchet-shaped blades made sculling much easier. But getting in and out of the boat was initially a major effort. To get in the boat, I would grab the oars with my left hand, crouch on the dock, lean back supported by my right arm, and place my feet in the stretchers. Then I would scoot onto the seat. On the water, turning the boat around was surprisingly painful, as backing on one side put tremendous pressure on the tops of my thighs. I expected blisters on my hands, but my legs ached like they never did fifty years ago. But all these complaints dissipated when I got the boat moving against an unsuspecting old-timer who didn't know that I was racing her.

Every year the Paddling and Rowing Club hosts a 3000-meter time-trial for human-propelled boats of all types. By 2021 I had been practicing for more than two years to beat the 17:39 single sculls time set by a very skilled woman in my age bracket. I was able to get close to her time, and once I was a few seconds under. Thus, I decided to enter the time-trial along with boats ranging from stand-up paddleboards to very fast racing kayaks.

Launching boats for time trial at Berkeley's Aquatic Park.[O-174]

The weather was good for racing: a warm November day with only a slight breeze blowing down the course. We assembled at the starting line near the dock and took off for the other end of the lagoon, 1500 meters away. I remember making the U-turn and heading back for the dock, far behind several racing kayaks. When I crossed the finish line, I thought I looked at my watch, thinking that my time was not bad. That must have been a hallucination: I never would have risked a slow beginning by looking at my watch at the start. I couldn't know the time.

Elaine Baden, Club President, was supervising the time trial.[O-173] As she stood on the dock watching the finish, a Club member commented that I looked tired, that my strokes were not clean or strong. It turned out that I was having a heart attack. That explained why my time was a disappointing 18:22.

I don't remember stopping the boat, which was required because the bank was close to the finish line. Nor do I remember turning the boat around and heading for the dock. I must have been rowing by reflex. Elaine noted that I looked increasingly uncoordinated and erratic as I slowly approached the dock.

Twenty-eight boats were in my heat, resulting in a backup at the dock. I waited, perhaps thirty feet from the dock, for space to land the boat. Roughly ten minutes after I crossed the finish line, Elaine saw my boat slowly roll over as I collapsed and went upside down in the water. Soon an air bubble surfaced, but I did not. Elaine immediately recognized a serious situation and began yelling for help and for someone to call 911. She then shouted at nearby racers to get me out of the water.

John Dye and Paul MacIntyre, two of the closest racers, didn't hesitate to jump into the water with bare feet, not knowing whether they would strike glass, rocks, or other sharp objects on the lagoon bottom.

John later wrote that as he approached the dock on his stand-up paddleboard, he saw that I was about two boat lengths off the dock when I gently rolled over into the water. [O-173a] I didn't appear in distress, but he thought this was very odd. He started to maneuver around my boat to see whether I needed help. Maybe three to five seconds passed when he heard Elaine yell from the dock, "Call 911!" He saw that my feet were still strapped into the foot supports of the shell and my head and torso were under water. A few air bubbles came up as he jumped off his board to get me up. It was another five to ten seconds before he reached me and raised my head above water.

Paul had also jumped in, reaching me about the same time as John, but on the other side of my boat. He had been only a few feet away and thought I tipped over to cool off after the race. He looked across my boat and saw that I was face-up under the water with my feet still attached to the boat. He reached across my racing shell to pull me up in a maneuver used for sea kayak rescues. As he pulled and John lifted, the weight on the fragile racing shell was too much—the boat broke. Paul rolled me onto my left side while they supported me. I seemed to be breathing a bit, but unconscious and unresponsive. He and John untangled me from the shell, being mindful of the boat's splintered fiberglass that was directly below the three of us.

Other boaters on the dock jumped into the water to help drag me to the dock. While others supported me, John held the now crumpled shell away from us. Many hands lifted me onto the dock.

Broken racing shell after parts were pushed together for repair. Left:
top view. Right: bottom view. In both views, bow is to the left.[O-184]

Dr. Jean Hayward brought her boat into the dock area a
minute after John and Paul jumped into the water. She immediately took control of the medical response, yelling instructions
before she landed. After I was laid on the dock, John ran to the
boathouse to get the defibrillator (fortunately a Club member had
subsidized the purchase of one several years earlier). Dr. Dimitri
Lerner stepped in to help with chest compression, as did Frank
Griffo, a parent of one of the paddlers from Petaluma.

Frank had participated in CPR classes, but he was surprised
that working on a human is not the same as working on a practice
doll. The doll maintains its shape and gives a decisive click when
you apply the proper pressure. I was quite flexible, soft and mal-
leable. The bending of the cartilage in my ribs made it difficult
to know how hard to push. Nevertheless, Frank quickly got his
bearings. A carotid pulse appeared, and skin color improved.
My lungs were full of water that chest compression brought up,
followed by a continuing stream of tan foam.

Meanwhile, Jean shocked me three times, gave me CPR, and
performed mouth-to-mouth resuscitation without regard for her
own safety (Covid-19 was prevalent at the time, and she had no
way of knowing what other infection I might have carried, either
personally or in either the dirty lagoon water or the tan foam
bubbling from my lips). We were all on a metal dock, and Jean
had on only one shoe—she administered the shocks standing on
the foot with the shoe, hoping not to shock herself in the process.

After each shock I gasped and coughed. Each time, she felt a faint pulse for a few seconds, but it was soon lost.

Frank recalled that after several rounds I began to breathe on my own. He briefly stopped to check the pulse and there it was: a nice strong beat sustaining on its own. He was so excited. But within 20-30 seconds the pulse faded, and they were back working the chest. Frank began to get tired and discouraged as he watched a cyanotic pallor spread across my skin; EMS was nowhere to be found. He later wrote, "This is why we work in teams!"

Dimitri relieved Frank, and Frank sat by my side to rest and monitor my pulse, recalling, "I could feel a very strong pulse (stronger than any I have ever felt) with each compression Dimitri applied. The compressions were doing their job."

Since blankets were unavailable, Jean shouted for someone to run to the boathouse and get dry towels. Audrey Johnson, a 13-year-old paddler, responded.

Audrey recalled,[O-185] "I had just climbed out of my racing kayak onto the dock at the Berkeley Mixer race, right after the first heat. Suddenly, officials on the dock started screaming, "Call 911! Call 911!" It didn't register with me what was happening for a few seconds, as I couldn't see what the emergency was. There was only a large clump of boats chatting to each other about the race they just finished. An adult was yelling at us to get off the dock and take our boats with us. Get your shoes later. When I walked up the gangway, I saw tons of people talking on their phones. When I heard another yell about getting towels, I felt a rush of adrenaline that overtook being tired from the race. I turned, handed my boat to someone and said, 'Hold this for a second.' Then I sprinted barefoot across the sharp gravel to find towels. I still didn't know what for, but based on the screaming and running around, I knew it was important.

"On land, it was like a whole other world, because the news of the emergency hadn't reached others yet. They were very confused by my yelling, 'Give me any towels you can see!' I ran back with my arms full of towels, and someone said, 'We need more towels! Bring more!' I now saw lots of people jumping into the relatively shallow water, a snapped rowing shell, and some rowing shoes still clipped to the footplate. I knew that meant that someone is possibly seriously hurt underwater, and I ran even faster than I had the previous time to find towels. I was shoving people aside (sorry) and stealing towels out of peoples' hands (sorry again) to find anything. Then, I remembered the restrooms had showers, so I grabbed all of the towels off of the pegs in the room. Running back, I gave the huge pile of towels to someone in the huge crowd surrounding the mystery person. They told me that they had enough towels now, so I shakily walked back up the ramp.

"At the boathouse, I stopped to have something to eat. A few of my teammates had left due to their fear of the situation and some grief because everyone was worried that someone had just died. I overheard a group of men that presumably knew the mystery person saying that they hope that they get to die in a somewhat nice way on a sunny day, out on the water doing what they love. I felt like I wanted to cry, but I couldn't. I believe it was because I was still in shock at what had just happened.

"Sirens were getting closer, and an ambulance came to take this person away. I wanted to go home after experiencing something so terrifying up close, but I didn't leave. After the race had been delayed, I went on with the day after agreeing with one of my coaches to race again in the third heat. I could begin to forget the empty, shaky feeling that I could not get rid of. Just being on the water made things seem okay for a while.

"Everything kept replaying in the back of my mind for a few days after, and then at one of my workouts, a coach told us that 'Karl' from the Berkeley Mixer was alive. It took me a minute to connect the dots that Karl was the name of the person who I thought had died at the race. I felt so much relief and happiness that he was okay. Some more time passes, and we hear that Karl is awake. A bit later, we receive a thank you letter from him for saving his life, and in the card, he said that he knew that a young lady had gotten her feet hurt while helping him. I was so happy he knew about me that I cried once I got home."

Running barefoot over sharp gravel had cut Audrey's feet. In school the next day, she asked her PE teacher to excuse her from class because her feet hurt. Helping to save a man's life was her reason. That excuse was a new one for the teacher—the school principal needed to hear this one. The principal found the story novel enough to telephone Audrey's mother for confirmation.

As the emergency response was developing on the dock, Frank's wife Vicki ran to the entrance of Aquatic Park to direct the Berkeley Fire Department Rescue Unit. But the following ambulance made a wrong turn directed by a GPS inaccuracy, and firemen had to call it back down the entrance ramp to the I-80 freeway. Nevertheless, the ambulance finally arrived and transported me to Alta Bates Summit Medical Center.

I was intubated and heavily sedated for three or four days.[O-182] During that time my heart was assisted by a helium-filled balloon in my leg and my body was subjected to several-hour cycles of cooling and warming. Each day they reduced the sedation to see whether I regained consciousness. After two days I began to twitch but without a response to commands. Antibiotics were administered because my lungs had taken up polluted lake water.

By day three I regained consciousness and some ability to move my arms and legs. I could nod and shake my head in response to questions. The ventilator was removed the next day, and I began to ask questions, such as what antibiotic was I receiving? By day five my thoughts were still scattered, but I was becoming more lucid.

Exploratory surgery revealed that stents would be inadequate; after a week in the hospital, I underwent heart surgery, a triple bypass. Somehow the stress test I had taken several months

384 BITTEN *by the* ROWING BUG

earlier failed to catch the problem. After a month in the hospital, I resumed work on the rowing archive, thanks to such skilled and selfless teammates. And Jean Hayward could rack up her second save (the first was in an airport).

The racing shell I rowed had been donated to the Club with the proviso that the boat would be carefully handled. The rescue seemed to render the boat a complete loss for racing, The donor was philosophical: a person's life is worth much more than an old rowing shell. But Mike Fennelly, the country's premier boatman, brought the shell back to life without a sign of damage.

Time Line[*]

1926 Two 8-oared shells obtained from the University of California

1927 Dock lost to flood that was so high it reached the middle of Corvallis

1928-29 J.C. Othus was volunteer coach; beat Washington frosh crew

1928 New dock built on west bank, shed rented; *Rho Dammit Rho I* training barge built

1929 Oregon State Rowing Club formed; credit for PE crew at OAC

1931 EA Stevens becomes coach, part-time instructor for PE crew

1932 Oregon Electric Depot obtained as crew house

1936-41 An OSU crew beat Portland Rowing Club and UW frosh; Drlica as cox broke a shell on the bridge; 10% of male student body participating in rowing at any given time

1937 *Rho Dammit Rho II* training barge built

1938-39 Stevens built two 4-oared shells for PE; later built 8-oared shell

1940 Drlica report to Langton shows Stevens needs assistant; World War II: competitive program halted

1947 Rowing restarted

1949 Senior class donates coaching launch (*49er*)

1950 Stevens retires, replaced by Drlica

1952 Women's intramural started

1952 John Beach farm purchased for golf course and recreational

---

[*]   sources J-1; J-7

area, negotiated by Stevens, Drlica, and Morris Robertson

1953 Rowing tank proposed

1954 Launch house completed

1950s Beach barn refurbished, classroom, weight training, rowing machines, shell and canoe storage

1955 Training barge *Rho Dammit Rho III* completed

1956 Barge house completed

1957 Western Crew Coaches Association started by 7 coaches including Drlica; Stevens passed away

1958 First Pocock shell (*Mike Zahorski*) purchased

1959 Second Pocock shell (*William Eskew*) purchased; work on Quonset hut started

1960 Western Sprint Championship Regatta started; nine antique small boats obtained from Portland Rowing Club (3 singles, 3 doubles, 3 fours); shell trailer built

1961 Quonset hut work continued; third Pocock shell (*Chuck Smith* purchased; 2 lighters (barges) received from Tongue Point Naval Depot

1963 Drlica designed program to fund club (non-Athletic Department) sports; Oregon Electric Depot demolished and portion salvaged as shower/locker room; Beach farmhouse demolished for new bridge; Navy barge moorage completed; small-boats float completed

1964 EA Stevens locker room built; old locker room to women's crew; first Corvallis Invitational Regatta; PE rowing classes for women; Astrid Hancock coaches first extramural women's crew

1966 National Women's Rowing Association constitutional convention in Corvallis, OSU women charter members of NWRA, first college crew in NWRA, first away race for OSU women; first NWRA championships in Seattle

1967 Heavyweight men's crew joins Athletic Department

1967 Women's intramural rowing terminated

1968 Styrofoam in floats

1969 Men's crew placed 10th in first national competition for OSU (IRA)

1972 Men's crew placed 3rd in national competition (IRA); Title IX legislation passed

1975 Men's four-oared crew placed first in national competition (IRA); Kate Gribskov at selection camp for national team

1976 Robert Zagunis on US Olympic team

1977 Oregon Sports Writers and Sports Broadcasters Merit Award to Drlica; men's four-oared crew placed first in national competition (IRA); women's and men's lightweight crews join Men's Athletic Department

1978 Two men on a national team

1979 Tom Woodman on PanAm team

1980 Tom Woodman on US Olympic team; women second in collegiate national championship, first in senior eight and elite eight; four and pair place third in women's nationals

1980 Drlica retired from active coaching

1991 Drlica entered OSU Sports Hall of Fame

1993 Robert Zagunis entered OSU Sports Hall of Fame

2003 Tom Woodman entered OSU Sports Hall of Fame

2006 Drlica passed away

2018 Rowing archive to OSU Valley Library

2020 Ralph Mathison and 1980 women's crew entered OSU Sports Hall of Fame

2022 Astrid Hancock and 14 women rowers entered OSU Sports Hall of Fame[O-189]

Acknowledgements

During the writing of *Bitten by the Rowing Bug* I resumed single sculling and suffered a life-threatening event. Without the lifesaving efforts of fellow boaters, led by Elaine Baden, Jean Hayward, John Dye, Paul MacIntyre, Frank Griffo, and Audrey Johnson, the book would not have been completed. Many paddlers and rowers contributed to a perfect rescue. I can never thank you enough for giving me another birthday. Of course, without the outstanding work of the medical team at Alta Bates Summit Medical Center, the rescue would have gone for naught. Special thanks go to Connie Cheung, Claudia Cordero, and Ole Dierks.

With respect to the production of the book, I am particularly indebted to Robert Harris and Diane Deblois for preventing me from throwing the archive into the garbage and to Astrid Hancock for recollections and for performing the thankless task of editing multiple versions. Kaitlyn Kernek Beattie provided many outstanding editorial insights: she changed my approach to the story. Other friends and relatives also stepped forward to help. Their recollections enriched the work, their encouragement kept me going, and their critical comments forced me to revise many times. For this help I thank Elaine Baden, James Berger, Tim Blower, Carl Bower, John Carnegie, James Carruthers, Alex Drlica-Wagner, Brian Finn, Wayne Fogle, Jean Hayward, Barry Hilt, Kirk Hutchinson, Cynthia Jackson, Robert Jackson, Audrey Johnson, Tracy Johnson, Shweta Karambelkar, Karen Drlica Kernek, Clyde Kernek, Sterling Kernek, Bill Knudson, Larry Landis, Liz Lee,

Dianne Drlica Lewis, Christopher Mathews, Karl McCreary, Joseph Michalek, Oliver O'Reily, Robert Poole, Melissa Kernek Rame, Dennis Searcy, Carol Simpson Sanoff, Steve Schaffran, Dan Smith, Ilene Wagner, and David Williams.

Notes and Citations

Coaches Stevens and Drlica maintained collections of crew-related documents that constitute the basis for *Bitten*. Most of the original documents reside in the Karl F. Drlica Papers, OSU Libraries Special Collections and Archives Research Center, as indicated below. To facilitate access, electronic copies have been prepared and numbered.

A-1 Two photos of Ed Stevens as a student at Cornell University, 1909. In one, it appears that Stevens is part of a soccer team. Photographer is unknown. Karl F. Drlica Papers, OSU Libraries Special Collections and Archives Research Center.

A-2 *Rowing as an Experience in Democracy* by Karl F. Drlica in *J. Am. Assoc. for Health-Physical Education-Recreation* June 1953 (also C-67 with more detail). Karl F. Drlica Papers, OSU Libraries Special Collections and Archives Research Center.

A-3. Article (*Common Sense Crew Program*) and photo from the *Oregon Stater* (OSU alumni magazine) May, 1952. Photographer is unknown. This article describes the philosophy of Stevens and Drlica. Karl F. Drlica Papers, OSU Libraries Special Collections and Archives Research Center.

A-4 Letter from E.C. Sammons to Coach Stevens, October 22, 1934. Sammons mentions the favorable response of the State Board of Education to Brands' report (A-67), indicating that Sammons was on the Board. Karl F. Drlica Papers, OSU Libraries Special Collections and Archives Research Center.

A-5 Photo of Coach Stevens building a racing shell, 1935. Photographer is unknown. Stevens had no prior experience with boat building and he was not paid to build boats. Karl F. Drlica Papers, OSU Libraries Special Collections and Archives Research Center.

A-6 Multiple photos of boathouse renovation. Photographer is unknown. The original Oregon Electric Depot was raised several feet, and a boat repair shop was added along one side. Funds for much of the work came from Federal work programs during the Great Depression. Karl F. Drlica Papers, OSU Libraries Special Collections and Archives Research Center.

A-7 Clipping from *The Morning Oregonian*, December 28, 1923. Stevens' coaching methods at Harvard are said to be unusual. Karl F. Drlica Papers, OSU Libraries Special Collections and Archives Research Center.

A-8 Article on training for crew and photo of Coach Fred Newell leading Harvard crew in a run; article in *The Boston Globe* March 5, 1924. Running was not a usual part of training for rowing at the time. Photographer is unknown. Karl F. Drlica Papers, OSU Libraries Special Collections and Archives Research Center.

A-9 Unidentified newspaper clipping concerning plans for crews in Boston area. Karl F. Drlica Papers, OSU Libraries Special Collections and Archives Research Center.

A-10 Unidentified newspaper clipping referring to Coach Stevens being awarded honorary degree from Harvard. Karl F. Drlica Papers, OSU Libraries Special Collections and Archives Research Center.

A-11 Unidentified newspaper clipping; local news reporting Ed Stevens visiting home from Cornell University. Karl F. Drlica Papers, OSU Libraries Special Collections and Archives Research Center.

A-12 Clipping from the *Harvard Crimson*, December 11, 1923 referring to training during Christmas break. Reference is made to the installation of a motor to move water in the rowing tank. Karl F. Drlica Papers, OSU Libraries Special Collections and Archives Research Center.

A-14 Unidentified newspaper clipping regarding beginning of season at Harvard. Mention is made of the football captain being on the crew. Karl F. Drlica Papers, OSU Libraries Special Collections and Archives Research Center.

A-15 Clippings from the *Harvard Crimson* regarding crew training, early 1924. Running was stressed. Karl F. Drlica Papers, OSU Libraries Special Collections and Archives Research Center.

A-16 Clipping from the Boston Globe, February 25, 1924, briefly updates progress with the crew. Karl F. Drlica Papers, OSU Libraries Special Collections and Archives Research Center.

A-17 Personal letter from Fred Newell to Ed Stevens, August 19, 1923, congratulating Stevens on behalf of the Portland Rowing Club on obtaining the Harvard job. Karl F. Drlica Papers, OSU Libraries Special Collections and Archives Research Center.

A-18 Clipping from the *Morning Oregonian*, December 24, 1923. Stevens comments on his chances to beat Yale in the spring. Karl F. Drlica Papers, OSU Libraries Special Collections and Archives Research Center.

A-19 Newspaper clipping concerning rowing tank and class crews at Harvard. Article includes a photo of the motor installed in the rowing tank. Karl F. Drlica Papers, OSU Libraries Special Collections and Archives Research Center.

A-20 Stevens testing the ice that is preventing the crew from rowing. Photo from the *Boston Globe*. Photographer is unknown. Karl F. Drlica Papers, OSU Libraries Special Collections and Archives Research Center.

A-21 Race program from regatta at Wigwam Inn, Canada; August 16, 1919. The Inn was a luxury resort located near Vancouver, B.C. Portland Rowing Club won the four-oared race. Karl F. Drlica Papers, OSU Libraries Special Collections and Archives Research Center.

A-22 *Heave Together*, official organ of Northwest Steel and Northwest Bridge and Iron Companies' Employees of Portland, Oregon. Photos of Stevens by unknown photographer. Also included is a newspaper clipping. Results of the race at Wigwam Inn are detailed along with a poem about Stevens. Karl F. Drlica Papers, OSU Libraries Special Collections and Archives Research Center.

A-24 Photo of two of Stevens' cattle. *Heave Together*, official organ of Northwest Steel and Northwest Bridge and Iron Companies' Employees of Portland, Oregon. Photographer is unknown. Karl F. Drlica Papers, OSU Libraries Special Collections and Archives Research Center.

A-25 Photo of frame-bending team, including Stevens, from *Heave Together*, official organ of Northwest Steel and Northwest Bridge and Iron Companies' Employees of Portland, Oregon. Photographer is unknown. The article mentions that Stevens was on the football team at Cornell. Karl F. Drlica Papers, OSU Libraries Special Collections and Archives Research Center.

A-26 Photo of lithograph by Carl Walters called "The Frame Benders." Copy taken from *Heave Together*, official organ of Northwest Steel and Northwest Bridge and Iron Companies' Employees of Portland, Oregon. Vol. 2 number 19; October 1, 1919. Karl F. Drlica Papers, OSU Libraries Special Collections and Archives Research Center.

A-27 Unidentified newspaper clipping noting that Cornell coach John Hoyle was making racing shells in the winter. Also mentioned is the use of an observation train running along

race courses. Karl F. Drlica Papers, OSU Libraries Special Collections and Archives Research Center.

A-28 Unidentified newspaper clipping (probably the *Daily Barometer*) noting activities at Oregon State College; photo of Coach Stevens and students. Photographer is unknown. Karl F. Drlica Papers, OSU Libraries Special Collections and Archives Research Center.

A-29 Clipping from the *Harvard Crimson,* February 18, 1924. Stevens stresses that the oarsmen must work hard. Karl F. Drlica Papers, OSU Libraries Special Collections and Archives Research Center.

A-30 Clipping from the *Harvard Crimson*, December 19, 1923. The end of the fall season is described as the crew prepares for winter ice. Karl F. Drlica Papers, OSU Libraries Special Collections and Archives Research Center.

A-31 Clippings from the *Syracuse Journal* indicating that Ed Stevens had been in the first boat the previous year but early in the season was being dropped to the second boat. Karl F. Drlica Papers, OSU Libraries Special Collections and Archives Research Center.

A-32 *Heave Together*, official organ of Northwest Steel and Northwest Bridge and Iron Companies' Employees of Portland, Oregon. The company is bragging about the productivity of the frame benders. Karl F. Drlica Papers, OSU Libraries Special Collections and Archives Research Center.

A33 Dr. Clair V. Langton, ca. 1930s. He became head of physical education at Oregon State about the time Stevens arrived. Langton was a strong supporter of crew. From Oregon Digital HC0272, OSU Libraries Special Collections & Archives Research Center.

A-34 Photo of Coach Stevens and rowing machines from an unidentified publication. The article discusses Stevens' boat building.

Photographer is unknown. Karl F. Drlica Papers, OSU Libraries Special Collections and Archives Research Center.

A-35 Photo of Stevens and Drlica working on a racing shell in the boathouse, *Oregon Sunday Journal*, 1939. Photographer is unknown. Karl F. Drlica Papers, OSU Libraries Special Collections and Archives Research Center.

A-36 Photo of training barge with crew rowing. Photographer is unknown. Karl F. Drlica Papers, OSU Libraries Special Collections and Archives Research Center.

A-37 Rowing Club letter requesting rental of shed for boathouse, 1930. The term was a little more than a month, and the rental fee was two tickets to all Oregon State home football games. Karl F. Drlica Papers, OSU Libraries Special Collections and Archives Research Center.

A-38 Photo of Coach Stevens, his wife Irene, and varsity crew members, 1949. Stevens was an avid gardener, and in the 1930s he ran a nursery. As a teenager the author pulled weeds for Irene. Photographer is unknown. Karl F. Drlica Papers, OSU Libraries Special Collections and Archives Research Center.

A-39 Photo of OSU boathouse, circa 1960, taken from the approach to Van Buren Street Bridge. The boathouse was originally a train depot that was repurposed in about 1933 and demolished for the Harrison Street Bridge in 1963. Racing shells were stored in the right-hand portion of the building. The approach to the bridge is on the right; the river is out of view, 200 yards to the left. Photographer is unknown. Karl F. Drlica Papers, OSU Libraries Special Collections and Archives Research Center.

A-40 Photo of the inboard coaching launch *49er*. This was the first reliable coaching boat at Oregon State. Photographer is unknown. Karl F. Drlica Papers, OSU Libraries Special Collections and Archives Research Center.

A-41 Barge house and training barge, April 1958. The shed, which was constructed on large logs, was considered necessary to keep rain from filling the barge with water. Photographer is unknown. Karl F. Drlica Papers, OSU Libraries Special Collections and Archives Research Center.

A-42 Crew on boathouse roof thanking the Class of 1949 for the gift of a coaching launch. Photographer is unknown. Karl F. Drlica Papers, OSU Libraries Special Collections and Archives Research Center.

A-43 Coach Drlica handwritten recollections of Coach Stevens at Oregon State. This was probably written when Drlica was more than 80 years old. Karl F. Drlica Papers, OSU Libraries Special Collections and Archives Research Center. A reference to Pop Courtney is made; Courtney is described separately in Wikipedia.

A-44 History of Oregon State Rowing Club, 1927 to 1935, written by Ed Stevens and edited by Arthur Orr. Includes material from latter part of 1930s. Karl F. Drlica Papers, OSU Libraries Special Collections and Archives Research Center.

A-45 History of Oregon State crew, written by Al Cook, 1933. Includes perspective not captured by the Stevens history (A-44). Karl F. Drlica Papers, OSU Libraries Special Collections and Archives Research Center.

A-46 Handwritten letter from Coach Stevens to Ted Carlson, Assistant Alumni Director, April 1952. This letter discusses Stevens' coaching philosophy and provides a reference for how Drlica's approach differed from that of Stevens. Karl F. Drlica Papers, OSU Libraries Special Collections and Archives Research Center.

A-47 Newspaper clippings, Stevens' obituary and other topics. Naming of the crew house was approved by the State of Oregon. Karl F. Drlica Papers, OSU Libraries Special Collections and Archives Research Center.

A-48 History of crew at Oregon State. This is a transcribed version of A-44, probably prepared by Coach Drlica. Karl F. Drlica Papers, OSU Libraries Special Collections and Archives Research Center.

A-49 Letter from Fred Newell to Coach Drlica, June 11, 1962. The letter includes discussion of the "old days". Karl F. Drlica Papers, OSU Libraries Special Collections and Archives Research Center.

A-51 Personal letter from Fred Newell to Coach Drlica, December 2, 1961. Karl F. Drlica Papers, OSU Libraries Special Collections and Archives Research Center.

A-52 History of the Portland Rowing Club and photo of Fred Newell, 1960, printed in *Boating News*, a magazine published by Durham & Downey Printers, Portland Oregon. Photographer is unknown. Karl F. Drlica Papers, OSU Libraries Special Collections and Archives Research Center.

A-53 Personal letter from Fred Newell to Coach Drlica, November 8, 1961. Karl F. Drlica Papers, OSU Libraries Special Collections and Archives Research Center.

A-54 Series of letters from Fred Newell to Coach Drlica regarding gift of shells from Portland Rowing Club to Oregon State College, 1960. Karl F. Drlica Papers, OSU Libraries Special Collections and Archives Research Center.

A-56 Series of letters from Coach Drlica to Fred Newell regarding small boats, 1962. Karl F. Drlica Papers, OSU Libraries Special Collections and Archives Research Center.

A-57 Letters from Fred Newell to Robert Young, 1929. Unsolicited advice on rowing style. Karl F. Drlica Papers, OSU Libraries Special Collections and Archives Research Center.

A-58 Letter from Robert Young acknowledging effort to name the boathouse after him. Karl F. Drlica Papers, OSU Libraries Special Collections and Archives Research Center.

A-59 Collection of letters written by Arthur Orr, 1935, as President of the Rowing Club. Karl F. Drlica Papers, OSU Libraries Special Collections and Archives Research Center.

A-60 The OAC *Daily Barometer*, November 20, 1926 and other clippings regarding racing shells. Clippings include instructions for handling the boats by Ky Ebright, searching for boathouse, funding the building of a training barge, and Coach Othus. Karl F. Drlica Papers, OSU Libraries Special Collections and Archives Research Center.

A-61 Letter to Rowing Club from Drlica as president, 1940. The letter illustrates the enthusiasm of oarsmen. Karl F. Drlica Papers, OSU Libraries Special Collections and Archives Research Center

A-61a Letter from Oliver Batcheller to Robert Young stating that the Club was not allowed to name the boathouse honoring Young, May 24, 1935. Karl F. Drlica Papers, OSU Libraries Special Collections and Archives Research Center.

A-62 Collection of correspondence requesting block awards for partication in competitive rowing crews. Karl F. Drlica Papers, OSU Libraries Special Collections and Archives Research Center.

A-64 Carl Clogstrom, report on crew to the Varsity O in an attempt to make rowing a part of the Varsity O, circa 1948. Karl F. Drlica Papers, OSU Libraries Special Collections and Archives Research Center.

A-65 Type-written letters from oarsmen to OSC student newspaper requesting donation from class of 1949 for new coaching launch. Karl F. Drlica Papers, OSU Libraries Special Collections and Archives Research Center.

A-66 Letter from Joseph Dyer regarding the *Yellow Peril*, March 1936. Karl F. Drlica Papers, OSU Libraries Special Collections and Archives Research Center.

A-67 Letter from C.E. Brands to the State Board of Education describing progress at the boathouse, October 22, 1934. Karl F. Drlica Papers, OSU Libraries Special Collections and Archives Research Center.

A-68 Letters between Fred Newell and Coach Drlica, 1964-5. Karl F. Drlica Papers, OSU Libraries Special Collections and Archives Research Center.

A-69 *The Timberman*, August 1941. Article and photos describe plywood racing shells being constructed and rowed. PT boat is sketched as an ad for waterproof glue. Photographer is unknown. Karl F. Drlica Papers, OSU Libraries Special Collections and Archives Research Center.

A-73 Coach Drlica comments on Campbell boat design and resistance data. November 5, 1997. Karl F. Drlica Papers, OSU Libraries Special Collections and Archives Research Center.

A-74 *Time*, February 7, 1969, page 58. Article on long-chain polymers reducing drag with naval vessels. Karl F. Drlica Papers, OSU Libraries Special Collections and Archives Research Center.

A-75 Letter from Peter Ayling to Coach Drlica regarding polymers affecting drag, December 1968. Karl F. Drlica Papers, OSU Libraries Special Collections and Archives Research Center.

A-76 Progress report by Coach Drlica regarding experiments with fiberglass racing shell parts, 1958. Karl F. Drlica Papers, OSU Libraries Special Collections and Archives Research Center.

A-78 Correspondence concerning friction-reducing material, 1969. Karl F. Drlica Papers, OSU Libraries Special Collections and Archives Research Center.

A-80 Photo of 1939 crew. Dean Painter was coxswain and President of Rowing Club. Photographer is unknown. Karl F. Drlica Papers, OSU Libraries Special Collections and Archives Research Center.

A-81 Letter from Robert Young to Karl Brandt, president of rowing club, 1959. Karl F. Drlica Papers, OSU Libraries Special Collections and Archives Research Center.

B-1 Photo of senior class crew 1929. This crew beat a University of Washington freshman crew in Corvallis. Shown is Robert Young, founder of Oregon State crew. Photographer is unknown. Karl F. Drlica Papers, OSU Libraries Special Collections and Archives Research Center.

B-3 Newspaper clippings, 1928 and 1929 races. Karl F. Drlica Papers, OSU Libraries Special Collections and Archives Research Center.

B-6 Newspaper clippings, 1928 and 1929 races. Karl F. Drlica Papers, OSU Libraries Special Collections and Archives Research Center.

B-7c,d Photo of 1934 crew and photo showing construction of the training barge. *The Oregon Stater*, May 1957. Photographer is unknown. Karl F. Drlica Papers, OSU Libraries Special Collections and Archives Research Center.

B-8 Newspaper clipping regarding JC Othus becoming rowing coach at the University of Portland, March 14, 1948. Karl F. Drlica Papers, OSU Libraries Special Collections and Archives Research Center.

B-9 Oregon State College Weekend Brochure, 1929, showing photos of Young, Othus, and crew. Karl F. Drlica Papers, OSU Libraries Special Collections and Archives Research Center.

C-1 Photos of Rowing Club Presidents and varsity letters early 1960s. Photographer is unknown. Karl F. Drlica Papers, OSU Libraries Special Collections and Archives Research Center.

C-2 Photo of racecourse in 1963 fundraising brochure and postcard used for publicity. The photo was probably from Western Ways, an aerial photography business in the Corvallis, Oregon area. Karl F. Drlica Papers, OSU Libraries Special Collections and Archives Research Center.

C-3 Instructions for Homecoming 1935, Art Orr and Oliver Batcheller. Includes sketch of training barge. Karl F. Drlica Papers, OSU Libraries Special Collections and Archives Research Center.

C-4 Photo of Jim Carruthers, 2001, *Daily Astorian and Chinook Observer*, October 2001. Photographer is unknown. Karl F. Drlica Papers, OSU Libraries Special Collections and Archives Research Center.

C-5 Photo of 1940 crew. Photo courtesy of Jim Bell. Karl F. Drlica Papers, OSU Libraries Special Collections and Archives Research Center.

C-6 Photo of painting house numbers on street curbs. Don Pearson, Gary Ray, circa 1961. Photographer is unknown. Karl F. Drlica Papers, OSU Libraries Special Collections and Archives Research Center.

C-7 Photo showing loading oars on Stevens' car for crew trip, 1940. Photographer is unknown. Karl F. Drlica Papers, OSU Libraries Special Collections and Archives Research Center.

C-9 Letter from Governor of Oregon Mark Hatfield to Rowing Club President, Joe Michalek, April 22, 1959. Karl F. Drlica Papers, OSU Libraries Special Collections and Archives Research Center.

C-11 Clipping from the *Daily Barometer* describing 11th annual Corvallis Regatta. Karl F. Drlica Papers, OSU Libraries Special Collections and Archives Research Center.

C-12 Newspaper clippings, 1980 Corvallis Regatta. Karl F. Drlica Papers, OSU Libraries Special Collections and Archives Research Center.

C-13 Newspaper clippings, 1980 Corvallis Regatta. Karl F. Drlica Papers, OSU Libraries Special Collections and Archives Research Center.

C-14 Kent Atwood, letter-to-the-editor column, *Daily Barometer,* November 1, 1978. Karl F. Drlica Papers, OSU Libraries Special Collections and Archives Research Center.

C-15 Notebook dividers used for fundraising and local publicity. Karl F. Drlica Papers, OSU Libraries Special Collections and Archives Research Center.

C-16 OSU crew recruiting poster; photo of the author building a single. Photographer is unknown. Karl F. Drlica Papers, OSU Libraries Special Collections and Archives Research Center.

C-17 Letters from Rowing Club, Langton, and Robert Young regarding naming of the boathouse, 1935. Karl F. Drlica Papers, OSU Libraries Special Collections and Archives Research Center.

C-18 Collection of letters to and from Arthur Orr/Oliver Batcheller and Oregon State President and faculty regarding learning to row. 1935. Karl F. Drlica Papers, OSU Libraries Special Collections and Archives Research Center.

C-19 Letter from Arthur Orr to University of Portland, 1935. Karl F. Drlica Papers, OSU Libraries Special Collections and Archives Research Center.

C-20 Arthur Orr letters of resignation to Coach Stevens and the Rowing Club, 1935. Karl F. Drlica Papers, OSU Libraries Special Collections and Archives Research Center.

C-21 Letter from Dean Dubach to Arthur Orr, 1935. Karl F. Drlica Papers, OSU Libraries Special Collections and Archives Research Center.

C-22 Letter from Arthur Orr to Coach Stevens, 1935. Karl F. Drlica Papers, OSU Libraries Special Collections and Archives Research Center.

C-23 Photo of the author building a one-person racing shell. October 1963. Photographer is unknown. Karl F. Drlica

Papers, OSU Libraries Special Collections and Archives Research Center.

C-24 Rowing Club members working on the alumni mailing list, circa 1963. Photographer is unknown. Karl F. Drlica Papers, OSU Libraries Special Collections and Archives Research Center.

C-25 Photo of Jim Carruthers, 1963. Photographer is unknown. Karl F. Drlica Papers, OSU Libraries Special Collections and Archives Research Center.

C-26 Photo of Assistant Coach Carl Bower working on barge. Bower performed all major renovations to the barges. Photographer is unknown. Karl F. Drlica Papers, OSU Libraries Special Collections and Archives Research Center.

C-27 Photo of Barry Hilt, 1965. Photographer is unknown. Karl F. Drlica Papers, OSU Libraries Special Collections and Archives Research Center.

C-28 Photo of Bob Janz. 1965. Photographer is unknown. Karl F. Drlica Papers, OSU Libraries Special Collections and Archives Research Center.

C-31 Photo of Jim Carruthers (upper left) and crew. Photographer is unknown. Karl F. Drlica Papers, OSU Libraries Special Collections and Archives Research Center.

C-32 Photo of the author in home-made single, January 1964. Photographer is unknown. Karl F. Drlica Papers, OSU Libraries Special Collections and Archives Research Center.

C-33 Photo of Coach Drlica preparing a mold for a fiberglass single. Photographer is unknown. Karl F. Drlica Papers, OSU Libraries Special Collections and Archives Research Center.

C-34 Oarsmen working on ramp to float. Photographer is unknown. Karl F. Drlica Papers, OSU Libraries Special Collections and Archives Research Center.

C-35 Photo of 1980 crew, Kent Atwood in bow. Photographer

is unknown. Karl F. Drlica Papers, OSU Libraries Special Collections and Archives Research Center.

C-36 Letter from OSC President Strand to Coach Drlica regarding the benefit of adversity. Karl F. Drlica Papers, OSU Libraries Special Collections and Archives Research Center.

C-42 Newspaper clipping (*Daily Barometer*, October 12, 1979) regarding crew seeking funding to replace broken boat. Karl F. Drlica Papers, OSU Libraries Special Collections and Archives Research Center.

C-48 Clipping from OSU *Daily Barometer*, April, 1963, describing Jim Carruthers' river trip in which he struck a rock. Karl F. Drlica Papers, OSU Libraries Special Collections and Archives Research Center.

C-49 Handwritten letter from Mel Monroe, 1997, recalling crew trip to California, 1940. Karl F. Drlica Papers, OSU Libraries Special Collections and Archives Research Center.

C-52 Letter from Paul Knoll to Coach Drlica, May 1952, chastising him for returning women students to their living groups 10 minutes late. At the time, women students were required to be in their living groups by 10 p.m. Karl F. Drlica Papers, OSU Libraries Special Collections and Archives Research Center.

C-53 Sketch of oarsman, artist was probably Harry Hanna. The sketch accompanies a certificate for the Deek Society, a loose organization formed in about 1965 for single scullers who met racing criteria. The sketch is reminiscent of Ed Stevens as an oarsman. The original source is unknown. Karl F. Drlica Papers, OSU Libraries Special Collections and Archives Research Center.

C-54 Letter from Fred Sterk to Gerald Frank. Karl F. Drlica Papers, OSU Libraries Special Collections and Archives Research Center.

C-55 Newspaper clipping 1971 Corvallis Regatta, photo of Coach Drlica. Photographer is unknown. Also race results of 1965 regatta. Karl F. Drlica Papers, OSU Libraries Special Collections and Archives Research Center.

C-56 Clipping from the *Daily Astorian*, May 9,1991, describing Carruthers' workouts towing ships' chains, carrying rocks in a backpack, and pushing his car in a parking lot. Karl F. Drlica Papers, OSU Libraries Special Collections and Archives Research Center.

C-60 Coach Drlica memo to crew "What the Small Boats Program Is." 1966. Karl F. Drlica Papers, OSU Libraries Special Collections and Archives Research Center.

C-64 Correspondence regarding fundraising for the *Zahorski*, 1956-1958, the first shell purchased by the rowing club. Karl F. Drlica Papers, OSU Libraries Special Collections and Archives Research Center.

C-65a Photo of Corvallis Regatta, taken from bridge. Photograph by Astrid Hancock. Karl F. Drlica Papers, OSU Libraries Special Collections and Archives Research Center.

C-67 Photo of Stevens coaching from the dock published in *Rowing as an experience in democracy* by Karl F. Drlica in *J. Am. Assoc. for Health-Physical Education-Recreation* June 1953 (also A-2). Photo caption indicated that Oregon State had 12 racing shells. No photo credits were published. Karl F. Drlica Papers, OSU Libraries Special Collections and Archives Research Center.

C-68 Letters from Paul Hemrich, 1959, to members of the crew. Letters regard crew lineups and boats from University of Washington. Karl F. Drlica Papers, OSU Libraries Special Collections and Archives Research Center.

C-69 Photo of crew taken from recruiting brochure, 1976. Photographer is unknown. Karl F. Drlica Papers, OSU Libraries Special Collections and Archives Research Center.

D-1 Regatta program, 1967 women's national championship.

Photos of crews, coaches, and regatta committee. OSU photo by Astrid Hancock. Karl F. Drlica Papers, OSU Libraries Special Collections and Archives Research Center.

D-3a "A History of Women's Crew at Oregon State University" by Juli Phillips, winter 1984. Karl F. Drlica Papers, OSU Libraries Special Collections and Archives Research Center.

D-4a Coach Astrid Hancock history of OSU women's crew, recollections of women rowers. Karl F. Drlica Papers, OSU Libraries Special Collections and Archives Research Center.

D-10 Letter from Coach Drlica to George Pasero, Sports Editor, *Oregon Journal*, April 14, 1972. Karl F. Drlica Papers, OSU Libraries Special Collections and Archives Research Center.

D-11 Newspaper clipping (*Daily Barometer*). Karl F. Drlica Papers, OSU Libraries Special Collections and Archives Research Center.

D-12 Coach Drlica response to Vicky Brown letter, December 3, 1971. Karl F. Drlica Papers, OSU Libraries Special Collections and Archives Research Center.

D-13 Anonymous letter from "A crew fan" to Coach Drlica, April 3, 1972. Karl F. Drlica Papers, OSU Libraries Special Collections and Archives Research Center.

D-14 Letter from Coach Don Costello to Coach Drlica, February 4, 1972 and response. Karl F. Drlica Papers, OSU Libraries Special Collections and Archives Research Center.

D-15 Letter from Coach Don Costello to Coach Drlica March 17, 1972, indicating results of coaches' poll. Karl F. Drlica Papers, OSU Libraries Special Collections and Archives Research Center.

D-16 Letter from Coach Dick Erickson to Coach Drlica, March 13, 1972. Karl F. Drlica Papers, OSU Libraries Special Collections and Archives Research Center.

D-17 Handwritten letter from Jan Pennington to Coach Drlica, March 30, 1972 and response. Karl F. Drlica Papers, OSU Libraries Special Collections and Archives Research Center.

D-18 Coach Drlica recollections concerning the "girl cox", 2002. Karl F. Drlica Papers, OSU Libraries Special Collections and Archives Research Center.

D-19 Letter from Coach Drlica to NAAO President, April 1, 1972. Karl F. Drlica Papers, OSU Libraries Special Collections and Archives Research Center.

D-20 Letter from Coach Ed Lickiss to Coach Don Costello, March 10, 1972. Karl F. Drlica Papers, OSU Libraries Special Collections and Archives Research Center.

D-21 Letter from Coach Don Costello to West Coast crew coaches, March 3, 1972 describing the reasons why a female coxswain should be allowed in a male crew. Karl F. Drlica Papers, OSU Libraries Special Collections and Archives Research Center.

D-23 Letter from Victoria Brown to Coach Drlica, December 1, 1971. Karl F. Drlica Papers, OSU Libraries Special Collections and Archives Research Center.

D-24 Handwritten letter from Mrs. A.L. Babb to Coach Drlica, April 3, 1972 and response. Karl F. Drlica Papers, OSU Libraries Special Collections and Archives Research Center.

D-25 Newspaper clipping, *Portland Oregonian*, April 25, 1972. Karl F. Drlica Papers, OSU Libraries Special Collections and Archives Research Center.

D-26 Letter from Doug Bamford to Coach Drlica, April 2, 1972. Karl F. Drlica Papers, OSU Libraries Special Collections and Archives Research Center.

D-27 Collection of newspaper and magazine clippings regarding Vicky Brown as coxswain. 1972. Karl F. Drlica Papers, OSU

Libraries Special Collections and Archives Research Center.

D-28 Letter from Jim Barratt (OSU Athletic Director) to Coach Drlica, February 8, 1972 regarding female coxswain controversy. Response from Coach Don Costello. Karl F. Drlica Papers, OSU Libraries Special Collections and Archives Research Center.

D-29 Letter from Coach John Lind to Coach Don Costello, March 10, 1972 regarding female coxswains in male crews. Karl F. Drlica Papers, OSU Libraries Special Collections and Archives Research Center.

D-32a Letter from Coach Kitzman to women's crew describing the events of the past summer regarding banishment from the boathouse, October 1976. Karl F. Drlica Papers, OSU Libraries Special Collections and Archives Research Center.

D-33 Letter from the author to Cal varsity crew coach, May, 1969. Copied to Cal Athletic Director. The letter refers to women using rowing equipment at Aquatic Park in Berkeley. Karl F. Drlica Papers, OSU Libraries Special Collections and Archives Research Center.

D-35 Letter from Coach Drlica announcing termination of women's intramural rowing, 1967. Karl F. Drlica Papers, OSU Libraries Special Collections and Archives Research Center.

D-37 Author's handwritten notes circa 2005 about Cal Women's Crew. Karl F. Drlica Papers, OSU Libraries Special Collections and Archives Research Center.

D-38 Letter from Coach Astrid Hancock to Women's Intercollegiate Athletics, January 29, 1976, seeking admission of women's crew to the WIA. Karl F. Drlica Papers, OSU Libraries Special Collections and Archives Research Center.

D-39 Clipping from the *Oregon Stater* (alumni magazine) September, 1980. Karl F. Drlica Papers, OSU Libraries Special Collections and Archives Research Center.

D-41 Letter from Sylvia Moore to Coach Kitzman denying admission to WIA, February 27, 1976. Karl F. Drlica Papers, OSU Libraries Special Collections and Archives Research Center.

D-42 Women's Athletic Department rejection letter to Jan Brown, Women's Crew Coach, April 15, 1975. Karl F. Drlica Papers, OSU Libraries Special Collections and Archives Research Center.

D-43 Letters from Dean Long to Ruth Stiehl (February 6, 1975) and to Milosh Popovich (September 17, 1974) regarding budget problems. Karl F. Drlica Papers, OSU Libraries Special Collections and Archives Research Center.

D-44 Coach Drlica, short essay "How the National Women's Rowing Association Began". Karl F. Drlica Papers, OSU Libraries Special Collections and Archives Research Center.

D-45 Coach Drlica recollections, 1997. Karl F. Drlica Papers, OSU Libraries Special Collections and Archives Research Center.

D-46a Letter from Coach Judy Kitzman to Coach Astrid Hancock, circa Feb 2015, responding to a request for biographical information. Karl F. Drlica Papers, OSU Libraries Special Collections and Archives Research Center.

D-47a Email from Susan Taylor to Coach Astrid Hancock recalling struggles to gain recognition for women's crew, March 2018. Karl F. Drlica Papers, OSU Libraries Special Collections and Archives Research Center.

D-48 Letter from James Long to Board of Women's Intercollegiate Athletics regarding budget considerations, November 20, 1974, and memo from Chair of Women's Intercollegiate Athletics, January 3, 1976. Karl F. Drlica Papers, OSU Libraries Special Collections and Archives Research Center.

D-49 Letter from Wiles Hallock, PAC-8 executive, February 17, 1972 regarding female coxswains in men's crews. PAC-8 minutes had a rule against mixing genders in varsity activities. He intended to revisit the issue at the May meeting of

PAC-8 representatives. Karl F. Drlica Papers, OSU Libraries Special Collections and Archives Research Center.

D-50 Historical material from Philadelphia Girl's Rowing Club website, copy. Karl F. Drlica Papers, OSU Libraries Special Collections and Archives Research Center.

D-51 Photo of Coach Astrid Hancock's uncle as single sculler. Karl F. Drlica Papers, OSU Libraries Special Collections and Archives Research Center.

D-57 Poem by Ellen Drake as newspaper clipping, letter-to-the-editor, OSU *Daily Barometer.* Karl F. Drlica Papers, OSU Libraries Special Collections and Archives Research Center.

D-60 Photo of Coach Judy Kitzman, 1975. Photo courtesy of Astrid Hancock. Karl F. Drlica Papers, OSU Libraries Special Collections and Archives Research Center.

D-62 Internet article reporting Coach Judy Kitzman's response to having her name on a racing shell. Karl F. Drlica Papers, OSU Libraries Special Collections and Archives Research Center.

D-63 Photo of USA women's quadruple sculls by Sy Cromwell from *The Sport of Rowing: Age of Enlightenment,* Chapter 127 by Peter Mallory.

D-65 Recollections of Carol Simpson, stroke of initial women's crew at the University of California and member of early USA entry in international races. She was also a member of the Women's Rowing Olympic Committee. Karl F. Drlica Papers, OSU Libraries Special Collections and Archives Research Center.

D-66 Email from Coach Astrid Hancock regarding historical details, 2018. Karl F. Drlica Papers, OSU Libraries Special Collections and Archives Research Center.

D-67 Memorandum from Coach Kitzman to Coach Drlica, referring to the rug being pulled out from under her by OSU administration. Karl F. Drlica Papers, OSU Libraries Special Collections and Archives Research Center.

D-68 Memorandum from Coach Kitzman to Coach Drlica, February 21, 1976. Karl F. Drlica Papers, OSU Libraries Special Collections and Archives Research Center.

D-69 Memorandum from Coach Drlica to Coach Kitzman regarding edits to a document being written by Kitzman. June 2, 1976. Karl F. Drlica Papers, OSU Libraries Special Collections and Archives Research Center.

D-73 Letter from Coach Kitzman to Pearl Gray, Chair of Affirmative Action, OSU, June 11, 1976. Karl F. Drlica Papers, OSU Libraries Special Collections and Archives Research Center.

D-74 Letter from Coach Kitzman, June 11, 1976, to crew supporters to seek re-evaluation of Dean Long's budget and prohibition of women's crew from using the docks. This is probably the letter referred to in D-69. Karl F. Drlica Papers, OSU Libraries Special Collections and Archives Research Center.

D-76 Response from Dean Long to Coach Kitzman regarding budget re-evaluation, June 25, 1976. Karl F. Drlica Papers, OSU Libraries Special Collections and Archives Research Center.

D-77 Letter from Vanessa Rennewitz to OSU President MacVicar with copies to state politicians, July 6, 1976. Karl F. Drlica Papers, OSU Libraries Special Collections and Archives Research Center.

D-78 Letter from Coach Drlica to Charlotte Lambert, Head PE Department, July 24, 1976. Karl F. Drlica Papers, OSU Libraries Special Collections and Archives Research Center.

D-79 Women's crew financial report, June 1976. Karl F. Drlica Papers, OSU Libraries Special Collections and Archives Research Center.

D-80 Letter from Coach Kitzman seeking letter-writing campaign to support admission of women's crew to the WIA, January 23, 1977. Karl F. Drlica Papers, OSU Libraries Special Collections and Archives Research Center.

D-81 Memorandum from Sandy Neeley stating that women's crew would be accepted into the WIA, June 2, 1977, on a one-year basis. Karl F. Drlica Papers, OSU Libraries Special Collections and Archives Research Center.

D-82 Women's crew spring newsletter, June 1977, recounting history behind admission to Women's Intercollegiate Athletics. Karl F. Drlica Papers, OSU Libraries Special Collections and Archives Research Center.

D-83 Support letters for maintaining women's crew, July 1976. Karl F. Drlica Papers, OSU Libraries Special Collections and Archives Research Center.

D-84 Letter from Coach Drlica to Dean James Long detailing inaccuracies in Long's budget statements concerning crew, June 17, 1976. Karl F. Drlica Papers, OSU Libraries Special Collections and Archives Research Center.

D-85 Package submitted to Women's Intercollegiate Athletics Department seeking admission for women's crew. Karl F. Drlica Papers, OSU Libraries Special Collections and Archives Research Center.

D-86 Handwritten letter from Coach Kitzman to OSU President MacVicar, November 1, 1977, with accompanying counternotes from Coach Drlica Karl F. Drlica Papers, OSU Libraries Special Collections and Archives Research Center.

D-87 Typewritten update on women's rowing from Coach Kitzman to Coach Drlica. Karl F. Drlica Papers, OSU Libraries Special Collections and Archives Research Center.

D-88 National Women's Rowing Association newsletter, 1964, documenting the beginning of the NWRA and resistance to the attitude that women need protection from strenuous physical activity. Karl F. Drlica Papers, OSU Libraries Special Collections and Archives Research Center.

D-89 Handwritten memorandum from Coach Kitzman to Coach Drlica, January 18, 1977. Karl F. Drlica Papers, OSU Libraries Special Collections and Archives Research Center.

D-90 Photo of Coach Astrid Hancock from recruiting brochure for OSU crew. Karl F. Drlica Papers, OSU Libraries Special Collections and Archives Research Center.

D-92 Unidentified magazine article on Lake Merritt Women's Rowing, mostly comprised of students from Mills College. Circa 1965. Karl F. Drlica Papers, OSU Libraries Special Collections and Archives Research Center.

D-95 Photo of barn used for physical training. Photographer is unknown. Karl F. Drlica Papers, OSU Libraries Special Collections and Archives Research Center.

D-96 Photo of women's locker room. Photo by Astrid Hancock. Karl F. Drlica Papers, OSU Libraries Special Collections and Archives Research Center.

D-98 Photo of Dean James Long, from *Daily Barometer*, December 5, 1975; includes text regarding controversy. Photographer is unknown. Karl F. Drlica Papers, OSU Libraries Special Collections and Archives Research Center.

D-99 Photo of Jan Brown, Kate Gribskov, and Coach Ralph Mathison, Northwest Regional Championship Regatta, 1975. Brown and Gribskov placed second in the national championship regatta. Photo courtesy of Astrid Hancock. Karl F. Drlica Papers, OSU Libraries Special Collections and Archives Research Center.

D-100 Photo of Coaches Drlica and Dave Prodehl. Photo by Astrid Hancock. Karl F. Drlica Papers, OSU Libraries Special Collections and Archives Research Center.

D-102 Photo of presentation of varsity letter awards to women rowers and dedication of *Astrid Hancock* racing shell, 2014. Photo courtesy of Astrid Hancock. Karl F. Drlica Papers, OSU Libraries Special Collections and Archives Research Center.

D-104 Photo of Oregon State women's crew, 1964 Corvallis Regatta. Photo shows how coxswains control the rudder; also shown is the center pier of the Van Buren Street Bridge. Photo by Astrid Hancock. Karl F. Drlica Papers, OSU Libraries Special Collections and Archives Research Center.

D-108 Photo of OSU crews that raced on Mom's Weekend 1965 (women's crew and men dressed as women). Photo by Astrid Hancock. Karl F. Drlica Papers, OSU Libraries Special Collections and Archives Research Center

D-109 Photo of training barge and the Aquathusiasts' boathouse, 1964. Photo by Astrid Hancock. Karl F. Drlica Papers, OSU Libraries Special Collections and Archives Research Center.

D-110a Photo of Coach Fred Mann and women's crew, 1975 Northwest Regional Regatta. Full shot shows women's oar blades (also D-110b). Photo by Kirk Hutchinson. Karl F. Drlica Papers, OSU Libraries Special Collections and Archives Research Center.

D-111 Photo of Coach Judy Kitzman. Photo courtesy of Astrid Hancock. Karl F. Drlica Papers, OSU Libraries Special Collections and Archives Research Center.

D-112 Photo of Coach Ralph Mathison, Northwest Regional Championship Regatta, 1975. Photo courtesy of Astrid Hancock. Karl F. Drlica Papers, OSU Libraries Special Collections and Archives Research Center.

D-113 Reports on passing of Julia Shew, 2012. Karl F. Drlica Papers, OSU Libraries Special Collections and Archives Research Center.

D-114 Coach Drlica, "The Launching of the National Women's Rowing Association", 1998. Karl F. Drlica Papers, OSU Libraries Special Collections and Archives Research Center.

D-115 Coach Drlica history of women's crew at Oregon State, 1997. Karl F. Drlica Papers, OSU Libraries Special Collections and Archives Research Center.

D-116 Coach Drlica notes on conversations with Ralph Mathison. Karl F. Drlica Papers, OSU Libraries Special Collections and Archives Research Center.

D-117 Photo of the author as Assistant Professor, Department of Biology, University of Rochester, 1977. The author's research focused on DNA supercoiling. Photographer is unknown. Karl F. Drlica Papers, OSU Libraries Special Collections and Archives Research Center.

D-118 Three photos of OSU crew at 1980 National Championship Regatta. Photos by Coach Kirk Hutchinson. Karl F. Drlica Papers, OSU Libraries Special Collections and Archives Research Center.

D-119 Letter from Coach Kitzman to Dean James Long requesting a budget re-evaluation, June 14, 1976. Karl F. Drlica Papers, OSU Libraries Special Collections and Archives Research Center.

D-120 Letter from Don Sanderson to Coach Drlica (June 1, 1976) stating that women's crew and the lightweight crew must vacate the boathouse facilities. Karl F. Drlica Papers, OSU Libraries Special Collections and Archives Research Center.

D-121 Minutes of Recreational Sports Committee, February 10, 1975. Karl F. Drlica Papers, OSU Libraries Special Collections and Archives Research Center.

D-122 Coach Drlica article regarding women rowing, in *Rowing News*, June 1958, page 18. Karl F. Drlica Papers, OSU Libraries Special Collections and Archives Research Center.

D-124 *row2k* interview with Tanner Mathison, written by Eric Dresser, January 19, 2010. https://www.row2k.com/features/447/Dartmouth-s-Tanner-Mathison/. Copy in Karl F. Drlica Papers, OSU Libraries Special Collections and Archives Research Center.

D-125 Newspaper clipping of column by sports editor of Seattle Post-Intelligencer, June 22, 1969 describing reactions to women's rowing at NWRA regatta on Green Lake in Seattle. Karl F. Drlica Papers, OSU Libraries Special Collections and Archives Research Center.

D-126 Email to Coach Astrid Hancock, 2018, recollections from Kate Engel about Coach Ralph Mathison. Karl F. Drlica Papers, OSU Libraries Special Collections and Archives Research Center.

D-128 Newspaper article describing 1980 women's championship races, Oak Ridge, TN, by Woody Cade in the *OakRidger*, June 23, 1980. Karl F. Drlica Papers, OSU Libraries Special Collections and Archives Research Center.

D-129 Wedding photo, Coach Art Sachs and Judy DeVries, 1967. Karl F. Drlica Papers, OSU Libraries Special Collections and Archives Research Center.

D-130 Photo of "Seahorses", taken from race program, 1953. Karl F. Drlica Papers, OSU Libraries Special Collections and Archives Research Center.

D-131 Photo of sorority crew, taken from race program, 1955. Aquathusiats' boathouse, which was taken by a flood, is in the background. Karl F. Drlica Papers, OSU Libraries Special Collections and Archives Research Center.

D-133 Newspaper article (*Daily Barometer*, February 27, 1975) describing women's crew fundraising. Karl F. Drlica Papers, OSU Libraries Special Collections and Archives Research Center.

D-134 Newspaper article on Kate (Diane) Gribskov, *Daily Barometer*, October 8, 1975. Karl F. Drlica Papers, OSU Libraries Special Collections and Archives Research Center.

D-135 Newspaper article concerning the finances of the field hockey team, *Daily Barometer*. Karl F. Drlica Papers, OSU Libraries Special Collections and Archives Research Center.

D-136 Newspaper clipping regarding fundraising by women's crew; *Daily Barometer*, February 19, 1975. Karl F. Drlica Papers, OSU Libraries Special Collections and Archives Research Center.

D-137 Letter-to-the-editor (*Daily Barometer*, November 22, 1977) by Coach Kitzman, who was upset by the lack of a women's coach. Karl F. Drlica Papers, OSU Libraries Special Collections and Archives Research Center.

D-138 Photo of OSU crew, 1968 or 1969, with Ralph Mathison rowing number 7. Photographer is unknown. Karl F. Drlica Papers, OSU Libraries Special Collections and Archives Research Center.

D-139 Newspaper clipping describing women's crew fundraiser, row to Salem, January 1975. Karl F. Drlica Papers, OSU Libraries Special Collections and Archives Research Center.

D-141 Photos and newspaper clippings, Janet Schoenborn, 1967. Photo by Astrid Hancock. Karl F. Drlica Papers, OSU Libraries Special Collections and Archives Research Center.

D-142 Photo of 1978 women's lightweight crew. Photographer is unknown. Karl F. Drlica Papers, OSU Libraries Special Collections and Archives Research Center.

D-147 Photo of Coach Ralph Mathison from the *Corvallis Gazette Times* April 19, 1976. Photographer is Tom Warren. Karl F. Drlica Papers, OSU Libraries Special Collections and Archives Research Center.

D-150 OSU Women's crew roster, 1980. Includes height, weight, year in school, and hometown. Karl F. Drlica Papers, OSU Libraries Special Collections and Archives Research Center.

D-153 Police Officer's Report (R.L. Swall), Oregon State University Police Department, March 3, 1973, regarding Coach Ralph Mathison at the boathouse late at night. Karl F. Drlica Papers, OSU Libraries Special Collections and Archives Research Center.

D-154 Photo of men's crew in drag for race with women, Mom's Weekend, 1965. Photo by Astrid Hancock. Karl F. Drlicam-Papers, OSU Libraries Special Collections and Archives Research Center.

D-155 Photo of men's locker room (Stevens Crewhouse). Photo courtesy of Astrid Hancock. Karl F. Drlica Papers, OSU Libraries Special Collections and Archives Research Center.

D-156 Report on women's intramural crew, written by the author, 1962. All committee chairpersons were required to submit written reports. Karl F. Drlica Papers, OSU Libraries Special Collections and Archives Research Center.

D-158 OSU Conciliation Agreement for Sex Equity In Intercollegiate Athletics, July 1980. Karl F. Drlica Papers, OSU Libraries Special Collections and Archives Research Center.

D-159 Letter from Charlotte Lambert, Chair of Women's Physical Education Department, OSU, June 14, 1971, to Herman Forslund, Chair of Recreational Sports Board, OSU. Part of this long clarification letter illustrated the protective attitude taken toward women's athletics such that women were not to participate in cut-throat varsity level sports. This letter was written one year before Title IX. Karl F. Drlica Papers, OSU Libraries Special Collections and Archives Research Center.

D-160 Resignation letter from Coach Ralph Mathison to Athletic Director Andros, July 3, 1980. Karl F. Drlica Papers, OSU Libraries Special Collections and Archives Research Center.

D-161 Letters between Judy Loosley and Jerry Ward regarding transfer of women's crew money to field hockey, draft letter from Coach Drlica. December, 1977. Karl F. Drlica Papers, OSU Libraries Special Collections and Archives Research Center.

F-1 Newspaper article by Michael Rollins (*Daily Barometer*, December 9, 1975) regarding debate between Coach Drlica and Dean Long. Karl F. Drlica Papers, OSU Libraries Special Collections and Archives Research Center.

F-2 Coach Drlica's draft history of crew, athletic department, and Dean James Long. Karl F. Drlica Papers, OSU Libraries Special Collections and Archives Research Center.

F-3 Newspaper clippings, towel service reinstated January 12, 1976; Yale women bare bodies. Karl F. Drlica Papers, OSU Libraries Special Collections and Archives Research Center.

F-4 Series of newspaper articles concerning towel service at the boathouse, December, 1975. Karl F. Drlica Papers, OSU Libraries Special Collections and Archives Research Center.

F-5 Newspaper article by Michael Rollins (*Daily Barometer*, September 26, 1976) regarding inadequate budget for crew. Karl F. Drlica Papers, OSU Libraries Special Collections and Archives Research Center.

F-6 Newspaper photo of Athletic Director Dee Andros in a racing shell. Photo by Don Ryan, *Daily Barometer* Apr.15, 1976. Karl F. Drlica Papers, OSU Libraries Special Collections and Archives Research Center.

F-7 Photo of Robert MacVicar and President's message regarding women's sports, probably in the *Oregon Stater*, 1978. Karl F. Drlica Papers, OSU Libraries Special Collections and Archives Research Center.

F-7a Newspaper clippings regarding towel service and showers at boathouse. Karl F. Drlica Papers, OSU Libraries Special Collections and Archives Research Center.

F-8 Newspaper clippings regarding towel service at boathouse, October 1976. Includes Karl Brandt's letter to *Daily Barometer*. Karl F. Drlica Papers, OSU Libraries Special Collections and Archives Research Center.

F-9 Photo of 1960s crew, left to right Dennis Searcy, Karl Drlica, unidentified,, Gary Ray, Bill Ruzicka, Don Pearson, Andy Paul, cox: Joe Jacobs. Karl F. Drlica Papers, OSU Libraries Special Collections and Archives Research Center.

F-9a "Title IX and American Collegiate Women's Rowing" by Tina Fisher Ford, *American Rowing*, March/April 1990, p.27-31. Copy in Karl F. Drlica Papers, OSU Libraries Special Collections and Archives Research Center.

F-12 Several newspaper clippings regarding discontinuing crew due to budget issues, including letter-to-the-editor by Dennis Searcy. March/April 1975. Karl F. Drlica Papers, OSU Libraries Special Collections and Archives Research Center.

F-13 Several newspaper clippings regarding towel service, quantitative statement. Karl F. Drlica Papers, OSU Libraries Special Collections and Archives Research Center.

F-14 Letter-to-the-editor, *Daily Barometer*, November 10, 1975, attacking Dean James Long and seeking student support for women's crew. Karl F. Drlica Papers, OSU Libraries Special Collections and Archives Research Center.

F-15 Letter from Coach Drlica to Sandy Neeley, Chairperson of Willamette River Facilities Committee, October 29, 1976. Karl F. Drlica Papers, OSU Libraries Special Collections and Archives Research Center.

F-16 Letter from Coach Drlica to Wilbur Cooney, Chair of Board of Intercollegiate Athletics, March 27, 1975. Karl F. Drlica Papers, OSU Libraries Special Collections and Archives Research Center.

F-17 Letter from Eldred Halsey to Coach Drlica, November 19, 1976, including Halsey's budget for October 1929. Karl

F. Drlica Papers, OSU Libraries Special Collections and Archives Research Center.

F-18 Letter from Sheriff Jack Dolan to OSU President MacVicar, November 14, 1975. Karl F. Drlica Papers, OSU Libraries Special Collections and Archives Research Center.

F-19 Letter from Coach Drlica to Jim and Nancy Young, January 23, 1975 regarding Long's memo to President MacVicar advising that the crew program be discontinued. Karl F. Drlica Papers, OSU Libraries Special Collections and Archives Research Center.

F-20 Letter from Tim Hayden to Coach Drlica, February 5, 1975 regarding communication with OSU President MacVicar and threat to discontinue rowing. Karl F. Drlica Papers, OSU Libraries Special Collections and Archives Research Center.

F-21 Letter from Karl Brandt to OSU President MacVicar, February 5, 1975 regarding threat to discontinue rowing. Karl F. Drlica Papers, OSU Libraries Special Collections and Archives Research Center.

F-22 Letter from Coach Fred Mann to crew supporters seeking lobbying effort with OSU administration regarding discontinuing rowing, March 19, 1975. Karl F. Drlica Papers, OSU Libraries Special Collections and Archives Research Center.

F-23 Letter from Coach Drlica to Fred Decker, March 13, 1975. This letter suggests that MacVicar is seeking to be forced to maintain crew. Karl F. Drlica Papers, OSU Libraries Special Collections and Archives Research Center.

F-24 Letter from Coach Drlica to crew supporters in Klamath Falls, March 13, 1975. Karl F. Drlica Papers, OSU Libraries Special Collections and Archives Research Center.

F-28a Photo of Tim Hayden. Photographer is unknown. Karl F. Drlica Papers, OSU Libraries Special Collections and Archives Research Center.

F-32 Letter from John R. Davis to OSU President MacVicar regarding full-time teaching equivalents assigned to Athletic Department coaches, February 12, 1974; document prepared by Coach Drlica. The conclusion was that the current situation is realistic and need not be changed. Karl F. Drlica Papers, OSU Libraries Special Collections and Archives Research Center.

F-33 Notes on meeting of Athletic Board to consider the problem of crew. Coach Drlica comments on Dean Long's budget, May 18, 1976. Karl F. Drlica Papers, OSU Libraries Special Collections and Archives Research Center.

F-34 Letter from Jack Dolan, Sheriff, to Coach Fred Mann, November 20, 1974. Karl F. Drlica Papers, OSU Libraries Special Collections and Archives Research Center.

F-37 Letter from Dean Long to OSU President MacVicar regarding maintenance budget for crew, November 26, 1974. Karl F. Drlica Papers, OSU Libraries Special Collections and Archives Research Center.

F-38 Letter from Coach Drlica to Dean James Long listing maintenance required at crew facilities, September 10, 1974. Karl F. Drlica Papers, OSU Libraries Special Collections and Archives Research Center.

F-40 Request for Oregon State crew to be in the NCAA, October 4, 1979. Karl F. Drlica Papers, OSU Libraries Special Collections and Archives Research Center.

F-41 Letter from Coach Drlica to OSU administration arguing for saving the barges, June 2, 1980. Karl F. Drlica Papers, OSU Libraries Special Collections and Archives Research Center.

F-42 Correspondence concerning the facilities problems. Karl F. Drlica Papers, OSU Libraries Special Collections and Archives Research Center.

F-44 Letter from Coach Drlica to OSU President MacVicar encouraging the construction of part 2 of the Stevens Crewhouse,

November 4, 1975, as work toward compliance with Title IX. Karl F. Drlica Papers, OSU Libraries Special Collections and Archives Research Center.

F-45 Directive from Northern Division of PAC-8 with memo from OSU Athletic Director regarding budget restrictions, June 10, 1974. Karl F. Drlica Papers, OSU Libraries Special Collections and Archives Research Center.

G-1 Photo of Oregon Electric Railway Depot showing the building being raised. The boat is probably not the Yellow Peril, since this photo probably predates delivery of that boat. Karl F. Drlica Papers, OSU Libraries Special Collections and Archives Research Center.

G-3 Coach Drlica description of Columbus Day Storm. Karl F. Drlica Papers, OSU Libraries Special Collections and Archives Research Center. (also J-15)

G-4 Correspondence regarding barge transfer from the Navy. Karl F. Drlica Papers, OSU Libraries Special Collections and Archives Research Center.

G-6 Comprehensive history of financial issues with crew written by Coach Drlica (1979 or 1980), memos regarding the expense of maintaining the barges, 1977. Karl F. Drlica Papers, OSU Libraries Special Collections and Archives Research Center.

G-8 Draft of letter from Coach Drlica to Vice President, OSU, arguing for keeping the barges. 1980. Karl F. Drlica Papers, OSU Libraries Special Collections and Archives Research Center.

G-9 Notes from interview with Coach Drlica, circa 2005. Karl F. Drlica Papers, OSU Libraries Special Collections and Archives Research Center.

G-10 Overview photo from Tenth Annual Corvallis Regatta race brochure, 1973. The aerial photo was probably taken by

Western Ways. Karl F. Drlica Papers, OSU Libraries Special Collections and Archives Research Center.

G-11 Shell trailer with accommodation for coaching launch. Photographer is unknown. Karl F. Drlica Papers, OSU Libraries Special Collections and Archives Research Center.

G-12 Photo (circa 1960) of rowing machines in barn with Mike Oxborrow, front. Photographer is unknown. Karl F. Drlica Papers, OSU Libraries Special Collections and Archives Research Center.

G-13 Coach Drlica document laying out vision for rowing program, including rowing tank details, 1953. Karl F. Drlica Papers, OSU Libraries Special Collections and Archives Research Center.

G-14 Coach Drlica statement about rowing tank being an appropriate senior class gift. Karl F. Drlica Papers, OSU Libraries Special Collections and Archives Research Center.

G-16 Interior of Quonset hut. Larry Birke, John Hamstreet, Fred Sterk. Circa 1962. Photographer is unknown Drlica Papers, OSU Libraries Special Collections and Archives Research Center.

G-17 Photo of placing styrofoam in floats. Photographer is unknown. Karl F. Drlica Papers, OSU Libraries Special Collections and Archives Research Center.

G-18 Photo of moving the locker room portion of the old boathouse. In the background are the Hickman house (home of the caretaker of the Beach farm) and the garage expanded for storage of the shell trailer. Photographer is unknown. Karl F. Drlica Papers, OSU Libraries Special Collections and Archives Research Center.

G-19 Photo of barges upon arrival in Corvallis. The photographer is unknown. Karl F. Drlica Papers, OSU Libraries Special Collections and Archives Research Center.

G-20 Photo of flood, January 1965 showing pontoons used to support ramps and Coaches Drlica and Bower pushing off debris with pike poles upstream from the barge house. Also shown are launch house and barge house. Photographer is unknown. Karl F. Drlica Papers, OSU Libraries Special Collections and Archives Research Center.

G-21 Photo showing sit-up boards and rowing machines in the barn hayloft. Photographer is unknown. Karl F. Drlica Papers, OSU Libraries Special Collections and Archives Research Center.

G-22 Photo of Richard Shafer, *Daily Barometer* April 17, 1975. Karl F. Drlica Papers, OSU Libraries Special Collections and Archives Research Center.

G-25 Photos of driving piling for barges and completed piling. One shows up-river end of northern barge where several people were sucked under the barge. Also shown are launch house and barge house. Photographer is unknown. Karl F. Drlica Papers, OSU Libraries Special Collections and Archives Research Center.

G-26 Photo of placing styrofoam in floats. Photographer is unknown. Karl F. Drlica Papers, OSU Libraries Special Collections and Archives Research Center.

G-27 Photo of placing styrofoam in floats. Photographer is unknown. Karl F. Drlica Papers, OSU Libraries Special Collections and Archive Research Center.

G-28 Photo of removing materials from old boathouse. Photographer is unknown. Karl F. Drlica Papers, OSU Libraries Special Collections and Archives Research Center.

G-29 Photo of barge house under construction or repair, with oil barrel on dock. Photographer is unknown. Karl F. Drlica Papers, OSU Libraries Special Collections and Archives Research Center.

G-30 Photo of removing materials from old boathouse by Cameron Brown and others. Photographer is unknown. Karl F. Drlica Papers, OSU Libraries Special Collections and Archives Research Center.

G-31 Two photos of crew house demolition, 1963. Photographer is unknown. Karl F. Drlica Papers, OSU Libraries Special Collections and Archives Research Center.

G-32 Photo of oil barrel holding up barge house. Photographer is unknown. Karl F. Drlica Papers, OSU Libraries Special Collections and Archives Research Center.

G-33 Three photos of garage damaged by pickup truck, circa 1970. Photographer is unknown. Karl F. Drlica Papers, OSU Libraries Special Collections and Archives Research Center.

G-44 Barn used for physical training with external staircase added. Photographer is unknown. Karl F. Drlica Papers, OSU Libraries Special Collections and Archives Research Center.

H-1 Series of newspaper clippings regarding selection of Steve Adler as coach, complaints by oarsmen about Coach Drlica, 1979, 1980. Karl F. Drlica Papers, OSU Libraries Special Collections and Archives Research Center.

H-2 Xerox copies of historical photos. Karl F. Drlica Papers, OSU Libraries Special Collections and Archives Research Center.

H-2a Draft of statement prepared by Coach Drlica for Athletic Board, June 11, 1980. Karl F. Drlica Papers, OSU Libraries Special Collections and Archives Research Center

H-4 Survey of rower opinions taken by Coach Drlica. Karl F. Drlica Papers, OSU Libraries Special Collections and Archives Research Center.

H-7 Kelly Moore resignation letter. Karl F. Drlica Papers, OSU Libraries Special Collections and Archives Research Center.

H-8 Newspaper clipping, *Daily Barometer*, new crew coach.

Karl F. Drlica Papers, OSU Libraries Special Collections and Archives Research Center.

H-9 Newspaper clipping, *Daily Barometer,* Coach Drlica responds to rower complaints. Karl F. Drlica Papers, OSU Libraries Special Collections and Archives Research Center.

H-10 Letter from Frank Zagunis, Beaver Crew Association to Athletic Director Andros, January 21, 1980. Karl F. Drlica Papers, OSU Libraries Special Collections and Archives Research Center.

H-11 Coach Drlica personal notes. Karl F. Drlica Papers, OSU Libraries Special Collections and Archives Research Center.

H-12 Coach Drlica photo by Tom Bernard in Daily Barometer, January 15,1980. Karl F. Drlica Papers, OSU Libraries Special Collections and Archives Research Center.

H-13 Petitions to Coach Drlica and Athletic Director Andros from rowers seeking to hire a new men's coach for on-the-water responsibility. December 1979. Karl F. Drlica Papers, OSU Libraries Special Collections and Archives Research Center.

H-15 Supportive letter from Coach Ed Lickiss to Coach Drlica, March 7, 1980 stating that he had the same problem. Karl F. Drlica Papers, OSU Libraries Special Collections and Archives Research Center.

H-16 Letter-to-the-editor Daily Barometer, March 2, 1979 complaining about Coach Drlica's competence as a rowing coach. Karl F. Drlica Papers, OSU Libraries Special Collections and Archives Research Center.

H-24 Letter from Coach Drlica to the author, October 30, 1980. Karl F. Drlica Papers, OSU Libraries Special Collections and Archives Research Center.

H-28 Coach Drlica notes on conversation with oarsman, January

4, 1979. Karl F. Drlica Papers, OSU Libraries Special Collections and Archives Research Center.

H-31 Changes in style to be inserted into Drlica's text *Ready All, Row*. Karl F. Drlica Papers, OSU Libraries Special Collections and Archives Research Center.

H-32 Coach Drlica notes on conversation with oarsman Bob Small, February 20, 1980. Karl F. Drlica Papers, OSU Libraries Special Collections and Archives Research Center.

H-39 Coach Drlica notes regarding survey of oarsmen. Karl F. Drlica Papers, OSU Libraries Special Collections and Archives Research Center

H-40 Coach Drlica draft farewell statement to Board of Directors, Intercollegiate Athletics, Oregon State University, June 11, 1980. Karl F. Drlica Papers, OSU Libraries Special Collections and Archives Research Center.

H-42a Coach Drlica notes on conversation with Ralph Mathison, February 20, 1980. Karl F. Drlica Papers, OSU Libraries Special Collections and Archives Research Center.

H-45 Letters from OSU coaches to Coach Drlica regarding missing boats and requesting use of facilities, June 6, 1982 and response letter. Karl F. Drlica Papers, OSU Libraries Special Collections and Archives Research Center.

H-45a University policy statement about the use of facilities, March 15, 1978. Karl F. Drlica Papers, OSU Libraries Special Collections and Archives Research Center.

H-47 Letter-to-the-editor *Daily Barometer*, February 15, 1979 concerning Coach Drlica's fitness as coach of rowing. Karl F. Drlica Papers, OSU Libraries Special Collections and Archives Research Center.

H-55 Letter to Coach Drlica from Station L Rowing Club, October 30, 1975 regarding burned boat. Karl F. Drlica Papers, OSU

Libraries Special Collections and Archives Research Center.

H-55a Letter to Coach Drlica from Station L Rowing Club, September 25, 1975. Includes photo of burned boat. Karl F. Drlica Papers, OSU Libraries Special Collections and Archives Research Center.

H-59 Series of newspaper clippings regarding dissatisfaction of rowers with Coach Drlica. Karl F. Drlica Papers, OSU Libraries Special Collections and Archives Research Center.

I-1 Cartoon from K.F. Drlica *Ready All Row*. Karl F. Drlica Papers, OSU Libraries Special Collections and Archives Research Center.

J-1 Coach Drlica draft of crew history. Karl F. Drlica Papers, OSU Libraries Special Collections and Archives Research Center.

J-2 *Shipwreck,* an essay written by Coach Drlica for adult writing class. This piece describes the foundering of the training barge. Karl F. Drlica Papers, OSU Libraries Special Collections and Archives Research Center.

J-4 Coach Drlica draft of crew history. Karl F. Drlica Papers, OSU Libraries Special Collections and Archives Research Center.

J-5 Coach Drlica crew history. Karl F. Drlica Papers, OSU Libraries Special Collections and Archives Research Center.

J-7 Crew timeline prepared by Coach Drlica. Karl F. Drlica Papers, OSU Libraries Special Collections and Archives Research Center.

J-8 Coach Drlica May 21, 1987, summary of activities. Karl F. Drlica Papers, OSU Libraries Special Collections and Archives Research Center.

J-9 Coach Drlica notes on incidents for rowing history. Karl F. Drlica Papers, OSU Libraries Special Collections and Archives Research Center.

J-10 Important dates for OSU crew, compiled by Coach Drlica.

Karl F. Drlica Papers, OSU Libraries Special Collections and Archives Research Center.

J-12 Coach Drlica text titled "Crew Trips", November, 1991. Karl F. Drlica Papers, OSU Libraries Special Collections and Archives Research Center.

J-13 Coach Drlica proposal for writing a history of OSU crew. Karl F. Drlica Papers, OSU Libraries Special Collections and Archives Research Center.

J-14 Coach Drlica crew history, second draft, written for continuing education course. Karl F. Drlica Papers, OSU Libraries Special Collections and Archives Research Center.

J-15 Coach Drlica description of Columbus Day Storm. Karl F. Drlica Papers, OSU Libraries Special Collections and Archives Research Center. (also G-3)

J-17 Collection of newsletters by Coach Drlica to alumni and summary of the beginnings of women's crew. Karl F. Drlica Papers, OSU Libraries Special Collections and Archives Research Center.

J-19 Collection of Coach Drlica contributions to *Rowing News*. Karl F. Drlica Papers, OSU Libraries Special Collections and Archives Research Center.

J-21 Draft of speech "History of Crew at OSU", Karl F. Drlica, May 28, 1991. Karl F. Drlica Papers, OSU Libraries Special Collections and Archives Research Center.

J-22 Coach Drlica crew history. This and other drafts indicate that the extremely high water was in 1929. Internet records indicate that it was more likely in 1927. Karl F. Drlica Papers, OSU Libraries Special Collections and Archives Research Center.

J-23 Coach Drlica crew history, revised 1998. Karl F. Drlica Papers, OSU Libraries Special Collections and Archives Research Center.

J-24 Drlica report to Langton, August, 1940. Karl F. Drlica Papers, OSU Libraries Special Collections and Archives Research Center.

J-25 Coach Drlica history of women's crew at Oregon State. Some discussion of the Corvallis Regatta. Karl F. Drlica Papers, OSU Libraries Special Collections and Archives Research Center.

K-1 Aerial Photo from race program, Corvallis Regatta, April 28, 1972. The original source is probably Western Ways, a commercial aerial photography company owned and operated by the Terway family from the 1950s to the 1980s. Karl F. Drlica Papers, OSU Libraries Special Collections and Archives Research Center.

K-2 Photo of Van Buren Street Bridge turntable pier, Corvallis. Photographer is unknown. Karl F. Drlica Papers, OSU Libraries Special Collections and Archives Research Center.

K-3 Photo, flood of 1965 showing barn. Photographer is unknown. Karl F. Drlica Papers, OSU Libraries Special Collections and Archives Research Center.

K-5 Photo of crews on the river. Photo by Pam Davis (OSU Athletic Department). Karl F. Drlica Papers, OSU Libraries Special Collections and Archives Research Center.

K-6 Photo, flood of 1965 showing flooded field, women's locker-room, and portion of Harrison Street Bridge. Photographer unknown. Karl F. Drlica Papers, OSU Libraries Special Collections and Archives Research Center.

K-7 Debris from flood of 1965. Photographer is unknown. Karl F. Drlica Papers, OSU Libraries Special Collections and Archives Research Center.

K-9 Photo, flood of 1964 showing flooded fields, the author sculling a single, and the garage used to house the boat trailer. Photographer is unknown. Karl F. Drlica Papers, OSU Libraries Special Collections and Archives Research Center.

K-11 Photo of moving newly constructed training barge from boathouse to the river. Photographer is unknown. Karl F. Drlica Papers, OSU Libraries Special Collections and Archives Research Center.

K-12 Photo of Carl Bower and a 1963 varsity crew. Also shown is how high the Van Buren Street Bridge is off the water. Photographer is unknown. Karl F. Drlica Papers, OSU Libraries Special Collections and Archives Research Center.

K-13 Photo of barge washed downriver, 1974. Coach Drlica, photographer. Karl F. Drlica Papers, OSU Libraries Special Collections and Archives Research Center.

K-14 Photo of barge house washed up on river bank, 1974. Coach Drlica, photographer. Karl F. Drlica Papers, OSU Libraries Special Collections and Archives Research Center.

K-15 Photo of Coach Drlica. Tom George, photographer. Karl F. Drlica Papers, OSU Libraries Special Collections and Archives Research Center.

K-16 Photo of Drlica and University of Washington coach, Dick Erickson, discussing race course. Photographer is unknown. Karl F. Drlica Papers, OSU Libraries Special Collections and Archives Research Center.

K-17 Photo of cox with rain gear. Photographer is unknown. Karl F. Drlica Papers, OSU Libraries Special Collections and Archives Research Center.

K-17a Portion of K-17 to illustrate knockers. Karl F. Drlica Papers, OSU Libraries Special Collections and Archives Research Center.

K-18 Listing of Hell Divers, part 2. Karl F. Drlica Papers, OSU Libraries Special Collections and Archives Research Center.

K-19 Newspaper clipping describing river rescue by Coach Drlica (acknowledged in K-22). Two adults and a 2-year-old were in a canoe that capsized in the Willamette River. They had climbed onto a snag and were stranded. Drlica maneuvered his motor boat in fast, shallow water to execute the rescue. Karl F. Drlica Papers, OSU Libraries Special Collections and Archives Research Center.

K-20 Author's handwritten notes regarding water skier accident, August 1962. Karl F. Drlica Papers, OSU Libraries Special Collections and Archives Research Center.

K-21 Coach Drlica, Old Man River Just Keeps Rollin' Along was written for adult writing class, 1998. This piece describes floods and several anecdotes involved with high water. Karl F. Drlica Papers, OSU Libraries Special Collections and Archives Research Center.

K-22 Letter from OSU President MacVicar acknowledging the river rescue (K-19) April 27, 1973. Karl F. Drlica Papers, OSU Libraries Special Collections and Archives Research Center.

K-23 *The River Itself*, Coach Drlica recollections. Karl F. Drlica Papers, OSU Libraries Special Collections and Archives Research Center.

K-24 Listing of Hell Divers, part 1. Karl F. Drlica Papers, OSU Libraries Special Collections and Archives Research Center.

K-25 Letters regarding dredging, control of river. Karl F. Drlica Papers, OSU Libraries Special Collections and Archives Research Center.

K-26 Letters between Coach Drlica and Eben Carruthers regarding the double scull broken when it went under the dock. Karl F. Drlica Papers, OSU Libraries Special Collections and Archives Research Center.

K-27 Letter from Coach Drlica to Dean James Long, 1979 regarding flood damage. Karl F. Drlica Papers, OSU Libraries Special Collections and Archives Research Center.

Notes and Citations 435

K-28 Coach Drlica, "All in a Day's Work", recollections about getting wet. Karl F. Drlica Papers, OSU Libraries Special Collections and Archives Research Center.

K-29 Newspaper clipping in 1990 recalling the flood of 1964. Karl F. Drlica Papers, OSU Libraries Special Collections and Archives Research Center.

K-30 Newspaper photo (*Corvallis Gazette Times*, January 30, 1974) and article about barge house going downriver. Coach Drlica, photographer. Karl F. Drlica Papers, OSU Libraries Special Collections and Archives Research Center.

K-33 Report on racing shell accident by Coach Drlica to OSU Athletic Department. 1977 plus letters regarding repairs. Karl F. Drlica Papers, OSU Libraries Special Collections and Archives Research Center.

K-34 Memo from Coach Drlica to Dee Andros, OSU Athletic Director, May 1980, regarding a water skier demand for an apology from Coach Adler. Karl F. Drlica Papers, OSU Libraries Special Collections and Archives Research Center.

K-37 Letter from Coach Drlica to Jerry Ward, Athletic Department, 1977, regarding snag removal, includes diagram and plan. Karl F. Drlica Papers, OSU Libraries Special Collections and Archives Research Center.

L-3 Photo of 1977 IRA champions. Photographer is unknown. Karl F. Drlica Papers, OSU Libraries Special Collections and Archives Research Center.

L-6 Photo of 1975 IRA champions. Photographer is unknown. Karl F. Drlica Papers, OSU Libraries Special Collections and Archives Research Center.

M-2 Clipping from the *Oregon Stater* (alumni magazine), April 1977, regarding awards for Coach Drlica. Also acceptance of women's crew into the Athletic Department. Karl F. Drlica Papers, OSU Libraries Special Collections and Archives Research Center.

M-16 Photo of lightweight doubles, Bruce Chapin bow. Photographer is unknown. Karl F. Drlica Papers, OSU Libraries Special Collections and Archives Research Center.

N-7 Letter from Richard Erickson, University of Washington coach, to Dee Andros stating that Oregon State has a real crew this year, May 24, 1977. Karl F. Drlica Papers, OSU Libraries Special Collections and Archives Research Center.

N-8 Correspondence between Coaches Don Costello and Drlica regarding crew at the University of Oregon, 1969 and 1971. Karl F. Drlica Papers, OSU Libraries Special Collections and Archives Research Center.

N-10 Newspaper article and photo regarding shell that was broken when falling off a van carrying it. Karl F. Drlica Papers, OSU Libraries Special Collections and Archives Research Center.

N-12 Correspondence between Coaches Conn Findlay and Drlica. Karl F. Drlica Papers, OSU Libraries Special Collections and Archives Research Center.

O-1 Photo of Jeff Young and Skip Spiering in pair-oared shell. Photographer is unknown. Karl F. Drlica Papers, OSU Libraries Special Collections and Archives Research Center.

O-2 Oral history interview of Sylvia Moore "Building a Foundation for Women's Athletics at OSU", March 31, 2015. Karl F. Drlica Papers, OSU Libraries Special Collections and Archives Research Center.

O-3 *Sunday Oregonian*, Portland, Oregon, May 5, 1907, describing a footrace that involved Fred Newell against the Native American school. Karl F. Drlica Papers, OSU Libraries Special Collections and Archives Research Center.

O-4 Newsletter to Beaver Crew Association regarding the article by Roy Gault concerning turning off the showers at the boathouse, October 29, 1976. Karl F. Drlica Papers, OSU Libraries Special Collections and Archives Research Center.

O-5 Coach Drlica notes regarding discussion with an administrator in the PE Department, May 22, 1976. The conversation concerned reduction in class listings for rowing. Karl F. Drlica Papers, OSU Libraries Special Collections and Archives Research Center.

O-6 Letter from Coach Drlica to Sandy Neeley pointing out that OSU is charging a user fee for services that are not being provided, October 29, 1976. Karl F. Drlica Papers, OSU Libraries Special Collections and Archives Research Center.

O-6a Memo from Dr. Lambert, subordinate to James Long, concerning withdrawal of request that PE class credit no longer be given to varsity athletes, November 17, 1975. Karl F. Drlica Papers, OSU Libraries Special Collections and Archives Research Center.

O-7 Letter from Dean Long to Coach Drlica regarding towel service at boathouse, November 12, 1975. Karl F. Drlica Papers, OSU Libraries Special Collections and Archives Research Center.

O-11 Article from *Heave Together*, volume 2 issue 1 January 1, 1919, Official Organ of the Northwest Steel Company, Portland, Oregon, transcribed from internet version. The piece concerns racing by Stevens. Karl F. Drlica Papers, OSU Libraries Special Collections and Archives Research Center.

O-15 Coach Stevens first-hand account of race against Washington, 1928 or 1929. Transcribed from the original. Karl F. Drlica Papers, OSU Libraries Special Collections and Archives Research Center.

O-16 Photos of OSU women rowers, 1971. Photo by Astrid Hancock. Karl F. Drlica Papers, OSU Libraries Special Collections and Archives Research Center.

O-17 Drlica testimony regarding renaming of Riverfront Park, 1983. Karl F. Drlica Papers, OSU Libraries Special Collections and Archives Research Center.

438 BITTEN *by the* ROWING BUG

O-18 Letter from the author to OSU President MacVicar, February 19, 1975. Karl F. Drlica Papers, OSU Libraries Special Collections and Archives Research Center.

O-19 Obituary of James Long in the *Oregon Stater*, October, 1997. Karl F. Drlica Papers, OSU Libraries Special Collections and Archives Research Center.

O-20 *Corvallis Gazette Times* article by Roy Gault concerning showers at the boathouse, October 26, 1976. Photo by John Bragg. Karl F. Drlica Papers, OSU Libraries Special Collections and Archives Research Center.

O-21a President Robert W. MacVicar, ca. 1970. From the Presidents of Oregon State University, OSU Libraries Special Collections & Archives Research Center. Identifier: MacVicar_P151_0047. Also in the *Daily Barometer* March 4, 1975. Article recommends that crew compete on a regional basis. Karl F. Drlica Papers, OSU Libraries Special Collections and Archives Research Center.

O-22 Dennis Searcy Letter-to-the-editor, *Daily Barometer*, April 9, 1975. Karl F. Drlica Papers, OSU Libraries Special Collections and Archives Research Center.

O-23 Ed Stevens obituary, *Corvallis Gazette Times*, 1957. Karl F. Drlica Papers, OSU Libraries Special Collections and Archives Research Center.

O-25 Memo from Dean James Long to Women's Intercollegiate Athletics, November 20, 1974 and Letter from James Long to Ruth Stiehl, Chair of Recreational Sports Committee, February 6, 1975. Karl F. Drlica Papers, OSU Libraries Special Collections and Archives Research Center.

O-26 Clipping from the *Harvard Crimson*, February 21, 1924. Coach Stevens' notes in margins. Karl F. Drlica Papers, OSU Libraries Special Collections and Archives Research Center.

O-27 Coach Drlica notes on interactions with assistant coach.

Karl F. Drlica Papers, OSU Libraries Special Collections and Archives Research Center.

O-28 Letter from Milosh Popovich stating that maintenance money for crew facilities is unavailable. 1968. Karl F. Drlica Papers, OSU Libraries Special Collections and Archives Research Center.

O-30 Official report to Langton regarding training barge foundering, May 1952. Karl F. Drlica Papers, OSU Libraries Special Collections and Archives Research Center.

O-31 Coach Carl Bower recollections, 2018. Karl F. Drlica Papers, OSU Libraries Special Collections and Archives Research Center.

O-32 Photo of 1971-72 OSU women's crew pushing off from dock. Photo by Astrid Hancock. Karl F. Drlica Papers, OSU Libraries Special Collections and Archives Research Center.

O-33 Photo of locking oar in oarlock, illustrating tape on shorts. 1971-72. Photo by Astrid Hancock. Karl F. Drlica papers, OSU Libraries Special Collections and Archives Research Center.

O-34 Letter from Jim Carruthers to author, 2018, concerning Coach Drlica Karl F. Drlica Papers, OSU Libraries Special Collections and Archives Research Center.

O-35 Newspaper clipping from the *Daily Barometer*, January 26, 1962, concerning strong winds and ice on crew. Karl F. Drlica Papers, OSU Libraries Special Collections and Archives Research Center.

O-37 Newspaper clipping about women's race at Aquatic Park, 1965. *Berkeley Gazette*. Article includes details about a dock and shed at the Rod and Gun Club at Aquatic Park. Karl F. Drlica Papers, OSU Libraries Special Collections and Archives Research Center.

O-38 Cartoon and news article concerning female coxswain,

Daily Barometer, April 6, 1972. Karl F. Drlica Papers, OSU Libraries Special Collections and Archives Research Center.

O-39 Newspaper clippings regarding 1966 Corvallis Regatta that included the race between Bob Janz and the author. Karl F. Drlica Papers, OSU Libraries Special Collections and Archives Research Center.

O-40 Example of flood. Aerial photo *Corvallis Gazette Times*, Jan. 22, 1974. Western Ways, photographer. Karl F. Drlica Papers, OSU Libraries Special Collections and Archives Research Center.

O-42 Newspaper (February 1961) clipping showing Paul Hemrich and J.R. Goerke cutting the bow off the *Orange Owl*. Article mentions the *Beaver* sinking in 1951. Photographer is unknown. Karl F. Drlica Papers, OSU Libraries Special Collections and Archives Research Center.

O-43 Newspaper clipping describing moving the float from land to water (November 1961). Karl F. Drlica Papers, OSU Libraries Special Collections and Archives Research Center.

O-44 Newspaper article and photo of fire at boathouse (*Corvallis Gazette Times*, April 8, 1955). Karl F. Drlica Papers, OSU Libraries S pecial Collections and Archives Research Center.

O-45 Article on plywood racing shells, Photo showing application of planking. *Science and Mechanics*, Spring 1943 p. 46-47. Photographer is unknown. Karl F. Drlica Papers, OSU Libraries Special Collections and Archives Research Center

O-46 Newspaper clippings, photo of Arthur Orr and Coach Stevens. Photographer is unknown. Karl F. Drlica Papers, OSU Libraries Special Collections and Archives Research Center.

O-47 Photo showing landscaping at the boathouse. Photo includes Coach Stevens and a view of the Beach farmhouse. Photographer is unknown. Karl F. Drlica Papers, OSU Libraries Special Collections and Archives Research Center.

O-48 Several photos of crew in the snow, March 1951. Photographer is unknown. Karl F. Drlica Papers, OSU Libraries Special Collections and Archives Research Center.

O-50 Photo of OSU boathouse, 1996. Photographer is unknown. Karl F. Drlica Papers, OSU Libraries Special Collections and Archives Research Center.

O-51 Photo of Karl F. Drlica, 1936 yearbook, Benson Polytechnical High School, Portland, Oregon. Karl F. Drlica Papers, OSU Libraries Special Collections and Archives Research Center.

O-53 Photo of 1962 varsity crew taken from race program. Crew includes Jim York and Chuck Emerick. Photographer is unknown. Karl F. Drlica Papers, OSU Libraries Special Collections and Archives Research Center.

O-54 Photo of Lake Merritt, Oakland California; unidentified source. Karl F. Drlica Papers, OSU Libraries Special Collections and Archives Research Center.

O-57 Results from University-wide donation campaign, 2019. Karl F. Drlica Papers, OSU Libraries Special Collections and Archives Research Center.

O-59 Photo of the author from 1965 Yearbook, International House, University of California, Berkeley. Photographer is unknown. Karl F. Drlica Papers, OSU Libraries Special Collections and Archives Research Center.

O-60 Corvallis population trends. Karl F. Drlica Papers, OSU Libraries Special Collections and Archives Research Center.

O-61 *The Club News: A Journal of Water Sports.* January 1923, Vol 13, Number 145, page 10. The piece describes Stevens and Newell taking over at Harvard. Karl F. Drlica Papers, OSU Libraries Special Collections and Archives Research Center.

O-62 Photos of Cal Women's Crew at Lake Merritt Rowing Club in Oakland. Also Aquatic Park, Berkeley photos by Wayne

Fogle. Karl F. Drlica Papers, OSU Libraries Special Collections and Archives Research Center.

O-63 Songs and recollections from early OSU women rowers; race records, photos of strong crews of both men and women. Karl F. Drlica Papers, OSU Libraries Special Collections and Archives Research Center.

O-69 Photo of Marcia Morley, Coach Drlica, and Coach Astrid Hancock, 1966 Women's Rowing National Regatta. Photo courtesy of Astrid Hancock. Karl F. Drlica Papers, OSU Libraries Special Collections and Archives Research Center.

O-71 *The Shell Game* by Stephen Kiesling, 1982, 1994, 2002 Nordic Knight Press, Ashland OR. The book provides an excellent description of preparations for *The Race*.

O-72 Coach Drlica cartoon, Bro Kirk, artist, *The Sunday Oregonian*, March 27, 1977. Karl F. Drlica Papers, OSU Libraries Special Collections and Archives Research Center.

O-73 Wikipedia article on Pop Courtney; photo at O-105. Copy in Karl F. Drlica Papers, OSU Libraries Special Collections and Archives Research Center.

O-74 Arthur M. Arlett, full text of "Ky Ebright: crew coach for the University of California and the Olympics: oral history transcript and related material, 1967-1968" University of California Berkeley, University of California Bancroft Library/Berkeley, Regional Oral History Office, Berkeley, 1968. Karl F. Drlica Papers, OSU Libraries Special Collections and Archives Research Center.

O-76 Jim Lemmon, 1989, *The Log of Rowing at the University of California Berkeley 1870-1987*, Western Heritage Press, Berkeley CA, 144 pp.

O-77 Unidentified newspaper clippings concerning E.C. Sammons. Karl F. Drlica Papers, OSU Libraries Special Collections and Archives Research Center.

O-78 Photo of first training barge in *Oregon State College Orange and Black*, Book 3, page 116, authored by Bud Forrester. From OSU Libraries Special Collections & Archives Research Center. https://ir.library.oregonstate.edu/concern/technical_reports/qn59q8355

O-79 Kip Carlson "When OSU Women Shocked the World" in *Oregon Stater* Spring 2020 p.52-54. This piece describes the victories at the national championships. Karl F. Drlica Papers, OSU Libraries Special Collections and Archives Research Center.

O-80 Photograph of Ilene Wagner, sculling at Aquatic Park, Berkeley, 1969. Photo by Wayne Fogle. Karl F. Drlica Papers, OSU Libraries Special Collections and Archives Research Center.

O-81 K.F. Drlica, 1990. Non-rowing history of Coach Drlica. Karl F. Drlica Papers, OSU Libraries Special Collections and Archives Research Center.

O-82 Craig Lambert, *Mind Over Water*, 1998. Mariner Books.

O-83 Drlica, K.F. "Rescue on the River". Coach Drlica's description of the rescue at the tree in the middle of the river. Karl F. Drlica Papers, OSU Libraries Special Collections and Archives Research Center.

O-84 Camp Mudjekeewis and Wellesley College. Photos by Astrid Hancock. Karl F. Drlica Papers, OSU Libraries Special Collections and Archives Research Center.

O-84a Float Night at Camp Mudjekeewis. Photo by Astrid Hancock. Karl F. Drlica Papers, OSU Libraries Special Collections and Archives Research Center.

O-84b Shells waiting for crews at Wellesley College. Photo by Astrid Hancock. Karl F. Drlica Papers, OSU Libraries Special Collections and Archives Research Center.

O-85 Background on Camp Mudjekeewis from *Yesterday's News,* Lovell Historical Society, volume 17, number 3, 2010. Includes photo of original boathouse. Copy in Karl F. Drlica Papers, OSU Libraries Special Collections and Archives Research Center.

O-86a Dotty Brown, *Boathouse Row: Waves of Change in the Birthplace of American Rowing* 2016; Chapter 6 includes a description of male discrimination against women rowers in Philadelphia. Copy of relevant portion in Karl F. Drlica Papers, OSU Libraries Special Collections and Archives Research Center.

O-89 Peter Mallory, *The Sport of Rowing—The Age of Enlightenment,* Chapter 127. Long Beach Rowing Assn., the Next Generation; pages 1619-1620. https://www.row2k.com/content/Women_in_the_70s.pdf; copy in Karl F. Drlica Papers, OSU Libraries Special Collections and Archives Research Center.

O-90 Astrid Hancock personal recollections. Karl F. Drlica Papers, OSU Libraries Special Collections and Archives Research Center.

O-91 Carol Simpson Sanoff personal recollections. Karl F. Drlica Papers, OSU Libraries Special Collections and Archives Research Center.

O-92 William G. Robbins, *The Oregon Encyclopedia.* Biography of Fred Milton. Karl F. Drlica Papers, OSU Libraries Special Collections and Archives Research Center.

O-93 Hubert Lindsey *Bless Your Dirty Heart* Logos International, publisher, 1972.

O-94 Dennis Searcy personal recollections. Karl F. Drlica Papers, OSU Libraries Special Collections and Archives Research Center.

O-97 Photo of Wellesley College crew from https://www.wellesley.edu/youarehere/renew/crew. Copy in Karl F. Drlica Papers, OSU Libraries Special Collections and Archives Research Center.

O-98 Front Street, Portland Oregon 1910. This image comes from *Portland Oregon Its History and Builders,* by Joseph Gaston, published in 1911. Copy in Karl F. Drlica Papers, OSU Libraries Special Collections and Archives Research Center. Also https://vintageportland.files.wordpress.com/2019/02/ ap-7080-city-auditor-archives-records-management-auditor-s-historical-records-view-of-front-ave.jpg

O-99 Downtown Corvallis, 1939. Photo from Puget Sound Theatre Organ Society http://www.pstos.org/instruments/or/corvallis/ whiteside_streetscene-1939-l.jpg 1 of 1 6/5/202. Photographer is unknown. Copy in Karl F. Drlica Papers, OSU Libraries Special Collections and Archives Research Center.

O-102 Photo of Van Buren Street Bridge at Corvallis, 1930s, showing a crew race between Oregon State and the University of California. Spectators cover the bridge. The boats, known to be 60 feet long, can be used to estimate that the width of the river is about 300 feet. Photo by Lloyd Jacobs. From Oregon Digital HC3420, OSU Libraries Special Collections & Archives Research Center.

O-103 Photo of Willamette River at Corvallis showing eddies below the bridge. Photographer is unknown. Copy in Karl F. Drlica, OSU Libraries Special Collections and Archives Research Center.

O-104 Photo of Ky Ebright, 1930. https://upload.wikimedia. org/wikipedia/commons/thumb/3/35/Ky_Ebright_1930. jpg/260px-Ky_Ebright_1930.jpg

O-105 Pop Courtney, photo taken between 1910 and 1915. https://upload.wikimedia.org/wikipedia/commons/ thumb/7/75/Charles_Courtney_%28LOC%29.jpg/500px-Charles_Courtney_%28LOC%29.jpg

O-106 Photo of single sculls race, Corvallis Regatta, April 1964. Photo by Astrid Hancock. Black shirt: the author; white shirt:

Art Sachs. Karl F. Drlica Papers, OSU Libraries Special Collections and Archives Research Center.

O-107 Short article in *Popular Mechanics*, October 1942, page 31, concerning Coach Stevens bending plywood. Copy in Karl F. Drlica Papers, OSU Libraries Special Collections and Archives Research Center.

O-109 Photo of race including OSU women's crew, Corvallis Regatta 1964. OSU won the race. Photo by Astrid Hancock. Karl F. Drlica Papers, OSU Libraries Special Collections and Archives Research Center.

O-110 Photo of snag attached to bridge pier. Photographer is unknown. Karl F. Drlica Papers, OSU Libraries Special Collections and Archives Research Center.

O-111 Recollections of Robert Poole. Karl F. Drlica Papers, OSU Libraries Special Collections and Archives Research Center.

O-112 Recollections of Astrid Hancock regarding varsity letters for women. Karl F. Drlica Papers, OSU Libraries Special Collections and Archives Research Center.

O-113 Letter from Kirk Hutchinson to Astrid Hancock, circa 2016. Karl F. Drlica Papers, OSU Libraries Special Collections and Archives Research Center.

O-114 Barry Hilt, personal recollections. Karl F. Drlica Papers, OSU Libraries Special Collections and Archives Research Center.

O-115a Press photo of E.A. Stevens the new Harvard Coach, 1923. Photo by Underwood & Underwood, New York City. Copy in Karl F. Drlica Papers, OSU Libraries Special Collections and Archives Research Center.

O-116 Sketch of sliding seat, prepared by the author. The seat moved on four pairs of wheels connected by axles held in place by copper strips (cages) screwed to a wooden support. These copper cages were easily distorted. The wooden support was attached to the seat. Steel strips were attached to the bottom of the supports to serve as bearing surfaces for the axles, which could roll about 4 inches. Grooves would form in the steel strips that would grab the axles and impede smooth movement of the seats. Holes in the seat reduced weight. Karl F. Drlica Papers, OSU Libraries Special Collections and Archives Research Center.

O-117 Sketch of portion of racing shell, top view, and seat; prepared by the author. The rower or sculler sits on a "sliding" seat that allows a long reach and the use of leg muscles in the stroke. The seat rests on the axels of four pairs of wheels. The wheels roll along a metal strip, guided by a wooden rail that fits between the wheels of each pair. Rower's feet are tied into supports called stretcher boots; their position can be adjusted for different leg lengths. The wheel axels are held in place by a thin strip of copper that acts as a cage. Each cage holds an axel. Karl F. Drlica Papers, OSU Libraries Special Collections and Archives Research Center.

O-118a Photo of log boom upstream from the southern barge used to store racing shells. Photo was taken when the water level was low. Photographer is unknown. Karl F. Drlica Papers, OSU Libraries Special Collections and Archives Research Center.

O-119a Photo of Beach farmhouse, which was demolished during construction of the Harrison Street Bridge, 1963. Photographer is unknown. Karl F. Drlica Papers, OSU Libraries Special Collections and Archives Research Center.

O-120 Photo of portion of port-side racing shell oar, 1960, top view. Blade is to the right, perpendicular to the plane of the page or the water surface. Strip of leather fits in the oarlock and protects the oar from wear. Brass nails hold the edges of the leather in position. The flat side of the oar shaft fits against a flat arm of an oarlock to establish the pitch of the blade while in the water. When the oar is removed from the water, the oar is rolled 90° relative to the water surface, placing the flat side of the shaft against the flat bottom of the oarlock to establish the pitch of the blade when out of the water (arrow indicates direction of rotation for oar). A leather collar, called a button, is pushed against the oarlock to establish the distance from the oarlock to the handle and to the blade. Oars are balanced at the oarlocks, thereby requiring no effort to keep the oar in position. Photo by the author. Karl F. Drlica Papers, OSU Libraries Special Collections and Archives Research Center.

O-122 Log dump, in Railroad Line Forums, from The Gallery: May 2007 "From Logging to Lumber". Copy in Karl F. Drlica Papers, OSU Libraries Special Collections and Archives Research Center.

O-124d Photo of sculling oarlock, circa 2020. Photo by the author. Karl F. Drlica Papers, OSU Libraries Special Collections and Archives Research Center.

O-125 Early stage in racing shell construction. Upper, shell is upside down. Long wooden stringers are flat on the workbench with the keelson arching above the plane of the workbench. Planking is shown on a portion, steamed, glued, and nailed in place. Lower, shell is shown right side up; keelson sits on the workbench. Karl F. Drlica Papers, OSU Libraries Special Collections and Archives Research Center.

O-126 New boathouse, Wellesley College. Photo courtesy of Astrid Hancock. Karl F. Drlica Papers, OSU Libraries Special Collections and Archives Research Center.

O-127 Wellesley College docks, 1962. Photo by Astrid Hancock. Karl F. Drlica Papers, OSU Libraries Special Collections and Archives Research Center.

O-129 Comparison of rowing styles. Sketch comparing the old lay-back style [top] and the newer leg-drive style [bottom]. The left figures show rower at the catch when the oar is placed in the water. During the pull-through [center], the old style quickly pushes the seat leftward toward the bow, while in the new style the rower applies full body weight to the oar and rises off the seat [exaggerated]. At the finish [right] the old style involves heaving on the oar, laying far toward the bow; in the new style the body remains more upright.

O-130 William Jasper Kerr, 1934. From the Presidents of Oregon State University, OSU Libraries Special Collections & Archives Research Center. Identifier: Kerr_P001_009.

O-132 Photo of winning coxswain being thrown into the river by women's intramural crew, 1964. Photo by Astrid Hancock. Karl F. Drlica Papers, OSU Libraries Special Collections and Archives Research Center.

O-133a. The author in a racing shell in the Willamette River at Corvallis. Photo by Astrid Hancock. Karl F. Drlica Papers, OSU Libraries Special Collections and Archives Research Center.

O-134 Photo of Sheriff Jack Dolan by Sue Wehnert Guss. Karl F. Drlica Papers, OSU Libraries Special Collections and Archives Research Center.

O-135 Recollections of Brian Finn. Karl F. Drlica Papers, OSU Libraries Special Collections and Archives Research Center.

O-136 Photo of race course on Dexter Reservoir, Oregon. (https://www.oarowing.org/oardexter). Copy in Karl F. Drlica Papers, OSU Libraries Special Collections and Archives Research Center.

O-137 Internet post by Steve Mims, *Eugene Register Guard*, October 26, 2019. This piece reflects on the girl cox issue of 1972. Copy in Karl F. Drlica Papers, OSU Libraries Special Collections and Archives Research Center.

O-138 Arshay Cooper, *A Most Beautiful Thing,* Flatiron Books, 2015.

O-139 Diary entry, Drlica 1937. First Sinking. Description of collision with bridge pier with Coach Drlica as coxswain. Karl F. Drlica Papers, OSU Libraries Special Collections and Archives Research Center.

O-140 Karl F. Drlica, *Reforming the Rising Sun*, Xlbris, 2005. This memoir describes teaching democracy in Occupied Japan.

O-141 Coach Drlica on his bicycle in undated photo. Photographer is unknown. Karl F. Drlica Papers, OSU Libraries Special Collections and Archives Research Center.

O-142 Coach Drlica standing on front porch of his home in Corvallis, circa 1960. Photographer is unknown. Karl F. Drlica Papers, OSU Libraries Special Collections and Archives Research Center.

O-143 Karen Drlica, mid-1950s. Photographer is unknown. Karl F. Drlica Papers, OSU Libraries Special Collections and Archives Research Center.

O-144 Oregon Electric Depot in flood of 1923. Caption indicates water was two feet higher the night before the photo was taken. Oregon Digital. Copy in Karl F. Drlica Papers, OSU Libraries Special Collections and Archives Research Center.

O-145 Sketch of PT boat as advertisement for waterproof wood glue. Published in *The Timberman*, August 1941, page 30. Copy in Karl F. Drlica Papers, OSU Libraries Special Collections and Archives Research

O-146 Ted Nash, Olympic gold medalist 1960. https://www.row2k.com/features/498/Rowing-History--Lake-Washington-RC-1960-Coxless-Four---Ted-Nash---The-Last-Great-LWRC-Boat/. Copy in Karl F. Drlica Papers, OSU Libraries Special Collections and Archives Research Center.

O-147 Cal Women's Crew, 1969 at Aquatic Park, Berkeley, CA. Karl F. Drlica Papers, OSU Libraries Special Collections and Archives Research Center.

O-149 E.C. Sammons, 1919, included with obituary. Source: https//www.findagrave.com/memorial. Sammons' papers are housed at the Oregon Historical Society, Portland, Oregon. Copy of this photo is in Karl F. Drlica Papers, OSU Libraries Special Collections and Archives Research Center.

O-151 Photos of debris following a flood, probably 1950s. Photographer is unknown. Karl F. Drlica Papers, OSU Libraries Special Collections and Archives Research Center.

O-152 Notes on conversation with Kirk Hutchinson, August 2021. Karl F. Drlica Papers, OSU Libraries Special Collections and Archives Research Center

O-153 Snag in the Willamette River immediately upstream from bridges. Photo by the author. Karl F. Drlica Papers, OSU Libraries Special Collections and Archives Research Center.

O-156 Sign on Drlica Building on Hawthorne Avenue, Portland, Oregon. Photo by the author. Karl F. Drlica Papers, OSU Libraries Special Collections and Archives Research Center.

O-157 Marker for bicycle trail near boathouse in Corvallis memorializing Suzanne Wilkins. Photo by the author. Karl F. Drlica Papers, OSU Libraries Special Collections and Archives Research Center.

O-160 *Playboy*, September 1969, page 169. Photo shows Astrid in the background. Karl F. Drlica Papers, OSU Libraries Special Collections and Archives Research Center.

O-161 Photo of rowing on the Willamette River at Corvallis in the 1930s. Courtesy of Mary Gallagher, Benton County Historical Society. Photographer is unknown.

O-162 Rex Lardner, "How They Row in Ratzeburg", *Sports Illustrated*, May 20, 1963. Copy in Karl F. Drlica Papers, OSU Libraries Special Collections and Archives Research Center.

O-163b Passing a loaded log truck in Oregon. Photo by Ilene Wagner. Karl F. Drlica Papers, OSU Libraries Special Collections and Archives Research Center.

O-164 Newspaper clipping, 1974 NWRA Regatta, *Daily Barometer*, June 20, 1974. Karl F. Drlica Papers, OSU Libraries Special Collections and Archives Research Center.

O-166 Race results (partial) 1974 NWRA Regatta. *The Oarsman*, July/August 1974. Karl F. Drlica Papers, OSU Libraries Special Collections and Archives Research Center.

O-166a Long Beach racing shirt, 1960s. The specific race for this shirt is unknown. Karl F. Drlica Papers, OSU Libraries Special Collections and Archives Research Center.

O-169 Wedding of Ilene Wagner and the author, 1967. Julia Shew is front left. Photographer is unknown. Karl F. Drlica Papers, OSU Libraries Special Collections and Archives Research Center.

O-170 Estimating boat speed. The distance between the number two and number eight puddles was 26 feet. The drawing shows the number two puddle from the previous stroke being passed by the number eight oar. The distance *x* between where the number eight oar enters the water and the previous number two puddle was called spacing. Spacing plus 26 feet [distance between arrow heads] indicated how many feet the boat traveled per stroke. Feet per stroke times strokes per minute [determined with a stopwatch held by the cox] gave feet per minute. Direction of travel is from left to right.

O-171a Photo of Aquathusiasts' dock showing hydroplane and the fiberglass boat made by Coach Drlica during night school. The photo is taken from a race program in which the Oregon State Rowing Club and the Aquathusiasts hosted a series of races. The view is downriver on the Corvallis side. Karl F. Drlica Papers, OSU Libraries Special Collections and Archives Research Center.

O-172 Recollections of Suzi Wong Swint as a coxswain for women's crews. Karl F. Drlica Papers, OSU Libraries Special Collections and Archives Research Center.

O-173 and O-173a Notes on near drowning including incident reports by Elaine Baden, John Dye, and Frank Griffo. Karl F. Drlica Papers, OSU Libraries Special Collections and Archives Research Center.

O-174 Photo of dock at Aquatic Park as boats launch for time trial. Photo by Elaine Baden. Karl F. Drlica Papers, OSU Libraries Special Collections and Archives Research Center.

O-175 Photo of Tom Bolles, Washington Freshman Coach, 1926-1937, PRC4.2.11.1.3, Poughkeepsie Regatta Collection, Marist College Archives & Special Collections, Poughkeepsie, NY, USA.

O-177 Notes on Dr. Milosh Popovich. Karl F. Drlica Papers, OSU Libraries Special Collections and Archives Research Center.

O-178 Notes concerning Dr. Robert MacVicar, President of OSU. Karl F. Drlica Papers, OSU Libraries Special Collections and Archives Research Center.

O-179 Obituary of Ellen T. Drake. Karl F. Drlica Papers, OSU Libraries Special Collections and Archives Research Center.

O-180 Carol Simpson Sanoff recollections. Karl F. Drlica Papers, OSU Libraries Special Collections and Archives Research Center.

O-182 Notes on hospitalization of the author after heart attack during a rowing time trial. Karl F. Drlica Papers, OSU Libraries Special Collections and Archives Research Center.

O-183 Recollections from Karen Drlica Kernek, 2022. Karl F. Drlica Papers, OSU Libraries Special Collections and Archives Research Center.

O-184 Photos of single scull broken during rescue. The photos were to guide repair work, so the pieces have been pushed together. Photos by Steve Schaffran. Karl F. Drlica Papers, OSU Libraries Special Collections and Archives Research Center.

O-186a Fiberglass motorboat constructed by Coach Drlica, 1957. Photo by Marc Drlica-Wagner. Karl F. Drlica Papers, OSU Libraries Special Collections and Archives Research Center.

O-187b Wooden single scull built by George Pocock, 1973. Photo courtesy of Rowable Classics https://rowableclassics.com.

O-188 Rook Lid. Photo, reproduced by permission, is part of a spectacular collection of hats found at hansonhats.com. "The Hanson Collection Vintage Fashion Hats" contains 1500 images of hats. The Rook Lid is found under Albums by Style/Just Fun Hats.

O-189 List of inductees into the 2022 Oregon State University Sports Hall of Fame. Listed are Astrid Hancock as a coach and 14 women rowers of the early years. Copy of induction program in Karl F. Drlica Papers, OSU Libraries Special Collections and Archives Research Center.

O-190 Gail Hufford, 1940. Wedding picture. Photographer is unknown. Karl F. Drlica Papers, OSU Libraries Special Collections and Archives Research Center

Glossary

Aft: toward the stern.

Beehive burner: An enclosed, quasi-conical metal structure associated with sawmills. The structures were about 25 feet high; the upper part was typically composed of a heavy mesh screen. Wood scraps and other wood waste products are burned inside the structures.

Blade: portion of oar that enters the water.

Bow: front

Button: enlarged portion of an oar handle that keeps the oar positioned in the oarlock.

Catch: portion of the stroke at which the oar is placed in the water.

Cockpit: portion of a racing shell that is not covered by decking; contains sliding seats and footrests.

Coxswain: person responsible for steering a boat; abbreviated as cox.

Crab: failure to properly remove the oar from the water at the end of a stroke; can result in oar blade being forced into a position along the side of the racing shell (see also reverse crab).

Decking cloth: covering, often varnished silk, that keeps water out of bow and stern portions of a racing shell.

Double sculls. Crew racing event in which two persons each hold two sculling oars.

Douglas fir: a tall, straight tree common to Western Oregon.

Eddy: portion of a river immediately downstream from an obstruction, such as a large rock or bridge pier; current can run upstream in an eddy.

Eddy line: where the upstream eddy current meets the main, downstream current.

Elite racing category: crew in which one or more members has been a competing member of the USRowing Senior National Team or any country's Senior National Team (includes being a spare) or a medalist at the U23 World Championships.

Feather: as verb, to turn the oar blade parallel to the water surface.

Float: a term for a dock supported by floating logs.

Gunnel, gunnel boards: portion of a racing shell that extends the length of the cockpit above the waterline.

Hold: command from the coxswain to push oar blades under the water to stop the boat or if on one side, to turn the boat.

Keel: portion of a boat that projects below the hull to provide stability and minimize sideways slippage.

Keelson: strip of wood extending the full length of the racing shell inside the planking; provides a support for nailing the planking in place.

Keeper bar: metal bar that locks an oar into an oarlock.

Knocker: wooden dowel, about six-inches long, that is hit against the side of the shell to signal strategies such as changing the stroke rate; also used to grip a rudder line.

Leather: a portion of an oar handle that fits in an oarlock. The leather protects the oar from wear.

Letter: an award for participating in a varsity sport. A letter was typically a large (8-inch), single letter of the alphabet representative of each school. For example, an orange "O" represented Oregon State. To "letter" in a sport means sufficient participation to earn a letter that could be worn on a special sweater or jacket as a status symbol.

List: tip, tilt; in a boat toward one side.

Log: the trunk of a tree after the tree has been cut down and the branches removed.

Log dump: area along a river bank where logs are removed from log trucks and rolled down the bank into the river.

Log raft: an organized collection of logs in a river, generally used to move logs to a saw mill.

Oarlock: metal, U-shaped structure that holds an oar in place.

Open water: a term describing the lead one crew has on another in a race; open water is observed when one shell is ahead by more than one boat length, for then the boats do not overlap. Open water is specified in units of boat lengths (if a crew has a lead of one length of open water, it is two boat lengths ahead).

Outrigger: metal projection from a racing shell that supports an oarlock.

Pair-oar: rowing event in which two persons each row with a single sweep oar.

Peavey: a short (6-foot), stout pole used to roll logs; the end contains a spike and a swiveled hook for grabbing a log.

Pike pole: a long (10-12 foot) pole used for positioning floating logs; the end contains a spike and hook.

Planking: skin of a racing shell.

Pocock: brand name of commercial racing shells constructed in Seattle, initially by George Pocock.

Puddle: whirl-pool like disturbance in water created by pulling on an oar.

Port: left side facing forward.

Quadruple sculls. Rowing event involving four persons each rowing with two oars.

Rail: wooden strip attached to a track to guide wheels of sliding seat.

Reach: extension of arms by rower to catch the water during a stroke.

Recovery: portion of the stroke beginning with removal of an oar from the water and ending when the oar is placed in the water.

Regatta: organized set of boat races on water.

Reverse crab: failure to keep the oar out of the water during the recovery phase of the stroke; occurs when the oar blade is caught by the water and the oar handle is driven sharply into the chest of the rower, often ejecting the rower from the shell.

Rigger: outrigger or a person responsible for racing shell maintenance.

Run: distance a racing shell moves between strokes.

Sculling: propelling a boat with two oars, one in each hand.

Shear pin: a metal pin that is part of a propeller assembly; if the propeller strikes an object, the pin breaks, saving the motor from damage.

Shell barge: a wide-bodied shell used for training.

Skeg: the fin on a racing shell.

Slack water: a portion of a river where the current is less than the major portion of the river.

Slide: seat in a racing shell

Snag: partially submerged tree stuck on the bottom of the river or on a bridge pier.

Spacing: distance between the number 2 puddle and the number 8 puddle of the next stroke; spacing plus 26 feet (the distance between the number 2 and 8 outriggers) equals the distance an eight-oared shell moves in one stroke.

Stake boat: small boat anchored at the starting line; a person in a stake boat holds the stern of a racing shell prior to the start of a race.

Starboard: right side facing forward.

Stern: rear

Stretcher, stretch boot, foot stretcher: foot support in which rower ties feet.

Stroke: rower seated in the stern who sets the rowing pace, also the process of putting an oar blade in the water, pulling on it, taking it out of the water, and preparing to put it in the water again.

Stroke rate: strokes per minute

Stroke watch: a stop watch calibrated to read out strokes per minute determined by the time required for three strokes.

Sweep oar: long oar, gripped with two hands and used for rowing.

Towel room: a heated room in a boathouse where wet rowing clothes and towels were hung on racks to dry. In Oregon, almost daily rain made drying clothing necessary.

Track: metal strip on which wheels of the sliding seat run.

Training barge: large, stable rowed boat containing sliding seats and outriggers for approximately 18 rowers. A walkway between two sets of rowers allows a coach to move from one rower to the next.

Washing out: pulling the oar blade out of the water before completing the stroke; this loss of contact with the water on one side of the boat will allow the boat to tip to the other side.

Weigh all or Weigh 'nuf: command from the coxswain to stop rowing and place oar blades on the water surface.

White cap: a frothy foam arising when a strong wind causes a wave to break.

Index

Rowing songs, poems 43, 131, 303
Rowing tank 46, 178, 374, 376, 393, 425
Ruzicka, Bill, 239, 421

S

Sachs, Art 278, 279, 280, 289, 307, 337, 417, 446
Sacramento Junior College 72, 79, 95
Salisbury, Mr. 162, 163
Salmon King 237
Sammons, Ed 81, 82, 84, 92, 183, 184, 391, 442, 451
Sanderson, Don 321, 322, 323, 325, 416
Savercool, Pat, 285
Schissler, Paul 61
Schlueniger, Bene 336
Schmitt, Carol 274
Schoenborn, Janet 268, 269, 418
School Board 372
Seahorses 146, 417
Searcy, Dennis 212, 227, 228, 346, 421, 438, 444
Seat race 121
Seberg, Frank 133
Seen, Eva 259
Severns, Kathy 271
Shafer, Richard 182, 426
Shaw, Sam 45, 49, 50
Shell barge 92, 93, 256
Shew, Julia 270, 415, 452
Simpson, Carol 280, 281, 285, 293, 297, 411, 444, 454
Sissul, Tom 359
Smith, Fred 203
Smith, Sherry 266
Smith, Sydney 285
Snag 127, 159, 167, 376
Spiering, Skip 222, 436
Sports Illustrated 307, 452
Sproul Plaza 278, 279
Stanford University 57, 79, 149, 173, 227, 248, 290
Station L Rowing Club 347, 371, 429, 430
Stephenson, Becky 334, 336
Sterk, Fred 129, 191, 239, 405, 425

237, 293, 306, 307, 309, 320, 337, 341, 353, 369, 373, 385, 401,
406, 433, 436, 437, 453
University of Wisconsin 77, 255, 335

V

Van Blom, John 295, 297
Van Buren Street Bridge 17, 56, 112, 113, 191, 237, 376, 396, 415,
432, 433, 445
Vancouver Lake 374
Vision, poor 108, 114, 365

W

Wagner, Ilene v, 284, 285, 292, 443, 452
Wahlstrom, Jim 138, 170
Ward, Jerry 243, 420, 435
Wellesley College 253, 255, 256, 263, 276, 443, 444, 448
Werner, Mary 200
Western Crew Coaches Association 301, 304, 386
Western, Sam 371
White Whale 153, 212
Wilkins, Suzanne 31
Woodman, Tom 359, 387

Y

Yale University 50, 52, 68, 321, 393, 420
Yellow Peril 101, 111, 112, 138, 399, 424
York, Jim 248, 249
Young, George 83
Young, Robert 55, 61, 63, 66, 67, 69, 71, 72, 73, 78, 80, 130, 398, 399,
401, 403

Z

Zagunis, Frank 428
Zagunis, Robert 359, 387
Zahorski 236, 237, 386, 406
Zahorski family 235

About the Author

KARL DRLICA is a molecular biologist who has written three science books for the general public, most notably Understanding DNA and Gene Cloning: A Guide for the Curious. He has been named an Alumni Fellow at Oregon State University where he learned to row. He also coached a women's crew at the University of California, Berkeley. He now sculls as a member of the Berkeley Paddling and Rowing Club. The richness of an archive he inherited compelled him to write *Bitten by the Rowing Bug*. He and his wife, Ilene Wagner, who also rowed, live in Northern California; they have two adult sons.

Made in United States
North Haven, CT
29 March 2024

50662554R00264